GILCHRIST ON BLAKE

D0743784

CLASSIC BIOGRAPHIES
EDITED BY RICHARD HOLMES

Defoe on Sheppard and Wild
Johnson on Savage
Godwin on Wollstonecraft
Southey on Nelson
Gilchrist on Blake
Scott on Zélide

GILCHRIST ON BLAKE

Life of William Blake
Pictor Ignotus

by
Alexander Gilchrist

EDITED WITH AN INTRODUCTION BY
RICHARD HOLMES

HARPER PERENNIAL
London, New York, Toronto and Sydney

Harper Perennial
An imprint of HarperCollins*Publishers*
77–85 Fulham Palace Road,
Hammersmith, London w6 8jb

www.harperperennial.co.uk

This Classic Biography published by Harper Perennial 2005

Life of William Blake first published 1863

Introduction copyright © Richard Holmes 2005

A catalogue record for this book is
available from the British Library

ISBN 978-0-00-711171-8

Set in PostScript Linotype Adobe Caslon
and Spectrum Display by
Rowland Phototypesetting Ltd,
Bury St Edmunds, Suffolk

All rights reserved. No part of this publication may be
reproduced, stored in a retrieval system, or transmitted,
in any form or by any means, electronic, mechanical,
photocopying, recording or otherwise, without the prior
permission of the publishers.

This book is sold subject to the condition that it shall not,
by way of trade or otherwise, be lent, re-sold, hired out or
otherwise circulated without the publisher's prior consent
in any form of binding or cover other than that in which it
is published and without a similar condition including this
condition being imposed on the subsequent purchaser.

CONTENTS

v

CONTENTS

vi

INTRODUCTION

1

When William Blake died in London in 1827, he was already a forgotten man. He had been living in two-room lodgings in Fountain Court, in the Middle Temple, off Fleet Street. His engraved and hand-painted *Songs of Innocence and of Experience*, had sold less than twenty copies in thirty years. His Prophetic Books had disappeared almost without trace. A single mysterious poem – 'The Tyger' – had reached the anthologies. As a poet – once read in manuscript by Coleridge, Wordsworth and Charles Lamb – he was virtually unknown outside a small circle of disciples, a group of young men who pointedly called themselves 'The Ancients'. Robert Southey, the Poet Laureate, magnanimously dismissed him 'a man of great, but undoubtedly insane genius'.

As an artist, his reputation was little better. He was chiefly remembered as a one-time commercial engraver of grimly improving texts: Edward Young's *Night Thoughts*, Robert Blair's *The Grave*, the dark Biblical drama of the *Book of Job*, and Dante's *Inferno* still unfinished at the time of his death. In 1830 Blake was given a short and gently patronizing entry in Alan Cunningham's *Lives of the Most Eminent British Painters*. The illuminations to *The Songs of Innocence*, and the *Book of Job*, were mildly admired. 'The Tyger' was re-printed as an example of fascinating eccentricity.

But Cunningham damned him with faint praise. Blake was a lovable, minor eccentric: unworldly, self-taught and self-deluded. He produced work that was 'unmeaning, mystical and extravagant'. He was a man 'overmastered' by his own imagination. He confused 'the spiritual for the corporeal vision'. But for the stabilizing influence of his faithful – but 'illiterate' – wife Kate, William Blake would be remembered simply as 'a madman'.

Three years later, in March 1833, the *Monthly Magazine* wittily celebrated Blake's lunacies. 'Blake was an embodied sublimity. He held converse with Michael Angelo, yea with Moses; not in dreams, but in the placid still hour of the night – alone, awake – with such powers as he possessed in their full vigour . . . He chatted with Cleopatra, and the Black Prince sat to him for a portrait. He reveled in the past; the gates of the spiritual world were unbarred at his behest, and the great ones of bygone ages, clothed in the flesh they wore on earth, visited his studio.'

Blake was diagnosed as a sufferer of extreme and persistent visual hallucinations, a man who 'painted from spectres', and had lost his grasp on reality. 'His may be deemed the most extraordinary case of spectral illusion that has hitherto occurred. Is it possible that neither Sir Walter Scott, nor Sir David Brewster – the authors of *Demonology and Witchcraft* and *Natural Magic* – ever heard of Blake?'

This article had great success, and was copied by the smart Parisian magazine, *La Revue Britannique*, the following year. The translation was a little hurried, and opened with the assertion that not only was the 'spectral' William Blake still alive, but he was actually incarcerated in a London madhouse. 'The two most celebrated inmates of the madhouse of Bedlam in London are the arsonist Martin, estranged elder brother of the painter John Martin, and William Blake – nicknamed "The Seer".'

Twenty years after his death, 'mad' Blake's reputation was barely taken seriously at all. A large manuscript collection of his work was offered for private sale by a keeper at the British Museum in 1847. It consisted of a foolscap quarto sketchbook of 58 leaves, packed with Blake's unpublished poems and drawings. It would now be considered priceless, but then it was sold for a mere ten shillings and sixpence.

The purchaser was Dante Gabriel Rossetti. Vague plans to publish it by the Pre-Raphaelite brotherhood were mooted, and Dante's brother the critic William Rossetti, expressed an interest. But on examination it was put quietly aside as too difficult and obscure to interest the public. A whole generation had now elapsed, the surviving 'Ancients' were indeed growing old, and the memory of 'mad' Blake was dwindling to nothing. It is possible that the author of 'The Tyger' might have been entirely lost.

Then, thirteen years later, on 1 November 1860, Rossetti wrote to his friend the poet William Allingham with surprising news. 'A man (one Gilchrist, who lives next door to Carlyle) wrote to me the other day, saying he was writing a Life of Blake, and wanted to see my manuscript by that genius. Was there not some talk of *your* doing something by way of publishing its contents? I know William thought of doing so, but fancy it might wait long for his efforts ... I have not engaged myself in any way to the said Gilchrist on the subject, though I have told him he can see it here if he will give me a day's notice.'

When the 'said Gilchrist' finally visited in March 1861, Rossetti was surprised to encounter a long-haired, dreamy, moon-faced young man who looked rather as if he had stepped out of one of his own Pre-Raphaelite paintings. Alexander Gilchrist was thirty-two, a young writer and art critic, who announced quietly that he had been working on a Life of Blake for the last six years. Indeed, he had already signed a contract with the publisher Macmillan. He did not think William Blake was mad; in fact he thought he was a genius. He was going to transform his reputation, however long it took him, and whatever it cost him.

2

Who was Blake's unexpected champion? Born in the year after Blake's death in 1828, Alexander Gilchrist had trained as a barrister in the Middle Temple. Restless in his profession, bookish and not physically strong, but with great determination and independence of mind, Gilchrist sought freedom in magazine journalism and freelance art criticism. From 1849, when he was just twenty-one, he began to write regularly for the *Eclectic Review*, and quickly made his name as critic and reviewer. He was known for his fresh eye, his jaunty prose style, his meticulous background research, and his highly unorthodox views. He was also a young critic in search of a cause.

In 1850, he produced an outstanding article on the forgotten and unfashionable painter, William Etty. Etty had once been renouned as an exuberant painter of Romantic nudes, both male and female, and erotic scenes from classical history and mythology, such as his *Vision of Gyges*. Once admired by Regency critics, Victorian taste and propriety had turned against him, and his paintings were scoffingly referred to in Academy circles as 'Etty's bumboats'. Gilchrist accepted a speculative commission from a provincial publisher, David Bogue, to write a full-length biography. He undertook to re-establish Etty's reputation, and turn back the tide of priggish mockery and misunderstanding.

On the strength of the £100 commission, Alexander married his twenty-three year old sweetheart, Anne Burrows, in February 1851. They spent part of their honeymoon researching Etty's life in York, where the painter had lived and worked. They interviewed his friends, and examined his nude studies and historical pictures, now mostly housed in private collections. This unorthodox nuptial expedition greatly appealed to Anne, who was free-thinking in her views, and impatient with the conventions of her respectable Highgate upbringing. She too hoped one day to write.

Their first child was born in December 1851, and the large Etty biography was published in 1855, when Gilchrist was still only twenty-seven. The book, which was studiously written and safely deprived of all illustrations (apparently Bogue lost his nerve at the last moment), caused only a mild scandal in York. But in London it drew wholly unexpected praised from the sixty year-old doyen of biographical writing, Thomas Carlyle. It was written, the Sage announced, 'in a vigorous, sympathetic, vivacious spirit', and gave the 'delineation, actual and intelligible, of a man extremely well-worth knowing'. This rare mark of approval from the author of *On Heroes, Hero-Worship and the Heroic in History* (1841), confirmed Gilchrist in his new vocation as biographer.

After several visits to Chelsea, Gilchrist established himself as Carlyle's confidante and to some extent his biographical protégé. The Sage had recently published his influential *Life of John Sterling* (1851), which by sympathetically recounting the career of an apparent failure, indeed a kind of anti-Hero, gave the whole genre a new impulse. It was a time when biography was about to enter a new literary golden age, with John Forster's *Oliver Goldsmith* (1854), Mrs Gaskell's *Charlotte Bronte* (1857), Samuel Smiles's *Self-Help* (1859), G. H. Lewes's *Goethe* (1855) and Frederick Martin's *John Clare* (1866).

Carlyle noticed that Gilchrist's dreamy appearance was deceptive: the young lawyer had a capacity for relentless archival research, an almost forensic gift for tracking down rare books and documents. Carlyle was working, with many groans, on his multi-volume *Life of Frederick the Great*, and soon found Gilchrist bringing him numerous rare bibliographic finds. 'Beyond doubt you are one of the successfullest hunters up of Old Books now living,' beamed Carlyle, 'and one of the politest of obliging men!'

The bookish Gilchrist also took great delight in pursing his open-air researches. With Anne he took long walks in Kent, Dorset, and the Lake District. With Carlyle he wandered after midnight about the backstreets of Westminster, Soho, Lambeth or the City. He had an eye (not unlike the young Dickens) for old houses, forgotten buildings, crooked corners, and disappearing communities. Faced with some old church, said Anne, he would 'scan every stone' until it yielded up its 'quota of history'. Over long evenings of black tea and tobacco, Carlyle encouraged him to talk, speculate, and seek a daring new subject for his pen. A warm, if slightly wary, friendship also grew up between Anne and the older Jane Carlyle.

The subject of William Blake had probably been in Gilchrist's mind for more than a decade. As a young law student of the Middle Temple, Gilchrist had heard rumours of Blake as the eccentric erstwhile occupant of Fountain Court, which he passed through every day on the way to his legal chambers. He wrote a highly characteristic evocation of this place, its sacred Blakean associations overlaid by mid-Victorian seediness, that eventually appeared in Chapter 31 of his biography.

> Fountain Court, unknown by name, perhaps, to many who yet often pass it on their way through a great London artery, is a court lying a little out of the Strand, between it and the river, and approached by a dark narrow opening, or inclined plane, at the corner of Simpson's Tavern, and nearly opposite Exeter Hall. At one corner of the court, nearest the Strand, stands the Coal Hole Tavern, once the haunt of Edmund Kean and his 'Wolf Club' of *claquers*, still in Blake's time a resort of the Thespian race; not then promoted to the less admirable notoriety it has, in our days, enjoyed. Now the shrill tinkle of a dilapidate piano, accompaniment to a series of tawdry *poses plastiques*, wakes the nocturnal echoes, making night hideous in the quiet court where the poet and visionary once lived and designed the *Inventions of Job*.

Initially Gilchrist knew little of the poetry. As an art critic it was a copy of Blake's *Illustrations to the Book of Job*, found at the back of a London printshop, which first caught his eye. He never lost his sense of their astonishing power, and it was Blake's visual imagination which always remained for Gilchrist the key to his genius. Accordingly, in summer 1855 he decided to write to one of the surviving Ancients, the painter Samuel Palmer, by then aged sixty.

On 23 August 1855 Gilchrist received a long and engaging reply, which he later reprinted entire in Chapter 33 of his biography. While praising Blake's artistic integrity, Palmer carefully dispelled the notion of Blake's madness, and replaced it with the figure of a gentle, almost Christ-like sage. 'He was a man without a mask; his aim was single, his path straight-forwards, and his wants few ... His voice and manner were quiet, yet all awake with intellect ... He was gentle and affectionate, loving to be with little children, and to talk about them. 'That is heaven,' he said to a friend, leading him to a window, and pointing to a group of them at play.'

At the same time Palmer hinted at a prophet from the Old Testament, rather than the New: a formidable Blake who could be highly 'expressive' and emotional, 'quivering with feeling', capable of deep anger, and with a flashing glance that could be 'terrible' towards his enemies. 'Cunning and falsehood quailed under it.' He summed up these contradictions with a painterly example from the Italian Renaissance. 'His ideal home was with Fra Angelico: a little later he might have been a reformer, but after the fashion of Savonarola.' Gilchrist was captivated, and he and Palmer became fast friends.

A year later in 1856, the Gilchrist family moved in next to the Carlyles at No. 6 Cheyne Row. The pursuit of Blake's trail through London galleries, local museums, antique bookshops, and private collections now began in earnest. Gilchrist purchased Blake prints, and borrowed what he could not buy. Anne started her own collection of Blake's watercolours. Together they tracked down Blake's various lodgings and workshops north and south of the river, in Soho and Lambeth, and meticulously researched his three year sojourn at Felpham, by the sea in Sussex.

Having established friendly contact with the affable Samuel Palmer, Gilchrist moved on to the other surviving Ancients. They were not all so easy to deal with. The painter John Linnell, was helpful but bossy, suggesting the possibilities of a collaboration. He had eleven precious letters from Blake, written at the very end of his life. The sculptor Frederick Tatham, having written his own private Memoir, and taken to religion, was strange and touchy. The artist George Richmond (only fifteen when he met Blake) was now a well-meaning but gushing middle-aged raconteur.

Gilchrist engaged them in correspondence and interviewed them where he could, minutely compiling anecdotes and stories, trying to sift the true from the apocryphal. He talked to Francis Oliver Finch and Flaxman's younger sister Maria Denman. He was particularly interested in the relations between Blake and his wife Catherine. Original letters from Blake were the one thing Gilchrist found it almost impossible to discover, apart from Linnell's.

Gilchrist's greatest diplomatic triumph was to pierce the peppery reserve of the retired journalist, Henry Crabb Robinson, then in his eighties. Robinson – once the intimate friend of Wordsworth, Coleridge and Lamb – had kept extensive diary accounts of the whole Romantic circle during his time. They were admiring, but sceptical and extremely shrewd. In 1811 he had published a rare appreciation of Blake's work in a German magazine published in Hamburg: 'William Blake: Artist, Poet, and Religious Dreamer'. Moreover, his unpublished Journals for 1825–7 contained a unique series of interviews with the older Blake. Robinson paid particular attention to the question of Blake's visions, the logic (or otherwise) of his explanations, and the significance of his eccentricities. Gilchrist managed to obtain all this material, and use it with brilliant effect in Chapter 36.

In the winter of 1859, Gilchrist submitted an outline draft of his *Life of Blake* to the publisher Macmillan. He was offered an £150 contract, and an advance on research expenses of £20. Compared with the Etty commission, these terms marked a small but not very generous increase. After all, this was a time when popular biographies by Mrs Gaskell and John Forster were being commissioned for well over £1,000. But of course Blake's name was still worth nothing. Undeterred, Gilchrist worked on through 1860, continuing to support his family with freelance journalism. But it must have seemed an increasingly quixotic venture.

In March 1861, he finally met Dante Gabriel Rossetti, and the pace of research increased still further. The Blake manuscript notebook, purchased over fourteen years before, was at last revealed. Over several later meetings at the Cheshire Cheese tavern, in Fleet Street, the new poems and drawings were discussed. Gilchrist quickly passed muster with the pre-Raphaelite brotherhood, all of whom were suddenly excited by the prospect of the forthcoming book. Rossetti's friendship also brought him into contact with Swinburne, who now discovered a passion for Blake.

Most enthusiastic of all was Dante Gabriel's brother, the art critic William Michael Rossetti, who encouraged Gilchrist to think in terms of an even more ambitious project. After the biography perhaps he could edit a companion volume of Blake's poems and a catalogue of his art work? Spurred on by these late supporters, Gilchrist promised Macmillan to deliver the completed biography by spring 1862.

But after six years, the work was now close to exhausting him. Money was short, and by now the Gilchrists had four children. Gilchrist's constitution, never strong, began to fail. He was frequently ill and depressed, harassed by his weekly art reviews. Sometimes he collapsed, unable to work on Blake for days on end. It was in this growing professional crisis that Anne Gilchrist began quietly to assert herself.

Anne had probably been working as Alexander's part-time research assistant ever since the Etty days. But now she became his full-time amanuensis. She took dictation, copied Blake's manuscripts, checked facts and dates at the British Museum, and prepared an index. She admired Gilchrist's perfectionism, always pursuing one more source or reference. But sometimes she felt he would never complete the book at all.

Nonetheless, by late summer 1861, Gilchrist told Macmillan that he had a draft of the whole biography. Although he was continually slipping in extra materials and anecdotes, the basic structure of the book was secure. It was lucidly organized in thirty-eight short chapters, and he was ready to start sending it in batches to the printer, for setting up in proof. This was the usual procedure for a large book.

Macmillan was delighted and urged him to begin. Accordingly, Gilchrist sent the first eight chapters to the printers in September 1861, taking Blake's Life up to the *Poetic Sketches* and the 'Notes on Lavater' made when Blake had just turned thirty. He promised to send in the next batch by November, with the aim of having the complete work in proof by the following spring. He was under great pressure, but believed that with Anne's help he could just about fulfil his deadlines.

On 20 November 1861, Gilchrist wrote to his publisher that he had been unable to send the next 'big mass of copy', consisting of the next dozen or so chapters (taking Blake up to forty and his most productive years). He explained that 'domestic troubles have during the last month stood in the way'. For six weeks his eldest daughter, seven year old Beatrice, had been lying dangerously ill at Cheyne Row with scarlet fever. His wife Anne had insisted on a 'rigid quarantine', remaining alone in the child's sickroom to carry out all the nursing herself. There was great fear of infection. Gilchrist was only allowed in once an evening, to make up the fire, while Anne stood back

xvii

by the window. Meanwhile, he tried to look after the other three young children with the help of one (frequently drunk) domestic.

At the end of his letter, Gilchrist unburdened himself to his publisher.

> We have been in great misery at times, aggravated by our having a doctor in whom we had not implicit confidence ... My wife has during all this time been confined to the sickroom, without help! ... Of hired nurses we have a horror; our friends have mostly children and others regard for whom makes them dread crossing the threshold of a scarlatina infected house. Forgive this closing matter.
>
> Yours faithfully,
> Alexander Gilchrist.

A week later, just as his little daughter Beatrice began to pull through, Gilchrist was himself struck down. Jane Carlyle sent notes offering help to Anne, and Thomas Carlyle brought a fashionable physician, who looked at Gilchrist from the distance of the sickroom door and hastily departed. After that, events unfolded quickly. Ten days after he had sent his desperate, apologetic letter to his publisher Macmillan, Alexander Gilchrist slipped into a coma.

Anne later wrote: 'The brain was tired with stress of work; the fever burned and devastated like a flaming fire: to four days of delirium succeeded one of exhaustion, of stupor; and then the end; without a word, but not without a look of loving recognition. It was on a wild and stormy night, 30 November 1861, that his spirit took flight.'

Alexander Gilchrist died at the age of thirty-three. His great biography of Blake, his labour of love, had been wonderfully researched and written in draft. But it was unfinished.

3

With her peculiar force and independence, Anne Gilchrist immediately determined to finish the biography for him. Less than a week after Alexander's death, she wrote to Macmillan on 6 December 1861, 'I try to fix my thoughts on the one thing that remains for me to do for my dear Husband. I do not think that anyone but myself can do what has to be done to the Book. I was his amanuensis . . .'

She packed up his papers, returned a mass of borrowed pictures and manuscripts, refused Jane's invitation to move in with the Carlyles, and took the children and the unfinished book down to a clapboard cottage in tiny village of Shottermill, a mile from Haslemere in Sussex.

To understand what happened next, we have to turn to Anne Gilchrist's own story. She had always been an independent spirit. She was born Annie Burrows in February 1828 in Gower Street, London, but was partly brought up in the country at Colne in Essex. Here, when she was nine years old, her beloved elder brother Johnnie saved her life. The incident, as re-told, has a curious fairy-tale-like quality. While exploring a secret part of the garden, little Annie fell backwards into a deep well, and would have certainly drowned, had not Johnnie reached down and just managed to hold her up by the hair, until help finally came. Over thirty years later she put this strangely symbolic tale of survival into a children's story, *Lost in the Woods* (1861).

Anne's father was a London lawyer, strict and demanding, who died aged fifty-one in 1839, when she was only eleven. From then on, the family were on their own, and Anne was in some sense a liberated spirit. They moved to Highgate, where Anne

xix

went to school, a handsome tomboy, clever and rebellious. She was musical, well-read, and free-thinking. At seventeen she was surprised by the local vicar, when reading Rousseau's sexually explicit *Confessions* on a tombstone in Highgate Cemetery. Embarrassment was avoided (according to Anne) when the vicar misheard the title as St Augustine's *Confessions*.

At nineteen she became fascinated by scientific ideas, a further unladylike development. She announced to a friend that the intellectual world was divided between Emerson and Comte, between the spiritual and the materialist, and she was tending towards the latter.

In 1847 (the year Rossetti bought the Blake manuscript), she was devastated by the death of her 'angel brother', Johnnie. A year later, aged twenty, she announced her engagement to one of Johnnie's friends, a handsome young law student, Alexander Gilchrist, 'great, noble and beautiful'. In a way, he was probably a substitute brother. She deeply admired him, but from what she said later, she was never truly in love. What Alexander offered was the chance of freedom and independence. Their unorthodox Etty honeymoon was a promise of things to come.

After the birth of their four children – Percy, Beatrice, Herbert, and Grace – she set herself to earn additional household money by writing small pieces for the monthly magazines, and *Chambers Encyclopaedia*. The first of these, 'A Glance at the Vegetable Kingdom', was published in *Chambers* in spring 1857, shortly after they moved into Cheyne Row.

Unexpectedly, Anne made a specialty of popular science subjects. Moreover, she was remarkably successful. In 1859, the year of Darwin's *Origin of Species*, she wrote a controversial article on the newly discovered gorilla, 'Our Nearest Relation', comparing its skills and habits to *homo sapiens*. It was published in

Charles Dickens' magazine, *All the Year Round*. Next she wrote on 'Whales and Whaling', and in the following years she produced several further young person's guides to scientific topics: 'What is Electricity?', 'What is a Sunbeam?', and 'The Indestructibility of Force'. Her ability to research, organize and explain technical subjects for the general reader was highly unusual.

Her role as Gilchrist's amanuensis was therefore more that it might superficially appear. She seems to have become a genuine literary partner. Anne claimed the subsequent work on the biography came to her as a kind of posthumous collaboration. 'Alex's spirit is with me ever – presides in my home; speaks to me in every sweet scene; broods over the peaceful valleys; haunts the grand wild hill tops; shines gloriously forth in setting sun, and moon and stars.'

This may have been true, but she was also driven by other, though no less powerful emotions. Essentially, she seems to have felt guilty about Gilchrist's death. She felt that she had never been his true wife. Nearly a decade later, in September 1871, she wrote a remarkable confession of her own. 'I think . . . my sorrow was far more bitter, though not so deep, as that of a loving tender wife. As I stood by him in the coffin, I felt such remorse I had not, could not have, been more tender to him – such a conviction that if I had loved him as he deserved to be loved he would not have been taken from us. To the last my soul dwelt apart and unmated, and his soul dwelt apart and unmated.'

Her drive to complete his biography of Blake was, therefore, far more than a show of pious sentiment, a widow's tender offering. It was more like an uneasy debt of honour, the recognition of a difficult but sacred trust. Anne already knew much of Alexander's method of working, and his perfectionism. What she did not know was whether she could match it. She wrote to Macmillan: 'Many things were to have been inserted – anecdotes etc. collected during the last year, which he used to say would be the best things in the book. Whether I shall be able to rightly use the rough notes of these and insert them in the fittest places I cannot yet tell. He altered chapter by chapter as he sent it to the printers . . .'

Three months later, in March 1862 she again wrote Macmillan that, to her surprise, she had completed sorting and arranging all of Alexander's remaining material for the book. It would be faithfully completed. 'You shall not find me dilatory or unreliable; least of all in this sacred trust.' Fiercely defensive of every word of Alexander's existing text, she carefully began to pull together the drafts of the outstanding chapters. She made regular visits to the British Museum, catching the London train up from Haslemere station. She checked his facts and polished his style. She defended him against Macmillan's charges of sometimes writing too flamboyantly, like Carlyle.

Most crucially, she turned for help to the Rossettis. She did not want them to touch the text of Alex's biography, but she wanted help with the companion volume: the catalogue of Blake's pictures and an anthology of his poetry. She proposed to Macmillan that he commission a second volume, to consist of an annotated catalogue of Blake's visual work compiled by Michael Rossetti, and a selection of Blake's poetry edited by Dante Gabriel. This was agreed, and the whole project now advanced rapidly on its new footing.

The sudden death of Dante Gabriel's own wife, Lizzie Siddal, that same spring of 1862, added a peculiar intensity to the work of selection. ('I feel forcibly', he wrote to Anne, 'the bond of misery that exists between us.') He moved back into bachelor lodgings, which he shared with Meredith and the young Swinburne, and they too acted as unofficial Blake readers and selectors. Even Christina Rossetti came to stay at the Shottermill cottage.

So not only had the whole Rossetti family now rallied round Anne's 'Herculean labour', but the two volume work had almost become a group enterprise, a Pre-Raphaelite project to restore Blake, and to do honour to his young idealistic biographer. As Dante Gabriel wrote to Anne, 'I would gladly have done it for Blake's or gladly for your husband's or gladly for your own sake, and moreover, had always had a great wish of my own to do something in this direction . . .'

The twin volumes were to be delivered twelve months later, in spring 1863.

4

Who, then, finally wrote Gilchrist's Life of William Blake?

It is clear from their correspondence, that the Rossettis almost entirely confined themselves to the editorial work on the second volume alone. Dante Gabriel was asked to write a 'Supplementary' summary (Chapter 39, no longer included); and to fill in a missing description of Blake's *Book of Job* (Chapter 32), ironically the very work that had first drawn Gilchrist to Blake. Apart from that, they touched virtually nothing in the first volume, because they were not permitted to. Anne regarded the text of the biography as a sacred to Gilchrist's memory. She was its sole guardian. 'I think you will not find it hard to forgive me a little reluctance,' she wrote to William Rossetti, 'that *any* living tones should blend with that voice which here speaks for the last time on earth.'

But how far she herself added new materials from Alexander's notes, or made stylistic changes, must remain more problematic. In April 1862 she was speaking of 'incorporating *all* the additional matter contained in the notes' into a final draft, which sounds quite radical. But by the end of May, the position was almost reversed. 'I am glad to say I find the Manuscript even more complete than I anticipated, and that a large mass of Notes which I had thought contained new matter, were merely for reference and verification.' To the end of her days Anne insisted that she was nothing more than her husband's 'editor'. But since Gilchrist's original manuscript has not survived, there is no way of knowing precisely how she understood this role.

However, it is difficult to find evidence of any large editorial additions or interventions. For example, Alexander had frequently lamented his failure to develop any proper critical commentary on the poetry (as opposed to the illuminations) of Blake's 'Prophetic Books'. Anne was clearly tempted to remedy this. 'I found the only grave omission in the book – the only place where dear Alec had left an absolute blank that *must* be filled in – was for some account of Blake's mystic writings, or 'Prophetic Books', as he called them.'

But although she consulted with Rossetti, she did not in the end attempt to add any significant commentary, writing ruefully: 'I could heartily wish the difficult problem presented by these strange Books had been successfully grappled with, or indeed grappled with at all. Hardly anything has now been attempted beyond bringing together a few readable extracts . . . They are at least psychologically curious and important.' The omission is very clear, for example in the desultory remarks on *Jerusalem* in Chapter 21, despite the fact that Anne had meticulously copied out the entire text by hand, from a rare copy loaned with great reluctance ('only for a week') by Monckton Milnes.

In fact, she seems to have conceived her main role as protecting what Alexander had written and quoted. There was some need for this. The genial Palmer was desperate to avoid anything that hinted at 'blasphemy', while Macmillan was acutely nervous of Blake's erotic writing; he anxiously read every line of the proofs, and questioned even single lines from the poems, especially those from 'The Daughters of Albion'. William Rossetti wrote: 'The pervading idea of "The Daughters of Albion" is one which was continually seething in Blake's mind, and flustering Propriety in his writings ... It is the idea of the unnatural and terrible result in which, in modern society, ascetic doctrines in theology and morals have involved the relations of the sexes ... in [this] cause he is never tired of uprearing the banner of heresy and non-conformity.'

Anne replied on 3 October 1862: 'I am afraid you will be vexed with me ... But it was no use to put in what I was perfectly certain Macmillan (who reads all the proofs) would take out again ... It might be well to mention to Mr Swinburne that it would be perfectly useless to attempt to handle this side of Blake's writings – that Mr Macmillan in far more inexorable against any shade of heterodoxy in morals, than in religion ... in fact poor "flustered Propriety" has to be most tenderly and indulgently dealt with.'

She was beset by other diplomatic problems. One of the original Ancients, the painter John Linnell, offered to oversee all the proofs, but made it clear that he would alter the text where he did not approve of it. Anne knew that Alexander had already rejected this idea long before: 'the bare notion of it filled him with horror: I do not think he ever showed proof or manuscript to the most congenial friend even.' This was a policy that Anne clearly intended to continue.

Alexander had made the 'most minute notes' of all Linnell told him, but believed there was 'considerable divergency' in their view of the facts. 'Besides,' concluded Anne, 'a biographer's duty often is to balance the evidence of conflicting witnesses.' To have acceded to Linnell would, she felt sure, have been 'a most imprudent, and indeed treacherous thing on my part.'

There were other difficulties among the survivors, and keepers of the flame. Frederick Tatham had quarreled with Linnell over the ownership of some of Blake's Dante drawings, and Anne believed that Tatham had also imposed on Blake's widow by silently selling off many of his engraved books over 'thirty years'. Such post-mortem disputes between the Ancients were peculiarly confusing to Anne. Yet she retained absolute confidence in Alexander's view of the situation. 'My husband, who had sifted the matter, and knew both parties, thought Linnell an upright and truthful, if somewhat hard man, and that towards Blake his conduct had been throughout admirable. He also inclined to think, that Mrs Blake retained one trait of an uneducated mind – an unreasonable suspiciousness...' Here, she was in fact quoting Gilchrist's own words from the biography.

She was however dismayed to discover that Tatham, in a fit of religious zeal, had much later destroyed many of Blake's manuscripts. For a biographer this was itself the ultimate sin, and would have appalled Alexander. She wrote angrily to Rossetti, saying that Tatham had come to believe that Blake was indeed inspired, 'but quite from a wrong quarter – by Satan himself – and was to be cast out as an "unclean spirit".' This was a ghastly parody of Gilchrist's subtle, secular, psychological appreciation of Blake's profound eccentricity and originality. She would have nothing to do with it.

The most challenging editorial problem arrived last. In January 1863, when the biography was already printing, Anne was sent ten precious letters of Blake's to his young publisher and patron, Thomas Butts. At a stroke, this doubled the number of surviving letters. They all dated from the crucial – and little known – period of creative renewal, when Blake retired to a tiny cottage in Felpham, Sussex, between 1800 and 1804. These gave a wholly new insight into Blake's character, his views of his art and patronage, and some wonderful examples of his most limpid but visionary prose.

> The villagers of Felpham are not mere rustics; they are polite and modest. Meat is cheaper than in London; but the sweet air and the voices of winds, trees, and birds, and the odours of the happy ground, make it a dwelling for immortals. Work will go on here with God-speed. A roller and two harrows lie before my window. I met a plough on my first going out at my gate the first morning of my arrival, and the ploughboy said to the Ploughman, 'Father, the gate is open.'

One letter even gave a long and detailed account, from Blake's point of view, of the fracas with a soldier in the garden at Felpham which lead to his trial for 'seditious and treasonable utterance' in 1804. This was one of the most dramatic events in Blake's life, and perhaps a turning point in his professional career. Gilchrist had already given up a whole chapter to describing the incident. His account was based on Catherine's memories, Hayley's letters, and a local Sussex newspaper report of the trial. While defending Blake as certainly not guilty of real treason, Gilchrist allowed it to be tacitly understood that Blake did treat the soldier with some violence, 'in a kind of inspired frenzy', and probably did shout some ill-advised political things at him: '"Damn the King, and you too," said Blake with pardonable emphasis.' Blake's own account was far more exculpatory, and intriguingly different.

How should Anne handle this unexpected biographical windfall? Macmillan claimed he was too far advanced with the printing to allow Anne to insert these letters at such a late stage. However, since they were discovered nine months before the book was finally published, it seems that Anne herself was loath to disrupt Alexander's narrative. Yet the letters were extremely revealing, and Anne could not bear to omit them. 'I have all but finished copying Blake's letters; a task of real enjoyment, for they are indeed supremely interesting, admitting one as far as anything he ever wrote into the "inner precincts" of his mind . . .'

In the end, the solution she chose was to print the 'LETTERS TO THOMAS BUTTS' separately, as an appendix to the Life (where they can now be found). This perhaps gives the clearest indication of the subsidiary way she saw her own editorial function. This solution (although clearly not ideal) allowed her carefully to retain Alexander's perceptive narrative of the Sussex period without interruption (Chapters 16 to 19). But it also allowed her to appear modestly in her own role of Editor, remarking on the light that the letters now threw on 'the undercurrents of Blake's life', and wishing only that Alexander had seen them before he died.

By autumn 1863, Anne had surmounted all these difficulties. Far from finding the work burdensome, she later said characteristically, that it had proved a support and a consolation to her in the time of mourning. 'That beloved task (the Blake) kept my head above water in the deep sea of affliction, and now that it is ended I sometimes feel like to sink – to sink, that is, into pining discontent – and a relaxing of the hold upon all high aims . . .' The Life was finally published in two volumes in October 1863.

5

Two thousand copies were printed, and reviews appeared rapidly. There were some initial doubts whether the biography would, as Anne put it, 'shock devout minds'. One reviewer observed evenly: 'a more timid biographer might have hesitated about making so open an exhibition of his hero's singularities.' But it was soon clear that the book would be a triumph. It was widely admired by the entire Pre-Raphaelite circle, Robert Browning wrote a fan letter, and Samuel Palmer spoke for the Ancients when he described it as 'a treasure'. He added thoughtfully, 'I do hope it may provoke a lively art-controversy in the periodicals, unless people have gone quite to sleep'. He had 'read wildly everywhere', and concluded tenderly, 'already it is certain to be an *imperishable monument* of the dear Biographer.'

It was loyally hailed by Carlyle: 'thankfulness is one clear feeling; not only to you from myself, but to you for the sake of another who is not here now.' He considered it 'right well done – minute knowledge well-arranged, lively utterance, brevity, cheerful lucidity'. Later he told Anne, with a tact surely designed to please the editor, that the whole biography was remarkable for 'the acuteness and thoroughness with which the slightest clues had been followed out in gathering the materials, and with all this toil and minute accuracy on the writer's part, nothing but pleasure for the reader – no tediousness.'

The great strengths of the work, which Anne had so faithfully

xxix

preserved, were quickly apparent. Gilchrist's approach is lively, personal, enthusiastic and often humourous – quite unlike much over-earnest mid-Victorian biography. The quick, informal, darting style of his prose lends a sense of continual discovery and excitement to the narrative, and yet allows for virtuoso passages of description and summary.

It is extraordinarily well-researched, especially in the use made of the previous memoirs by Malkin, Tatham, Linnell, Palmer, Crabb Robinson, and others. Although he had lacked the Butts Letters, Gilchrist draws effectively on some original correspondance with Flaxman in the early years, and the expressive series of short notes to John Linnell at Hampstead in the last years. He also quotes brilliantly throughout from Blake's own works, both prose and poetry, much of it quite unknown to contemporary readers, such as the early 'Notes on Lavater' and the 'Proverbs of Hell'. He was, too, the first Victorian writer to pick out and reprint in full Blake's great 'Jerusalem' hymn from the preface to *Milton*, 'And did those feet in ancient times', in Chapter 21.

There are two qualities in Gilchrist's writing, which make him such an exceptionally vivid biographer. The first is his sense of physical place. Gilchrist had a gift for evoking particular London streets, characteristic clusters of buildings or courtyards, and beyond them certain rural landscapes and secluded villages, where Blake had lived and worked. He captured their appearance, mood and atmosphere, and gave hints of their visionary meanings, or auras, for Blake.

Gilchrist had spent endless days researching and identifying them, following meticulously in Blake's footsteps. He could also add fascinating observations of how these sacred places had changed in the subsequent fifty or so years, giving a sense of historical continuity. In this way, the biography first gave Blake's extraordinary imaginative life 'a local habitation and a name'. The descriptions of the gothic interior of Westminster Abbey, or of Hercules Building (and its garden) in Lambeth, or of the cottage and seashore at Felpham, and the last, hidden lodgings at Fountain Court are especially evocative in this respect.

The second quality is his power to conjure up Blake's pictures and designs for the reader. Only few of these were actually illustrated in black and white engravings, so a great deal depended on Gilchrist's verbal descriptions. He found a remarkable way of bringing these to life in virtuoso passages of exquisite prose 'dramatization', the energy of his syntax matching the energy of Blake's line, which became a major feature of his biography. Here the young art critic comes into his own. This, for example, is how he brilliantly evoked the life and movement of the thirteen designs for 'A Memorable Fancy', in Chapter 10.

> The ever-fluctuating colour, the spectral pigmies rolling, flying, leaping among the letters; the ripe bloom of quiet corners, the living light and bursts of flame, the spires and tongues of fire vibrating with the full prism, make the page seem to move and quiver within its boundaries, and you lay the book down tenderly, as if you had been handling something sentient. A picture has been said to be midway between a thing and a thought; so in these books over which Blake had brooded, with the brooding of fire, the very paper seems to come to life as you gaze upon it – not with a mortal life, but with a life indestructible, whether for good or evil.

Gilchrist made the defense of Blake's eccentricity, and the rejection of his supposed insanity, a commanding theme from the beginning of the biography.

> On Peckham Rye (by Dulwich Hill) it is, as he will in after years relate, that while quite a child, of eight or ten perhaps, he has

his 'first vision'. Sauntering along, the boy looks up and sees a tree filled with angels, bright angel wings bespangling every bough like stars. Returned home he relates the incident, and only through his mother's intercession escapes a thrashing from his honest father, for telling a lie . . . If these traits of childish years be remembered, they will help to elucidate the visits from the spiritual world of later years, in which the grown man believed as unaffectedly as ever had the boy of ten.

Gilchrist reverts continually to these visions: calmly asking what exactly they were, how Blake described them, and how they should be accounted for. Much apparently outlandish behaviour, such as the 'scandalous' Adam and Eve nude sunbathing incident at Lambeth, is given a reasonable and detailed explanation, in this case with a amusing reminder about the poet Shelley's enthusiasm for the early naturist movement. It is interesting that clearly Anne had been able to prevent Macmillan from censoring this particular account.

Later, Blake's poverty, social isolation and professional difficulties are shrewdly shown to have exacerbated the oddities of his temperament. Of the quarrel with the commercial publisher Cromek in 1815, a frankly 'discordant episode', Gilchrist writes, 'In Blake's own mind, where all should have been, and for the most part was, peace, the sordid conflict left a scar. It left him more tetchy than ever; more disposed to willful exaggeration of individualities already too prominent, more prone to unmeasured violence of expression. The extremes he gave way to in his designs and writings – mere ravings to such as had no key to them – did him no good with that portion of the public the illustrated *Blair* had introduced him to . . . Now, too, was established for him the damaging reputation "Mad".'

All this is summarised in the decisive Chapter 35, boldly

entitled: 'Mad or Not Mad'. In many way this chapter is the psychological key to the entire biography. Here Gilchrist carefully defines the 'special faculty' of Blake's imagination, and vindicates the profound spiritual sanity of the 'gentle yet fiery-hearted mystic'. One after another, he calls to witness all Blake's circle of friends, from Flaxman and Fuseli to Palmer and Linnell. In a robust passage Gilchrist rejects any modish Victorian interpretation of Blake's visions. 'No man, by the way, would have been more indifferent or averse than he (wide and tolerant as was his faith in supernatural revelations) towards the table-turning, wainscot-knocking, bosh-propounding "Spiritualism" of the present hour.' Instead Gilchrist finally champions Blake in terms that Carlyle would have recognised: 'Does not prophet or hero always seem "mad" to the respectable mob, and to polished men of the world . . . ?'

Gilchrist's remaining narrative problem lay in the dearth of material during Blake's 'dark years' in London in the decade between 1808 and 1818, when he met his great patron and supporter, the young painter John Linnell, the first of the Ancients. Broadly his solution is to introduce the engaging stories of some of the more colourful characters who knew Blake during this time: the rapacious art dealer Cromek; the exuberant astrologer John Varley (for whom Blake painted the visionary portrait of the Flea); and the dandy art critic and poisoner (later championed by Oscar Wilde), Thomas Wainewright.

The last chapters are structured round the unpublished *Reminiscences* of Crabb Robinson from 1825, and the interviews with Palmer, Richmond and Tatham who knew Blake in the last years at Fountain Court. Here, from Chapter 34 onwards ('Personal Details'), the biography is at its most intimate and moving. The final picture of Blake 'chaunting Songs' to Catherine, as he lay on his deathbed in the little upper room above the Thames, is unforgettable.

6

Gilchrist's biography was immediately taken up by the Pre-Raphaelites and their circle. William Rossetti established himself as the leading nineteenth-century Blake scholar, and edited the first collection of Blake's *Poetical Works*, published in the Aldine series in 1874. Algernon Swinburne, inspired by Gilchrist, wrote the first detailed assessment of Blake as a poet, which appeared as a long monograph, *William Blake: A Critical Essay* in 1868. In his Preface Swinburne spoke with admiration of Gilchrist's 'trained skill' and 'sense of selection' as a biographer, and his 'almost incomparable capacity of research and care in putting to use the results of such long and refined labour'.

Like Palmer, he felt the biography would endure, despite the tragic circumstances of its composition. 'This good that he did is likely to live after him; no part of it is likely to be interred in his grave.' In saying this, Swinburne also gently re-opened the question of the posthumous collaboration between Anne and Alexander. 'For the book, unfinished, was not yet incomplete, when the writer's work was broken short off. All or nearly all the biographical part had been carried through to a good end. It remained for other hands to do the editing; to piece together the loose notes left, and to supply all that was requisite or graceful in the way of remark or explanation.' Anne however remained strenuous in her denial of having contributed anything more than 'editorial' work.

Interest in Blake steadily revived, and within fifteen years

Macmillan was ready to undertake a new edition. Anne Gilchrist had spent the previous four years in America with her children, writing about the work of Walt Whitman and forming an intense personal friendship with the poet. But on her return to England in June 1879, almost her first act was undertake the revision of the Blake biography for Macmillan. She had remained in close touch with the Rossettis, and with their advice began to correct minor errors of fact and dates. By March 1880 the work was being 'pushed energetically through'.

Her son Herbert remarked: 'Anne Gilchrist's task of editing the second edition was not an easy one. It was a tradition in the family to avoid notes; to recast the text rather than to use them. Thus, too, as a consequence, her work as editor is not apparent.' This is curious, as her editorial hand is much more evident in the 1880 edition, and its impact much more marked.

Her main task was to find a place for another major cache of correspondence, some forty newly discovered letters from Blake to his patron William Hayley. Thirty-four of them had been auctioned at Sotheby's in 1878, and bought by the Rossettis. Dante Gabriel regarded them as 'rather disappointing', and largely concerned with mundane business matters. But together with the twelve letters to Thomas Butts, they filled in the picture of Blake's middle years between 1800 and 1805. Clearly these could no longer be left in an Appendix.

Anne determined that they should be fully integrated into the narrative of the text. She inserted them with extraordinary skill between Chapter 16 and Chapter 20, adding short linking sentences, but largely allowing them to speak for themselves. By comparing the two editions, one can see how ingenuously she kept to Alexander's original wording (often by the device of altering the order of his paragraphs), and how little she added of her own. She was, however, forced to delete a large part of Alexander's account of the 'soldier' incident at Felpham, allowing it to be replaced by Blake's own self-justifying letter to Butts. This was the one major cut she made in the entire biography, and it was not a happy one. It produced a smoother but more anodyne account.

Indeed overall, the changes in the second edition had a curiously muffling effect. The dramatic story of Blake's Sussex period nearly doubled in length, but also halved in biographical impact. The picture of Blake's strange inner life, was swamped and blurred by the mundane superfluity of Hayley materials. The fifty extra pages slowed the pace of the entire narrative.

This loss of pace was further increased by newly extended citations from the Prophetic Books. Though she still regarded any attempt to interpret Blake's mythology as 'a reckless adventure', Anne hopefully read and re-read *Jerusalem*, finding 'several more coherent and indeed beautiful passages', and relating the poetry to the 'sublime influence of the sea' on Blake at Felpham. Finally she added half-a-dozen new extracts from both *Jerusalem* and *Milton* to Chapter 21, with a brief commentary on Blake's use of names. She also referred the reader to Swinburne's critical essay, as a possible guide 'through the dark mazes of these labyrinthine, spectre-haunted books'. Further expansions included more quotations from the 'Proverbs of Hell', and further brief reflections on Blake's mysticism.

But she also made cuts at certain points of controversy. She slightly shortened the 'Adam and Eve' incident in Chapter 12, in deference to its supposed immorality. She also removed some of Alexander's reflection on the sexual symbolism of 'The Daughters of Albion', the old point of disagreement with Macmillan and 'flustered Propriety'. Finally she censored a few of his more vivid but risqué phrases, such as the memorable reference to the music hall nude shows near Fountain Court.

Altogether the addition of the new letters, together with Anne's expanded quotations from the Prophetic Books, and her prudential cuts, gave the second edition of 1880 greater authority as a work of reference. But it also damaged much of its original charm and energy as a biography.

The second edition was longer, slower and more ponderous. The elegant, lively narrative structure with its short concentrated chapters, as Alexander had originally devised it, was weakened and made more conventional. It lost something of the passionate excitement and directness of its original youthful conception. Ironically for all Anne's sense of holding a sacred trust to her husband's work, Alexander's own voice is muted and dissipated. The second edition became more like a standard high Victorian volume of Life and Letters.

Nonetheless, the edition of 1880 continued the task of re-establishing Blake's reputation on both sides of the Atlantic. Praise for Gilchrist's heroic work was now universal, and Walt Whitman for one, saluted the rise of a new informal English style of biography, comparing it to the work of J.A. Froude. 'The Blake book is charming for the same reason that we find Froude's *Carlyle* fascinating – it is minute, it presents the man as he was, it gathers together little things ordinarily forgotten; portrays the man as he walked, talked, worked, in his simple capacity as a human being. It is just in such touches – such significant details – that the profounder, conclusive, art of biographical narrative lies.'

Anne would still make no claims other than that of being 'editor' of Alexander's work. Instead she added a long and passionate Memoir, praising his supreme dedication as a biographer. In it she made this thoughtful observation: 'If I could briefly sketch a faithful portrait of Blake's biographer, the attempt would need no apology; for if the work be of interest, so is the worker. A biographer necessarily offers himself as the mirror in which his hero is reflected; and we judge all the better of the truth and adequacy of the image by a closer acquaintance with the medium through which it comes to us.' In the use of that one word 'medium', she might, at least unconsciously, have been calling attention to herself.

7

Anne Gilchrist later wrote the Blake entry for Leslie Stephen's *Dictionary of National Biography* in 1882, and also a well-judged Life of Mary Lamb for the new and influential *Eminent Women of Letters* series, published by Allen Lane in 1883. She had other literary plans, including Lives of Wordsworth and Thomas Carlyle. But her heart was broken by the sudden and tragic death of her favourite daughter Beatrice.

This was the child they had nursed through scarlet fever at Cheyne Row, while Alexander was struggling to complete the biography. She was always closely associated in Anne's mind with the early shared work on Blake. True to her mother's early leanings towards science, Beatrice had been training in Edinburgh to qualify as one of Britain's first women doctors. Possibly as the result of an unhappy love affair, she committed suicide at the age of twenty-five by taking cyanide in July 1881. Anne Gilchrist never really recovered from the death of Beatrice, so shortly after the publication of the second edition of Blake. She contracted cancer and died at Hampstead four years later in November 1885, aged only fifty-three, all her other literary plans unfulfilled.

Gilchrist's original *Life of William Blake*, with its combative subtitle *Pictor Ignotus* ('The Unknown Painter'), is one of the most influential of all the great mid-Victorian biographies. It rescued its subject from almost total obscurity, challenged the notion of Blake's madness, and first defined his genius as both an artist and visionary poet combined. It set the agenda for modern Blake studies, and remains the prime source for all modern Blake biographies. It remains wonderfully readable today, and salvaged from death, it still vibrates with extraordinary life.

Yet like so many works of art, it was produced at great cost, and under mysterious conditions. In the absence of an original manuscript of the 1863 biography, the mystery will always remain just how much of this first, ground-breaking text we really owe to Alexander Gilchrist or to Anne; or to some indefinable Blakean collaboration between the two.

The text printed here is that of the first edition of 1863, together with the letters to Thomas Butts in an Appendix.

SELECT CHRONOLOGY

1757 (28 November) Blake born at 28 Broad Street, Soho, London

1766 Sees angels on Peckham Rye

1782 Marries Catherine Boucher in Battersea

1784 Death of father, opens his own printshop

1787 Death of beloved brother Robert, aged 19

1789 Fall of the Bastille in Paris. Engraves *Songs of Innocence*

1790 Writing *The Marriage of Heaven and Hell*
Moves to Hercules Buildings, Lambeth

1793 Engraves *Visions of the Daughters of Albion*

1794 *Songs of Innocence and of Experience*

1800 Moves to cottage in Felpham, Sussex

1803 Returns to London, to 17 South Molton Street

1804 Tried for sedition and treason at Chichester
Begins to write and engrave *Jerusalem*

1807 Quarrels with Cromek

1809 His Exhibition and *Descriptive Catalogue*, criticized as 'insane'
Beginning of Blake's lost decade

1810 Engraves *Milton*, with the hymn 'Jerusalem' in Preface

1811 Article by Crabb Robinson, 'William Blake, Painter, Poet and Religious Dreamer' published in Germany

1817 Aged sixty

1818 Befriended by the young painter John Linnell

xli

1820 Finishes *Jerusalem*, his last Prophetic Book, and illustrates Virgil's *Pastorals*

1821 Moves to 3 Fountain Court, Strand

1824 Adopted by his young disciples, 'the Ancients' (including Samuel Palmer, George Richmond, Frederick Tatham)

1825 Interviewed by Crabb Robinson, and visited by Coleridge

1826 Illustrates the *Book of Job* and *Pilgrim's Progress*

1827 Starts to illustrate Dante's *Divina Comedia* Blake dies on 12 August

1828 Alexander Gilchrist born at Newington Green, London Anne Burrows born in Gower Street, London

1830 Alan Cunningham's *Lives of the British Painters*

1847 D.G. Rossetti buys Blake's manuscript notebook

1851 Alexander Gilchrist and Anne Burrows married

1855 Alexander Gilchrist's *Life of William Etty RA* The Gilchrists meet Thomas and Jane Carlyle The Gilchrists meet Samuel Palmer

1856 The Gilchrists move to No. 6 Cheyne Row, Chelsea

1859 Anne Gilchrist, 'Our Nearest Relation', in *All the Year Round*

1861 (March) The Gilchrists meet the Rossettis (November) Death of Alexander Gilchrist

1862 Anne Gilchrist moves to Shottermill, near Haslemere, Surrey

1863 (October) Publication of Alexander Gilchrist's *Life of Blake*

1871 Anne Gilchrist and family leave for America

1880 Publication of the second edition of *Life of Blake*

1881 (July) Death of Beatrice Gilchrist

1883 Publication of Anne Gilchrist's *Life of Mary Lamb*

1885 (November) Death of Anne Gilchrist

LIFE OF
WILLIAM BLAKE

I assert, for myself, that I do not behold the outward creation, and that to me it is hindrance and not action. 'What!' it will be questioned, 'when the sun rises, do you not see a round disc of fire somewhat like a guinea?' Oh! no, no! I see an innumerable company of the heavenly host crying 'Holy, holy, holy is the Lord God Almighty!' I question not my corporeal eye any more than I would question a window concerning a sight. I look through it, and not with it.

BLAKE.—*A Vision of the Last Judgment.*

ONE

Preliminary

From nearly all collections or beauties of 'The English Poets,' catholic to demerit as these are, tender of the expired and expiring reputations, one name has been hitherto perseveringly exiled. Encyclopædias ignore it. The Biographical Dictionaries furtively pass it on with inaccurate despatch, as having had some connexion with the Arts. With critics it has had but little better fortune. The *Edinburgh Review*, twenty-seven years ago, specified as a characteristic sin of 'partiality' in Allan Cunningham's pleasant *Lives of British Artists*, that he should have ventured to include this name, since its possessor could (it seems) 'scarcely be considered a painter' at all. And later, Mr Leslie, in his *Handbook for Young Painters*, dwells on it with imperfect sympathy for awhile, to dismiss it with scanty recognition.

Yet no less a contemporary than Wordsworth, a man little prone to lavish eulogy or attention on brother poets, spake in private of the *Songs of Innocence and Experience* of William Blake, as 'undoubtedly the production of insane genius,' (which adjective we shall, I hope, see cause to qualify), but as to him more significant than the works of many a famous poet. 'There is something in the madness of this man,' declared he (to Mr Crabb Robinson), 'which interests me more than the sanity of Lord Byron and Walter Scott.'

3

Of his *Designs*, Fuseli and Flaxman, men not to be imposed on in such matters, but themselves sensitive – as Original Genius must always be – to Original Genius in others, were in the habit of declaring with unwonted emphasis, that 'the time would come' when the finest 'would be as much sought after and treasured in the portfolios' of men discerning in art, 'as those of Michael Angelo now.' 'And ah! Sir,' Flaxman would sometimes add, to an admirer of the designs, 'his poems are grand as his pictures.'

Of the books and designs of Blake, the world may well be ignorant. For in an age rigorous in its requirement of publicity, these were in the most literal sense of the words, *never published* at all: not published even in the mediæval sense, when writings were confided to learned keeping, and works of art not unseldom restricted to cloister-wall or coffer-lid. Blake's poems were, with one exception, not even printed in his life-time; simply *engraved* by his own laborious hand. His drawings, when they issued further than his own desk, were bought as a kind of charity, to be stowed away again in rarely opened portfolios. The very copper-plates on which he engraved, were often used again after a few impressions had been struck off; one design making way for another, to save the cost of new copper. At the present moment, Blake drawings, Blake prints, fetch prices which would have solaced a life of penury, had their producer received them. They are thus collected, chiefly because they *are* (naturally enough) already 'RARE,' and 'VERY RARE.' Still hiding in private portfolios, his drawings are there prized or known by perhaps a score of individuals, enthusiastic appreciators, – some of their singularity and rarity, a few of their intrinsic quality.

At the Manchester Art-Treasures Exhibition of 1857, among the select thousand water-colour drawings, hung two modestly tinted designs by Blake, of few inches size: one the *Dream of Queen Catherine*, another *Oberon and Titania*. Both are remarkable displays of imaginative power, and finished examples in the artist's peculiar manner. Both were unnoticed in the crowd, attracting few gazers, fewer admirers. For it needs to be *read* in Blake, to have familiarized oneself with his unsophisticated, archaic, yet spiritual 'manner,' – a style *sui generis* as no other artist's ever was, – to be able to sympathize with, or even understand, the equally individual strain of thought, of which it is the vehicle. And one must almost be *born* with a sympathy for it. He neither wrote nor drew for the many, hardly for work'y-day men at all, rather for children and angels; himself 'a divine child,' whose playthings were sun, moon, and stars, the heavens and the earth.

In an era of academies, associations, and combined efforts, we have in him a solitary, self-taught, and as an artist, *semi-*taught Dreamer, 'delivering the burning messages of prophecy by the stammering lips of infancy,' as Mr Ruskin has said of Cimabue and Giotto. For each artist and writer has, in the course of his training, to approve in his own person the immaturity of expression Art has at recurrent periods to pass through as a whole. And Blake in some aspects of his art never emerged from infancy. His Drawing, often correct, almost always powerful, the *pose* and grouping of his figures often expressive and sublime, as the sketches of Raffaelle or Albert Dürer, often, on the other hand, range under the category of the 'impossible;' are crude, contorted, forced, monstrous, though none the less efficient in conveying the visions fetched by the guileless man from Heaven, from Hell itself, or from the intermediate limbo tenanted by hybrid nightmares. His prismatic colour, abounding in the purest, sweetest melodies to the eye, and always expressing a sentiment, yet, looks to the casual observer slight, inartificial, arbitrary.

Many a cultivated spectator will turn away from all this, as from mere ineffectualness, – Art in its second childhood. But see this sitting figure of *Job in his Affliction*, surrounded by the bowed figures of wife and friend, grand as Michael Angelo, nay, rather as the still, colossal figures fashioned by the genius of old Egypt or Assyria. Look on that simple composition of *Angels Singing aloud for Joy*, pure and tender as Fra Angelico, and with an austerer sweetness.

It is not the least of Blake's peculiarities, that instead of expressing himself, as most men have been content to do, by help of the prevailing style of his day, he, in this, as every other matter, preferred to be independent of his fellows; partly by choice, partly from the necessities of imperfect education as a painter. His Design has conventions of its own: in part, its own, I should say, in part, a return to those of earlier and simpler times.

Of Blake, as an Artist, we will defer further talk. His Design can ill be translated into words, and very inadequately by any engraver's copy. Of his Poems, tinged with the very same ineffable qualities, obstructed by the same technical flaws and impediments – a semi-utterance as it were, snatched from the depths of the vague and unspeakable – of these remarkable Poems, never once yet fairly placed before the reading public, specimens shall by-and-bye speak more intelligibly for themselves. Both form part in a Life and Character as new, romantic, pious – in the deepest natural sense – as they: romantic, though incident be slight; animated by the same unbroken simplicity, the same high unity of sentiment.

TWO

Childhood, 1757–71

William Blake, the most spiritual of artists, a mystic poet and painter, who lived to be a contemporary of Cobbett and Sir Walter Scott, was born 28th November, 1757, the year of Canova's birth, two years after Stothard and Flaxman; while Chatterton, a boy of five, was still sauntering about the winding streets of antique Bristol. Born amid the gloom of a London November, at 28, Broad Street, Carnaby Market, Golden Square, (market now extinct), he was christened on the 11th December – one in a batch of six – from Grinling Gibbons' ornate font in Wren's noble Palladian church of St James's. He was the son of James and Catherine Blake, the second child in a family of four.

His father was a moderately prosperous hosier of some twenty years' standing, in a then not unfashionable quarter. Broad Street, half private houses, half respectable shops, was a street (only shorter) much such as Wigmore Street is now. Dashing Regent Street as yet was not, and had more than half a century to wait for birth; narrow Swallow Street in part filling its place. All that Golden Square neighbourhood, – Wardour Street, Poland Street, Brewer Street, held then a similar status to the Cavendish Square district say, now: an ex-fashionable, highly respectable condition, not yet sunk into the seedy category. The

7

Broad Street of present date is a dirty, forlorn-looking thorough-fare; one half of it twice as wide as the other. In the wider portion stands a large, dingy brewery. The street is a shabby miscellany of oddly assorted occupations, – lapidaries, pickle-makers, manufacturing trades of many kinds, furniture-brokers, and nondescript shops. 'Artistes' and artizans live in the upper stories. Almost every house is adorned by its triple or quadruple row of brass bells, bright with the polish of frequent hands, and yearly multiplying themselves. The houses, though often disguised by stucco, and some of them refaced, date mostly from Queen Anne's time; 28, now a 'trimming shop,' is a corner house at the narrower end, a large and substantial old edifice.

The mental training which followed the physical one of swaddling-clothes, go-carts, and head-puddings, was, in our Poet's case, a scanty one, as we have cause to know from Blake's writings. All knowledge beyond that of reading and writing, was evidently self-acquired. A 'new kind' of boy was soon sauntering about the quiet neighbouring streets – a boy of strangely more romantic habit of mind than that neighbourhood had ever known in its days of gentility, has ever known in its dingy decadence. Already he passed half his time in dream and imagin-ative reverie. As he grew older the lad became fond of roving out into the country, a fondness in keeping with the romantic turn. For what written romance can vie with the substantial one of rural sights and sounds to a town-bred boy! Country was not, at that day, beyond reach of a Golden Square lad of nine or ten. On his own legs he could find a green field without the exhaustion of body and mind which now separates such a boy from the alluring haven as rigorously as prison bars. After West-minster Bridge – the 'superb and magnificent structure' now defunct then a new and admired one, – came St George's Fields,

8

open fields and scene of 'Wilkes and Liberty' riots in Blake's boyhood; next the pretty village of Newington Butts, undreaming its nineteenth century bad eminence in the bills of cholera-mortality; and then, unsophisticate green field and hedgerow opened on the child's delighted eyes. A mile or two further through the 'large and pleasant village' of Camberwell with its grove (or avenue) and famed prospect, arose the sweet hill and vale and 'sylvan wilds' of rural Dulwich, a 'village' even now retaining some semblance of its former self. Beyond, stretched, to allure the young pedestrian on, yet fairer amenities: southward, hilly Sydenham; eastward, in the purple distance, Blackheath. A favourite day's ramble of later date was to Blackheath, or south-west, over Dulwich and Norwood hills, through the antique rustic town of Croydon, type once of the compact, clean, cheerful Surrey towns of old days, to the fertile verdant meads of Walton-upon-Thames; much of the way by lane and footpath. The beauty of those scenes in his youth was a life-long reminiscence with Blake, and stored his mind with life-long pastoral images.

On Peckham Rye (by Dulwich Hill) it is, as he will in after years relate, that while quite a child, of eight or ten perhaps, he has his 'first vision.' Sauntering along, the boy looks up and sees a tree filled with angels, bright angelic wings bespangling every bough like stars. Returned home he relates the incident, and only through his mother's intercession escapes a thrashing from his honest father, for telling a lie. Another time, one summer morn, he sees the hay-makers at work, and amid them angelic figures walking. If these traits of childish years be remembered, they will help to elucidate the visits from the spiritual world of later years, in which the grown man believed as unaffectedly as ever had the boy of ten.

One day, a traveller was telling bright wonders of some foreign city. 'Do you call *that* splendid?' broke in young Blake; 'I should call a city splendid in which the houses were of gold, the pavements of silver, the gates ornamented with precious stones.' At which outburst, hearers were already disposed to shake the head and pronounce the speaker crazed: a speech natural enough in a child, but not unlikely to have been uttered in maturer years by Blake.

To say that Blake was born an artist, is to say of course that as soon as the child's hand could hold a pencil it began to scrawl rough likeness of man or beast, and make timid copies of all the prints he came near. He early began to seek opportunities of educating hand and eye. In default of National Gallery or Museum, for the newly founded *British* Museum contained as yet little or no sculpture, occasional access might freely be had to the Royal Palaces. Pictures were to be seen also of noblemen's and gentlemen's houses in the sale-rooms of the elder Langford in Covent Garden, and of the elder Christie: sales exclusively filled as yet with the pictures of the 'old and dark' masters, sometimes genuine, oftener spurious, demand for the same exceeding supply. Of all these chances of gratuitous instruction the boy is said to have sedulously profited: a clear proof other schooling was irregular.

The fact that such attendances were permitted, implies that neither parent was disposed, as so often happens, to thwart the incipient artist's inclination; bad, even for a small tradesman's son, as at that time were an artist's outlooks, unless he were a portrait-painter. In 1767, (three years after Hogarth's death), Blake being then ten years old, was 'put to Mr Pars' drawing-school in the Strand.' This was the preparatory school for juvenile artists then in vogue: preparatory to the Academy of Painting and Sculpture in St Martin's Lane, of the 'Incorporated Society of Artists,' the Society Hogarth had helped to found. The *Royal* Academy of intriguing Chambers' and Moser's founding, for which George the Third legislated, came a year later. 'Mr Pars' drawing-school in the Strand' was located in 'the great room,' subsequently a show-room of the Messrs Ackermann's – name once familiar to all buyers of prints – in their original house, on the left-hand side of the Strand, as you go citywards, just at the eastern corner of Castle Court: a house and court demolished when Agar Street and King William Street were made. The school was founded and brought into celebrity by William Shipley, painter, brother to a bishop, and virtual founder also, in 1754, of the still-extant Society of Arts, – in that same house, where the Society lodged until migrating to its stately home over the way, in the Adelphi.

Who *was* Pars? Pars, the Leigh or Cary of his day, was originally a chaser and son of a chaser, the art to which Hogarth was apprenticed, one then going out of demand, unhappily, – for the fact implied the loss of a decorative art. Which decadence it was led this Pars to go into the juvenile Art-Academy line, *vice* Shipley retired. He had a younger brother, William, a portrait painter, and one of the earliest *Associates* or inchoate R. A.'s, who was extensively patronized by the Dilettanti Society, and by the *dilettante* Lord Palmerston of that time. The former sent him to Greece, there for three years to study ruined temple and mutilated statue, and to return with portfolios, a mine of wealth to cribbing 'classic' architects, – contemporary Chamber's, and future Soanes.

At Pars' school as much drawing was taught as is to be learned by copying plaster-casts after the Antique, but no drawing from the living figure. Blake's father bought a few casts, from which the boy could continue his drawing-lessons at home: the *Gladiator*, the *Hercules*, the *Venus de Medici*, various heads, and the usual models of hand, arm, and foot. After a time, small sums of money were indulgently supplied wherewith to make a collection of Prints for study. To secure these, the youth became a frequenter of the print-dealers' shops and the sales of the auctioneers, who then took *threepenny* biddings, and would often knock down a print for as many shillings as pounds are now given, thanks to ever-multiplying Lancashire fortunes.

In a scarce, probably almost unread book, affecting – despite the unattractive literary peculiarities of its pedagogue author – from its subject and very minuteness of detail, occurs an account, from which I have begun to borrow, of Blake's early education in art, derived from the artist's own lips. It is a more reliable story than Allan Cunningham's pleasant mannered generalities, easy to read, hard to verify. The singular biography to which I allude, is Dr Malkin's *Father's Memoirs of his Child* (1806), illustrated by a frontispiece of Blake's design. The Child in question was one of those hapless 'prodigies of learning' who, – to quote a good-natured friend and philosopher's consoling words to the poor Doctor, – 'commence their career at three, become expert linguists at four, profound philosophers at five, read the Fathers at six, and die of old age at seven.'

'Langford,' writes Malkin, called Blake 'his little connoisseur, and often knocked down a cheap lot with friendly precipitation.' Amiable Langford! The great Italians, – Raffaelle, Michael Angelo, Giulio Romano, – the great Germans, – Albert Dürer, Martin Hemskerk, – with others similar, were the exclusive objects of his choice; a sufficiently remarkable one in days when Guido and the Caracci were the gods of the servile crowd. Such a choice was 'contemned by his youthful companions, who were accustomed to laugh at what they called his *mechanical* taste!' 'I am happy,' wrote Blake himself in later life (*MS. notes to Reynolds*), 'I cannot say that Raffaelle ever was from my earliest childhood hidden from me. I saw and I knew immediately the difference between Raffaelle and Rubens.'

Between the ages of eleven and twelve, if not before, Blake had begun to write original irregular verse; a rarer precocity than that of sketching, and rarer still in alliance with the latter tendency. Poems composed in his twelfth year, came to be included in a selection privately printed in his twenty-sixth. Could we but know which they were! *One*, by Malkin's help, we *can* identify as written before he was fourteen: the following ethereal piece of sportive Fancy, 'Song' he calls it:

> How sweet I roam'd from field to field,
> And tasted all the summer's pride,
> Till I the prince of Love beheld,
> Who in the sunny beams did glide!
>
> He shew'd me lilies for my hair,
> And blushing roses for my brow;
> He led me through his gardens fair,
> Where all his golden pleasures grow.
>
> With sweet May-dews my wings were wet,
> And Phœbus fir'd my vocal rage;
> He caught me in his silken net,
> And shut me in his golden cage.
>
> He loves to sit and hear me sing,
> Then, laughing, sports and plays with me;
> Then stretches out my golden wing,
> And mocks my loss of liberty.

This may surely be reckoned equal precocity to that so much lauded of Pope and Cowley. It is not promise, but fulfilment. The grown man in vain might hope to better such sweet playfulness, – playfulness as of a 'child angel's' penning – any more than noon can reproduce the tender streaks of dawn. But criticism is idle. How analyse a violet's perfume, or dissect the bloom on a butterfly's wing?

THREE

Engraver's Apprentice 1771–78
[ÆT. 14–21]

The preliminary charges of launching Blake in the career of a Painter, were too onerous for the paternal pocket; involving for one thing, a heavy premium to some leading artist for instruction under his own roof, then the only attainable, always the only adequate training. The investment, moreover, would not after all be certain of assuring daily bread for the future. English engravers were then taking that high place they are now doing little to maintain. Apprenticeship to one would secure, with some degree of artistic education, the cunning right hand which can always keep want at arm's length: a thing artist and *littérateur* have often had cause to envy in the skilled artisan. The consideration was not without weight in the eyes of an honest shopkeeper, to whose understanding the prosaic craft would more practically address itself than the vague abstractions of Art, or those shadowy promises of Fame, on which alone a mere artist had too often to feed. Thus it was decided for the future designer, that he should enter the to him enchanted domain of Art by a back door as it were. He is not to be dandled into a Painter, but painfully to win his way to an outside place. Daily through life, he will have to marry his shining dreams to the humblest, most irksome realities of a virtually artisan life. Already it had been decreed that an inspired Poet should be endowed with barely grammar enough to compose with school-boy accuracy.

At the age of fourteen, the drawing-school of Mr Pars in the Strand, was exchanged for the shop of engraver Basire in Great Queen Street, Lincoln's Inn Fields. There had been an intention of apprenticing Blake to Ryland, a more famous man than Basire; an artist of genuine talent and even genius, who had been well educated in his craft; had been a pupil of Ravenet, and after that (among others) of Boucher, whose *stipple* manner he was the first to introduce into England. With the view of securing the teaching and example of so skilled a hand, Blake was taken by his father to Ryland; but the negotiation failed. The boy himself raised an unexpected scruple. The sequel shows it to have been a singular instance – if not of absolute prophetic gift or second-sight – at all events of natural intuition into character and power of forecasting the future from it, such as is often the endowment of temperaments like his. In after life this involuntary faculty of reading hidden writing continued to be a characteristic. 'Father,' said the strange boy, after the two had left Ryland's studio, 'I do not like the man's face: *it looks as if he will live to be hanged!*' Appearances were at that time utterly against the probability of such an event. Ryland was then at the zenith of his reputation. He was engraver to the king, whose portrait (after Ramsay) he had engraved, receiving for his work an annual pension of 200*l*. An accomplished and agreeable man, he was the friend of poet Churchill and others of distinguished rank in letters and society. His manners and personal appearance were peculiarly prepossessing, winning the spontaneous confidence of those who knew or even casually saw him. But, twelve years after this interview, the unfortunate artist will have got into embarrassments, will commit a forgery on the East India Company: – and the prophecy will be fulfilled.

The Basire with whom ultimately Blake was placed, was James Basire, the second chronologically and in merit first of four Basires; all engravers, and the three last in date (all bearing one Christian name) engravers to the Society of Antiquaries. This Basire, born in London, 1730, now therefore forty-one, and son of Isaac Basire, had studied design at Rome. He was the engraver of Stuart and Revett's *Athens* (1762), of Reynolds' *Earl Camden* (1766), of West's *Pylades and Orestes* (1770). He had also executed two or three plates after some of the minor and later designs of Hogarth: the frontispiece to Garrick's *Farmer's Return* (1761), the noted political caricature of *The Times*, and the portrait sketch of Fielding (1762), which Hogarth himself much commended, declaring 'he did not know his own drawing from a proof of the plate.' The subjects of his graver were principally antiquities and portraits of men of note, – especially portraits of antiquaries: hereditary subjects since with the Basire family. He was official engraver to the Royal as well as the Antiquarian Society. Hereafter he will become still more favourably known in his generation, as the engraver of the illustrations to the slow-revolving *Archæologia* and *Vetusta Monumenta* of the Society of Antiquaries, – then in a comparatively brisk condition, – and to the works of Gough and other antiquarian big-wigs of the old, full-bottomed sort. He was an engraver well grounded in drawing, of dry, hard, monotonous, but painstaking, conscientious style; the lingering representative of a school already getting old-fashioned, but not without staunch admirers, for its 'firm and correct outline,' among antiquaries; whose confidence and esteem, – Gough's in particular, – Basire throughout possessed.

In the days of Strange, Woollett, Vivares, Bartolozzi, better models, if more expensive in their demands might have been found though also worse. Basire was a superior, liberal-minded man, ingenuous and upright; and a kind master. The lineaments of his honest countenance (set off by a bob-wig) may be studied in the portrait by his son, engraved as frontispiece to the ninth volume of Nichols's *Literary Anecdotes*. As a Designer, Blake was, in essentials, influenced by no contemporary; as engraver alone influenced by Basire, and that strongly – little as his master's style had in common with his own genius. Even as engraver, he was thus influenced, little to his future advantage in winning custom from the public. That public, in Blake's youth, fast outgrowing the flat and formal manner inherited by Basire, in common with Vertue (engraver to the Society of Antiquaries before him), and the rest, from the Vanderguchts, Vanderbanks, and other naturalized Dutchmen and Germans of the bob-wig and clipped-yew era, will now readily learn to enjoy the softer, more agreeable one of M'Ardell, Bartolozzi, Sherwin.

His seven years' apprenticeship commenced in 1771, year of the Academy's first partial lodgement in Old Somerset Palace – and thus (eventually) in the National Pocket. As he was constitutionally painstaking and industrious, he soon learned to draw carefully and copy faithfully whatever was set before him, – altogether to the Basire taste, and to win, as a good apprentice should, the approval and favour of his master. One day, by the way (as Blake ever remembered), Goldsmith walked into Basire's. It must have been during the very last years of the poet's life: he died in 1774. The boy – as afterwards the artist was fond of telling – mightily admired the great author's finely marked head as he gazed up at it, and thought to himself how much *he* should like to have such a head when he grew to be a man. Another still more memorable figure, and a genius singularly german to Blake's own order of mind, the 'singular boy of fourteen,' during the commencement of his apprenticeship, *may* 'any day have met unwittingly in London streets, or walked beside: a placid, venerable, thin man of eighty-four, of erect figure and abstracted air, wearing a full-bottomed wig, a pair of long ruffles, and a curious-hilted sword, and carrying a gold-headed cane, – no Vision, still flesh and blood, but himself the greatest of modern Vision Seers, – Emanuel Swedenborg by name; who came from Amsterdam to London, in August 1771, and died at No. 26, Great Bath Street, Coldbath Fields, on the 29th of March, 1772.' This Mr Allingham pleasantly suggests, in a note to his delightful collection of lyrical poems, *Nightingale Valley* (1860), in which (at last) occur a specimen or two of Blake's verse. The coincidence is not a trivial one. Of all modern men the engraver's apprentice was to grow up the likest to Emanuel Swedenborg; already by constitutional temperament and endowment was so: in faculty for theosophic dreaming, for the seeing of visions while broad awake, and in matter of fact hold of spiritual things. To *savant* and to artist alike, while yet on earth, the Heavens were opened. By Swedenborg's theologic writings, the first English editions of some of which appeared during Blake's manhood, the latter was considerably influenced; but in no slavish spirit. These writings, in common with those of Jacob Boehmen, and of the other select mystics of the world, had natural affinities to Blake's mind, and were eagerly assimilated. But he hardly became a proselyte or 'Swedenborgian' proper; though his friend Flaxman did. In another twenty years we shall find him freely and as true believers may think – heretically criticising the Swedish seer from the spiritualist not the rationalist point of view: as being a Divine Teacher, whose truths however were 'not new,' and whose falsehoods were 'all old.'

Among the leading engravings turned out by Basire, during

the early part of Blake's apprenticeship, may be instanced in 1772, one after B. Wilson (*not* Richard), *Lady Stanhope as the Fair Penitent* (her *rôle* in certain amateur theatricals by the Quality); and in 1774, *The Field of the Cloth of Gold and Interview of the two Kings*, after a copy for the Society of Antiquaries by 'little Edwards' of Anecdote fame, from the celebrated picture at Windsor. The latter print was celebrated for one thing, if no other, as the *largest* ever engraved up to that time on one plate – copper, let us remember, – being some 47 inches by 27; and paper had to be made on purpose for it.

'Two years passed over smoothly enough,' writes Malkin, 'till two other apprentices were added to the establishment, who completely destroyed its harmony.' Basire said of Blake, '*he* was too simple and they too cunning.' He, lending I suppose a too credulous ear to their tales, 'declined to take part with his master against his fellow-apprentices;' and was therefore sent out of harm's way into Westminster Abbey and the various old churches in and near London, to make drawings from the monuments and buildings Basire was employed by Gough the antiquary to engrave: 'a circumstance he always mentioned with gratitude to Basire.' The solitary study of authentic English history in stone was far more to the studious lad's mind than the disorderly wrangling of mutinous comrades. It is significant of his character, even at this early date, for zeal, industry, and moral correctness, that he could be trusted month after month, year after year, unwatched, to do his duty by his master in so independent an employment.

The task was singularly adapted to foster the romantic turn of his imagination, and to strengthen his natural affinities for the spiritual in art. It kindled a fervent love of Gothic, – itself an originality then, – which lasted his life, and exerted enduring influences on his habits of feeling and study; forbidding, once for all, if such a thing had ever been possible to Blake, the pursuit of fashionable models, modern excellencies, technic and superficial, or of any but the antiquated essentials and symbolic language of imaginative art.

From this time forward, from 1773 that is, the then 'neglected works of art, called Gothic monuments,' were for years his daily companions. The warmer months were devoted to zealous sketching, from every point of view, of the Tombs in the Abbey; the enthusiastic artist 'frequently standing on the monument and viewing the figures from the top.' Careful drawings were made of the regal forms, which for five centuries had lain in mute majesty, – once amid the daily presence of reverent priest and muttered mass, since in awful solitude, – around the lovely Chapel of the Confessor, the austere sweetness of Queen Eleanor, the dignity of Philippa, the noble grandeur of Edward the Third, the gracious stateliness of Richard the Second and his Queen. Then, came drawings of the glorious effigy of Aymer de Valence, and of the beautiful though mutilated figures which surround his altar-tomb; drawings in fact, of all the mediæval tombs. He pored over all with a reverent good faith, which, in the age of Stuart and Revett, taught the simple student things our Pugins and Scotts had to learn near a century later. 'The heads he considered as portraits,' – not unnaturally, their sculptors showing no overt sign of idiocy; – 'and all the ornaments appeared as miracles of art to his gothicized imagination,' as they have appeared to other imaginations since. He discovered for himself then, or later, the important part once subserved by *Colour* in the sculptured building, the living help it had rendered to the once radiant Temple of God, – now a bleached dishonoured skeleton.

Shut up alone with these solemn memorials of far off centuries, – for, during service and in the intervals of visits from strangers, the vergers turned the key on him, – the Spirit of the past became his familiar companion. Sometimes his dreaming eye saw more palpable shapes from the phantom past: once a vision of 'Christ and the Apostles,' as he used to tell; and I doubt not others. For, as we have seen, the visionary tendency, or faculty, as Blake more truly called it, had early shown itself.

During the progress of Blake's lonely labours in the Abbey, on a bright day in May, 1774, the Society for which, through Basire, he was working, perpetrated, by royal permission, on the very scene of those rapt studies, a highly interesting bit of antiquarian sacrilege: on a more reasonable pretext, and with greater decency, than sometimes distinguish such questionable proceedings. A select company formally and in strict privacy opened the tomb of Edward the First, and found the embalmed body 'in perfect preservation and sumptuously attired,' in 'robes of royalty, his crown on his head, and two sceptres in his hands.' The antiquaries saw face to face the 'dead conqueror of Scotland;' had even a fleeting glimpse – for it was straightway re-enclosed in its cerecloths – of his very visage: a recognizable likeness of what it must have been in life. I cannot help hoping that Blake may (unseen) have assisted at the ceremony.

In winter the youth helped to engrave selections from these Abbey Studies, in some cases executing the engraving single-handed. During the evenings, and at over hours, he made drawings from his already teeming Fancy, and from English History. 'A great number,' it is said, were thrown off in such spare hours. There is a scarce engraving of his dated so early as 1773, the second year of his apprenticeship, remarkable as already to some extent evincing in style – as yet, however, heavy rather than majestic – still more in choice of subject, the characteristics of later years. In one corner at top we have the inscription (which sufficiently describes the design), 'Joseph of Arimathea among the Rocks of Albion;' and at bottom, 'engraved by W. Blake, 1773, from an old Italian drawing;' 'Michael Angelo, Pinxit.' Between these two lines, according to a custom frequent with Blake, is engraved the following characteristic effusion, which reads like an addition of later years:– 'This' (he is venturing a wild theory as to Joseph), 'is One of the Gothic Artists who built the Cathedrals in what we call the Dark Ages, wandering about in sheepskins and goatskins; of whom the World was not worthy. Such were the Christians in all ages.'

The 'prentice work as assistant to Basire of these years (1773–78) may be traced under Basire's name in the *Archæologia*, in some of the engravings of coins, &c., to the *Memoirs of Hollis* (1780), and in Gough's *Sepulchral Monuments*, not published till 1786 and 1796. The Antiquaries were alive and stirring then; and enthusiastic John Carter was laying the foundations in English Archæology on which better-known men have since built. In the *Sepulchral Monuments, vol.* 1, *pt* 2 (1796), occurs a capital engraving as to drawing and feeling, 'Portrait of Queen Philippa from her Monument,' with the inscription *Basire delineavit et sculpsit*; for which, as in many other cases, we may safely read 'W. Blake.' In fact, Stothard often used to mention this drawing as Blake's, and with praise. The engraving is in Blake's forcible manner of decisively contrasted light and shade, but simple and monotonous manipulation. It is to a large scale, and gives the head and shoulders merely. Another plate, with a perspective view of the whole monument and a separate one of the effigy, accompanies it. In Part I. (1786) are similar 'Portraits' of Queen Philippa, of Edward III. &c.

From Basire, Blake could only acquire the mechanical part of Art, even of the engraver's art; for Basire had little more to communicate. But that part he learned thoroughly and well. Basire's acquirements as an engraver were of a solid though not a fascinating kind. The scholar always retained a loyal feeling towards his old master; and would stoutly defend him and his style against that of more attractive and famous hands, – Strange, Woollett, Bartolozzi. Their ascendancy, indeed, led to no little public injustice being done throughout, to Blake's own sterling style of engraving. A circumstance which intensified the artist's aversion to the men. In a MS. descriptive *Advertisement* (1810) to his own *Canterbury Pilgrimage* (the engraving not the picture), Blake expresses his contempt for them very candidly – and intemperately perhaps. There too, he records the impression made on him personally, when as a boy he used to see some of them in Basire's studio. 'Woollett,' he writes, 'I knew very intimately by his intimacy with Basire, and knew him to be one of the most ignorant fellows I ever met. A machine is not a man, nor a work of art: it is destructive of humanity and of art. Woollett, I know, did not know how to grind his graver. *I know this.* He has often proved his ignorance before me at Basire's by laughing at Basire's knife-tools, and ridiculing the forms of Basire's other gravers, till Basire was quite dashed and out of conceit with what he himself knew. But his impudence had a contrary effect on me.' West, for whose reputation Woollett's graver did so much, 'asserted' continues Blake, 'that Woollett's prints were superior to Basire's, because they had more labour and care. Now this is contrary to the truth. Woollett did not know how to put so much labour into a hand or a foot as Basire did; he did not know how to draw the leaf of a tree. All his study was clean strokes and mossy tints . . . Woollett's best works

24

were etched by Jack Brown; Woollett etched very ill himself. The *Cottagers*, and *Jocund Peasants*, the *Views* in Kew Gardens, *Foot's Cray*, and *Diana and Actæon*, and, in short, all that are called Woollett's were etched by Jack Brown. And in Woollett's works the etching is all; though even in these a single leaf of a tree is never correct. Strange's prints were, when I knew him, all done by Aliamet and his French journeymen, whose names I forget. I also knew something of John Cooke, who engraved after Hogarth. Cooke wished to give Hogarth what he could take from Raffaelle; that is, outline, and mass, and colour; but he could not.' Again, in the same one-sided, trenchant strain: – 'What is called the English style of engraving, such as proceeded from the toilettes of Woollett and Strange (for theirs were Fribble's toilettes) can never produce character and expression.' Drawing – 'firm, determinate outline' – is in Blake's eyes, all in all: – 'Engraving is drawing on copper and nothing else. But, as Gravelot once said to my master, Basire, "*De English may be very clever in deir own opinions, but day do not draw.*"'

Before taking leave of Basire, we will have a look at the house in Great Queen Street, in which Blake passed seven years of his youth; whither Gough, Tyson, and many another enthusiastic dignified antiquary, in knee-breeches and powdered wig, so often bent their steps to have a chat with their favourite engraver. Its door has opened to good company in its time, to engravers, painters, men of letters, celebrated men of all kinds. Just now we saw Goldsmith enter. When Blake was an apprentice, the neighbourhood of Lincoln's Inn Fields, though already antique, was a stately and decorous one, through which the tide of fashionable life still swayed on daily errands of pleasure or business. The house can yet be identified as No. 31, one of two occupied by Messrs Corben and Son, the coach-builders, which firm, or rather their predecessors, in Basire's time occupied only No. 30. It stands on the northern side of the street, opposite – to the west or Drury Lane-ward of – Freemasons' Tavern; almost exactly opposite New Yard and the noticeable ancient house at one side of that yard, with the stately Corinthian pilasters in well wrought brick. Basire's is itself a seventeenth century house refaced early in the Georgian era, the parapet then put up half hiding the old dormar windows of the third story. Originally, it must either have been part of a larger mansion, or one of a uniformly built series, having continuous horizontal brick mouldings; as remnants of the same on its neighbours testify. Outside, it remains pretty much as it must have looked in Blake's time; old-fashioned people having (Heaven be praised!) tenanted it ever since the first James Basire and after him his widow ended their days there. With its green paint, old casements, quiet old-fashioned shop-window, and freedom from the abomination of desolation (stucco), it retains an old-world genuine aspect, rare in London's oldest neighbourhoods, and not at war with the memories which cling around the place.

FOUR

A Boy's Poems 1768–77
[ÆT. 11–20]

The poetical essays of the years of youth and apprenticeship, are preserved in the thin octavo, *Poetical Sketches by W. B.*, printed by help of friends in 1783, and now so rare, that after some years' vain attempt, I am forced to abandon the idea of myself owning the book. I have had to use a copy borrowed from one of Blake's surviving friends. In such hands alone, linger, I fancy, the dozen copies or so still extant. There is (of course) none where, at any rate, there should be one – in the British Museum.

'Tis hard to believe these poems were written in the author's teens, harder still to realize how some of them, in their unforced simplicity, their bold and careless freedom of sentiment and expression, came to be written at all in the third quarter of the eighteenth century: the age 'of polished phraseology and subdued thought,' – subdued with a vengeance. It was the generation of Shenstone, Langhorne, Mason, Whitehead, the Wartons; of obscurer Cunningham, Lloyd, Carter. Volumes of concentrated *Beauties of English Poetry*, volumes as fugitive often as those of original verse, are literary straws which indicate the set of the popular taste. If we glance into one of this date, – say into that compiled towards the close of the century, by one Mr Thomas Tompkins, and which purports to be a collection (expressly compiled 'to enforce the practice of Virtue') of 'Such poems as

27

have been universally esteemed the first ornaments of our language,' – who are the elect? We have in great force the names just enumerated, and among older poets then read and honoured, to the exclusion of Chaucer and the Elizabethans, so imposing a muster-roll as – Parnell, Mallett, Blacklock, Addison, Gay; and, ascending to the highest heaven of the century's Walhalla, Goldsmith, Thomson, Gray, Pope; with a little of Milton and Shakspere thrown in as make-weight.

Where, beyond the confines of his own most individual mind, did the hosier's son find his model for that lovely web of rainbow fancy already quoted? I know of none in English literature. For the *Song* commencing

'My silks and fine array,'

with its shy evanescent tints and aroma as of pressed rose-leaves, parallels may be found among the lyrics of the Elizabethan age: an alien though it be in its own. The influence of contemporary models, unless it be sometimes Collins or Thompson, is nowhere in the volume discernible; but involuntary emulation of higher ones partially known to him: of the *Reliques* given to the world by Percy in 1760; of Shakspere, Spenser, and other Elizabethans. For the youth's choice of masters was as unfashionable in Poetry as in Design. Among the few students or readers in that day of Shakspere's *Venus and Adonis, Tarquin and Lucrece*, and *Sonnets*, of Ben Jonson's *Underwoods* and *Miscellanies*, the boy Blake was, according to Malkin, an assiduous one. The form of such a poem as

'Love and harmony combine,'

is inartificial and negligent; but incloses the like intangible spirit of delicate fancy: a lovely blush of life as it were, suffusing the

28

enigmatic form. Even schoolboy blunders against grammar, and schoolboy complexities of expression, fail to break the musical echo, or mar the naïve sweetness of the two concluding stanzas; which, in practised hands, might have been wrought into more artful melody, with little increase of real effect. Again, how many reams of scholastic Pastoral have missed the simple gaiety of one which does not affect to be a 'pastoral' at all:—

'I love the jocund dance.'

Of the remarkable *Mad Song* extracted by Southey in his *Doctor*, who probably valued the thin octavo, as became a great Collector, for its rarity and singularity, that poet has said nothing to show he recognized its dramatic power, the daring expression of things otherwise inarticulate, the unity of sentiment, the singular truth with which the key-note is struck and sustained, or the eloquent, broken music of its rhythm.

The 'marvellous Boy' that 'perished in his pride,' (1770) while certain of these very poems were being written, amid all *his* luxuriant promise, and memorable displays of Talent, produced few so really original as some of them. There are not many more to be instanced of quite such rare quality. But all abound in lavish if sometimes unknit strength. Their faults are such alone as flow from youth, as are inevitable in one whose intellectual activity is not sufficiently logical to reduce his imaginings into sufficiently clear and definite shape. As examples of poetic power and freshness quickening the imperfect, immature *form*, take his verses *To the Evening Star*, in which the concluding lines subside into a reminiscence, but not a slavish one, of Puck's Night Song in *Midsummer Night's Dream*; or the lament *To the Muses*, – not inapposite surely, when it was written; or again, the full-coloured invocation *To Summer*.

In a few of the poems, the influence of Blake's contemporary, Chatterton, – of the *Poems of Rowley, i.e.*, is visible. In the *Prologue to King John, Couch of Death, Samson*, &c., all written in measured prose, the influence is still more conspicuous of Macpherson's *Ossian*, which had taken the world by storm in Blake's boyhood, and in his manhood was a ruling power in the poetic world. In the 'Prophetic' and too often incoherent rhapsodies of later years this influence increases unhappily, leading the prophet to indulge in vague, impalpable personifications, as dim and monotonous as a moor in a mist. To the close of his life, Blake retained his allegiance to Ossian and Rowley. 'I believe,' writes he, in a MS. note (1826) on Wordsworth's *Supplementary Essay*, 'I believe both Macpherson and Chatterton: that what they say is ancient, is so.' And again, when the Lake Poet speaks contemptuously of Macpherson, 'I own myself an admirer of Ossian equally with any other poet whatever; of Rowley and Chatterton also.'

The longest piece in this volume, the most daring, and perhaps considering a self-taught boy wrote it, the most remarkable, is the Fragment, or single act, of a Play on the high historic subject of *King Edward III*: one of the few in old English history accidentally omitted from Shakspere's cycle. In *his* steps it is, not in those of Addison or Home, the ambitious lad strives as a dramatist to tread; and, despite halting verse, confined knowledge, and the anachronism of a modern tone of thought, not unworthily, – though of course with youthful unsteady stride. The manner and something of the spirit of the *Historical Plays* is caught, far more nearly than by straining Ireland in his forgeries.

Fully to appreciate such poetry as the lad Blake composed in the years 1768–77, let us call to mind the dates at which first peeped above the horizon, the cardinal lights which people our modern poetic Heavens; those once more wakening into life the dull corpse of English song. Five years later than the last of these dates was published a small volume of *Poems*, 'By William Cowper of the Middle Temple.' Nine years later (1786), *Poems in the Scottish Dialect*, by Robert Burns, appealed to a Kilmarnock public. Sixteen years later (1793), came the poems Wordsworth afterwards named *Juvenile*, written between the ages of eighteen and twenty-two: *The Evening Walk*, and the *Descriptive Sketches*, with their modest pellucid merit, still in the fettered eighteenth century manner. Not till twenty-one years later (1798), followed the more memorable *Lyrical Ballads*, including for one thing, the *Tintern Abbey* of Wordsworth; for another, *The Ancient Mariner* of Coleridge.

All these Poems had their influence, prompt or tardy, widening eventually into the universal. All were at any rate *published*. Some, – those of Burns, – appealed to the feelings of the people, and of *all* classes; those of Cowper to the most numerous and influential section of an English community. The unusual notes struck by William Blake, in any case appealing but to one class and a small one, were fated to remain unheard, even by the Student of Poetry, until the process of regeneration had run its course, and, we may say, the Poetic Revival gone to seed again: seeing that the virtues of simplicity and directness the new poets began by bringing once more into the foreground, are those least practised now.

FIVE

Student and Lover 1778–82
[ÆT. 21–25]

Apprenticeship to Basire having ended, Blake, now (1778) twenty-one, studied for awhile in the newly formed Royal Academy: just then in an uncomfortable chrysalis condition, having had to quit its cramped lodgings in Old Somerset Palace (pulled down in 1775); and awaiting completion of the new building in which more elbow-room was to be provided. He commenced his course of study at the Academy (in the Antique School) 'under the eye of Mr Moser,' its first Keeper, who had conducted the parent Schools in St Martin's Lane. Moser, like Kauffman and Fuseli, was Swiss by birth: a sixth of our leading artists were still foreigners; as lists of the Original Forty testify. By profession he was a chaser, unrivalled in his generation, medallist – he modelled and chased a great seal of England, afterwards stolen – and enamel-painter, in days when costly watch-cases continued to furnish ample employment for the enamel-painter. He was, in short, a skilled decorative artist during the closing years of Decorative Art's existence as a substantive fact in England, or Europe. The thing itself – the very notion that such art was wanted – was about to expire; and be succeeded, for a dreary generation or two, by a mere blank negation. Miss Moser, afterwards Mrs Lloyd 'the celebrated flower painter,' another of the original members of the Academy, was George

32

Michael Moser's daughter. Edwards, in his *Anecdotes of Painters*, obscurely declares of the honest Switzer, that he was 'well skilled in the construction of the human figure, and as an instructor in the Academy, his manners, as well as his abilities, rendered him a most respectable master to the students.' A man of plausible address, as well as an ingenious, the quondam chaser and enameller was, evidently: a favourite with the President (Reynolds), a favourite with royalty. On the occasion of one royal visit to the Academy, after 1780 and its instalment in adequate rooms in the recently completed portion of Chambers' 'Somerset Palace,' Queen Charlotte penetrated to the old man's apartment, and made him sit down and have an hour's quiet chat in German with her. To express his exultation at such 'amiable condescension,' the proud Keeper could ever after hardly find broken English and abrupt gestures sufficiently startling and whimsical. He was a favourite, too, with the students; many of whom voluntarily testified their regard around his grave in the burial-ground of St Paul's, Covent Garden, when the time came to be carried thither in January, 1783.

The specific value of the guidance to be had by an ingenuous art-student from the venerable Moser, now a man of seventy-three, is suggestively indicated by a reminiscence afterwards noted down in Blake's MS. commentary on Reynolds' *Discourses*. 'I was once,' he there relates, 'looking over the prints from Raffaelle and Michael Angelo in the Library of the Royal Academy. Moser came to me, and said, – "You should not study these old, hard, stiff and dry, unfinished works of art: stay a little and *I* will show you what you should study." He then went and took down Le Brun and Rubens' *Galleries*. How did I secretly rage! I also spake my mind! I said to Moser, "These things that you call finished are not even begun: how then can

33

they be finished?" The man who does not know the beginning cannot know the end of art.' Which observations 'tis to be feared Keeper Moser accounted hardly dutiful. For a well-conducted Student ought, in strict duty, to spend (and in such a case lose) his evening in looking through what his teacher sets before him. It has happened to other Academy students under subsequent Keepers and Librarians, I am told, to find themselves in a similarly awkward dilemma to this of Blake's.

With the Antique, Blake got on well enough, drawing with 'great care all or certainly nearly all the noble antique figures in various views.' From the living figure he also drew a good deal; but early conceived a distaste for the study, as pursued in Academies of Art. Already 'life,' in so factitious, monotonous an aspect of it as that presented by a Model artificially *posed* to enact an artificial part – to maintain in painful rigidity some fleeting gesture of spontaneous Nature's – became, as it continued, 'hateful,' looking to him, laden with thick-coming fancies, 'more like death' than life; nay (singular to say) 'smelling of mortality' – to an imaginative mind! 'Practice and opportunity,' he used afterwards to declare, 'very soon teach the language of art:' as much, that is, as Blake ever acquired, not a despicable if imperfect quantum. 'Its spirit and poetry, centred in the imagination alone, never can be taught; and these make the artist:' a truism, the fervid poet already began to hold too exclusively in view. Even at their best – as the vision-seer and instinctive Platonist tells us in one of the very last years of his life (*MS. notes to Wordsworth*) – mere 'Natural Objects *always did and do* weaken, deaden and obliterate imagination in me!'

The student still continued to throw off drawings and verses for his own delight; out of his numerous store of the former engraving two designs from English history. One of these

34

engravings, *King Edward and Queen Eleanor*, 'published' by him at a later date (from Lambeth), I have seen. It is a meritorious but heavy piece of business, in the old-fashioned plodding style of line-engraving, wherein the hand monotonously hatched line after line, now struck off by machine. The design itself and the other water-colour drawings of this date, all on historical subjects, which now lie scattered among various hands, have little of the quality or of the mannerism we are accustomed to associate with Blake's name. They remind one rather of Mortimer, *the* historical painter (now obsolete) of that era, who died, high in reputation with his contemporaries for fancy and correct drawing of the human figure, but neglected by patrons, about this very time, viz. in 1779, at the early age of forty. Of Mortimer, Blake always continued to entertain a very high estimate. The designs of this epoch in his life are correctly drawn, prettily composed, and carefully coloured, in a clear uniform style of equally distributed positive tints. But the costumes are vague and mythical, without being graceful and credible; what mannerism there is is a timid one, such as reappears in Hamilton always, in Stothard often; the general effect is heavy and uninteresting, – and the net result a yawn. One drawing dating from these years (1778–9), *The Penance of Jane Shore* in St Paul's Church, thirty years later was included in Blake's Exhibition of his own Works (1809). In the *Descriptive Catalogue* he speaks of it with some complacency as 'proving to the author, and he thinks to any discerning eye, that the productions of our youth and of our maturer age, are equal in all essential points.' To me, on inspecting the same, it proves nothing of the kind; though it be a very exemplary performance in the manner just indicated. The central figure of Jane Shore has however much grace and sweetness; and the intention of the whole composition is clear and decisive. One extrinsic circumstance materially detracts from the appearance of this and other water-colour drawings from his hand of the period: viz. that, as a substitute for glass, they were all eventually, in prosecution of a hobby of Blake's, *varnished*, – of which process, applied to a water-colour drawing, nothing can exceed the disenchanting, not to say destructive effect.

There is a scarce engraving inscribed 'W. B. *inv.* 1780' which, within certain limitations, has much more of the peculiar Blake quality and intensity about it. The subject is evidently a personi-fication of Morning, or Glad Day: a nude male figure, with one foot on earth, just alighted from above; a flood of radiance still encircling his head; his arms outspread, – as exultingly bringing joy and solace to this lower world, – not with classic Apollo-like indifference, but with the divine chastened fervour of an angelic minister. Below crawls a caterpillar, and a hybrid kind of night-moth takes wing.

Meanwhile, the Poet and Designer, living under his father the hosier's roof, 28, Broad Street, had not only to educate himself in high art, but to earn his livelihood by humbler art – engraver's journey-work. During the years 1779 to 1782 and onwards, one or two booksellers gave him employment in engraving from afterwards better known fellow designers. Harri-son of Paternoster Row employed him for his *Novelists' Maga-zine*, or collection of approved novels; for his *Ladies' Magazine*, and perhaps other serials; J. Johnson, a constant employer during a long series of years, for various books; and occasionally other booksellers, – Macklin, Buckland, and (later) Dodsley, Stock-dale, the Cadells. Among the first in date of such prints, was a well-engraved frontispiece after Stothard, bold and telling in light and shade ('The four Quarters of the Globe'), to a *System of Geography* (1779); and another after Stothard, ('Clarence's

Dream'), to Enfield's *Speaker*, published by Johnson in 1780. Then came with sundry miscellaneous, eight plates after some of Stothard's earliest and most beautiful designs for the *Novelists' Magazine*. The designs brought in young Stothard, hitherto an apprentice to a Pattern-draftsman in Spitalfields, a guinea a piece, – and established his reputation: their intrinsic grace, feeling, and freshness being (for one thing) advantageously set off by very excellent engraving, of an infinitely more robust and honest kind than the smooth style of Heath and his School, which succeeded to it, and eventually brought about the ruin of line-engraving for book illustrations. Of Blake's eight engravings, all thorough and sterling pieces of workmanship, two were illustrations of *Don Quixote*, one, of the *Sentimental Journey* (1782), one, of Miss Fielding's *David Simple*, another, of *Launcelot Greaves*, three, of *Grandison* (1782–3).

One Trotter, a fellow-engraver who received instructions from Blake, who engraved a print or two after Stothard, and was also draftsman to the calico printers, had introduced Blake to Stothard, the former's senior by nearly two years, and then lodging in company with Shelly, the miniature painter, in the Strand. Stothard introduced Blake to Flaxman, who after seeing some of the early graceful plates in the *Novelists' Magazine*, had of his own accord made their designer's acquaintance. Flaxman, of the same age and standing as Stothard, was as yet subsisting by his designs for the first Wedgwood, and also living in the Strand, with his father; who there kept a well-known plaster-cast shop when plaster-cast shops were rare. A wistful remembrance of the superiority of 'old Flaxman's' casts still survives among artists. In 1781 the sculptor married, taking house and studio of his own at 27, Wardour Street, and becoming Blake's near neighbour. He proved – despite some passing clouds which for a time

37

obscured their friendship at a later era – one of the best and firmest friends Blake ever had; as great artists often prove to one another in youth. The imaginative man needed friends; for his gifts were not of the bread-winning sort. He was one of those whose genius is in a far higher ratio than their talents: and it is Talent which commands worldly success. Amidst the miscellaneous journey-work which about this period kept Blake's graver going, if not his mind, may be mentioned the illustrations to a show-list of Wedgwood's productions: specimens of his latest novelties in earthenware and porcelain – tea and dinner services, &c. Seldom have such very humble essays in Decorative Art – good enough in form, but not otherwise remarkable – tasked the combined energies of a Flaxman and a Blake! To the list of the engraver's friends was afterwards added Fuseli, of maturer age and acquirements, man of letters as well as Art; a multifarious and learned author. From intercourse with minds like these, much was learned by Blake, in his art and out of it. In 1780, Fuseli, then thirty-nine, just returned from eight years' sojourn in Italy, became a neighbour, lodging in Broad Street, where he remained until 1782. In the latter year, his original and characteristic picture of *The Nightmare* made 'a sensation' at the Exhibition: the first of his to do so. The subsequent engraving gave him a European reputation. Artists' homes as well as studios abounded then in Broad Street and its neighbourhood. Bacon the sculptor lived in Wardour Street, Paul Sandby in Poland Street, the fair R.A., Angelica Kauffman, in Golden Square, Bartolozzi, with his apprentice Sherwin, in Broad Street itself, and at a later date John Varley, 'father of modern Water Colours,' in the same street (No. 15). Literary celebrities were not wanting: in Wardour Street, Mrs Chapone; in Poland Street, pushing, pompous Dr Burney, of Musical *History* notoriety.

In the catalogue of the now fairly established Royal Academy's Exhibition for 1780, its *twelfth*, and first at Somerset House – all previous had been held in its 'Old Room' (originally built for an auction room), on the south side of Pall Mall East – appears for the first time a work by 'W. Blake.' It was an Exhibition of only 489 'articles,' in all, waxwork and 'designs for a fan' inclusive among its leading exhibitors, boasting Sir Joshua Reynolds and Mary Moser, R.A., Gainsborough and Angelica Kauffman, *R.A.*, Cosway and Loutherbourg, Paul Sandby and Zoffany, Copley (Lyndhurst's father), and Fuseli, not yet Associate. Blake's contribution is the *Death of Earl Goodwin*, a drawing probably; being exhibited in 'The Ante-room,' devoted to flower-pieces, crayons, miniatures, and water-colour landscapes – some by Gainsborough. This first Exhibition in official quarters went off with much *éclat*, netting double the average amount realized by its predecessors: viz. as much as 3,000*l.*

In the sultry, early days of June, 1780, the Lord George Gordon No-Popery Riots rolled through Town. Half London was sacked, and its citizens for six days laid under forced contributions, by a mob some forty thousand strong, of boys, pickpockets, and 'roughs.' In this outburst of anarchy, Blake long remembered an involuntary participation of his own. On the third day, Tuesday, 6th of June, 'the Mass-houses' having already been demolished – one, in Blake's near neighbourhood, Warwick Street, Golden Square – and various private houses also; the rioters, flushed with gin and victory, were turning their attention to grander schemes of devastation. That evening, the artist happened to be walking in a route chosen by one of the mobs at large, whose course lay from Justice Hyde's house near Leicester Fields, for the destruction of which less than an hour had sufficed, through Long Acre, past the quiet house of Blake's old master, engraver Basire, in Great Queen Street, Lincoln's Inn Fields, and down Holborn, bound for Newgate. Suddenly, he encountered the advancing wave of triumphant Blackguardism, and was forced (for from such a great surging mob there is no disentanglement) to go along in the very front rank, and witness the storm and burning of the fortress-like prison, and release of its three hundred inmates. This was a peculiar experience for a spiritual poet; not without peril, had a drunken soldier chanced to have identified him during the after weeks of indiscriminate vengeance: those black weeks when strings of boys under fourteen were hung up in a row to vindicate the offended majesty of the Law. '*I never saw boys cry so!*' observed Selwyn, connoisseur in hanging, in his diary.

It was the same Tuesday night, one may add, that among the obnoxious mansions of magistrate and judge gutted of furniture, and consigned to the flames, Lord Mansfield's in Bloomsbury Square was numbered. That night, too – every householder having previously chalked the talisman, 'No Popery,' on his door, (the very Jews inscribing 'This House True Protestant!') every house showing blue flag, every wayfarer having donned the blue cockade – that night the Londoners with equal unanimity illuminated their windows. Still wider stupor of fear followed next day: and to it, a still longer sleepless night of prison-burning, drunken infatuation, and onsets from the military, let slip at last from civil leash. Six-and-thirty fires are to be seen simultaneously blazing in one new neighbourhood (Bloomsbury), not far from Blake's and still nearer to Basire's; whence are heard the terrible shouts of excited crowds, mingling with the fiercer roar of the flames, and with the reports of scattered musket-shots at distant points from the soldiery. Some inhabitants catch up their household effects and aimlessly run up and down the streets with them; others cheerfully pay their guinea a mile for a vehicle to carry them beyond the tumult. These were *not* favourable days for designing, or even quiet engraving.

Since his twentieth year, Blake's energies had been 'wholly directed to the attainment of excellence in his profession' as artist: too much so to admit of leisure or perhaps inclination for poetry. Engrossing enough was the indispensable effort to master the difficulties of Design, with pencil or in water-colours. With the still tougher mechanical difficulties of oil-painting he never fairly grappled; but confined himself to water-colours and *tempera* (on canvas), with in after years a curious modification of the latter – which he daringly christened 'fresco.' Original invention now claimed more than all his leisure. His working-hours during the years 1780 to 1782 were occupied by various book-plates for the publications already named. These voluminous, well-illustrated serials are infrequently stumbled on by the Collector at the second-hand booksellers. Very few are to be found in our Museum Library, professedly miscellaneous as that collection is. In the Print Room exists a fine series of engravings after Stothard; which, however, being undated, affords little help to those wishing to learn something about the engravers of them.

These were days of Courtship, too. And the course of Blake's love did not open smoothly. 'A lively little girl' in his own, or perhaps a humbler station, the object of his first sighs readily allowed him, as girls in a humble class will, meaning neither marriage nor harm, to 'keep company' with her; to pay his court, take mutual walks, and be as lovesick as he chose; but nowise encouraged the idea of a wedding. In addition to the pangs of fruitless love, attacks of jealousy had stoically to be borne. When he complained that the favour of her company in a stroll had been extended to another admirer, 'Are you a fool?' was the brusque reply – with a scornful glance. 'That cured me of jealousy,' Blake used naïvely to relate. One evening at a friend's house he was bemoaning in a corner his love-crosses. His listener, a dark-eyed, generous-hearted girl, frankly declared 'She pitied him from her heart.' '*Do* you pity me?' '*Yes!* I do, most sincerely.' 'Then I love you for that!' he replied, with enthusiasm: – such soothing pity is irresistible. And a second more prosperous courtship began. At this, or perhaps a later meeting, followed the confession, I dare say in lower tones, '*Well! and I love you!*' – always, doubtless, a pretty one to hear.

The unsophisticated maiden was named Catherine Sophia Boucher – plebeian corruption, probably, of the grand historic name, Bourchier; – daughter of William and Mary Boucher of Battersea. So at least the Register gives the name: where, within less than ten years, no fewer than seven births to the same parents, including two sets of twins in succession, immediately precede hers. Her position and connexions in life were humble, humbler than Blake's own; her education – as to book-lore – neglected, not to say omitted. For even the (at first) paltry makeshift of National Schools had not yet been invented; and Sunday Schools were first set going a little after this very time, namely, in 1784. When, by-and-by, Catherine's turn came, as bride, to sign the Parish Register, she, as the same yet mutely testifies, could do no more than most young ladies of her class then, or than the Bourchiers, Stanleys, and magnates of the land four centuries before could do – viz. make a X as 'her mark:' her surname on the same occasion being mis-spelt for her and vulgarized into Butcher, and her second baptismal name omit- ted. A bright-eyed, dark-haired brunette, with expressive fea- tures and a slim graceful form, can make a young artist and poet overlook such trifles as defective scholarship. Nor were a fair outside and a frank accessible heart deceptive lures in this instance. Catherine – Christian namesake, by the way, of Blake's mother – was endowed with a loving loyal nature, an adaptive open mind, capable of profiting by good teaching, and of enabling her, under constant high influence, to become a meet companion to her imaginative husband in his solitary and way-ward course. Uncomplainingly and helpfully, she shared the low and rugged fortunes which over-originality insured as his unvarying lot in life. She had mind and the ambition which follows. Not only did she prove a good housewife on straitened means, but in after-years, under his tuition and hourly com-panionship, she acquired besides the useful arts of reading and writing, that which very few uneducated women with the honestest effort ever succeed in attaining: some footing of equality with her husband. She, in time, came to work off his engravings, as though she had been bred to the trade; nay, imbibed enough of his very spirit to reflect it in Design which might almost have been his own.

Allan Cunningham says she was a neighbour. But the mar-riage took place at Battersea, where I trace relatives of Blake's father to have been then living. During the course of the court-ship many a happy Surrey ramble must have been taken towards and around the pleasant village of the St Johns. The old family-seat, spacious and venerable, still stood, in which Lord Boling-broke had been born and died, which Pope had often visited. The village was 'four miles from London' then, and had just begun to shake hands with Chelsea, by a timber bridge over the Thames; the river bright and clear there at low tide as at Rich-mond now, with many a placid angler dotting its new bridge. Green meadow and bright cornfield lay between the old-fashioned winding High Street and the purple heights of Wimbledon and Richmond. In the volume of 1783, among the poems which have least freshness of feeling, being a little alloyed by false notes as of the poetic Mocking Bird, are one or two love-poems anticipating emotions as yet unfelt. And love, it is said, must be felt ere it can be persuasively sung. One or two stanzas, if we did not know they had been written long before, might well have been allusive to the 'black-eyed maid' of present choice, and the 'sweet village' where he wooed her.

> When early morn walks forth in sober grey,
> Then to my black-ey'd maid I haste away;
> When evening sits beneath her dusky bow'r
> And gently sighs away the silent hour,
> The village-bell alarms, away I go,
> And the vale darkens at my pensive woe.
>
> To that sweet village, where my black-ey'd maid
> Doth drop a tear beneath the silent shade,
> I turn my eyes; and pensive as I go,
> Curse my black stars, and bless my pleasing woe.
>
> Oft when the summer sleeps among the trees,
> Whisp'ring faint murmurs to the scanty breeze,
> I walk the village round; if at her side
> A youth doth walk in stolen joy and pride,
> I curse my stars in bitter grief and woe,
> That made my love so high and me so low.

*   *   *

The last is an inapplicable line to the present case, – decidedly *un*prophetic. In a better, more Blake-like manner is the other poem, apposite to how many thousand lovers, in how many climes, since man first came into the planet.

*   *   *

My feet are wing'd while o'er the dewy lawn
I meet my maiden risen with the morn:
Oh, bless those holy feet, like angel's feet!
Oh, bless those limbs beaming with heavenly light!

As when an angel glitt'ring in the sky
In times of innocence and holy joy,
The joyful shepherd stops his grateful song
To hear the music of that angel's tongue:

So when *she* speaks, the voice of Heav'n I hear;
So when we walk, nothing impure comes near;
Each field seems Eden and each calm retreat;
Each village seems the haunt of holy feet.

But that sweet village where my black-ey'd maid
Closes her eyes in sleep beneath Night's shade,
Whene'er I enter, more than mortal fire
Burns in my soul, and does my song inspire.

The occasional hackneyed rhyme, awkward construction, and verbal repetition, entailed by the requirements of very inartificial verse, are technical blemishes any poetical reader may by ten minutes' manipulation mend, but such as clung to Blake's verse in later and maturer years.

The lovers were married, Blake being in his twenty-fifth year, his bride in her twenty-first, on a Sunday in August (the 18th), 1782, in the then newly rebuilt church of Battersea: a 'handsome edifice,' say contemporary topographers. Which, in the present case, means a whitey-brown brick building in the church-warden style, relying for architectural effect, externally, on a nondescript steeple, a low slate roof, double rows of circular-headed windows, and an elevated western portico in a strikingly picturesque and unique position: almost *upon* the river as it were, which here takes a sudden bend to the south-west, the body of the church stretching alongside it. The interior, with its galleries (in which are interesting seventeenth and eighteenth century mural tablets from the old church, one by Roubiliac), and elaborately decorated apsidal dwarf-chancel, has an imposing effect and a strongly marked characteristic *accent* (of its Day), already historical and interesting. There, standing above the vault wherein lies the coronetted coffin of Pope's Bolingbroke, the two plighted troth. The vicar who joined their hands, Joseph Gardnor, was himself an amateur artist of note in his day, copious 'honorary contributor' (not above customers) to the Exhibitions; sending 'Views from the Lakes,' from Wales, and other much-libelled Home Beauties, and even *Landscape Compositions* 'in the style of the Lakes,' whatever that may mean. Specimens of this master – pasteboard-like model of misty mountain, old manorial houses as of cards, perspectiveless diagram of lovely vale – may be inspected in Williams' plodding *History of Monmouthshire*, and in other books of topography. Engravers had actually to copy and laboriously bite in these young-lady-like Indian ink drawings. Conspicuous mementoes of the vicar's Taste and munificence still survive, parochially, in the 'handsome crimson curtains' trimmed with amber, and held up by gold cord with heavy gold tassels, festooned about the painted eastern window of the church: or rather in deceptively perfect *imitations* of such upholstery, painted ('tis said) by the clergyman's own skilled hand on the light-grained wall of the circular chancel. The window is an eighteenth century remnant piously preserved from the old church: a window literally *painted* not stained – the colours not burnt in, that is; so that a deluded cleaner on one occasion rubbed out a portion. The subjects are armorial bearings of the St Johns, and (at bottom) portraits of three august collateral connexions of the Family: Margaret Beauchamp, Henry VII and Queen Elizabeth. The general effect is good in colour, not without a tinge of ancient harmony, yellow being the predominating hue. From the vicar's hand, again, are the two small 'paintings on glass,' – *The Lamb* bearing the sacred monogram, and *The Dove* (descending), – which fill the two circular sidewindows, of an eminently domestic type, in the curvilinear chancel-wall: paintings so 'natural' and familiarly 'like,' an innocent spectator forgets perhaps their sacred symbolism – as possibly did the artist too! Did the future designer of *The Gates of Paradise*, the *Jerusalem*, and the *Job*, kneel beneath these trophies of religious art?

SIX

Introduction to the Polite World 1782–84
[ÆT. 24–27]

To his father, Blake's early and humble marriage is said to have been unacceptable; and the young couple did not return to the hosier's roof. They commenced housekeeping on their own account in lodgings, at 23, Green Street, Leicester Fields: in which Fields or Square, on the north side, the junior branches of Royalty had lately abode, on the east (near Green Street) great Hogarth. On the west side of it Sir Joshua in these very years had his handsome house and noble gallery. Green Street, then the abode of quiet private citizens, is now a nondescript street, given up to curiosity shops, shabby lodging-houses, and busy feet hastening to and from the Strand. No. 23, on the right-hand side going citywards, next to the house at the corner of the Square, is one – from the turn the narrow Street here takes – at right angles with and looking down the rest of it. At present, part tenanted by a shoemaker, the house is in an abject plight of stucco, dirt, and dingy desolation. In the previous year, as we have seen, friendly Flaxman had married and taken a house.

About this time, or a little earlier, Blake was introduced by the admiring sympathetic sculptor to the accomplished Mrs Mathew, his own warm friend. The 'celebrated Mrs Mathew?' Alas! for tenure of mortal Fame! This lady ranked among the distinguished blue-stockings of her day; was once known to half the Town, the polite and lettered part thereof, as the agreeable, fascinating, *spirituelle* Mrs Mathew, as, in brief, one of the most 'gifted and elegant' of women. As she does not, like her fair comrades, still flutter about the bookstalls among the half-remembered all-unread, and as no lettered contemporary has handed down her portrait, she has disappeared from us. Yet the lady, with her husband, the Rev. Henry Mathew, merit remembrance from the lovers of Art, as the first discoverers and fosterers of the genius of Flaxman, when a boy not yet in teens, and his introducer to more opulent patrons. Their son, afterwards Dr Mathew, was John Hunter's favourite pupil. Learned as well as elegant, she would read Homer in Greek to the future sculptor, interpreting as she went, while the child sat by her side sketching a passage here and there; and thus she stimulated him to acquire hereafter some knowledge of the language for himself. She was an encourager of musicians, a kind friend to young artists. To all of promising genius the doors of her house, 27, Rathbone Place, were open. Rathbone Place, not then made over to *papier-maché*, Artist's colours, toy-shops, and fancy-trades, was a street of private houses, stiffly genteel and highly respectable, nay, in a sedate way, *quasi* fashionable; the Westbourne Street of that day, when the adjacent district of Bloomsbury with its Square, in which (on the countryward side) was the Duke of Bedford's grand House, was absolutely fashionable and comparatively new, lying on the northern skirts of London; when Great Ormond Street, Queen's Square, Southampton Row, were accounted 'places of pleasure,' being 'in one of the most charming situations about town,' next the open fields, and commanding a 'beautiful landscape formed by the hills of Highgate and Hampstead and adjacent country.' Among the

49

residents of Rathbone Place, the rebel Lords Lovat, Kilmarnock, Balmarino had at one time numbered. Of the Mathews' house, by the way, now divided into two, both of them shops, the library or back parlour, garrulous Smith (Nollekens's biographer) in his *Book for a Rainy Day* tells us, was decorated by grateful Flaxman 'with models in putty and sand, of figures in niches in the Gothic manner:' *quære* if still extant? The window was painted 'in imitation of stained glass' – just as that in Battersea church, those at Strawberry Hill, and elsewhere were, the practice being one of the valued arts or artifices of the day – by Loutherbourg's assistant, *young* Oram, another *protégé*. The furniture, again, 'bookcases, tables, and chairs, were also ornamented to accord with the appearance of those of antiquity.'

Mrs Mathew's drawing-room was frequented by most of the literary and known people of the last quarter of the century, was a centre of all then esteemed enlightened and delightful in society. *Réunions* were held in it such as Mrs Montagu and Mrs Vesey had first set going, unconsciously contributing the word *bluestocking* to our language. There, in the list of her intimate friends and companions, would assemble those esteemed ornaments of their sex: unreadable Chapone, of well improved mind; sensible Barbauld; versatile, agreeable Mrs Brooke, novelist and dramatist; learned and awful Mrs Carter, a female Great Cham of literature, and protectress of 'Religion and Morality.' Thither, came sprightly, fashionable Mrs Montagu herself, Conyers Middleton's pupil, champion of Shakspere in his urgent need against rude Voltaire, and a letter-writer almost as vivacious and *piquante* in the modish style as her namesake Lady Wortley; her printed correspondence remaining still readable and entertaining. This is the lady whose powers of mind and conversation Dr Johnson estimated so highly, and whose good opinion he so highly valued, though at last to his sorrow falling out of favour with her. It was she who gave the annual May-Day dinner to the chimney sweeps, in commemoration of a well-known family incident. As illustrative of their status with the public, let us add, on Smith's authority, that the four last-named *beaux-esprits* figured as Muses in the Frontispiece to a *Lady's Pocket Book* for 1778 – a flattering apotheosis of nine contemporary female wits, including Angelica Kauffman and Mrs Sheridan. Perhaps pious, busy Hannah More, as yet of the world, as yet young and kittenish, though not without claws, also in her youth a good letter-writer in the woman-of-the-world style; perhaps, being of the Montagu circle, she also would make one at Mrs Mathew's, on her visits to town to see her publishers, the Cadells, about some ambling poetic 4to. *Florio and the Bas-bleu*, modest *Sacred Drama*, heavy 8vo. *Strictures on Female Education*, or other fascinating lucubration on

'Providence, foreknowledge, will and fate:'

dissertations, which, after having brought their author in some thirty thousand pounds sterling, a capricious public consumes with less avidity than it did. Good heavens! what a frowsy, drowsy 'party sitting in a parlour,' *now* 'all silent and all damned' (in a literary sense), these venerable ladies and great literary luminaries of their day, ladies once lively and chatty enough, seem to an irreverent generation, at their present distance from us. The spiritual interval is an infinitely wider one than the temporal; so foreign have mere eighteenth-century habits of thought and prim conventions become. Let us charitably believe the conversation of the fair was not so dull as their books; that there was the due enlivenment of scandal and small talk; and that Mrs Mathew – by far the most pleasant to think of, because she did not commit herself to a book – that she, with perhaps Mrs Brooke and Mrs Montagu, took the leading parts.

The disadvantages of a neglected education, such as Blake's, are considerable. But, one is here reminded, the disadvantages of a false one are greater: when the acquisition of a second nature of conventionality, misconception of high models and worship of low ones is the kind in vogue. An inestimable advantage for an original mind to have retained its freedom, the healthy play of native powers, of virgin faculties yet unsophisticate.

Mrs Mathew's husband was a known man, too, man of taste and *virtù*, incumbent of the neighbouring Proprietary Chapel, Percy Chapel, Charlotte Street, built for him by admiring lay friends; an edifice known to a later generation as the theatre of *Satan* Montgomery's displays. Mr Mathew filled also a post of more prestige as afternoon preacher at St Martin's-in-the-Fields; and 'read the church-service more beautifully than any other clergyman in London,' a lady who had heard him informs me – and as others too used to think – Flaxman for one. With which meagre biographic trait, the inquisitive reader must be satisfied. The most diligent search yields nothing further. That he was an amiable, kindly man we gather from the circumstances of his first notice of the child Flaxman in the father's cast-shop, coughing over his Latin behind the counter, and of his continued notice of the weakly child during the years which elapsed before he was strong enough to walk from the Strand to Rathbone Place, and be received into the sunshine of Mrs Mathew's smiles.

To that lady's agreeable and brilliant *conversazioni* Blake was made welcome. At one of them, a little later (in 1784), Nollekens Smith, most literal, most useful of gossips, then a youth of eighteen, first saw the poet-painter, and 'heard him read and sing several of his poems' – 'often heard him.' Yes! *sing* them; for Blake had composed airs to his verses. Wholly ignorant of the art of music, he was unable to note down these spontaneous melodies, and repeated them by ear: Smith reports that his tunes were sometimes 'most singularly beautiful,' and 'were noted down by musical professors;' Mrs Mathew's being a musical house. I wish one of these musical professors or his executors would produce a sample. Airs simple and ethereal to match the designs and poems of William Blake would be a novelty in music. One would fain hear the melody invented for

How sweet I roam'd from field to field –

or for some of the *Songs of Innocence*. 'He was listened to by the company,' adds Smith, 'with profound silence, and allowed by most of the visitors to possess original and extraordinary merit.' Phœnix amid an admiring circle of cocks and hens is alone a spectacle to compare mentally with this!

The accomplished hostess for a time took up Blake with much fervour. His poetic recitals kindled so much enthusiasm in her feminine bosom, that she urged her husband to join his young friend, Flaxman, in placing the poems – those of which we gave an account at the date of composition – in the clear light of print, and to assume half the cost. Which, accordingly, was done, in 1783, the year in which happened the execution for forgery of the gifted fellow-engraver – in whose face the boy Blake, twelve years before had so strangely deciphered omens of his fate – Ryland. This unfortunate man's prepossessing appearance and manners inspired on the other hand so much confidence in the governor of the prison in which he awaited trial, that on one occasion the former took him out for a walk,

53

implicitly trusting to his good faith that he would not avail himself of the opportunity to run away. Ryland's was the *last* execution at Tyburn, then still on the outside of London. This was the year, too, in which Barry published his *Account* of the *Pictures in the Adelphi*. On one copy I have seen a characteristic pencil recollection, from Blake's hand, of the strange Irishman's ill-favoured face: that of an idealized bulldog, with villainously low forehead, turn-up nose, and squalid *tout-ensemble*. It is strong evidence of the modest Flaxman's generous enthusiasm for his friend that, himself a struggling artist, little patronized, he should have made the first offer of printing these poems, and at his own charge; and that he now bore a moiety of the cost. The book only runs to 74 pages, 8vo., and its unpretending title-page stands thus: *Poetical Sketches; by W. B. London: Printed in the Year* 1783. The clergyman 'with his usual urbanity' penned a preface stating the youthful authorship of the volume, apologizing for 'irregularities and defects' in the poems, and hoping their 'poetic originality merits some respite from oblivion.'

The author's absence of leisure is pleaded, 'requisite to such a revisal of these sheets as might have rendered them less unfit to meet the public eye.' Little revisal certainly they had, not even correction of the press, apparently. The pamphlet, which has no printer's name to be discredited by it, is as carelessly printed as an old English play, evidently at an establishment which did not boast a 'reader.' Semicolons and fullstops where commas should be, misprints, such as 'beds of dawn' for 'birds,' by no means help out the meaning. The whole impression was presented to Blake to sell to friends or publish, as he should think best. Unfortunately, it never got published, and for all purposes except that of preservation, might as well have continued MS. As in those days there still survived, singular to say,

54

a *bonâ fide* market for even mediocre verse, publishers and editors actually handing over hard cash for it, just as if it were prose, Blake's friends would have done better to have gone to the Trade with his poems. The thin octavo did not even get so far as the *Monthly Review*; at all events, it does not appear in the copious and explicit *Index* of 'books noticed' in that periodical, now quite a manual of extinct literature.

The poems J.T. Smith, in 1784, heard Blake sing, can hardly have been those known to his hearers by the printed volume of 1783, but fresh ones, to the composition of which the printing of that volume had stimulated him: some doubtless of the memorable and musical *Songs of Innocence*, as they were subsequently named.

Blake's course of *soirées* in Rathbone Place was not long a smooth one. 'It happened unfortunately,' writes enigmatic Smith, whose forte is not grammar, 'soon after this period' – soon after 1784, that is, the year during which Smith heard him 'read and sing his poems' to an attentive auditory – 'that in consequence of his unbending deportment, or what his adherents are pleased to call his manly firmness of opinion, which certainly was not at all times considered pleasing by every one, his visits were not so frequent:' – and after a time ceased altogether, 'tis to be feared. One's knowledge of Blake's various originalities of thought on all subjects, his stiffness, when roused, in maintaining them, also his high, though at ordinary moments inobtrusive notions of his calling, of the dignity of it, and its superiority to all mere worldly distinctions, help to elucidate gossiping John Thomas. One readily understands that on more intimate acquaintance, when it was discovered by well-regulated minds that the erratic Bard perversely came to teach, not to be taught, nor to be gently schooled into imitative proprieties and condescendingly patted on the back, he became less acceptable to the polite world at No. 27, than when first started as a prodigy in that elegant arena.

SEVEN

Struggle and Sorrow 1782–87
[ÆT. 25–30]

Returning to 1782–3, among the engravings executed by Blake in those years, I have noticed after Stothard, four illustrations – two vignettes and two oval plates – to Scott of Amwell's *Poems*, published by Buckland (1782); two frontispieces to Dodsley's *Lady's Pocket-Book* – 'The morning amusements of H.R.H. the Princess Royal and her four sisters' (1782), and 'A Lady in full-dress' with another 'in the most fashionable undress now worn' (1783); – and *The Fall of Rosamond*, a circular plate in a book published by Macklin (1783). To the latter year also, the first after Blake's marriage, belong about eight or nine of the vignettes, after the purest and most lovely of the early and best designs of the same artist – full of sweetness, refinement, and graceful fancy – which illustrate Ritson's *Collection of English Songs* (3 vols 8vo.); others being engraved by Grignon, Heath, &c. In the first volume occur the best designs, and – what is remarkable – designs very Blake-like in feeling and conception; having the air of graceful translation of *his* inventions. Most in this volume are engraved by Blake, and very finely, with delicacy, as well as force. I may instance in particular one at the head of the *Love Songs*, a Lady singing, Cupids fluttering before her, a singularly refined composition; another, a vignette to *Jemmy Dawson*, which is, in fact, Hero awaiting

57

Leander; another to *When Lovely Woman*, a sitting figure of much dignity and beauty.

In after-years of estrangement from Stothard, Blake used to complain of this mechanical employment as engraver to a fellow-designer, who (he asserted) first borrowed from one that, in his servile capacity, had then to copy that comrade's version of his own inventions – as to motive and composition his own, that is. The strict justice of this complaint I can hardly measure, because I know not how much of the Design he afterwards engraved was actually being produced at this period – doubtless much. We shall hereafter have to point out that a good deal in Flaxman and Stothard may be traced to Blake, is indeed only Blake in the Vernacular, classicized and (perhaps half-unconsciously) adapted. His own compositions bear the authentic first-hand impress; those unmistakable traces, which no hand can feign, of genuineness, freshness, and spontaneity, the look as of coming straight from another world – that in which Blake's spirit lived. He, in his cherished visionary faculty, his native power and life-long habit of vivid Invention, was placed above all need or inclination to borrow from others. If, as happens to all, there occur occasional passages of unconscious reminiscence from the Old Masters, there is no cooking or disguise. His friend Fuseli, with characteristic candour, used to declare, 'Blake is d—d good to steal from!'

Certainly, Stothard, though even he could by utmost diligence only earn a moderate income – for if in request with the publishers he was neglected by picture-buyers – was throughout life, compared with Blake, a prosperous, affluent man. He had throughout, the advantage of Blake with the public. Hence early, some feeling of soreness in his uncompliant companion's bosom. Stothard had the advantage in the marketable quality of his genius, in his versatile talents, his superior technic attainments – or, rather, superior consistency of attainment; above all, in his inborn grace and elegance. He could make the refined Domestic groups he so readily conceived, whether all his own or in part borrowed, far more palatable to the many, the cultivated many – cultivated Rogers for example, his life-long patron – than Blake could ever make his Dantesque sublimity, wild Titanic play of fancy, and spiritually imaginative dreams. I think the latter, as we shall see when we come to the *Songs of Innocence and Experience*, was at this period of his life influenced to his advantage as a designer by contact with Stothard's graceful mind; but that any capability of grander qualities occasionally shown by Stothard was derived, and perhaps as unconsciously, from Blake. And Stothard's earlier style is far purer and more 'matterful,' to use an expression of Charles Lamb's, than the sugar-plum manner of his latter years. In Stothard as in Blake, however nominally various the subject, there is the tyrannous predominance of certain ruling ideas of the designer's. Stothard's tether was always shorter than Blake's; but within the prescribed limits, his performance was the more (superficially) perfect, as well as soft, and rounded.

In 1784 I find Blake engraving after Stothard and others in the *Wit's Magazine*. The *Wit's Magazine* was a 'Monthly Repository for the Parlour Window' – *not* designed (as the title in those free-speaking days might warrant a suspicion) to raise a blush on Lady's cheek: – a miscellany of innocently entertaining rather than strictly witty gleanings, and original contributions mostly amateur. A periodical curious to look back upon in days of a weekly *Punch!* It would be difficult now to find a literary parallel to Mr Harrison's plan of 'creating a spirit of emulation, and rewarding genius:' by awarding 'one silver medal' per month to the 'best witty tale, essay, or poem,' another to 'the best answer' to the munificent proprietor's 'prize enigmas.' A full list of the names and addresses of successful candidates for Fame is appended to each of the two octavo volumes to which the Magazine ran. A graceful grotesque, the *Temple of Mirth*, of Stothard's design, is the frontispiece to the first number: a folding sheet forcibly engraved by Blake in his characteristic manner of distributing strongly contrasted light and shade and tone. To it succeeded, month by month, four similar engravings by him after a noted caricaturist of the day, now forgotten, S. Collings: on broad-grin themes, such as *The Tithe in Kind, or the Son's Revenge, The Discomfited Duellists, The Blind Beggar's Hats*, and *May Day in London*. After which, an engraver of lower grade, one Smith, (*quære*, our friend Nollekens Smith?) executes the engravings; and after him a nameless one. The engraving caricatures, of the earth earthy, for this 'Library of Momus' was truly a singular task for a spiritual poet!

Some slight clue to the original Design of this period in a somewhat different key is given by the Exhibition-Catalogues, which report Blake as making a second appearance at the Academy in 1784. In that year, – the year of Reynolds' *Mrs Siddons as the Tragic Muse*, and *Fortune-Teller*, – hung in the 'Drawing and Sculpture Room,' two designs of Blake's: one, *War unchained by an Angel – Fire, Pestilence and Famine following*; the other, a *Breach in a City – The Morning after a Battle*. Companion-subjects, their tacit moral – the supreme despicableness of War – was one of which the artist, in all his tenets thorough-going, was a fervent propagandist in days when War was tyrannously in the ascendant. This, by the way, was the year of Peace with the tardily recognized North American States. I have not seen those two drawings. The same theme gave birth about twenty years later to four very fine water-colour drawings, – for Dantesque intensity, imaginative directness, and power of the terrible: illustrations of the doings of the Destroying Angels that War lets loose – *Fire, Plague, Pestilence*, and *Famine*. Another very grand and awe-inspiring illustration of still later date, of the same suggestive theme, is *Let loose the Dogs of War* – a Demon cheering on blood-hounds who seize a man by the throat; of which Mr Ruskin possesses the original pencil sketch, Mr Linnell the water-colour drawing.

During the summer of 1784, died Blake's father, an honest shopkeeper of the old school, and a devout man – a dissenter. He was buried in Bunhill Fields, on the fourth of July (a Sunday) says the Register. The eldest son, James, – a year and a half William's senior – continued to live with the widow Catherine, and succeeded to the hosier's business in Broad Street, still a highly respectable street, and a good one for trade, as it and the whole neighbourhood continued until the era of Nash and the 'first gentleman in Europe.' Golden Square was still the 'town residence' of some half-dozen M.P.'s – for county or rotten borough; Poland Street and Great Marlborough Street of others. Between this brother and the artist no strong sympathy existed, little community of sentiment or common ground (mentally) of any kind; although indeed, James – for the most part an humble matter-of-fact man – had his spiritual and visionary side too; would at times *talk Swedenborg*, talk of seeing Abraham and Moses, and to outsiders seem like his gifted brother 'a bit mad' – a mild madman instead of a wild and stormy.

On his father's death, Blake, who found Design yield no income, Engraving but a scanty one, returned from Green Street, Leicester Fields, to familiar Broad Street. At No. 27, next door to his brother's, he set up shop as printseller and engraver, in partnership with a former fellow-apprentice at Basire's: James Parker, a man some six or seven years his senior. An engraving by Blake after Stothard, *Zephyrus and Flora* (a long oval), was published by the firm 'Parker and Blake' this same year (1784). Mrs Mathew, still friendly and patronizing, though one day to be less eager for the poet's services as lion in Rathbone Place, countenanced, nay perhaps first set the scheme going – in an ill-advised philanthropic hour; favouring it, if Smith's hints may be trusted, with solid pecuniary help. It will prove an ill-starred speculation; Pegasus proverbially turning out an indifferent draught-horse. Mrs Blake helped in the shop; the poet busied himself with his graver and pencil still. William Blake behind a counter would have been a curious sight to see! His younger and favourite brother, Robert, made one in the family; William taking him as a gratis pupil in engraving. It must have been a singularly conducted commercial enterprise. No. 27 bears at present small trace – with its two quiet parlour-windows, apparently the same casements that have been there from the beginning – of having once been even temporarily a shop. The house is of the same character as No. 28: a good-sized three-storied one, with panelled rooms; its original aspect (like that of No. 28) wholly disguised, externally, by all-levelling stucco. It is still a private mansion; but let out (now) in floors and rooms to many families instead of one.

From 27, Broad Street, Blake in 1785 sent four water-colour drawings to the Academy-Exhibition, one, by the way, at which our old friend Parson Gardnor is still exhibiting – some seven *Views of Lake Scenery*. One of Blake's drawings is from Gray, *The Bard*. The others are subjects from the Story of Joseph: *Joseph's Brethren bowing before him*; *Joseph making himself known to them*; *Joseph ordering Simeon to be bound*. The latter series I have seen. The drawings are interesting for their imaginative merit, and as specimens, full of soft tranquil beauty, of Blake's earlier style: a very different one from that of his later and better-known works. Conceived in a dramatic spirit, they are executed in a subdued key of which, extravagance is the last defect to suggest itself. The design is correct and blameless, not to say tame (for Blake), the colour full, harmonious and sober. At the head of the Academy-Catalogues of those days, stands the stereotype notification, 'The Pictures &c. marked (*) are to be disposed of.' Blake's are not so marked: let us hope they were disposed of! The three *Joseph* drawings turned up within the last ten years in their original close rose-wood frames (a far from advantageous setting), at a broker's in Wardour Street, who had purchased them at a furniture-sale in the neighbourhood. Among Blake's fellow-exhibitors, it is now curious to note the small galaxy of still remembered names – Reynolds, Nollekens, Morland, Cosway, Fuseli, Flaxman, Stothard (the last three yet juniors) – sprinkling the mob of forgotten ones: among which such as West, Hamilton, Rigaud, Loutherbourg, Copley, Serre, Mary Moser, Russell, Dance, Farington Edwards, Garvey, Tomkins, are positive points of light. This year, by the way, Blake's friend Trotter exhibits a *Portrait of the late Dr Johnson*, 'a drawing in chalk from the life, about eighteen months before his death,' which should be worth something.

Blake's brother Robert, his junior by nearly five years, had been a playfellow of Smith's, whose father lived near (in Great Portland Street); and from him we hear that 'Bob, as he was familiarly called,' had ever been 'much beloved by all his companions.' By William he was in these years not only taught to draw and engrave, but encouraged to exert his imagination in original sketches. I have come across some of these tentative essays, carefully preserved by Blake during life, and afterwards forming part of the large accumulation of artistic treasure remaining in his widow's hands: the sole legacy, but not at all unproductive, he had to bequeath her. Some are in pencil, some in pen and ink outline thrown up by a uniform dark ground washed in with Indian ink. They unmistakably show the beginner – not to say the child – in art; are naïf and archaic-looking; rude, faltering, often puerile or absurd in drawing; but are characterized by Blake-like feeling and intention, having in short a strong family likeness to his brother's work. The subjects are from Homer and the poets. Of one or two compositions there are successive and each time enlarged versions. True imaginative *animus* is often made manifest by very imperfect means; in the composition of the groups, and the expressive disposition of the individual figure, or of an individual limb: as, *e.g.* (in one drawing) that solitary upraised arm stretched heaven-ward from out the midst of the panic-struck crowd of figures, who, embracing, huddle together with bowed heads averted from a Divine Presence. In another, a group of ancient men stand silent on the verge of a sea-girt precipice, beyond which they gaze towards awe-inspiring shapes and sights unseen by us. This last motive seems to have pleased Blake himself. One of his earliest attempts, if not his very earliest, in that peculiar stereotype process he soon afterwards invented, as a version of this very composition: marvellously improved in the treatment – in the disposition and conception of the figures (at once fewer and better contrasted), as well, of course, as in drawing; which was what Blake's drawing always was – whatever its *wilful* faults – not only full of grand effect, but firm and decisive, that of a Master.

With Blake and with his wife, at the print shop in Broad Street, Robert for two happy years and a half lived in seldom disturbed accord. Such domestications however, always bring their own trials, their own demands for mutual self-sacrifice. Of which the following anecdote will supply a hint, as well as testify to much amiable magnanimity on the part of both the younger members of the household. One day, a dispute arose between Robert and Mrs Blake. She, in the heat of discussion, used words to him, his brother (though a husband too) thought unwarrantable. A silent witness thus far, he could now bear it no longer, but with characteristic impetuosity – when stirred – rose and said to her: 'Kneel down and beg Robert's pardon directly, or you never see my face again!' A heavy threat, uttered in tones which, from Blake, unmistakably showed it was *meant*. She, poor thing! 'thought it very hard,' as she would afterwards tell, to beg her brother-in law's pardon when she was not in fault! But being a duteous, devoted wife, though by nature nowise tame or dull of spirit, she *did* kneel down and meekly murmur, '*Robert, I beg your pardon, I am in the wrong.*' 'Young woman, you lie!' abruptly retorted he: '*I* am in the wrong!'

At the commencement of 1787, the artist's peaceful happiness was gravely disturbed by the premature death, in his twenty-fifth year, of this beloved brother: buried in Bunhill Fields the 11th of February. Blake affectionately tended him in his illness, and during the last fortnight of it watched continuously day and night by his bedside, without sleep. When all claim had ceased with that brother's last breath, his own exhaustion showed itself in an unbroken sleep of three days' and nights' duration. The mean room of sickness had been to the spiritual man, as to him most scenes were, a place of vision and of revelation; for Heaven lay about him still, in manhood, as in Infancy it 'lies about us' all. At the last solemn moment, the visionary eyes beheld the released spirit ascend heavenward through the matter-of-fact ceiling, 'clapping its hands for joy' – a truly Blake-like detail. No wonder he could paint such scenes! With him they were work'a-day experiences.

In the same year, disagreements with Parker put an end to the partnership and to print-selling. This Parker subsequently engraved a good deal after Stothard, in a style which evinces a common Master with Blake as well as companionship with him: in particular, the very fine designs, among Stothard's most masterly, to the *Vicar of Wakefield* (1792), which are very admirably engraved; also most of those of Falconer's *Shipwreck* (1795). After Flaxman, he executed several of the plates to Homer's *Iliad*; after Smirke, *The Commemoration of* 1797; after Northcote, *The Revolution of* 1688, and others; and for Boydell's *Shakspeare*, eleven plates. He died 'about 1805,' according to the Dictionaries.

Blake quitted Broad Street for neighbouring Poland Street: the long street which connects Broad Street with Oxford Street, and into which Great Marlborough Street runs at right angles. He lodged at No. 28, (now a cheesemonger's shop, and boasting three brass bells), not many doors from Oxford Street on the right-hand side, going towards that thoroughfare; the houses at which end of the street are smaller and of later date than those between Great Marlborough and Broad Street. Henceforward Mrs Blake, whom he carefully instructed, remained his sole pupil – sole assistant and companion too; for the gap left by his brother was never filled up by children. In the same year – that of Etty's birth (March, 1787) amid the narrow streets of distant antique York – his friend Flaxman exchanged Wardour Street for Rome, and a seven years' sojourn in Italy. Already educating eye and mind in his own way, Turner, a boy of twelve, was hovering about Maiden Lane, Covent Garden, in which the barber's son

66

was born: some half mile – of (then) staid and busy streets – distant from Blake's Broad Street; Long Acre in which Stothard first saw the light lying between the two.

EIGHT

Meditation: Notes on Lavater 1788
[ÆT. 30–31]

One of Blake's engravings of the present period is a frontispiece after Fuseli to the latter's translation of the *Aphorisms* of his fellow-countryman, Lavater. The translation, which was from the original MS., was published by Johnson in 1788, the year of Gainsborough's death. If any deny merit to Blake as an engraver, let them turn from this boldly executed print of Fuseli's mannered but effective sitting figure, ostentatiously meditative, of Philosophic Contemplation, or whatever it may be, to the weak shadow of the same in the subsequent Dublin editions of this little book. For the Swiss enthusiast had then a European reputation. And this imposing scroll of fervid truisms and haphazard generalities, as often disputable as not, if often acute and striking, always ingenuous and pleasant, was, like all his other writings, warmly welcomed in this country. Now it as a whole reads unequal and monotonous, does not impress one as an elixir of inspired truth; induces rather, like most books of maxims, the ever recurring query, *cui bono*. And one readily believes what the English edition states, that the whole epitome of moral wisdom was the rapid 'effusion' of *one* autumn.

In the ardent, pious, but illogical Lavater's *character*, full of amiability, candour, and high aspiration, a man who in the eighteenth century believed in the continuation of miracles, of

68

witchcraft, and of the power of exorcizing evil spirits, who, in fact, had a *bonâ fide* if convulsive hold of the super-sensual, there was much that was germane to William Blake, much that still remains noble and interesting.

In the painter's small library the *Aphorisms* became one of his most favourite volumes. This well-worn copy contains a series of marginal notes, neatly written in pen and ink – it being his habit to make such in the books he read – which speak to the interest it excited in him. On the title-page occurs a naïve token of affection: below the name Lavater is inscribed 'Will. Blake,' and around the two names the outline of a heart.

Lavater's final Aphorism tells the reader, 'If you mean to know yourself, interline such of these as affected you agreeably in reading, and set a mark to such as left a sense of uneasiness with you, and then show your copy to whom you please.' Blake showed his notes to Fuseli; who said one assuredly could read their writer's character in *them.*

'*All Gold!*' 'This should be written in letters of gold on our temples,' are the endorsements accorded such an announcement as 'The object of your love is your God;' or again, 'Joy and grief decide character. What exalts prosperity? What embitters grief? What leaves us indifferent? What interests us? As the interest of man, so is God, as his God so is he.'

But the annotator sometimes dissents; as from this: 'You enjoy with wisdom or with folly, as the gratification of your appetites capacitates or unnerves your powers.' '*False!*' is the emphatic denial, 'for weak is the joy which is never wearied.' On one Aphorism, in which 'frequent laughing,' and 'the scarcer smile of harmless quiet,' are enumerated as signs respectively 'of a little mind,' or 'of a noble heart;' while the abstaining from laughter merely not to offend, &c. is praised as 'a power unknown to many a vigorous mind;' Blake exclaims, 'I hate scarce smiles; I love laughing!' 'A sneer is often the sign of heartless malignity,' says Lavater. '*Damn sneerers!*' echoes Blake. To Lavater's censure of the 'pietist who crawls, groans, blubbers, and secretly says to gold, Thou art my hope! and to his belly, Thou art my God,' follows a cordial assent. 'Everything,' Lavater rashly declares, 'may be mimicked by hypocrisy but humility and love united.' To which, Blake: 'All this may be mimicked very well. This Aphorism certainly was an oversight: for what are all crawlers but mimickers of humility and love?' 'Dread more the blunderer's friendship than the calumniator's envy,' exhorts Lavater. '*I doubt this!*' says the margin.

At the maxim, 'You may depend upon it that he is a good man, whose intimate friends are all good, and whose enemies are characters decidedly bad,' the artist (obeying his author's injunctions) reports himself '*Uneasy,*' fears he 'has not many enemies!' *Uneasy,* too, he feels at the declaration, 'Calmness of will is a sign of grandeur: the vulgar, far from hiding their *will,* blab their wishes – a single spark of occasion discharges the child of passion into a thousand crackers of desire.' Again: 'Who seeks those that are greater than himself, their greatness enjoys, and forgets his greatest qualities in their greater ones, is already truly great.' To this, Mr Blake: '*I hope I do not flatter myself that this is pleasant to me.*'

Some of Blake's remarks are not without a brisk candour: as when the Zurich philanthropist tells one, 'The great art to love your enemy consists in never losing sight of *man* in him,' &c.; and he boldly replies, 'None *can* see the man in the enemy. If he is ignorantly so, he is not truly an enemy: if maliciously so not a man. I cannot love my enemy, for my enemy is not a man but a beast. And if I have any, I can love him as a beast, and wish to beat him.' And again, to the dictum, 'Between passion and lie there is not a finger's breadth,' he retorts, 'Lie is contrary to passion.' Upon the aphorism, 'Superstition always inspires littleness; religion, grandeur of mind; the superstitious raises beings inferior to himself to deities,' Blake remarks at some length: 'I do not allow there is such a thing as superstition, taken in the true sense of the word. A man must first deceive himself before he is thus superstitious and so he is a hypocrite. No man was ever truly superstitious who was not as truly religious as far as he knew. True superstition is ignorant honesty, and this is beloved of God and man. Hypocrisy is as different from superstition as the wolf from the lamb.' And similarly when Lavater, with a shudder, alludes to 'the gloomy rock, on either side of which superstition and incredulity their dark abysses spread,' Blake says, 'Superstition has been long a bug-bear, by reason of its having been united with hypocrisy. But let them be fairly separated and then superstition will be honest feeling, and God, who loves all honest men, will lead the poor enthusiast in the path of holiness.' This was a cardinal thought with Blake, and almost a unique one in his century.

The two are generally of better accord. The since often-quoted warning, 'Keep him at least three paces distant who hates bread, music, and the laugh of a child!' is endorsed as the 'Best in the book.' Another, 'Avoid like a serpent him who speaks politely, yet writes impertinently,' elicits the ejaculation, '*A dog! get a stick to him!*' And the reiteration, 'Avoid him who speaks softly and writes sharply,' is enforced with, 'Ah, rogue, I would be thy hangman!' The assertion that 'A woman, whose ruling passion is not vanity, is superior to any man of equal faculties,' begets the enthusiastic comment, '*Such a woman I adore!*' At the foot of another, on woman, 'A great woman not imperious, a fair woman not vain, a woman of common talents not jealous, an accomplished woman who scorns to shine, are four wonders just great enough to be divided among the four corners of the globe,' Blake appends, 'Let the men do their duty and the women will be such wonders: the female life lives from the life of the male. See a great many female dependents and you know the man.'

In a higher key, when Lavater justly affirms that 'He only who has enjoyed immortal moments can reproduce them,' Blake exclaims, 'Oh that men would *seek* immortal moments! – that men would converse with God!' as he, it may be added, was ever seeking, ever conversing, in one sense. In another place Lavater declares, that 'He who adores an impersonal God, has none; and without guide or rudder launches on an immense abyss, that first absorbs his powers and next himself.' To which warm assent from the fervently religious Blake: 'Most superlatively beautiful, and most affectionately holy and pure. Would to God all men would consider it!' Religious, I say, but far from orthodox; for in one place he would show sin to be '*negative* not positive evil;' lying, theft, &c. 'mere privation of good,' a favourite idea with him, which, whatever its merit as an abstract position, practical people would *not* like written in letters of gold on their temples, for fear of consequences.

One of the most prolix of these aphorisms runs, 'Take from Luther his roughness and fiery courage, from this man one quality, from another that, from Raffaelle his dryness and nearly hard precision, and from Rubens his supernatural luxury of colours; detach his oppressive *exuberance* from each, and you will have something very correct and flat instead, as it required no conjuror to tell us.' Whereon Blake, whom I here condense: 'Deduct from a rose its red, from a lily its whiteness, from a diamond hardness, from an oak-tree height, from a daisy lowli-

72

ness, rectify everything in nature, as the philosophers do, and then we shall return to chaos, and God will he compelled to be eccentric in His creation. Oh! happy philosophers! Variety does not necessarily suppose deformity. Beauty is exuberant, but if ugliness is adjoined, it is not the exuberance of beauty. So if Raffaelle *is* hard and dry, it is not from genius, but an accident acquired. How can substance and accident be predicated of the same essence? Aphorism 47th speaks of the "heterogeneous" in works of Art and Literature, which all extravagance is; but exuberance is not. But,' adds Blake, 'the substance gives tincture to the accident, and makes it physiognomic.'

In the course of another lengthy aphorism, the 'knave' is said to be 'only an *enthusiast*, or *momentary fool*.' Upon which Mr Blake breaks out still more characteristically: 'Man is the ark of God: the mercy seat is above upon the ark; cherubim guard it on either side, and in the midst is the holy law. Man is either the ark of God or a phantom of the earth and water. If thou seekest by human policy to guide this ark, remember Uzzah. *2d Sam. 6th ch.* Knaveries are not human nature; knaveries are knaveries. This aphorism seems to lack discrimination.' In a similar tone, on Aphorism 630, commencing, '*A God*, an *animal, a plant*, are not companions of man; nor is the *faultless*, – then judge with lenity of all,' Blake writes, 'It is the God in *all* that is our companion and friend. For our God Himself says, "You are my brother, my sister, and my mother;" and St John, "Whoso dwelleth in love, dwelleth in God, and God in him." Such an one cannot judge of any but in love and his feelings will be attractions or repulsions. God is in the lowest effects as well as in the highest causes. He is become a worm that he may nourish the weak. For let it be remembered that creation is God descending according to the weakness of man; our Lord is the

73

Word of God, and everything on earth is the Word of God, and in its essence is God.'

Surely gold-dust may be descried in these notes; and when we remember it is a painter, not a metaphysician, who is writing, we can afford to judge them less critically. Another characteristic gleaming or two, ere we conclude. An ironical maxim, such as 'Take here the grand secret if not of pleasing all yet of displeasing none: court mediocrity, avoid originality, and sacrifice to fashion,' meets with the hearty response from an unfashionable painter, 'And go to hell.' When the Swiss tells him that 'Men carry their character not seldom in their pockets: you might decide on more than half your acquirance had you will or right to turn their pockets inside out,' the artist candidly acknowledges that he 'seldom carries money in his pockets: they are generally full of paper,' which we readily believe. Towards the close, Lavater drops a doubt that he may have 'perhaps already offended his readers;' which elicits from Blake a final note of sympathy. 'Those who are offended with anything in this book, would be offended with the innocence of a child, and for the same reason, because it reproaches him with the errors of acquired folly.'

Enough of the Annotations on Lavater, which, in fulfilment of biographic duty, I have thus copiously quoted; too copiously, the reader may think, for their intrinsic merit. To me they seem mentally physiognomic, giving a near view of Blake in his ordinary moments at this period. We, as through a casually open window, glance into the artist's room, and see him meditating at his work, graver in hand.

Lavater's *Aphorisms* not only elicited these comments from Blake, but set him composing aphorisms on his own account, of a far more original and startling character. In Lavater's book I trace the external accident to which the form is attributable

He ground and mixed his water-colours himself on a piece of statuary marble, after a method of his own, with common carpenter's glass diluted, which he had found out, as the early Italians had done before him, to be a good binder. Joseph, the sacred carpenter, had appeared in vision and revealed *that* secret to him. The colours he used were few and simple: indigo, cobalt, gamboge, vermilion, Frankfort-black freely, ultramarine rarely, chrome not at all. These he applied with a camel's-hair brush, not with a sable, which he disliked.

He taught Mrs Blake to take off the impressions with care and delicacy, which such plates signally needed, and also to help in tinting them from his drawings with right artistic feeling; in all which tasks she, to her honour, much delighted. The size of the plates was small, for the sake of economising copper; something under five inches by three. The number of engraved pages in the *Songs of Innocence* alone was twenty-seven. They were done up in boards by Mrs Blake's hand, forming a small octavo; so that the poet and his wife did everything in making the book, – writing, designing, printing, engraving, – everything except manufacturing the paper: the very ink, or colour rather, they did make. Never before surely was a man so literally the author of his own book. '*Songs of Innocence, the author and printer W. Blake, 1789,*' is the title. Copies still occur occasionally; though the two series bound together in one volume each with its own title-page, and a general one added, is the more usual state.

First of the Poems let me speak, harsh as seems their divorce from the Design which blends with them, forming warp and woof in one texture. It is like pulling up a daisy by the roots from the green sward out of which it springs. To me many years ago, first reading these weird Songs in their appropriate environment of equally spiritual form and hue, the effect was

of a remarkable portion – certain 'Proverbs of Hell,' as they were waywardly styled – of an altogether remarkable book, *The Marriage of Heaven and Hell*, engraved two years later; the *most* curious and significant book, perhaps, out of many, which ever issued from the unique man's press.

Turning from the Annotations on Lavater to higher, less approachable phases of this original Mind, the indubitably INSPIRED aspects of it, it is time to note that the practice of verse had, as we saw in 1784, been once more resumed, in a higher key and clearer tones than he had yet sounded. Design more original and more mature than any he had before realized; at once grand, lovely, comprehensible, was in course of production. It must have been during the years 1784–88, the Songs and Designs sprang from his creative brain, of which another chapter must speak.

NINE

Poems of Manhood 1788–89
[ÆT. 31–32]

Though Blake's brother Robert had ceased to be with him in the body, he was seldom far absent from the faithful visionary in spirit. Down to late age the survivor talked much and often of that dear brother; and in hours of solitude and inspiration his form would appear and speak to the poet in consolatory dream, in warning or helpful vision. By the end of 1788, the first portion of that singularly original and significant series of Poems, by which of themselves, Blake established a claim, however unrecognized, on the attention of his own and after generations, had been written; and the illustrative designs in colour, to which he wedded them in inseparable loveliness, had been executed. The *Songs of Innocence* form the first section of the series he afterwards, when grouping the two together, suggestively named *Songs of Innocence and of Experience*: But how publish? for standing with the public, or credit with the trade, he had none. Friendly Flaxman was in Italy; the good offices of patronizing blue-stockings were exhausted. He had not the wherewithal to publish on his own account; and though he could be his own engraver, he could scarcely be his own compositor. Long and deeply he meditated. How solve this difficulty with his own industrious hands? How be his *own* printer and publisher?

The subject of anxious daily thought passed – as anxious

76

meditation does with us all – into the domain of drea (in his case) of visions. In one of these a happy insp befell, not, of course, without supernatural agency. After thinking by day and dreaming by night, during long we months, of his cherished object, the image of the vanishe and brother at last blended with it. In a vision of the ni form of Robert stood before him, and revealed the wis secret, directing him to the technical mode by which c produced a fac-simile of song and design. On his risin morning, Mrs Blake went out with half-a-crown, all the they had in the world, and of that laid out 1s. 10d. on the materials necessary for setting in practice the new rev Upon that investment of 1s. 10d. he started what was t a principal means of support through his future life, – th of poems and writings illustrated by coloured plates, ofte finished afterwards by hand, – which became the most and durable means of revealing Blake's genius to the wor method, to which Blake henceforth consistently adh multiplying his works, was quite an original one. It cons a species of engraving in relief both words and desig verse was written and the designs and marginal embelli outlined on the copper with an impervious liquid, prob ordinary stopping out varnish of engravers. Then all th parts or lights, the remainder of the plate that is, we away with aquafortis or other acid, so that the outline and design was left prominent, as in stereotype. Fro plates he printed off in any tint, yellow, brown, blue, to be the prevailing, or ground colour in his fac-similes used for the letter-press. The page was then coloure hand in imitation of the original drawing, with mor variety of detail in the local hues.

77

as that of an angelic voice singing to oaten pipe, such as Arcadians tell of; or, as if a spiritual magician were summoning before human eyes, and through a human medium, images and scenes of divine loveliness; and in the pauses of the strain, we seem to catch the rustling of angelic wings. The Golden Age independent of Space or Time, object of vague sighs and dreams from many generations of struggling humanity – an Eden such as childhood sees, is brought nearer than ever poet brought it before. For this poet was in assured possession of the Golden Age, within the chambers of his own mind. As we read, fugitive glimpses open, clear as brief, of our buried childhood, of an unseen world present, past, to come; we are endowed with new spiritual sight, with unwanted intuitions, bright visitants from finer realms of thought, which ever elude us, ever hover near. We encounter familiar objects, in unfamiliar, transfigured aspects, simple expression and deep meanings, type and antitype. True, there are palpable irregularities, metrical licence, lapse of grammar, and even of orthography; but often the sweetest melody, most daring eloquence of rhythm, and, what is more, appropriate rhythm. They are *unfinished* poems: yet would finish have bettered their bold and careless freedom? Would it not have brushed away the delicate bloom? that visible spontaneity, so rare and great a charm, the eloquent attribute of our old English Ballads and of the early Songs of all nations. The most deceptively perfect wax-model is no substitute for the living flower. The form is, in these Songs, a transparent medium of the spiritual thought, not an opaque body. 'He has dared to venture,' writes Malkin, not irrelevantly, 'on the ancient simplicity, and feeling it in his own character and manners, has succeeded better than those who have only seen it through a glass.'

There is the same divine *afflatus* as in the Poetical Sketches,

79

but fuller: a maturity of expression, despite surviving negligences, and of thought and motive. The 'Child Angel,' as we ventured to call the Poet in earlier years, no longer merely sportive and innocently wanton, wears a brow of thought; a glance of insight has passed into

> 'A sense sublime
> Of something far more deeply interfused'

in Nature, a feeling of 'the burthen of the mystery of things; though still possessed by widest sympathies with all that is simple and innocent, with echoing laughter, little lamb, a flower's blossom, with 'emmet wildered and forlorn.'

These poems have a unity and mutual relationship, the influence of which is much impaired if they be read otherwise than as a whole.

Who but Blake, with his pure heart, his simple exalted character, could have transfigured a commonplace meeting of Charity Children at St Paul's, as he has done in the *Holy Thursday?* a picture at once tender and grand. The bold images, by a wise instinct resorted to at the close of the first and second stanzas and opening of the third, are in the highest degree imaginative; they are true as only Poetry can be.

How vocal is the poem *Spring*, despite imperfect rhymes. From addressing the child, the poet, by a transition not infrequent with him, passes out of himself into the child's person, showing a chameleon sympathy with childlike feelings. Can we not see the little three-year-old prattler stroking the white lamb, her feelings made articulate for her? – Even more remarkable is the poem entitled *The Lamb*, sweet hymn of tender infantine sentiment appropriate to that perennial image of meekness; to which the fierce eloquence of *The Tiger*, in the *Songs of Experi-*

ence, is an antitype. In *The Lamb*, the poet again changes person to that of a child. Of lyrical beauty, take as a sample *The Laughing Song* with its happy *ring* of merry innocent voices. This and *The Nurse's Song* are more in the style of his early poems, but, as we said, of far maturer execution. I scarcely need call attention to the delicate simplicity of the little pastoral, entitled *The Shepherd*: to the picturesqueness in a warmer hue, the delightful domesticity, the expressive melody of *The Echoing Green:* or to the lovely sympathy and piety which irradiate the touching *Cradle Song*. More enchanting still is the stir of fancy and sympathy which animates *The Dream*, that

> Did weave a shade o'er my angel guarded bed;

of an emmet that had

> Lost her way,
> Where on grass methought I lay.

Few are the readers, I should think, who can fail to appreciate the symbolic grandeur of *The Little Boy Lost* and *The Little Boy Found*, or the enigmatic tenderness of the *Blossom* and the *Divine Image*; and the verses *On Another's Sorrow*, express some of Blake's favourite religious ideas, his abiding notions on the subject of the Godhead, which surely suggest the kernel of Christian feeling. A similar tinge of the divine, colours the lines called *Night*, with its revelation of angelic guardians, believed in with unquestioning piety by Blake, who makes us in our turn conscious, as we read, of angelic noiseless footsteps. For a nobler depth of religious beauty, with accordant grandeur of sentiment and language, I know no parallel nor hint elsewhere of such a poem as *The Little Black Boy* –

> My mother bore me in the southern wild.

We may read these poems again and again, and they continue fresh as at first. There is something unsating in them, a perfume as of a growing violet, which renews itself as fast as it is inhaled.

One poem, *The Chimney Sweeper*, still calls for special notice. This and *Holy Thursday* are remarkable as an anticipation of the daring choice of homely subject, of the yet more daringly familiar manner, nay, of the very metre and trick of style adopted by Wordsworth in a portion of those memorable 'experiments in Poetry,' – the *Lyrical Ballads*: in *The Reverie of Poor Susan*, for instance (not written till 1797), the *Star Gazers*, and *The Power of Music* (both 1806). The little Sweep's dream has the spiritual touch peculiar to Blake's hand. This poem, I may add, was extracted thirty-five years later in a curious little volume (1824), of James Montgomery's editing, as friend of the then unprotected Climbing Boys. It was entitled *The Chimney Sweeper's Friend, and Climbing-Boy's Album*: a miscellany of verse and prose, original and borrowed, with illustrations by Robert Cruickshank. Charles Lamb, one of the living authors applied to by the kind-hearted Sheffield poet, while declining the task of rhyming on such a subject, sent a copy of this poem from the *Songs of Innocence*, communicating it as 'from a very rare and curious little work.' At line five, 'Little Tom Dacre' is transformed by a sly blunder of Lamb's into 'little Tom Toddy.' The poem on the same subject in the *Songs of Experience*, inferior poetically, but in an accordant key of gloom, would have been the more apposite to Montgomery's volume.

The tender loveliness of these poems will hardly reappear in Blake's subsequent writing. Darker phases of feeling, more sombre colours, profounder meanings, ruder eloquence, characterize the *Songs of Experience* of five years later.

ness, rectify everything in nature, as the philosophers do, and then we shall return to chaos, and God will he compelled to be eccentric in His creation. Oh! happy philosophers! Variety does not necessarily suppose deformity. Beauty is exuberant, but if ugliness is adjoined, it is not the exuberance of beauty. So if Raffaelle *is* hard and dry, it is not from genius, but an accident acquired. How can substance and accident be predicated of the same essence? Aphorism 47th speaks of the "heterogeneous" in works of Art and Literature, which all extravagance is; but exuberance is not. But,' adds Blake, 'the substance gives tincture to the accident, and makes it physiognomic.'

In the course of another lengthy aphorism, the 'knave' is said to be 'only an *enthusiast*, or *momentary fool*.' Upon which Mr Blake breaks out still more characteristically: 'Man is the ark of God: the mercy seat is above upon the ark; cherubim guard it on either side, and in the midst is the holy law. Man is either the ark of God or a phantom of the earth and water. If thou seekest by human policy to guide this ark, remember Uzzah. 2d *Sam*. 6th *ch*. Knaveries are not human nature; knaveries are knaveries. This aphorism seems to lack discrimination.' In a similar tone, on Aphorism 630, commencing, '*A God*, an *animal, a plant*, are not companions of man; nor is the *faultless*, – then judge with lenity of all,' Blake writes, 'It is the God in *all* that is our companion and friend. For our God Himself says, "You are my brother, my sister, and my mother;" and St John, "Whoso dwelleth in love, dwelleth in God, and God in him." Such an one cannot judge of any but in love and his feelings will be attractions or repulsions. God is in the lowest effects as well as in the highest causes. He is become a worm that he may nourish the weak. For let it be remembered that creation is God descending according to the weakness of man; our Lord is the

Word of God, and everything on earth is the Word of God, and in its essence is God.'

Surely gold-dust may be descried in these notes; and when we remember it is a painter, not a metaphysician, who is writing, we can afford to judge them less critically. Another characteristic gleaming or two, ere we conclude. An ironical maxim, such as 'Take here the grand secret if not of pleasing all yet of displeasing none: court mediocrity, avoid originality, and sacrifice to fashion,' meets with the hearty response from an unfashionable painter, 'And go to hell.' When the Swiss tells him that 'Men carry their character not seldom in their pockets: you might decide on more than half your acquirance had you will or right to turn their pockets inside out,' the artist candidly acknowledges that he 'seldom carries money in his pockets: they are generally full of paper,' which we readily believe. Towards the close, Lavater drops a doubt that he may have 'perhaps already offended his readers;' which elicits from Blake a final note of sympathy. 'Those who are offended with anything in this book, would be offended with the innocence of a child, and for the same reason, because it reproaches him with the errors of acquired folly.'

Enough of the Annotations on Lavater, which, in fulfilment of biographic duty, I have thus copiously quoted; too copiously, the reader may think, for their intrinsic merit. To me they seem mentally physiognomic, giving a near view of Blake in his ordinary moments at this period. We, as through a casually open window, glance into the artist's room, and see him meditating at his work, graver in hand.

Lavater's *Aphorisms* not only elicited these comments from Blake, but set him composing aphorisms on his own account, of a far more original and startling character. In Lavater's book I trace the external accident to which the form is attributable

74

of a remarkable portion – certain 'Proverbs of Hell,' as they were waywardly styled – of an altogether remarkable book, *The Marriage of Heaven and Hell*, engraved two years later; the *most* curious and significant book, perhaps, out of many, which ever issued from the unique man's press.

Turning from the Annotations on Lavater to higher, less approachable phases of this original Mind, the indubitably INSPIRED aspects of it, it is time to note that the practice of verse had, as we saw in 1784, been once more resumed, in a higher key and clearer tones than he had yet sounded. Design more original and more mature than any he had before realized; at once grand, lovely, comprehensible, was in course of production. It must have been during the years 1784–88, the Songs and Designs sprang from his creative brain, of which another chapter must speak.

NINE

Poems of Manhood 1788–89
[ÆT. 31–32]

Though Blake's brother Robert had ceased to be with him in the body, he was seldom far absent from the faithful visionary in spirit. Down to late age the survivor talked much and often of that dear brother; and in hours of solitude and inspiration his form would appear and speak to the poet in consolatory dream, in warning or helpful vision. By the end of 1788, the first portion of that singularly original and significant series of Poems, by which of themselves, Blake established a claim, however unrecognized, on the attention of his own and after generations, had been written; and the illustrative designs in colour, to which he wedded them in inseparable loveliness, had been executed. The *Songs of Innocence* form the first section of the series he afterwards, when grouping the two together, suggestively named *Songs of Innocence and of Experience*: But how publish? for standing with the public, or credit with the trade, he had none. Friendly Flaxman was in Italy; the good offices of patronizing blue-stockings were exhausted. He had not the wherewithal to publish on his own account; and though he could be his own engraver, he could scarcely be his own compositor. Long and deeply he meditated. How solve this difficulty with his own industrious hands? How be his *own* printer and publisher?

The subject of anxious daily thought passed – as anxious

meditation does with us all – into the domain of dreams and (in his case) of visions. In one of these a happy inspiration befell, not, of course, without supernatural agency. After intently thinking by day and dreaming by night, during long weeks and months, of his cherished object, the image of the vanished pupil and brother at last blended with it. In a vision of the night, the form of Robert stood before him, and revealed the wished-for secret, directing him to the technical mode by which could be produced a fac-simile of song and design. On his rising in the morning, Mrs Blake went out with half-a-crown, all the money they had in the world, and of that laid out $1s.$ $10d.$ on the simple materials necessary for setting in practice the new revelation. Upon that investment of $1s.$ $10d.$ he started what was to prove a principal means of support through his future life, – the series of poems and writings illustrated by coloured plates, often highly finished afterwards by hand, – which became the most efficient and durable means of revealing Blake's genius to the world. This method, to which Blake henceforth consistently adhered for multiplying his works, was quite an original one. It consisted in a species of engraving in relief both words and designs. The verse was written and the designs and marginal embellishments outlined on the copper with an impervious liquid, probably the ordinary stopping out varnish of engravers. Then all the white parts or lights, the remainder of the plate that is, were eaten away with aquafortis or other acid, so that the outline of letter and design was left prominent, as in stereotype. From these plates he printed off in any tint, yellow, brown, blue, required to be the prevailing, or ground colour in his fac-similes; red he used for the letter-press. The page was then coloured up by hand in imitation of the original drawing, with more or less variety of detail in the local hues.

He ground and mixed his water-colours himself on a piece of statuary marble, after a method of his own, with common carpenter's glass diluted, which he had found out, as the early Italians had done before him, to be a good binder. Joseph, the sacred carpenter, had appeared in vision and revealed *that* secret to him. The colours he used were few and simple: indigo, cobalt, gamboge, vermilion, Frankfort-black freely, ultramarine rarely, chrome not at all. These he applied with a camel's-hair brush, not with a sable, which he disliked.

He taught Mrs Blake to take off the impressions with care and delicacy, which such plates signally needed, and also to help in tinting them from his drawings with right artistic feeling; in all which tasks she, to her honour, much delighted. The size of the plates was small, for the sake of economising copper; something under five inches by three. The number of engraved pages in the *Songs of Innocence* alone was twenty-seven. They were done up in boards by Mrs Blake's hand, forming a small octavo; so that the poet and his wife did everything in making the book, – writing, designing, printing, engraving, – everything except manufacturing the paper: the very ink, or colour rather, they did make. Never before surely was a man so literally the author of his own book. '*Songs of Innocence, the author and printer W. Blake*, 1789,' is the title. Copies still occur occasionally; though the two series bound together in one volume each with its own title-page, and a general one added, is the more usual state.

First of the Poems let me speak, harsh as seems their divorce from the Design which blends with them, forming warp and woof in one texture. It is like pulling up a daisy by the roots from the green sward out of which it springs. To me many years ago, first reading these weird Songs in their appropriate environment of equally spiritual form and hue, the effect was as that of an angelic voice singing to oaten pipe, such as Arcadians tell of; or, as if a spiritual magician were summoning before human eyes, and through a human medium, images and scenes of divine loveliness; and in the pauses of the strain, we seem to catch the rustling of angelic wings. The Golden Age independent of Space or Time, object of vague sighs and dreams from many generations of struggling humanity – an Eden such as childhood sees, is brought nearer than ever poet brought it before. For this poet was in assured possession of the Golden Age, within the chambers of his own mind. As we read, fugitive glimpses open, clear as brief, of our buried childhood, of an unseen world present, past, to come; we are endowed with new spiritual sight, with unwanted intuitions, bright visitants from finer realms of thought, which ever elude us, ever hover near. We encounter familiar objects, in unfamiliar, transfigured aspects, simple expression and deep meanings, type and antitype. True, there are palpable irregularities, metrical licence, lapse of grammar, and even of orthography; but often the sweetest melody, most daring eloquence of rhythm, and, what is more, appropriate rhythm. They are *unfinished* poems: yet would finish have bettered their bold and careless freedom? Would it not have brushed away the delicate bloom? that visible spontaneity, so rare and great a charm, the eloquent attribute of our old English Ballads and of the early Songs of all nations. The most deceptively perfect wax-model is no substitute for the living flower. The form is, in these Songs, a transparent medium of the spiritual thought, not an opaque body. 'He has dared to venture,' writes Malkin, not irrelevantly, 'on the ancient simplicity, and feeling it in his own character and manners, has succeeded better than those who have only seen it through a glass.'

There is the same divine *afflatus* as in the Poetical Sketches, but fuller: a maturity of expression, despite surviving negligences, and of thought and motive. The 'Child Angel,' as we ventured to call the Poet in earlier years, no longer merely sportive and innocently wanton, wears a brow of thought; a glance of insight has passed into

> 'A sense sublime
> Of something far more deeply interfused'

in Nature, a feeling of 'the burthen of the mystery of things; though still possessed by widest sympathies with all that is simple and innocent, with echoing laughter, little lamb, a flower's blossom, with 'emmet wildered and forlorn.'

These poems have a unity and mutual relationship, the influence of which is much impaired if they be read otherwise than as a whole.

Who but Blake, with his pure heart, his simple exalted character, could have transfigured a commonplace meeting of Charity Children at St Paul's, as he has done in the *Holy Thursday?* a picture at once tender and grand. The bold images, by a wise instinct resorted to at the close of the first and second stanzas and opening of the third, are in the highest degree imaginative; they are true as only Poetry can be.

How vocal is the poem *Spring*, despite imperfect rhymes. From addressing the child, the poet, by a transition not infrequent with him, passes out of himself into the child's person, showing a chameleon sympathy with childlike feelings. Can we not see the little three-year-old prattler stroking the white lamb, her feelings made articulate for her? – Even more remarkable is the poem entitled *The Lamb*, sweet hymn of tender infantine sentiment appropriate to that perennial image of meekness; to which the fierce eloquence of *The Tiger*, in the *Songs of Experi-*

ence, is an antitype. In *The Lamb*, the poet again changes person to that of a child. Of lyrical beauty, take as a sample *The Laughing Song* with its happy *ring* of merry innocent voices. This and *The Nurse's Song* are more in the style of his early poems, but, as we said, of far maturer execution. I scarcely need call attention to the delicate simplicity of the little pastoral, entitled *The Shepherd*: to the picturesqueness in a warmer hue, the delightful domesticity, the expressive melody of *The Echoing Green:* or to the lovely sympathy and piety which irradiate the touching *Cradle Song*. More enchanting still is the stir of fancy and sympathy which animates *The Dream*, that

> Did weave a shade o'er my angel guarded bed;

of an emmet that had

> Lost her way,
> Where on grass methought I lay.

Few are the readers, I should think, who can fail to appreciate the symbolic grandeur of *The Little Boy Lost* and *The Little Boy Found*, or the enigmatic tenderness of the *Blossom* and the *Divine Image*; and the verses *On Another's Sorrow*, express some of Blake's favourite religious ideas, his abiding notions on the subject of the Godhead, which surely suggest the kernel of Christian feeling. A similar tinge of the divine, colours the lines called *Night*, with its revelation of angelic guardians, believed in with unquestioning piety by Blake, who makes us in our turn conscious, as we read, of angelic noiseless footsteps. For a nobler depth of religious beauty, with accordant grandeur of sentiment and language, I know no parallel nor hint elsewhere of such a poem as *The Little Black Boy* –

> My mother bore me in the southern wild.

We may read these poems again and again, and they continue fresh as at first. There is something unsating in them, a perfume as of a growing violet, which renews itself as fast as it is inhaled.

One poem, *The Chimney Sweeper*, still calls for special notice. This and *Holy Thursday* are remarkable as an anticipation of the daring choice of homely subject, of the yet more daringly familiar manner, nay, of the very metre and trick of style adopted by Wordsworth in a portion of those memorable 'experiments in Poetry,' – the *Lyrical Ballads*: in *The Reverie of Poor Susan*, for instance (not written till 1797), the *Star Gazers*, and *The Power of Music* (both 1806). The little Sweep's dream has the spiritual touch peculiar to Blake's hand. This poem, I may add, was extracted thirty-five years later in a curious little volume (1824), of James Montgomery's editing, as friend of the then unprotected Climbing Boys. It was entitled *The Chimney Sweeper's Friend, and Climbing-Boy's Album*: a miscellany of verse and prose, original and borrowed, with illustrations by Robert Cruickshank. Charles Lamb, one of the living authors applied to by the kind-hearted Sheffield poet, while declining the task of rhyming on such a subject, sent a copy of this poem from the *Songs of Innocence*, communicating it as 'from a very rare and curious little work.' At line five, 'Little Tom Dacre' is transformed by a sly blunder of Lamb's into 'little Tom Toddy.' The poem on the same subject in the *Songs of Experience*, inferior poetically, but in an accordant key of gloom, would have been the more apposite to Montgomery's volume.

The tender loveliness of these poems will hardly reappear in Blake's subsequent writing. Darker phases of feeling, more sombre colours, profounder meanings, ruder eloquence, characterize the *Songs of Experience* of five years later.

In 1789, the year in which Blake's hand engraved the *Songs of Innocence*, Wordsworth was finishing his versified *Evening Walk* on the Goldsmith model; Crabbe ('Pope in worsted stockings,' as Hazlitt christened him), famous six years before by his *Village*, was publishing one of his minor quartos, *The Newspaper*; and Mrs Charlotte Smith, not undeservedly popular, was accorded a fifth edition within five years, of her *Elegiac Sonnets*, one or two of which still merit the praise of being good sonnets, among the best in a bad time. In these years, Hayley, Mason, Hannah More, Jago, Downman, Helen Maria Williams, were among the active producers of poetry; Cumberland, Holcroft, Inchbald, Burgoyne, of the acting drama of the day; Peter Pindar, and *Pasquin* Williams, of the satire.

The designs, simultaneous offspring with the poems, which in the most literal sense illuminate the *Songs of Innocence*, consist of poetized domestic scenes. The drawing and draperies are grand in style as graceful, though covering few inches' space; the colour pure, delicate, yet in effect rich and full. The mere tinting of the text and of the free ornamental border often makes a refined picture. The costumes of the period are idealized, the landscape given in pastoral and symbolic hints. Sometimes these drawings almost suffer from being looked at as a book and held close, instead of at due distance as pictures, where they become more effective. In composition, colour, pervading feeling, they are lyrical to the eye, as the *Songs* to the ear.

On the whole, the designs to the *Songs of Innocence* are finer as well as more pertinent to the poems; more closely interwoven with them, than those which accompany the *Songs of Experience*. Of these in their place.

TEN

Books of Prophecy 1789–90
[ÆT. 32–33]

In the same year that the *Songs of Innocence* were published, Blake profited by his new discovery to engrave another illustrated poem. It is in a very different strain, one, however, analogous to that running through nearly all his subsequent writings, or 'Books,' as he called them. The *Book of Thel* is a strange mystical allegory, full of tender beauty and enigmatic meaning. Thel, youngest of 'the Daughters of the Seraphim' (personification of humanity, I infer), is afflicted with scepticism, with forebodings of life's brevity and nothingness:

> She in paleness sought the secret air
> To fade away like morning beauty from her mortal day;
> Down by the river of Adona her soft voice is heard,
> And thus her gentle lamentation falls like morning dew.

I will now simply give an Argument of it, by way of indicating its tenor, and to serve as a bridge for the reader across the eddying stream of abstractions which make up this piece of poetic mysticism.

Argument

Thel laments her transient life – The Lily of the Valley answers her – Pleads *her* weakness, yet Heaven's favour – Thel urges her own uselessness – A little cloud descends and taketh shape – Shows how he weds the evening dew and feeds the flowers of earth – Tells of Love and Serviceableness – Thel replies in sorrow still – The Cloud invokes the lowly worm to answer her – Who appears in the form of a helpless child – A clod of clay pities her wailing cry – And shows how in her lowliness she blesses and is blessed – She summons Thel into her house – The grave's gates open – Thel, wandering, listens to the voices of the ground – Hears a sorrowing voice from her own grave-plot – Listens, and flees back.

The fault of the poem is the occasional tendency to vagueness of motive, to an expression of abstract emotions, more legitimate for the sister art of music than for poetry, which must be definite, however deep and subtle. The tendency grew in Blake's after writings and overmastered him. But on this occasion the meaning which he is at the pains to define, with the beauty of much of the imagery and of the pervading sentiment, more than counterbalance any excess of the element of the Indefinite, especially when, as in the original, the poem is illumined by its own design, lucidly expository, harmonizing with itself and with the verse it illustrates.

The original quarto consists of seven engraved pages, including the title, in size some six inches by four and a quarter. Four are illustrated by vignettes, the other two by ornamental head or tail-piece. The designs – Thel, the virgin sceptic, listening to the lily of the valley in the humble grass; to the golden cloud 'reclining on his airy throne;' to the worm upon her dewy bed; or kneeling over the personified clod of clay, an infant wrapped in lily's leaf; or gazing at the embracing clouds – are of the utmost sweetness; simple, expressive, grand; the colour slight, but pure and tender. The more ornamental part of the title page, of which the sky forms the framework, is a study for spontaneous easy grace and unobtrusive beauty. The effect of the whole, poem and design together, is as of a wise, wondrous, spiritual dream, or angel's reverie. The engraving of the letter-press differs from that of the *Songs of Innocence*, the text (in colour red as before) being relieved by a white ground, which makes the page more legible if less of a picture. I may mention, in corroboration of a previous assertion of Stothard's obligations as a designer to Blake, that the copy of *Thel*, formerly Stothard's, bears evidence of familiar use on his part, in broken edges, and the marks of a painter's oily fingers. These few and simple designs, while plainly original, show all the feeling and grace of Stothard's early manner, with a tinge of sublimity superadded which was never Stothard's.

In the track of the mystical *Book of Thel* came in 1790 the still more mystical *Marriage of Heaven and Hell*, an engraved volume, illustrated in colour, to which I have already alluded as perhaps the most curious and significant, while it is certainly the most daring in conception and gorgeous in illustration of all Blake's works. As the title dimly suggests, it is an attempt to sound the depths of the mystery of Evil: to take a stand out of and beyond humanity, and view it, not in its relation to man here and now, but to the eternal purposes of God. Hence old words are wrested to new meanings (angel, devil, &c.), for language breaks down under so bold an enterprise. And we need hardly observe that Blake does not set up as an instructor of youth or of age either, but rather as one who loves to rouse, perplex, provoke; to shun safe roads and stand on dizzy brinks; to dare anything and everything, in short, if peradventure he might grasp a truth beyond the common reach, or catch a glimpse 'behind the veil.' Nor could there well be a harder task than the endeavour to trace out any kind of system, any coherent or consistent philosophy, in this or in any other of Blake's writings. He laid to heart very zealously and practically his favourite doctrine, that 'the man who never alters his opinion is like standing water, and breeds reptiles of the mind.' Hence antagonistic assertions may be found almost side by side.

The *Marriage of Heaven and Hell* opens with an 'Argument' in irregular unrhymed verse:

> Rintrah roars and shakes his fires in the burdened air;
> Hungry clouds swag on the deep.
>
> Once meek and in a perilous path
> The just man kept his course along
> The vale of death.
> Roses are planted where thorns grow,
> And on the barren heath
> Sing the honey bees.
>
> Then the perilous path was planted;
> And a river and a spring
> On every cliff and tomb;
> And on the bleached bones
> Red clay brought forth.
>
> Till the villain left the paths of ease
> To walk in perilous paths, and drive
> The just man into barren climes.
>
> Now the sneaking serpent walks
> In mild humility,
> And the just man rages in the wilds
> Where lions roam.
>
> Rintrah roars and shakes his fires in the burdened air;
> Hungry clouds swag on the deep.

The key-note is more clearly sounded in the following detached sentences:

Without contraries is no progression. Attraction and Repulsion, Reason and Energy, Love and Hate, are necessary to human existence. From these contraries spring what the religious call Good and Evil. Good is the passive, that obeys Reason. Evil is the active, springing from Energy. Good is Heaven. Evil is Hell.

The Voice of the Devil.

All Bibles or sacred codes have been the causes of the following errors:

1. That man has two real existing principles, viz. a Body and a Soul.
2. That Energy, called Evil, is alone from the Body, and that Heaven, called Good, is alone from the Soul.
3. That God will torment man in Eternity for following his energies.

But the following contraries to these are true:

1. Man has no Body distinct from his Soul, for that called Body is a portion of Soul discerned by the five senses, the chief inlets of Soul in this age.
2. Energy is the only Life, and is from the Body; and Reason is the bound or outward circumference of Energy.
3. Energy is Eternal Delight.

To this shortly succeeds a series of Proverbs or Aphorisms, fantastically called 'Proverbs of Hell,' of which, if some indeed contain the Wisdom of the Serpent, there are others wherein the wisdom is of a more terrestrial and innocent sort, while not a few possess a truly celestial meaning and beauty. These Proverbs we give almost entire.

In seed-time learn, in harvest, teach, in winter enjoy.

Drive your cart and your plough over the bones of the dead.

The road of excess leads to the palace of wisdom.

Prudence is a rich ugly old maid courted by Incapacity.

The cut worm forgives the plough.

Dip him in the river who loves water.

A fool sees not the same tree that a wise man sees.

He whose face gives no light, shall never become a star.

Eternity is in love with the productions of Time.

The busy bee has no time for sorrow.

The hours of Folly are measured by the clock, but of Wisdom no clock can measure.

All wholesome food is caught without a net or a trap.

Bring out number, weight, and measure, in a year of dearth.

The most sublime act is to set another before you.

If the fool would persist in his folly, he would become wise.

Shame is Pride's cloak.

Excess of sorrow laughs: excess of joy weeps.

The roaring of lions, the howling of wolves, the raging of the stormy sea, and the destructive sword, are portions of eternity too great for the eye of man.

The fox condemns the trap, not himself.

Joys impregnate, sorrows bring forth.

Let man wear the fell of the lion, woman the fleece of the sheep.

The bird a nest, the spider a web, man friendship.

The selfish smiling fool and the sullen frowning fool shall be both thought wise, that they may be a rod.

What is now proved was once only imagined.

The rat, the mouse, the fox, the rabbit, watch the roots; the lion, the tiger, the horse, the elephant, watch the fruits.

The cistern contains; the fountain overflows.

One thought fills immensity.

Always be ready to speak your mind, and a base man will avoid you.

Everything possible to be believed is an image of truth.

The eagle never lost so much time as when he submitted to learn of the crow.

The fox provides for himself, but God provides for the lion.

He who has suffered you to impose on him, knows you.

The tigers of wrath are wiser than the horses of instruction.

Expect poison from the standing water.

You never know what is enough, unless you know what is more than enough.

Listen to the fool's reproach; it is a kingly title!

The eyes of fire; the nostrils of air; the mouth of water; the beard of earth.

The weak in courage is strong in cunning.

The apple tree never asks the beech how he shall grow, nor the lion the horse how he shall take his prey.

The thankful receiver bears a plentiful harvest.

If others had not been foolish, we should be so.

The soul of sweet delight can never be defiled.

When thou seest an eagle, thou seest a portion of genius; lift up thy head!

One law for the lion and ox is oppression.

To create a little flower is the labour of ages.

Damn braces, Bless relaxes.

The best wine is the oldest, the best water the newest.

Prayers plough not! Praises reap not!

Joys laugh not! Sorrows weep not!

As the air to a bird, or the sea to a fish, so is contempt to the contemptible.

The crow wished everything was black, the owl that everything was white.

Exuberance is beauty.

Improvement makes straight roads, but the crooked roads without improvement are roads of Genius.

Where man is not, Nature is barren.

Truth can never be told so as to be understood, and not be believed.

Enough! or too much.

The remainder of the book consists of five distinct, but kindred prose compositions, not all following consecutively, each entitled a 'Memorable Fancy.' Half dream, half allegory, these wild and strange fragments defy description or interpretation. It would hardly occur, indeed, that they *were* allegorical, or that interpretation was a thing to be expected or attempted, but for an occasional sentence like the following: – 'I, in my hand, brought the skeleton of a body which in the mill was Aristotle's Analytics.' And we are sometimes tempted to exclaim with the angel who conducts the author to the mill: 'Thy phantasy has imposed upon me, and thou oughtest to be ashamed.' Throughout these 'Memorable Fancies,' there is a mingling of the sublime and grotesque better paralleled in art than literature – in that Gothic art with the spirit of which Blake was so deeply penetrated; where corbels of grinning and distorted faces support solemn overarching grandeurs, and quaint monsters lurk in foliaged capital or nook.

In the second 'Memorable Fancy,' of which we give a brief sample or two, he sees Isaiah and Ezekiel in a vision:

* * * Then I asked: 'Does a firm persuasion that a thing is so make it so?'

He replied, 'All poets believe that it does, and in ages of imagination this firm persuasion removed mountains; but many are not capable of a firm persuasion of anything.'

Then Ezekiel said: 'The philosophy of the East taught the first principles of human perception; some nations held one principle for the origin and some another; we of Israel taught that the Poetic Genius (as you now call it) was the first principle, and all the others merely derivative; which was the cause of our despising the priests and philosophers of other countries, and prophesying that all gods would at last be proved to originate in ours, and to be the tributaries of the Poetic Genius.

It was this that our great poet, King David, desired so fervently and invoked so pathetically, saying, "By this he conquers enemies, and governs kingdoms;" and we so loved our God, that we cursed in His name all the deities of surrounding nations, and asserted that they had rebelled. From these opinions, the vulgar came to think that all nations would at last be subject to the Jews.'

'This,' said he, 'like all firm persuasions, is come to pass, for all nations believe the Jews' code and worship the Jews' God; and what greater subjection can be?'

I heard this with some wonder, and must confess my own conviction.

* * *

If the doors of perception were cleansed, everything would appear to man as it is – infinite.

For man has closed himself up, till he sees all things through narrow chinks of his cavern.

* * *

A Memorable Fancy.

I was in a printing-house in hell, and saw the method in which knowledge is transmitted from generation to generation.

In the first chamber was a dragon-man, clearing away the rubbish from a cave's mouth; within, a number of dragons were hollowing the cave.

In the second chamber was a viper folding round the rock and the cave, and others adorning it with gold, silver, and precious stones.

In the third chamber was an eagle with wings and feathers of air; he caused the inside of the cave to be infinite. Around, were numbers of eagle-like men, who built palaces in the immense cliffs.

In the fourth chamber were lions of flaming fire raging around and melting the metals into living fluids.

In the fifth chamber were unnamed forms, which cast the metals into the expanse.

There they were received by men who occupied the sixth chamber, and took the forms of books, and were arranged in libraries.

The Giants who formed this world into its sensual existence, and now seem to live in it in chains, are, in truth, the causes of its life and the sources of all activity, but the chains are the cunning of weak and tame minds which have power to resist energy; according to the proverb, the weak in courage is strong in cunning.

Thus, one portion of being is the Prolific, the other the Devouring. To the devourer it seems as if the producer was in his chains, but it is not so; he only takes portions of existence and fancies that the whole.

But the Prolific would cease to be prolific, unless the devourer, as a sea, received the excess of his delights.

* * *

A Memorable Fancy.

An Angel came to me, and said, 'O pitiable, foolish young man! O horrible – O dreadful state! Consider the hot burning dungeon thou art preparing for thyself to all eternity, to which thou art going in such career.' I said, 'Perhaps you will be willing to show me my eternal lot, and we will contemplate together upon it, and see whether your lot or mine is most desirable.'

So he took me through a stable and through a church, and down into the church vault, at the end of which was a mill. Through the mill we went, and came to a cave: down the winding cavern we groped our tedious way till a void, boundless as a nether sky, appeared beneath us, and we held by the roots of trees, and hung over this immensity. But I said, 'If you please, we will commit ourselves to this void and see whether Providence is here also; if you will not, I will!' But he answered, 'Do not presume, O young man; but as we here remain, behold thy lot, which will soon appear when the darkness passes away.'

So I remained with him, sitting in the twisted root of an oak; he was suspended in a fungus which hung with the head downward into the deep.

By degrees we beheld the infinite Abyss, fiery as the smoke of a burning city. Beneath us, at an immense distance, was the sun, black but shining. Round it were fiery tracks, on which revolved vast spiders crawling after their prey, which flew or rather swam in the infinite deep, in the most terrific shapes of animals sprung from corruption; and the air was full of them, and seemed composed of them. These are Devils, and are called Powers of the Air. I now asked my companion which was my eternal lot? He said, 'Between the black and the white spiders.'

But now, from between the black and white spiders, a cloud of fire burst and rolled through the deep, blackening all beneath; so that the nether deep grew black as a sea, and rolled with a terrible noise. Beneath us was nothing now to be seen but a black tempest; till, looking east between the clouds and the waves, we saw a cataract of blood mixed with fur, and not many stones' throw from us appeared and sunk again the scaly fold of a monstrous serpent. At last to the east, distant about three degrees, appeared a fiery crest above the waves. Slowly it reared like a ridge of golden rocks, till we discovered two globes of crimson fire, from which the sea fled away in clouds of smoke, and now we saw it was the head of Leviathan. His forehead was divided into streaks of green and purple, like those on a tiger's forehead. Soon we saw his mouth and red gills hang just above the raging foam, tinging the black deep with beams of blood, advancing towards us with all the fury of a spiritual existence.

My friend the Angel climbed up from his station into the mill. I remained alone, and then this appearance was no more; but I found myself sitting on a pleasant bank beside a river by moonlight, hearing a harper who sung to the harp, and his theme was, 'The man who never alters his opinion is like standing water, and breeds reptiles of the mind.'

But I arose, and sought for the mill, and there I found my Angel; * * * but I by force suddenly caught him in my arms, and flew westerly through the night, till we were elevated above the earth's shadow. Then I flung myself with him directly into the body of the sun. Here I clothed myself in white, and, taking in my hand Swedenborg's volumes, sunk from the glorious clime, and passed all the planets till we came to Saturn. Here I stayed to rest, and then leaped into the void between Saturn and the fixed stars.

*   *   *

Soon we saw seven houses of brick; one we entered; in it were a number of monkeys, baboons, and all of that species, chained by the middle, grinning and snatching at one another, but with-held by the shortness of their chains. However, I saw that they sometimes grew numerous, and then the weak were caught by the strong, and with a grinning aspect devoured, by plucking off first one limb and then another, till the body was left a helpless trunk. This, after grinning and kissing it with seeming fondness, they devoured too; and here and there I saw one savourily picking the flesh off of his own tail. As the stench terribly annoyed us both, we went into the mill, and I in my hand brought a skeleton of a body, which in the mill was Aristotle's Analytics. So the Angel said: 'Thy phantasy has imposed upon me, and thou oughtest to be ashamed.'

I answered, 'We impose on one another, and it is but lost time to converse with you, whose works are only Analytics.'

Swedenborg boasts that what he writes is new; though it is only the contents or index of already published books.

* * *

Any man of mechanical talents may, from the writings of Paracelsus or Jacob Boehmen, produce ten thousand volumes of equal value with Swedenborg's, and from those of Dante or Shakespeare an infinite number.

But when he has done this, let him not say that he knows better than his master, for he only holds a candle in sunshine.

The power of these wild utterances is enhanced to the utmost by the rich adornments of design and colour in which they are set – design as imaginative as the text, colour which has the lustre of jewels.

A strip of azure sky surmounts, and of land divides, the words of the title page, leaving on each side scant and baleful trees, little else than stem and spray. Drawn on a tiny scale, lies a corpse, and one bends over it. Flames burst forth below and slant upward across the page, gorgeous with every hue. In their very core two spirits rush together and embrace. These beautiful figures appear to have suggested to Flaxman the delicately executed bas-relief on Collins' monument.

In the second design, to the right of the page, there runs up an almost lifeless tree. A man clinging to the thin stem, and holding by a branch, reaches its only cluster to a woman standing below. Distant are three figures reposing on the ground. At the top of the third, a woman with outspread arms is borne away on flames –

> 'like a creature native and indued
> Unto that element;'

beneath, two figures are rushing away from a female lying on the earth.

96

In the next, the sun sets over the sea in blood. A spirit, grasping a child, walks on the waves. Another, in the midst of fire, would fain rush to her, but an iron link clinches his ankle to the rock.

The fifth resembles the catastrophe of Phaëton, save that there is but one horse. Spires of flame are already kindling below.

Under the text of the sixth, an accusing demon, with bat-like wings, points fiercely to a scroll – a great parchment scroll across his knees. A figure sits on each side recording.

In the next design we have a little island of the sea, where an infant springs to its mother's bosom. From the birth-cleft ground a spirit has half emerged. Below, with outstretched arms and hoary beard, an awful ancient man rushes at you, as it were, out of the page.

At the top of the fourteenth page a spirit, with streaming locks, extends her arms across, pointing hither and thither. She hovers, poised over a corpse, which looks as if 'laid out,' the arms straight by the sides; helpless, uncoffined; flames are rolling onward to consume it.

The ninth design is of an eagle flying and gazing upwards: his talons gripe a long snake trailing and writhing. Both are flecked with gold, and coruscate as from a light within.

The tenth presents a huddled group of solemn figures seated on the ground. The next is a surging of mingled fire, water, and blood, wherein roll the volumes of a huge double-fanged serpent, his crest erect, his jaws wide open.

In the twelfth, the disembodied spirit, luminous and radiant, sits lightly upon its late prison house, gazing upwards whither it is about to soar. It is the same figure as that in Blair's *Grave*, where you see also the natural body, bent with years, tottering into the dark doorway beneath.

The thirteenth and last design gives Blake's idea of Nebuchadnezzar in the wilderness. Mr Palmer tells me that he has old German translations of Cicero and Petrarch, in which, among some wild and original designs, almost the very same figure occurs; but that many years had elapsed after making his own design before Blake saw the woodcut.

The designs are highly finished: Blake had worked upon them so much, and illuminated them so richly, that even the letterpress seems as if done by hand. The ever-fluctuating colour, the spectral pigmies rolling, flying, leaping among the letters; the ripe bloom of quiet corners, the living light and bursts of flame, the spires and tongues of fire vibrating with the full prism, make the page seem to move and quiver within its boundaries, and you lay the book down tenderly, as if you had been handling something sentient. A picture has been said to be midway between a thing and a thought; so in these books over which Blake had long brooded, with his brooding of fire, the very paper seems to come to life as you gaze upon it – not with a mortal life, but with a life indestructible, whether for good or evil.

The volume is an octavo, consisting of twenty-four pages; all of them illuminated. In some copies the letters are red, in others a golden brown. The engraved page is about six inches by four. Occasionally a deep margin was left so as to form a quarto.

As it was found inexpedient to reprint the *Marriage of Heaven and Hell* entire, I have brought together, in connexion with some account of the designs, the foregoing fragments, rather than isolate them in Part II. There are a few, doubtless, who will regret that the work is not given in its integrity. These I must refer to the original, though access to it, there being no copy at present in the British Museum, is difficult. Mr Monckton Milnes possesses a fire quarto, Mr Linnell an octavo copy.

ELEVEN

Bookseller Johnson's 1791–92
[ÆT. 34–35]

These were prolific years with Blake, both in poetry and design. In 1791 he even found a publisher, for the first and last time in his life, in Johnson of St Paul's Churchyard, to whom Fuseli had originally introduced him, and for whom he had already engraved. Johnson in this year – the same in which he published Mary Wollstonecraft's *Rights of Woman* – issued, without Blake's name, and unillustrated, a thin quarto, entitled *The French Revolution, a Poem in Seven Books. Book the First, One Shilling*. Of the Revolution itself, only the first book, ending with the taking of the Bastille, had as yet been enacted. In due time the remainder followed. Those of Blake's epic already written were never printed, events taking a different turn from the anticipated one.

The French Revolution, though ushered into the world by a regular publisher, was no more successful than the privately printed *Poetical Sketches*, or the privately engraved *Songs of Innocence* in reaching the public, or even in getting noticed by the monthly reviewers. It finds no place in their indices, nor in the catalogue of the Museum Library.

In this year Johnson employed Blake to design and engrave six plates to a series of *Tales for Children*, in the then prevailing Berquin School, by Johnson's favourite and *protégée*, Mary Wollstonecraft; tales new and in demand in the autumn of 1791, now unknown to the bookstalls. 'Original stories,' they are entitled, 'from real life, with conversations calculated to regulate the affections and form the mind to truth and goodness.' The designs, naïve and rude, can hardly be pronounced a successful competition with Stothard, though traces of a higher feeling are visible in the graceful female forms – benevolent heroine, or despairing, famishing peasant group. The artist evidently moves in constraint, and the accessories of these domestic scenes are as simply generalized as a child's: result of an inobservant eye for such things. They were not calculated to obtain Blake employment in a capacity in which more versatile hands and prettier designers, such as Burney and Corbould (failing Stothard), were far better fitted to succeed. The book itself never went to a second edition. More designs appear to have been made for this little work than were found available, and some of the best were among the rejected. He also illustrated for Johnson, in the same style, another book of pinafore precepts, called *Elements of Morality*, translated from the German of Salzmann by Mary Wollstonecraft; and among casual work engraved a plate for Darwin's *Botanic Garden – The Fertilization of Egypt* – after Fuseli.

Bookseller Johnson was a favourable specimen of a class of booksellers and men now a tradition: an open-hearted tradesman of the eighteenth century, of strict probity, simple habits, liberal in his dealings, living by his shop and in it, not at a suburban mansion. He was, for nearly forty years, Fuseli's fast and intimate friend, his first and best; the kind patron of Mary Wollstonecraft, and of many another. He encouraged Cowper over *The Task*, after the first volume of *Poems* had been received with indifference; and when *The Task* met its sudden unexpected success, he righteously pressed 1,000*l.* on the author, although both this and the previous volume had been assigned to him for nothing – as an equivalent, that is, for the bare cost of publication. To Blake, also, Johnson was friendly, and tried to help him, as far as he could help so unmarketable a talent.

In Johnson's shop – for booksellers' shops were places of resort then with the literary – Blake was, at this date, in the habit of meeting a remarkable coterie. The bookseller gave, moreover, plain but hospitable weekly dinners at his house, No. 72, St Paul's Churchyard, in a little quaintly shaped upstairs room, with walls not at right angles, where his guests must have been somewhat straitened for space. Hither came Drs Price and Priestley; and occasionally Blake; hither friendly, irascible Fuseli; hither precise doctrinaire Godwin, whose *Political Justice* Johnson will, in 1793, publish, giving 700*l.* for the copyright. Him, the author of the *Songs of Innocence* got on ill with, and liked worse. Here, too, he met formal, stoical Holcroft, playwright, novelist, translator, literary man-of-all-work, who had written verse 'to order' for our old friend *The Wits' Magazine*. Seven years hence he will be promoted to the Tower, and be tried for high treason with Hardy, Thelwall, and Horne Tooke, and one day will write the best fragment of autobiography in the language: a man of very varied fortunes. Here hard-headed Tom Paine, 'the rebellious needleman:' Mary Wollstonecraft also, who at Johnson's table commenced her ineffectual flirtation with already wedded, cynical Fuseli, their first meeting occurring here in the autumn of 1790. These and others of very 'advanced' political and religious opinions, theoretic republicans and revolutionists, were of the circle. The *First Part* of *The Rights of Man* had been launched on an applauding and indignant world, early in 1791; Johnson, whom the MS. had made the author's friend, having prudently declined to publish it, though he was Priestley's publisher. A few years hence their host, despite his caution, will, for his liberal sympathies, receive the honour of prosecution from a good old *habeas-corpus*-suspending Government; and, in 1798, be fined and imprisoned in the King's Bench for selling a copy of Gilbert Wakefield's *Reply to the Bishop of Llandaff's Address*, a pamphlet which every other bookseller in town sold, and continued to sell, with impunity. While in prison he still gave his weekly literary dinners – in the Marshal's house instead of his own; Fuseli remaining staunch to his old friend under a cloud.

Blake was himself an ardent member of the New School, a vehement republican and sympathiser with the Revolution, hater and contemner of kings and king-craft. And like most reformers of that era, – when the eighteenth century dry-rot had well-nigh destroyed the substance of the old English Constitution, though the anomalous *caput mortuum* of it was still extolled as the 'wisest of systems,' – he may have even gone the length of despising the 'Constitution.' Down to his latest days Blake always avowed himself a 'Liberty Boy,' a faithful 'Son of Liberty;' and would jokingly urge in self-defence that the shape of his forehead made him a republican. 'I can't help being one,' he would assure Tory friends, 'any more than you can help being a Tory: your forehead is larger above; mine, on the contrary, over the eyes.' To him, at this date, as to ardent minds everywhere, the French Revolution was the herald of the Millennium, of a new age of light and reason. He courageously donned the famous symbol of liberty and equality – the *bonnet-rouge* – in open day, and philosophically walked the streets with the same on his head. He is said to have been the only one of the set who had the courage to make that public profession of faith. Brave as a lion at heart was the meek spiritualist. Decorous Godwin, Holcroft, wily Paine, however much they might approve, paused before running the risk of a Church-and-King mob at their heels. All this was while the Revolution, if no longer constitutional, still continued muzzled; before, that is, the Days of Terror, in September '92, and subsequent defiance of kings and of humanity. When the painter heard of these September doings he tore off his white cockade, and assuredly never wore the red cap again. Days of humiliation for English sympathisers and republicans were beginning.

Though at one with Paine, Godwin, Fuseli, and the others, as to politics, he was a rebel to their theological or anti-theological tenets. Himself a heretic among the orthodox, here among the infidels he was a saint, and staunchly defended Christianity – the spirit of it – against these strangely assorted disputants.

In 1792 the artist proved, as he was wont to relate, the means of saving Paine from the vindictive clutches of exasperated 'friends of order.' Early in that year Paine had published his *Second Part* of *The Rights of Man*. A few months later, county and corporation addresses against 'seditious publications' were got up. The Government (Pitt's) answered the agreed signal by issuing a proclamation condemnatory of such publications, and commenced an action for libel against the author of *The Rights of Man*, which was to come off in September; all this helping the book itself into immense circulation. The 'Friends of Liberty' held their meetings too, in which strong language was used. In September, a French deputation announced to Paine that the Department of *Calais* had elected him member of the National Convention. Already as an acknowledged cosmopolitan and friend of man, he had been declared a citizen of France by the deceased Assembly. One day in this same month, Paine was giving at Johnson's an idea of the inflammatory eloquence he had poured forth at a public meeting of the previous night. Blake, who was present, silently inferred from the tenor of his report that those in power, now eager to lay hold of noxious persons, would certainly not let slip such an opportunity. On Paine's rising to leave, Blake laid his hands on the orator's shoulder, saying, 'You must not go home, or you are a dead man!' and hurried him off on his way to France, whither he was now, in any case bound, to take his seat as French legislator. By the time Paine was at Dover, the officers were in his house, or, as his biographer Mr Cheetham designates it, his 'lurking hole in the purlieus of London;' and some twenty minutes after the Custom House officials at Dover had turned over his slender baggage with, as he thought, extra malice, and he had set sail for Calais, an order was received from the Home Office to detain him. England never saw Tom Paine again. New perils awaited him: Reign of Terror and near view of the guillotine – an accidentally open door and a chalk mark on the wrong side of it proving his salvation. But a no less serious one had been narrowly escaped from the English Tories. Those were hanging days! Blake, on this occasion, showed greater sagacity than Paine, whom, indeed, Fuseli affirmed to be more ignorant of the common affairs of life than himself even. Spite of unworldliness and visionary faculty, Blake never wanted for prudence and sagacity in ordinary matters.

Early in this September died Blake's mother, at the age of seventy, and was buried in Bunhill Fields on the 9th. She is a shade to us, alas! in all senses: for of her character, or even her person, no tidings survive. Blake's associates in later years remember to have heard him speak but rarely of either father or mother, amid the frequent allusions to his brother Robert.

At the beginning of the year (February 23rd, 1792) had died

the recognised leader of English painters, Sir Joshua Reynolds, whom failing eyesight had for some time debarred from the exercise of his art. He was borne, in funeral pomp, from his house in Leicester Fields to Saint Paul's, amid the regrets of the great world, testified by a mourning train of ninety coaches, and by the laboured panegyric of Burke. Blake used to tell of an interview he had once had with Reynolds, in which our neglected enthusiast found the originator of a sect in art to which his own was so hostile, very pleasant personally, as most found him. 'Well, Mr Blake,' blandly remarked the President, who, doubtless, had heard strange accounts of his interlocutor's sayings and doings, 'I hear you despise our art of oil-painting.' 'No, Sir Joshua, I don't despise it; but I like fresco better.'

Sir Joshua's style, with its fine taste, its merely earthly graces and charms of colour, light, and shade, was an abomination to the poetic visionary – 'The Whore of Babylon' and 'Antichrist,' metaphorically speaking. For as it has been said, very earnest original artists make ill critics: of feeble sympathy with alien schools of feeling, they can no more be eclectic in criticism than, to any worthy result, in practice. Devout sectaries in art hate and contemn those of opposite artistic faith with truly religious fervour. I have heard of an eminent living painter in the New School, who, on his admiration being challenged for a superlative example of Sir Joshua's graceful, generalizing hand, walked up to it, pronounced an emphatic word of disgust, and turned on his heel: such bigoted mortals are men who paint!

It was hardly in flesh and blood for the unjustly despised author of the *Songs of Innocence*, who had once, as Allan Cunningham well says, thought, and not perhaps unnaturally, that 'he had but to sing beautiful songs, and draw grand designs, to become great and famous,' and in the midst of his obscurity feeling conscious of endowments of imagination and thought, rarer than those fascinating gifts of perception and expression which so readily won the world's plaudits and homage; it was hardly possible *not* to feel jealous, and as it were injured, by the startling contrast of such fame and success as Sir Joshua's and Gainsborough's.

Of this mingled soreness and antipathy we have curious evidence in some MS. notes Blake subsequently made in his copy of Sir Joshua's *Discourses*. Struck by their singularity, one or two of Blake's admirers in later years transcribed these notes. To Mr Palmer I am indebted, among many other courtesies, for a copy of the first half of them.

'This man was here,' commences the indignant commentator, 'to depress Art: this is the opinion of William Blake. My proofs of this opinion are given in the following notes. Having spent the vigour of my youth and genius under the oppression of Sir Joshua, and his gang of cunning, hired knaves – without employment, and, as much as could possibly be, without bread – the reader must expect to read, in all my remarks on these books, nothing but indignation and resentment. While Sir Joshua was rolling in riches, Barry was poor and unemployed, except by his own energy; Mortimer was called a madman, and only portrait painting was applauded and rewarded by the rich and great. Reynolds and Gainsborough blotted and blurred one against the other, and divided all the English world between them. Fuseli, indignant, almost hid himself. I AM HID.'

Always excepting the favoured portrait painters, these were, indeed, cold days for the unhappy British artist – the historical or poetic artist above all. Times have strangely altered within living memory. The case is now reversed. One can but sympathise with the above touching outburst; and Blake rarely complained aloud of the world's ill usage, extreme as it was: one can but sympathise, I say, even while cherishing the warmest love and admiration for Sir Joshua's and Gainsborough's delightful art. The glow of sunset need not blind us to the pure light of Hesperus. Admiration of a fashionable beauty, with her Watteau-like grace, should not dazzle the eye to exclusion of the nobler grace of Raphael or the Antique.

Of these notes more hereafter.

TWELVE

The Gates of Paradise, America, ETC. 1793
[ÆT. 36]

In 1793, Blake quitted Poland Street, after five years' residence there. The now dingy demi-rep street, one in which Shelley lodged in 1810, after his expulsion from Oxford, had witnessed the production of the *Songs of Innocence* and other Poetry and Design of a genus unknown, before or since, to that permanently foggy district. From the neighbourhood of his birth he removed across Westminster Bridge to Lambeth. There he will remain other seven years, and produce no less an amount of strange and original work. Hercules Buildings is the new abode; a row of houses which had sprung up, since his boyish rambles.

Within easy reach of the centre of London on one side, the favourite Dulwich strolls of early years were at hand on the other. Hercules Buildings, stretching diagonally between the Kennington Road and Lambeth Palace, was then a street of modest irregular sized houses, from one to three stories high, with fore-courts or little gardens in front, in the suburban style; a street indeed only for half its length, the remainder being a single row, or terrace. No. 13, Blake's, was among the humbler, one-storied houses, on the right hand side as you go from the Bridge to the Palace. It had a wainscoted parlour, pleasant low windows, and a narrow strip of real garden behind, wherein grew a fine vine. A lady, who as a girl used with her elders to call on the artist here, tells me Blake would on no account prune this vine, having a theory it was wrong and unnatural to prune vines: and the affranchised tree consequently bore a luxuriant crop of leaves, and plenty of infinitesimal grapes which never ripened. Open garden ground and field, interspersed with a few lines of clean, newly-built houses, lay all about and near; for brick and mortar was spreading even then. At back, Blake looked out over gardens towards Lambeth Palace, and the Thames, seen between gaps of Stangate Walk, – Etty's home a few years later. The city and towers of Westminster closed the prospect beyond the river, on whose surface sailing hoys were then plying once or twice a day. Vauxhall Gardens lay half a mile to the left; Dulwich and Peckham hills within view to the south-west. The street has since been partly rebuilt, partly re-named; the whole become now sordid and dirty. At the back of what was Blake's side has arisen a row of ill-drained, one-storied tenements bestridden by the arches of the South-Western Railway; while the adjacent main roads, grimy and hopeless looking, stretch out their long arms towards further mile on mile of suburb, – Newington, Kennington, Brixton.

In Hercules Buildings Blake engraved and 'published' – May, 1793, adding at the foot of the title-page Johnson's name to his own – *The Gates of Paradise*; a singularly beautiful and characteristic volume, pre-eminently marked by significance and simplicity. It is a little foolscap octavo, printed according to his usual method, but not coloured; containing seventeen plates of emblems, accompanied by verse, with a title or motto to each plate. *For Children*, the title runs, or, as some copies have it, *For the Sexes. The Gates of Paradise* – 'a sort of devout dream, equally wild and lovely,' Allan Cunningham happily terms it.

There is little in art which speaks to the mind directly and pregnantly as do these few, simple Designs, emblematic of so much which could never be imprisoned in words, yet of a kind more allied to literature than to art. It is plain, on looking on this little volume alone, from whom Flaxman and Stothard borrowed. Hints of more than one design of theirs might be found in it. And Blake's designs have, I repeat, the look of originals. A shock as of something wholly fresh and new, these typical compositions give us.

The verses at the commencement elucidate, to a certain extent, the intention of the Series, embodying an ever-recurrent canon of Blake's Theology:

> Mutual forgiveness of each vice,
> Such are the Gates of Paradise,
> Against the Accuser's chief desire,
> Who walked among the stones of fire.
> Jehovah's fingers wrote The Law:
> He wept! then rose in zeal and awe,
> And in the midst of Sinai's heat,
> Hid it beneath His Mercy Seat.
> O Christians! Christians! tell me why
> You rear it on your altars high?

'What is man?' – the frontispiece significantly inquires.

To the *Gates of Paradise* their author in some copies added what many another Book of his would have profited by, – the *Keys of the Gates*, in sundry wild lines of rudest verse, which do not pretend to be poetry, but merely to tag the artist's ideas with rhyme, and are themselves a little obscure, though they do help one to catch the prevailing *motives*. The numbers prefixed to the lines refer them to the plates which they are severally intended to explain.

CHAPTER TWELVE

The Keys of the Gates

The Caterpillar on the Leaf
Reminds thee of thy Mother's Grief.
1 My Eternal Man set in Repose,
   The Female from his darkness rose;
   And she found me beneath a Tree,
   A Mandrake, and in her Veil hid me.
   Serpent reasonings us entice,
   Of Good and Evil, Virtue, Vice.
2 Doubt self-jealous, Wat'ry folly,
3 Struggling through Earth's Melancholy.
4 Naked in Air, in Shame and Fear,
5 Blind in Fire, with Shield and Spear,
   Two Horrid Reasoning Cloven Fictions,
   In Doubt which is Self Contradiction,
   A dark Hermaphrodite I stood, –
   Rational Truth, Root of Evil and Good.
   Round me, flew the Flaming Sword;
   Round her, snowy Whirlwinds roar'd,
   Freezing her Veil, the mundane shell.
6 I rent the veil where the Dead dwell:
   When weary Man enters his Cave,
   He meets his Saviour in the Grave.
   Some find a Female Garment there,
   And some a Male, woven with care,
   Lest the Sexual Garments sweet
   Should grow a devouring Winding-sheet.
7 One Dies! Alas! the living and dead!
   One is slain! and one is fled!
8 In vainglory hatcht and nurst,
   By double spectres, self accurst.
   My Son! my Son! thou treatest me
   But as I have instructed thee.

112

9 On the shadows of the Moon,
   Climbing thro' night's highest noon:
10 In Time's Ocean falling, drown'd:
11 In Aged Ignorance profound,
   Holy and cold, I clipt the Wings
   Of all Sublunary Things:
12 And in depths of icy Dungeons
   Closed the Father and the Sons.
13 But when once I did descry
   The Immortal man that cannot Die,
14 Thro' evening shades I haste away
   To close the labours of my Day.
15 The Door of Death I open found,
   And the Worm weaving in the Ground:
16 Thou'rt my Mother, from the Womb;
   Wife, Sister, Daughter, to the Tomb:
   Weaving to Dreams the Sexual Strife,
   And weeping over the Web of Life.

Last follows an epilogue, or postscript, which perhaps explains itself, addressed

To the Accuser, who is the God of this World

Truly, my Satan, thou art but a dunce,
And dost not know the garment from the man;
Every harlot was a virgin once,
Nor canst thou ever change Kate into Nan.
Though thou art worshipped by the names divine
Of Jesus and Jehovah, thou art still
The Son of Morn in weary Night's decline,
The lost traveller's dream under the hill.

In this year, by the way, the first volume of a more famous poet, but a much less original volume than Blake's first, – the *Descriptive Sketches* of Wordsworth, followed by the *Evening*

Walk, – were published by Johnson, of St Paul's Churchyard. Neither reached a second edition; but by 1807, when the *Lyrical Ballads* had attracted admirers here and there, they had, according to De Quincey, got out of print, and scarce.

Other engraved volumes, more removed from ordinary sympathy and comprehension than the *Gates of Paradise*, were issued in the same year: dreamy 'Books of Prophecy' following in the wake of the *Marriage of Heaven and Hell*. First came *Visions of the Daughters of Albion*, a folio volume of Designs and rhymeless verse, printed in colour.

The eye sees more than the heart knows

is the key-note struck in the first page, to which follows the Argument:

> I loved Theotormon,
> And I was not ashamed;
> I trembled in my virgin fears,
> And I hid in Leutha's vale.
>
> I plucked Leutha's flower,
> And I rose up from the vale;
> But the terrible thunders tore
> My virgin mantle in twain.

The poem partakes of the same delicate mystic beauty as Thel, but tends also towards the incoherence of the writings which immediately followed it. Of the former qualities the commencement may be quoted as an instance –

> Enslaved, the daughters of Albion weep: a trembling lamentation
> Upon their mountains; in their valleys, sighs toward America.
>
> For the soft soul of America, – Oothoon, – wandered in woe
> Among the vales of Leutha, seeking flowers to comfort her:
> And thus she spoke to the bright marigold of Leutha's vale, –

'Art thou a flower? Art thou a nymph? I see thee now a flower;
And now a nymph! I dare not pluck thee from thy dewy bed!'

The golden nymph replied, 'Pluck thou my flower, Oothoon the
    mild,
Another flower shall spring, because the soul of sweet delight
Can never pass away.' – She ceased, and closed her golden shrine.

Then Oothoon plucked the flower, saying, – 'I pluck thee from
    thy bed,
Sweet flower, and put thee here to glow between my breasts,
And thus I turn my face to where my whole soul seeks.'

Over the waves she went, in wing'd exulting swift delight,
And over Theotormon's reign took her impetuous course.

But she is taken in the 'thunders,' or toils of Bromion, who
appears the evil spirit of the soil. Theotormon, in jealous fury,
chains them – 'terror and meekness' – together, back to back,
in Bromion's caves, and seats himself sorrowfully by. The lamen-
tations of Oothoon, and her appeals to the incensed divinity,
with his replies, form the burthen of the poem. The Daughters
of Albion, who are alluded to in the opening lines as enslaved,
weeping, and sighing towards America, 'hear her woes and echo
back her cries;' a recurring line or *refrain*, which includes all
they have to do.

We subjoin another extract or two:

Oothoon weeps not: she cannot weep! her tears are locked up!
But she can howl incessant, writhing her soft, snowy limbs,
And calling Theotormon's eagles to prey upon her flesh!

'I call with holy voice! kings of the sounding air!
Rend away this defiled bosom that I may reflect
The image of Theotormon on my pure transparent breast!'

The eagles at her call descend and rend their bleeding prey.
Theotormon severely smiles; her soul reflects the smile,

As the clear spring mudded with feet of beasts grows pure and
  smiles.

The Daughters of Albion hear her woes and echo back her
  sighs.

'Why does my Theotormon sit weeping upon the threshold?
And Oothoon hovers by his side persuading him in vain!
I cry, Arise, O Theotormon! for the village dog
Barks at the breaking day; the nightingale has done lamenting;
The lark does rustle in the ripe corn; and the Eagle returns
From nightly prey, and lifts his golden beak to the pure east,
Shaking the dust from his immortal pinions, to awake
The sun that sleeps too long! Arise, my Theotormon; I am
  pure!

* * *

'Ask the wild ass why he refuses burdens; and the meek camel
Why he loves man. Is it because of eye, ear, mouth, or skin,
Or breathing nostrils? No: for these the wolf and tiger have.
Ask the blind worm the secrets of the grave; and why her
  spires
Love to curl round the bones of death: and ask the ravenous
  snake
Where she gets poison; and the winged eagle, why he loves the
  sun:
And then tell me the thoughts of man that have been hid of
  old!

'Silent I hover all the night, and all day could be silent,
If Theotormon once would turn his loved eyes upon me;
How can I be defiled, when I reflect thy image pure?
Sweetest the fruit that the worm feeds on; and the soul prey'd on
  by woe.
The new washed lamb ting'd with the village smoke and the
  bright swan
By the red earth of our immortal river: I bathe my wings,

And I am white and pure, to hover round Theotormon's
  breast.'

Then Theotormon broke his silence, and he answered:

'Tell me what is the night or day to one o'erflow'd with woe?
Tell me what is a thought? and of what substance is it made?
Tell me what is a joy; and in what gardens do joys grow;
And in what rivers swim the sorrows; and upon what mountains
Wave shadows of discontent? And in what houses dwell the
  wretched,
Drunken with woe forgotten, and shut up from cold despair?
Tell me where dwell the thoughts forgotten till thou call them
  forth?
'Tell me where dwell the joys of old, and where the ancient
  loves?
And when they will renew again, and the night of oblivion
  pass?
That I may traverse times and spaces far remote, and bring
Comforts into a present sorrow, and a night of pain.'

The poem concludes thus:

The sea fowl takes the wintry blast for a covering to her limbs.
And the wild snake the pestilence, to adorn him with gems and
  gold.
And trees, and birds, and beasts, and men, behold their eternal
  joy.
Arise, you little glancing wings, and sing your infant joy!
Arise, and drink your bliss! For every thing that lives is holy.

  Thus every morning wails Oothoon, but Theotormon sits
  Upon the margined ocean, conversing with shadows dire.

The Daughters of Albion hear her woes, and echo back her
  sighs.

117

Formidable moral questions are, in an enigmatic way, occasionally opened up through the medium of this allegory, and in many another of Blake's writings: questions on which he had his own views, and gave fearless and glowing expression to them, – as the exemplary man had good right to do. But we will not enter on them here.

The designs to the *Visions of the Daughters of Albion* are magnificent in energy and portentousness. They are coloured with flat, even tints, not worked up highly. A frontispiece represents Bromion and Oothoon, chained in a cave that opens on the sea; Theotormon sitting near. The title-page is of great beauty; the words are written over rainbow and cloud, from the centre of which emerges an old man in fire, other figures floating round.

The other volume of this year's production at Lambeth, entitled *America, a Prophecy*, is a folio of twenty pages, of still more dithyrambic verse. It is verse hard to fathom; with far too little Nature behind it, or back-bone; a redundance of mere invention, – the fault of all this class of Blake's writings; too much wild tossing about of ideas and words. The very names – Urthona, Enitharmon, Ore, &c. are but Ossian-like shadows, and contrast oddly with those of historic or matter-of-fact personages occasionally mentioned in the poem, whom, notwithstanding the subject in hand, we no longer expect to meet with, after reading the *Preludium*:

The shadowy Daughter of Urthona stood before red Orc,
When fourteen suns had faintly journey'd o'er his dark abode:
His food she brought in iron baskets, his drink in cups of iron.
Crown'd with a helmet and dark hair, the nameless female stood.
A quiver with its burning stores, a bow like that of night
When pestilence is shot from heaven, – no other arms she
    needs, –

Invulnerable though naked, save where clouds roll round her loins
Their awful folds in the dark air. Silent she stood as night:
For never from her iron tongue could voice or sound arise;
But dumb from that dread day when Orc essay'd his fierce
    embrace.
'Dark virgin!' said the hairy youth, 'thy father stern, abhorr'd,
Rivets my tenfold chains, while still on high my spirit soars;
Sometimes an eagle screaming in the sky; sometimes a lion,
Stalking upon the mountains; and sometimes a whale, I lash
The raging, fathomless abyss; anon, a serpent folding
Around the pillars of Urthona, and round thy dark limbs,
On the Canadian wilds I fold.'

The poem itself opens thus:

The Guardian Prince of Albion burns in his nightly tent.
Sullen fires across the Atlantic glow to America's shore,
Piercing the souls of warlike men, who rise in silent night.
Washington, Franklin, Paine, Warren, Gates, Hancock and
    Green,
Meet on the coast, glowing with blood, from Albion's fiery
    prince.
Washington spoke: 'Friends of America, look over the Atlantic
    sea.
A bended bow is lifted in heaven, and a heavy iron chain
Descends link by link from Albion's cliffs across the sea to bind
Brothers and sons of America, till our faces pale and yellow,
Heads deprest, voices weak, eyes downcast, hands work-bruised,
Feet bleeding on the sultry sands, and the furrows of the whip,
Descend to generations that in future times forget.'
The strong voice ceased: for a terrible blast swept over the
    heaving sea,
The eastern cloud rent. On his cliffs stood Albion's wrathful
    Prince,
A dragon form clashing his scales: at midnight he arose,
And flamed red meteors round the land of Albion beneath.

His voice, his locks, his awful shoulders and his glowing
  eyes,
Appear to the Americans, upon the cloudy night.
Solemn heave the Atlantic waves between the gloomy
  nations.

One more extract shall suffice:

The morning comes, the night decays, the watchmen leave their
  stations;
The grave is burst, the spices shed, the linen wrapped up.
The bones of death, the covering clay, the sinews shrunk and
  dried,
Reviving shake, inspiring move, breathing! awakening!
Spring, – like redeemed captives when their bonds and bars are
  burst.
Let the slave grinding at the mill run out into the field;
Let him look up into the heavens and laugh in the bright air.
Let the enchained soul, shut up in darkness and in sighing,
Whose face has never seen a smile in thirty weary years,
Rise, and look out! – his chains are loose! his dungeon doors
  are open!

The poem has no distinctly seizable pretensions to a prophetic
character, being, like the rest of Blake's 'Books of Prophecy,'
rather a retrospect, in its mystic way, of events already transpired.
The American War of Independence is the theme; a portion of
history here conducted mainly by vast mythic beings, 'Orc,' the
'Angels of Albion,' the 'Angels of the thirteen states,' &c.; whose
movements are throughout accompanied by tremendous elemental commotion – 'red clouds and raging fire;' 'black smoke,
thunder,' and

Plagues creeping on the burning winds driven by flames of Orc, through which chaos the merely human agents show small and remote, perplexed and busied in an ant-like way. Strange to conceive a somewhile associate of Paine producing these 'Prophetic' volumes!

The *America* now and then occurs coloured, more often plain black, or occasionally blue, and white. The designs blend with and surround the verse; the mere grouping of the text, filled in here and there with ornament, often forming, in itself, a picturesque piece of decorative composition. Of the beauty of most of these designs, in their finished state, it would be quite impossible to obtain any notion, without the necessary adjunct of colour, Blake never intending any copies to go forth to the world until they had been coloured by hand.

Whatever may be the literary value of the work, the designs display unquestionable power and beauty. In firmness of outline and refinement of finish, they are exceeded by none from the same hand. We have more especially in view Mr Monckton Milnes's superb copy. Turning over the leaves, it is sometimes like an increase of daylight on the retina, so fair and open is the effect of particular pages. The skies of sapphire, or gold, rayed with hues of sunset, against which stand out leaf or blossom, or pendant branch, gay with bright plumaged birds; the strips of emerald sward below, gemmed with flower and lizard and enamelled snake, refresh the eye continually.

Some of the illustrations are of a more sombre kind. There is one in which a little corpse, white as snow, lies gleaming on the floor of a green overarching cave, which close inspection proves to be a field of wheat, whose slender interlacing stalks, bowed by the full ear and by a gentle breeze, bend over and inclose the dead infant. The delicate network of stalks (which is carried up one side of the page, the main picture being at the bottom), and the subdued yet vivid green light shed over the whole, produce a lovely decorative effect. Decorative effect is in fact never lost sight of, even when the *motive* of the design is ghastly or terrible. As for instance at page 13, which represents the different fate of two bodies drowned in the sea – the one, that of a woman, cast up by the purple waves on a rocky shore; an eagle, with outstretched wings, alighting on her bosom, his beak already tearing her flesh: the other, lying at the bottom of the ocean, where snaky loathsome things are twining round it, and open-mouthed fishes gathering greedily to devour. The effect is as of looking through water down into wondrous depths. One design in the volume was an especial favourite of Blake's: that of an old man entering Death's door. It occurs in the *Gates of Paradise* (Plate 15); in Blair's *Grave* (1805), and as a distinct engraving. There are also two other subjects repeated subsequently, – in the *Grave* and the *Job*. But one more design (we might expatiate on all) shall tempt us to loiter. It heads the last page of the book, and consists of a white-robed, colossal figure, bowed to the earth; about which, as on a huge snow-covered mass of rock, dwarf shapes are clustered here and there. Enhancing the weird effect of the whole, stand three lightning-scathed oaks, each of which, 'as if threatening heaven with vengeance, holds out a withered hand.' An exquisite piece of decorative work occupies the foot of the page.

In all these works the Designer's genius floats loose and rudderless; a phantom ship on a phantom sea. He projects himself into shapeless dreams, instead of into fair definite forms, as already in the *Songs of Innocence* he had shown that he could do; and hereafter will again in the tasks so happily prescribed by others: the illustrations to *Young*, to Blair's *Grave*, to *Job*, to

Dante. In these amorphous *Prophecies* are profusely scattered the unhewn materials of poetry and design: sublime hints are sown broad-cast. But alas! whether Blake were definite or indefinite in his conceptions, he was alike ignored. He had not the faculty to make himself popular, even with a far more intelligent public as to Art than any which existed during the reign of George the Third.

In 1794, Flaxman returned from his seven years' stay in Italy; with well-stored portfolios, with more than ever classicized taste, and at Rome having made for discerning patrons those designs from Homer, Æschylus, and Dante, which were afterwards to spread his fame through Europe. He returned to be promoted R.A. at once, and to set up house and studio in Buckingham Street, Fitzroy Square, – then a new, scantily-peopled region, lying open to the hills of Hampstead and Highgate. In these premises he continued till his death in 1826. Piroli, a Roman artist, had been engaged to engrave the abovementioned graceful compositions from the poets. His first set of plates, – those to the *Odyssey*, – were lost in the voyage to England, and Blake was obtained to make engravings in their stead, although Piroli's name still remained on the general title page (dated 1793); probably as being likelier credentials with the public. Piroli subsequently engraved the Outlines to *Æschylus*, to the *Iliad*, &c. Blake's engravings are much less telling, at the first glance, than Piroli's. Instead of hard, bold, decisive lines, we have softer, lighter ones. But on looking into them we find more of the artist in the one, – as in the beautiful *Aphrodite*, for instance, a very fine and delicate engraving, – more uniform mechanical effect in the other. Blake's work is like a drawing, with traces as of a pen; Piroli's the orthodox copperplate style.

Blake, in fact, at that time, etched a good deal more than do ordinary engravers.

One consistent patron there was, whom it has become time to mention. Without his friendly countenance, even less would have remained to show the world, or a portion of it, what manner of man Blake was. I mean Mr Thomas Butts, whose long friendship with Blake commenced at this period. For nearly thirty years he continued (with few interruptions) a steady buyer at moderate prices of Blake's drawings, temperas, and frescoes; the only large buyer the artist ever had. Occasionally he would take of Blake a drawing a week. He, in this way, often supplied the imaginative man with the bare means of subsistence when no others existed – at all events from his art. All honour to the solitary appreciator and to his zealous constancy! As years rolled by, Mr Butts' house in Fitzroy Square became a perfect Blake Gallery. Fitzroy Square, by the way built in great part by Adelphi Adams, was fashionable in those days. Noblemen were contented to live in its spacious mansions; among other celebrities, General Miranda, the South American hero, abode there.

Mr Butts was no believer in Blake's 'madness.' Strangers to the man, and they alone, believed in that. Yet he could give *piquant* accounts of his *protégé's* extravagances. One story in particular he was fond of telling, which has been since pretty extensively retailed about town. At the end of the little garden in Hercules Buildings there was a summer-house. Mr Butts calling one day found Mr and Mrs Blake sitting in this summerhouse, freed from 'those troublesome disguises' which have prevailed since the Fall. *'Come in!'* cried Blake; *'it's only Adam and Eve, you know!'* Husband and wife had been reciting passages from *Paradise Lost*, in character, and the garden of Hercules Buildings had to represent the Garden of Eden: a little to the scandal of wondering neighbours, on more than one occasion. However, they knew sufficient of the single-minded artist not wholly to misconstrue such phenomena. For my reader not to do so, but frankly to enter into the full simplicity and *naïveté* of Blake's character, calls for the exercise of a little imagination on his part. He must go out of himself for a moment, if he would take such eccentricities for what they are worth, and not draw false conclusions. If he or I – close-tethered as we are to the matter-of-fact world – were on a sudden to wander in so bizarre a fashion from the prescriptive proprieties of life, it would be time for our friends to call in a doctor, or apply for a commission *de lunatico*. But Blake lived in a world of Ideas; Ideas to him were more real than the actual external world. On this matter, as on all others, he had his own peculiar views. He thought that the Gymnosophists of India, the ancient Britons, and others of whom History tells, who went naked, were, in this, wiser than the rest of mankind, – pure and wise, – and that it would be well if the world could be as they. From the speculative idea to the experimental realization of it in his own person, was, for him, but a step; though the prejudices of Society would hardly permit the experiment to be more than temporary and private. Another of Blake's favourite fancies was that he could be, for the time, the historical person into whose character he projected himself: Socrates, Moses, or one of the Prophets. 'I am Socrates,' or 'Moses,' or 'the prophet Isaiah,' he would wildly say; and always, his glowing enthusiasm was mirrored in the still depths of his wife's nature. This incident of the garden illustrates forcibly the strength of her husband's influence over her, and the unquestioning manner in which she fell in with all he did or said. When assured by him that she (for the time) was Eve, she would not dream of contradiction – nay she in a sense believed it. If therefore the anecdote argues madness in one, it argues it in both.

The Blakes do not stand alone, however, in modern history as to eccentric tenets, and even practices, in the article of drapery. Jefferson Hogg, for instance, in his *Life of Shelley*, tells us of a 'charming and elegant' family in the upper ranks of society whose acquaintance the poet made about 1813, who had embraced the theory of 'philosophical nakedness.' The parents believing in an impending 'return to nature' and reason, the pristine state of innocence, prepared their children for the coming millennium, by habituating them to run naked about the house, a few hours every day; in which condition they would open the door to welcome Shelley. The mother herself, enthusiastic in the cause, – than whom there was 'never a more innocent or more virtuous lady,' – also rehearsed *her* part – in private. She would rise betimes, lock herself into her dressing-room, and there for some hours remain (without her clothes) reading and writing; naively assuring her friends afterwards that she 'felt so much the better for it; so innocent during the rest of the day.' Strange *dénouements* have happened to other believers in the high physical, moral, and æsthetic advantages of nudity. Hogg tells another story, – of Dr Franklin; who wrote, on merely sanitary grounds, in favour of morning 'air-baths.' The philosopher, by the daily habit of devoting the early hours to study undressed, had so familiarized himself with the practice of his theory, that the absence of mind natural to philosophers led him into inadvertences. Espying once a friend's maid-servant tripping quickly across the green with a letter in her hand – an important letter he had been eagerly expecting – the philosopher ran out to meet her: at which apparition she fled in terror, screaming. Again, no one ever accused hard-headed, canny Wilkie even of eccentricity. But he was a curious mixture of simplicity, worldliness, and almost fanatical enthusiasm in the practice of his art. One morning, the raw-boned young Scotchman was discovered by a caller (friend Haydon) drawing from the nude figure before a mirror; a method of study he pronounced 'verra improving,' as well as economical! Blake's vagary, then, we may fairly maintain to be not wholly without parallel on the part of sane men, when carried away by an idea, as at first blush it would seem.

At the period of the enactment of the scene from Milton, Mrs Blake was, in person, still a presentable Eve. A 'brunette' and 'very pretty' are terms I have picked up as conveying something regarding her appearance in more youthful days. Blake himself would boast what a pretty wife he had. She lost her beauty as the seasons sped, – 'never saw a woman so much altered' was the impression of one on meeting her again after a lapse of but seven years; a life of hard work and privation having told heavily upon her in the interim. In spirit, she was, at all times, a true Eve to her Adam; and might with the most literal appropriateness have used to him the words of Milton:

> 'What thou bid'st
> Unargued I obey; so God ordains:
> God is thy law, thou mine; to know no more
> Is woman's happiest knowledge and her praise.
> With thee conversing I forget all time;
> All seasons and their change, all please alike.'

To her he never seemed erratic or wild. There had indeed at one time been a struggle of wills, but she had yielded; and his was a kind, if firm rule. Surely never had visionary man so loyal and affectionate a wife.

THIRTEEN

The Songs of Experience 1794
[ÆT. 37]

In the *Songs of Experience*, put forth in 1794, as complement to the *Songs of Innocence*, of 1789, we come again on more lucid writing than the Books of Prophecy last noticed, – writing freer from mysticism and abstractions, if partaking of the same colour of thought. *Songs of Innocence and Experience, showing the Two Contrary States of the Human Soul: the author and printer, W. Blake*, is the general title now given. The first series, quite in keeping with its name, had been of far the more heavenly temper. The second, produced during an interval of another five years, bears internal evidence of later origin, though in the same rank as to poetic excellence. As the title fitly shadows, it is of grander, sterner calibre, of gloomier wisdom. Strongly contrasted, but harmonious phases of poetic thought are presented by the two series.

One poem in the *Songs of Experience* happens to have been quoted often enough, (first by Allan Cunningham, in connexion with Blake's name), to have made its strange old Hebrew-like grandeur, its Oriental latitude yet force of eloquence, comparatively familiar: *The Tyger*. To it Charles Lamb refers: 'I have heard of his poems,' writes he, 'but have never seen them. There is one to a tiger, beginning –

Tiger! Tiger! burning bright
In the forests of the night,

which is glorious!'

Of the prevailing difference of sentiment between these poems and the *Songs of Innocence*, may be singled out as examples *The Cold and the Pebble*, and even so slight a piece as *The Fly*; and in a more sombre mood, *The Garden of Love, The Little Boy Lost, Holy Thursday* (anti-type to the poem of the same title in *Songs of Innocence*), *The Angel, The Human Abstract, The Poison Tree*, and above all, *London*. One poem, *The Little Girl Lost*, may startle the literal reader, but has an inverse moral truth and beauty of its own. Another, *The Little Girl Lost, and Little Girl Found*, is a daringly emblematic anticipation of some future age of gold, and has the picturesqueness of Spenserian allegory, lit with the more ethereal spiritualism of Blake. Touched by

'The light that never was on sea or shore,'

is this story of the carrying off of the sleeping little maid by friendly beasts of prey, who gambol round her as she lies; the kingly lion bowing 'his mane of gold,' and on her neck dropping 'from his eyes of flame, ruby tears;' who, when her parents seek the child, brings them to his cave; and

They look upon his eyes,
Filled with deep surprise;
And wondering behold
A spirit armed in gold!

Well might Flaxman exclaim, 'Sir, his poems are as grand as his pictures,' Wordsworth read them with delight, and used the words before quoted. Blake himself thought his poems finer than his designs. Hard to say which are the more uncommon in kind. Neither, as I must reiterate, reached his own generation.

In Malkin's *Memoirs of a Child*, specimens from the *Poetical Sketches* and *Songs of Innocence and Experience* were given; for these poems struck the well-meaning scholar, into whose hands by chance they fell, as somewhat astonishing; as indeed they struck most who stumbled on them. But Malkin's *Memoirs* was itself a book not destined to circulate very freely; and the poems of Blake, even had they been really known to their generation, were not calculated in their higher qualities to win popular favour, – not if they had been free from technical imperfection. For it was an age of polish, though mostly polish of trifles; not like the present age, with its slovenliness and licence. Deficient finish was never a characteristic of the innovator Wordsworth himself, who started from the basis of Pope and Goldsmith; and whose matter, rather than manner, was obnoxious to critics. Defiant carelessness, though Coleridge in his Juvenile Poems was often guilty of it, did not become a characteristic of English verse, until the advent of Keats and Shelley; poets of imaginative virtue enough to cover a multitude of their own and other people's sins. The length to which it has since run (despite Tennyson), we all know.

Yet in this very inartificiality lies the secret of Blake's rare and wondrous success. Whether in design or in poetry, he does, in very fact, work as a man already practised in one art, beginning anew in another; expressing himself with virgin freshness of mind in each, and in each realizing, by turns, the idea flung out of that prodigal cornucopia of thought and image, *Pippa Passes:* 'If there should arise a new painter, will it not be in some such way by a poet, now, or a musician (spirits who have conceived and perfected an ideal through some other channel), transferring it to this, and escaping our conventional roads by pure ignorance of them?' Even Malkin, with real sense, observes of the poet in general, – his mind 'is too often at leisure for the mechanical prettinesses of cadence and epithet, when it ought to be engrossed by higher thoughts. Words and numbers present themselves unbidden when the soul is inspired by sentiment, elevated by enthusiasm, or ravished by devotion.' Yes! ravished by devotion. For in these songs of Blake's occurs devotional poetry, which is real poetry too – a very exceptional thing. Witness that simple and beautiful poem entitled *The Divine Image*, or that *On Another's Sorrow*. The *Songs of Innocence* are in truth animated by an uniform sentiment of deep piety, of reverent feeling, and may be said, in their pervading influence, to be one devout aspiration throughout. The *Songs of Experience* consist rather of earnest, impassioned arguments; in this differing from the simple *affirmations* of the earlier *Songs of Innocence*, – arguments on the loftiest themes of existence.

After the *Songs of Experience*, Blake never again sang to like angelic tunes; nor even with the same approach to technical accuracy. His poetry was the blossom of youth and early manhood. Neither in design did he improve on the tender grace of some of these illustrations; irregularities became as conspicuous in it, as in his verse; though in age he attained to nobler heights of sublimity, as the *Inventions to Job* will exemplify.

Let us again take a glance at what was going on contemporaneously in English literature during the years 1789–94. In novels, these were the days of activity of the famous Minerva Press, with Perdita Robinson and melancholy Charlotte Smith as leaders. Truer coin was circulated by Godwin (*St Leon* appeared in 1799), by *Zeluco* Moore, by Mrs Radcliffe (*The Mysteries of Udolpho*, in 1794), by Monk Lewis, the sisters Lee, Mrs Inchbald, and Mrs Opie. In verse, it was the hour of the sentimental Della Cruscans, Madame Piozzi, Mrs Robinson again, 'Mr Merry,' and others. On these poor butterflies, Gifford, in this very year, laid his coarse, heavy hand; himself as empty a versifier, if smarter. Glittering Darwin, whose *Loves of the Plants* delighted the reading world in 1789, smooth Hayley, Anna Seward, 'Swan of Lichfield,' were popular poets. In satire, Dr Wolcott was punctually receiving from the booksellers his unconscionably long annuity of two hundred and fifty pounds, for copious Peter Pindarisms, fugitive odes, and epistles. In the region of enduring literature, Cowper had closed his contributions to poetry by the translation of Homer. The third reprint of Burns's *Poems*, with *Tam O'Shanter* for one addition, had appeared at Edinburgh in 1793; and the poet himself took leave of this rude world in 1796. Crabbe had achieved his first success. Among rising juniors was Rogers, who had made his *début* in 1786, the same year as Burns; and in 1792, the *Pleasures of Memory* established a lasting reputation for its author, – a thing it would hardly do now. A little later (1799), stripling Campbell's *Pleasures of Hope* will leap through four editions in a year. Bloomfield is in 1793–4 jotting down *The Farmer's Boy;* Wordsworth shaping the first example, but a diffuse one, of that new kind of poetry which was hereafter to bring refreshment and happiness to many hearts, – *Guilt and Sorrow;* still one of his least read poems.

In the newly-opened fruitful domain of poetic antiquarianism, – the eighteenth century's best poetic bequest, – Bishop Percy had found a zealous follower in choleric, trenchant Joseph Ritson, who in 1791 published his *Pieces of Ancient Popular Poetry*, and in 1795 *Robin Hood*. In 1790 had appeared Ellis's *Specimens of the Early English Poets*.

Surely there was room for Blake's pure notes of song – still, in 1860, fresh as when first uttered – to have been heard. But it was fated otherwise. Half a century later, they attracted the attention of a sympathiser with all mystics and spiritualists, Dr Wilkinson, the editor of Swedenborg. Under his auspices, the *Songs of Innocence and Experience* were reprinted, or rather *first* printed, as a thin octavo, without illustrations, by Pickering, in Chancery Lane, and W. Newberry, in Chenies Street, both extinct publishers now. A very limited impression was taken off, and the reprint soon became almost as scarce as the costly and beautiful original. During the last few years, I have observed only three copies turn up – two at the fancy prices of £1 8s. and £1 7s. 6d.; the other, secured by myself at a more moderate outlay. Consisting, as they did, of loose sheets, the *Songs* have seldom been bound up twice alike, and are generally even numbered wrong. Dr Wilkinson printed them in an order of his own, and too often with words of his own; alterations which were by no means improvements always.

A few words of bibliographic detail may perhaps be permitted for the collector's sake, considering the extreme beauty, the singularity, and rarity of the original book.

The illustrated *Songs of Innocence and Experience* was issued to Blake's public, to his own friends that is, at the modest price of thirty shillings and two guineas. Its selling price *now*, when perfect, varies from ten and twelve guineas upwards. From the circumstance of its having lain on hand in sheets, and from some purchasers having preferred to buy or bind only select portions, the series often occurs short of many plates – generally wants one or two. The right number is fifty-four engraved pages.

Later in Blake's life, – for the sheets always remained in stock, – five guineas were given him, and in some cases, when intended as a delicate means of helping the artist, larger sums. Flaxman recommended more than one friend to take copies, a Mr Thomas among them, who, wishing to give the artist a present, made the price ten guineas. For such a sum Blake could hardly do enough, finishing the plates like miniatures. In the last years of his life, Sir Thomas Lawrence, Sir Francis Chantrey, and others, paid as much as twelve and twenty guineas; Blake conscientiously working up the colour and finish, and perhaps over-labouring them, in return; printing off only on one side of the leaf, and expanding the book by help of margin into a handsome quarto. If without a sixpence in his pocket, he was always too justly proud to confess it: so that, whoever desired to give Blake money, had to do it indirectly, to avoid offence, by purchasing copies of his works; which, too, might have hurt his pride, had he suspected the secret motive, though causelessly; for he really gave, as he well knew, far more than an intrinsic equivalent.

The early, low-priced copies, – Flaxman's for instance, – though slighter in colour, possess a delicacy of feeling, a freshness of execution, often lost in the richer, more laboured examples, especially in those finished after the artist's death, by his widow. One of the latter I have noticed, very full and heavy in colour, the tints laid on with a strong and indiscriminating touch.

Other considerable varieties of detail in the final touches by hand exist. There are copies in which certain minutiæ are finished with unusual care and feeling. The prevailing ground-colour of the writing and illustrations also varies. Sometimes it is yellow, sometimes blue, and so on. In one copy the *writing* throughout is yellow, not a happy effect. Occasionally the colour is carried further down the page than the ruled space; a stream say, as in *The Lamb*, is introduced. Of course, therefore, the degrees of merit vary greatly between one copy and another, both as a whole and in the parts. A few were issued plain, in black and white, or blue and white, which are more legible than the polychrome examples. In these latter, the red or yellow lettering being sometimes unrelieved by a white ground, we have, instead of contrasted hue, gradations of it, as in a picture.

Out of the destruction that has engulfed so large a portion of Blake's copper-plates, partly owing to the poverty which compelled him often to obliterate his own work, that the same metal might serve again, partly to the neglect, and worse than neglect, of some of those into whose hands they fell, we have happily ten plates, taking of sixteen impressions (a few having been engraved on both sides), – of the *Songs of Innocence and Experience*. The gentleman from whom they were obtained had once the entire series in his possession, but all save these ten were stolen by an ungrateful black he had befriended, who sold them to a smith as old metal.

FOURTEEN

Productive Years 1794–95
[ÆT. 37–38]

To the *Songs of Experience* succeeded from Lambeth the same year (1794) volumes of mystic verse and design, in the track of the *Visions of the Daughters of Albion*, and the *America*. One of them is a sequel to the *America*, and generally occurs bound up with it, sometimes coloured, sometimes plain. It is entitled *Europe, a Prophecy: Lambeth, printed by William Blake*, 1794; and consists of seventeen quarto pages, with designs of a larger size than those of *America*, occupying the whole page often. The frontispiece represents the 'Ancient of Days,' as shadowed forth in Proverbs viii. 27: 'when he set a compass upon the face of the earth;' and again, as described in *Paradise Lost*, Book vii. line 236: a grand figure, in an orb of light surrounded by dark clouds, is stooping down, with an enormous pair of compasses, to describe the world's destined 'orb,' Blake adopting with child-like fidelity, but in a truly sublime spirit, the image of the Hebrew and English poets. This composition was an especial favourite with its designer. When colouring it by hand, he 'always bestowed more time,' says Smith, 'and enjoyed greater pleasure in the task, than from anything else he produced.' The process of colouring his designs was never to him, however, a mechanical or irksome one. Very different feelings were his from those of a mere copyist. Throughout life, whenever

137

for his few patrons filling in the colour to his engraved books, he lived anew the first fresh, happy experiences of conception, as in the high hour of inspiration.

Smith tells us that Blake 'was inspired with the splendid grandeur of this figure, *The Ancient of Days*, by the vision which he declared hovered over his head at the top of his staircase' in No. 13, Hercules Buildings, and that 'he has been frequently heard to say that it made a more powerful impression upon his mind than all he had ever been visited by.' On that same staircase it was Blake, for the only time in his life, *saw a ghost*. When talking on the subject of ghosts, he was wont to say they did not appear much to imaginative men, but only to common minds, who did not see the finer spirits. A ghost was a thing seen by the gross bodily eye, a vision, by the mental. 'Did you ever see a ghost?' asked a friend. 'Never but once,' was the reply. And it befell thus. Standing one evening at his garden-door in Lambeth, and chancing to look up, he saw a horrible grim figure, 'scaly, speckled, very awful,' stalking downstairs towards him. More frightened than ever before or after he took to his heels, and ran out of the house.

It is hard to describe poems wherein the *dramatis personæ* are giant shadows, gloomy phantoms; the *scene*, the realms of space; the *time*, of such corresponding vastness, that eighteen hundred years pass as a dream:

Enitharmon slept.

* * *

She slept in middle of her nightly song,
Eighteen hundred years.

More apart from humanity even than the *America*, we are baffled in the endeavour to trace out any distinct subject, any

138

plan or purpose, in the *Europe*, or to determine whether it mainly relate to the past, present, or to come. And yet, though the natural impulse is to close such a book in despair, we can testify to the reader, that were it his lot, as it has been ours, to read and re-read many times this and other of the 'prophetic' volumes, he would do so with a deepening conviction that their incoherence has a grandeur about it, as that of a man whose eyes are fixed on strange and awful sights, invisible to bystanders. To use an expression of Blake's own, on a subsequent occasion, it is as if the 'Visions were angry,' and hurried in stormy disorder before his rapt gaze, no longer to bless and teach, but to bewilder and confound.

The *Preludium* will enable the reader to form some idea of the poem. There occurs an allusion to the Courts of Law at Westminster, which is a striking instance of that occasional mingling of the actual with the purely symbolic, before spoken of. Perhaps the broidery of spider's web which so felicitously embellishes the page, was meant to bear a typical reference to the same.

The 'nameless shadowy female,' with whose lamentation the poem opens, personifies Europe as it would seem; her head (the mountains) turbaned with clouds, and round her limbs, the 'sheety waters' wrapped; whilst Enitharmon symbolizes great mother Nature:

Preludium.

The nameless shadowy female rose from out
The breast of Orc,
Her snaky hair brandishing in the winds of Enitharmon:
And thus her voice arose:

'O mother Enitharmon, wilt thou bring forth other sons?
To cause my name to vanish, that my place may not be found?
For I am faint with travel!
Like the dark cloud disburdened in the day of dismal thunder.

'My roots are brandish'd in the heavens; my fruits in earth beneath,
Surge, foam, and labour into life! – first born, and first consum'd,
Consumed and consuming!
Then why shouldst thou, accursed mother! bring me into life?

'I weep! – my turban of thick clouds around my lab'ring head;
And fold the sheety waters as a mantle round my limbs.
Yet the red sun and moon
And all the overflowing stars rain down prolific pains.

'Unwilling I look up to heaven: unwilling count the stars,
Sitting in fathomless abyss of my immortal shrine.
I seize their burning power,
And bring forth howling terrors and devouring fiery kings!

'Devouring and devoured, roaming on dark and desolate
    mountains,
In forests of eternal death, shrieking in hollow trees,
Ah! mother Enitharmon!
Stamp not with solid form this vig'rous progeny of fire!

'I bring forth from my teeming bosom, myriads of flames,
And thou dost stamp them with a signet. Then they roam
    abroad,
And leave me, void as death.
Ah! I am drown'd in shady woe, and visionary joy.

'And who shall bind the infinite with an eternal band?
To compass it with swaddling bands? And who shall cherish it
With milk and honey?
I see it smile, and I roll inward, and my voice is past.'

She ceas'd; and rolled her shady clouds
Into the secret place.

So rapid was the production of this class of Blake's writings, that notwithstanding their rich and elaborate decoration, and the tedious process by which the whole had to be, with his own hand, engraved and afterwards coloured, the same year witnessed the completion of another, and the succeeding year, of two more 'prophetic books.' *The Book of Urizen* (1794), was the title of the next. The same may be said of it as of its predecessors. Like them, the poem is shapeless, unfathomable; but in the heaping up of gloomy and terrible images, the *America* and *Europe* are even exceeded. It throws however, some vivid though confused glimpses of light upon the speculative conceptions of Blake himself – conceptions not essentially undevout, but much the reverse, in their own audacious, iconoclastic way.

The following striking passage, which describes the appearing of the first woman, will serve as an example of *Urizen*:

> At length, in tears and cries, embodied
> A female form trembling and pale
> Waves before his deathly face.
>
> All Eternity shudder'd at sight
> Of the first female form, now separate,
> Pale as a cloud of snow,
> Waving before the face of Los!
>
> Wonder, awe, fear, astonishment,
> Petrify the eternal myriads
> At the first female form now separate.
> They call'd her Pity, and fled!
>
> 'Spread a tent with strong curtains around them:
> Let cords and stakes bind in the Void,
> That Eternals may no more behold them!'
>
> They began to weave curtains of darkness.
> They erected large pillars round the void;

With golden hooks fastened in the pillars;
With infinite labour, the Eternals
A woof wove, and called it Science.

The design, like the text, is characterized by a monotony of horror. Every page may be said as a furnace mouth to

'Cast forth redounding smoke and ruddy flame,'

in the midst of which are figures howling, weeping, writhing, or chained to rocks, or hurled headlong into the abyss. There are grand things among them. Of the more striking, we recal a figure that stoops over and seems breathing upon a globe enveloped in flames, the lines of fire flowing into those of his drapery and hair; an old, amphibious-looking giant, with rueful visage, letting himself sink slowly through the waters like a frog; a skeleton coiled round, resembling a fossil giant imbedded in the rock, &c. The colouring is rich, – a little overcharged perhaps in the copy I have seen, – and gold-leaf has been freely used, to heighten the effect.

Still another volume bears date 1794, – a small quarto, consisting of twenty-three engraved and coloured designs, without letter-press, explanation, or key of any kind. The designs are of various size, all fine in colour, all extraordinary, some beautiful, others monstrous, abounding in forced attitudes, and suspicious anatomy. The frontispiece, adopted from *Urizen*, is inscribed *Lambeth, printed by Will Blake*, 1794, and has the figure of an aged man, naked, with white beard sweeping the ground, and extended arms, each hand resting on a pile of books, and each holding a pen, wherewith he writes. The volume seems to be a carefully finished selection of favourite compositions from his portfolios and engraved books. Four are recognisable as the principal designs of the *Book of Thel*, modified in outline, and in colour richer and deeper. One occurs in the *Visions of the Daughters of Albion*. Another will hereafter re-appear in the illustrations to *The Grave*: 'The spirit of the strong wicked man going forth.'

The Song of Los (1795), is in metrical prose, and is divided into two portions, one headed *Africa*, the other *Asia*. In it, we again, as in the *America*, seem to catch a thread of connected meaning. It purports to show the rise and influence of different religions and philosophies upon mankind; but, according to Blake's wont, both action and dialogue are carried on, not by human agents, but by shadowy immortals, Orc, Sotha, Palamabron, Rintrah, Los, and many more:

> Then Rintrah gave abstract philosophy to Brama in the East;
> (Night spoke to the cloud –
> 'So these human-formed spirits in smiling hypocrisy war
> Against one another: so let them war on!
> Slaves to the eternal elements!')

Next, Palamabron gave an 'abstract law' to Pythagoras; then also to Socrates and Plato:

> Times roll'd on o'er all the sons of men,

till Christianity dawns. Monasticism is spoken of:

> *   *   *   The healthy built,
> Secluded places: *   *   *

Afterwards as becoming a fruitful source of spiritual corruption:

> Then were the churches, hospitals, castles, palaces,
> Like nets and gins and traps to catch the joys of eternity;
> And all the rest a desert,
> Till like a dream, eternity was obliterated and erased.

Prior to this, however –

> Antamon call'd up Leutha from her valleys of delight,
> And to Mahomet a loose Bible gave.
> But in the North to Odin, Sotha gave a code of war.

A gradual debasement of the human race goes on –

> Till a philosophy of five senses was complete!
> Urizen wept, and gave it into the hands of Newton and Locke.
>
> Clouds roll heavy upon the Alps round Rousseau and Voltaire.
> And on the mountains of Lebanon round the deceas'd gods of
>   Asia,
> And on the deserts of Africa round the Fallen Angels.
> The Guardian Prince of Albion burns in his nightly tent!

Under the symbol of the kings of Asia, the *Song* describes the misery of the old philosophies and despotisms; their bitter lament and prayer that by pestilence and fire the race may be saved; 'that a remnant may learn to obey':

> The Kings of Asia heard
> The howl rise up from Europe!
> And each ran out from his web,
> From his ancient woven den:
> For the darkness of Asia was startled
> At the thick-flaming, thought-creating fires of Orc.
> And the Kings of Asia stood
> And cried in bitterness of soul:
> 'Shall not the King call for Famine from the heath?
> Nor the Priest for Pestilence from the fen?
> To restrain! to dismay! to thin
> The inhabitants of mountain and plain!
> In the day of full-feeding prosperity,
> And the night of delicious songs?'

Urizen heard their cry:

> And stretched his clouds over Jerusalem:
> For Adam, a mouldering skeleton,
> Lay bleached on the garden of Eden;
> And Noah, as white as snow,
> On the mountains of Ararat.

He thunders desolately from the heavens; Orc rises 'like a pillar of fire above the Alps,' the earth shrinks, the resurrection of dry bones is described, and the poem concludes.

Orc, that spirit of most volcanic nature whom we hear of so frequently throughout the 'Prophetic Books,' seems (for a too positive assertion were unwise) to represent the wild energies of nature, and more especially of man: the 'natural man' in a state of permanent revolt and protest against the tyranny of Urizen, Theotormon, &c.

Of the illustrations, two are separate pictures occupying the full page; the rest surround and blend with the text in the usual manner; and if they have not all the beauty, they share a full measure of the spirit and force of Blake. The colour is laid on with an *impasto* which gives an opaque and heavy look to some of them, and the medium being oil, the surface and tints have suffered. Here as elsewhere, the designs seldom directly embody the subjects of the poem, but are independent though kindred conceptions – the right method perhaps.

As if the artist himself were at length beginning to grow weary, *The Book of Ahania* (1795), last of this series, is quite unadorned, except by two vignettes, one on the title, the other on the concluding page. The text is neatly engraved in plain black and white, without border or decoration of any kind. There are lines and passages of much force and beauty, but they emerge from surrounding obscurity like lightning out of a cloud:

'And ere a man hath power to say – Behold!
The jaws of darkness do devour it up.'

The first half of the poem is occupied with the dire warfare between Urizen and his rebellious son, Fuzon. Their weapons are thus described:

The broad disk of Urizen upheaved,
Across the void many a mile.
It was forged in mills where the winter
Beats incessant: ten winters the disk
Unremitting endured the cold hammer.

But it proves ineffectual against Fuzon's fiery beam:

* * * Laughing, it tore through
That beaten mass; keeping its direction,
The cold loins of Urizen dividing.

Wounded and enraged, Urizen prepares a bow formed of the ribs of a huge serpent – 'a circle of darkness' – and strung with its sinews, by which Fuzon is smitten down into seeming death. In the midst of the conflict, Ahania, who is called 'the parted soul of Urizen,' is cast forth:

She fell down, a faint shadow wand'ring
In chaos and circling dark Urizen,
As the moon anguish'd circles the earth;
Hopeless! abhorr'd! a death-shadow
Unseen, unbodied, unknown!
The mother of Pestilence!

Her lamentation, from which we draw our final extract, fills the concluding portion of the poem:

Ah, Urizen! Love!
Flower of morning! I weep on the verge

146

Of non-entity: how wide the abyss
Between Ahania and thee!

* * *

I cannot touch his hand,
Nor weep on his knees, nor hear
His voice and bow; nor see his eyes
And joy; nor hear his footsteps and
My heart leap at the lovely sound!
I cannot kiss the place
Whereon his bright feet have trod.
But I wander on the rocks
With hard necessity.

While intent on the composition and execution of these mystic books, Blake did not neglect the humble task-work which secured him a modest independence. He was at this very time busy on certain plates for a book of travels, Captain J. G. Stedman's *Narrative of a Five Years' Expedition against the Revolted Negroes of Surinam*. This work, 'illustrated with eighty elegant engravings from drawings made by the author,' was published by Johnson the following year (1796). Of these 'elegant engravings' Blake executed fourteen; Holloway and Bartolozzi were among those employed for the remainder. Negroes, monkeys, 'Limes, Capsicums, Mummy-apples,' and other natural productions of the country, were the chief subjects which fell to Blake's share.

Also among the fruit of this period should be particularized two prints in which the figures are on a larger scale than in any other engravings by Blake. They are both from his own designs. Under the first is inscribed: *Ezekiel: 'Take away from thee the desire of thine eyes.'* Ezek. xxiv. 17. *Painted and Engraved by W. Blake. Oct.* 27, 1794. 13, *Hercules Buildings*. Ezekiel kneels with arms crossed and eyes uplifted in stern and tearless grief, according to God's command: beside him is one of those solemn bowed figures, with hidden face, and hair sweeping the ground, Blake often, and with such powerful effect, introduces: and on a couch in the background lies the shrouded corpse of Ezekiel's wife.

The subject of the other, which corresponds in size and style, is from the Book of Job: 'What is man, that thou shouldst try him every moment?' It possesses a peculiar interest as being the first embodiment of Blake's ideas upon a theme, thirty years later, to be developed in that series of designs, – the *Inventions to the Book of Job*; which, taken as a grand harmonious whole, is an instance of rare individual genius, of the highest art with whatever compared, that certainly constitutes his masterpiece. The figure of Job himself, in the early design, is the same as that in the *Inventions*. But the wife is a totally different conception, being of a hard and masculine type.

FIFTEEN

At Work for the Publishers 1795–99
[ÆT. 38–42]

In 1795–6, Miller, the publisher, of Old Bond Street, employed Blake to illustrate a new edition in quarto, of a translation of Bürger's *Lenore*, by one Mr J. T. Stanley, F.R.S. The first edition (1786), had preceded by ten years Sir Walter Scott's translation, which came out at the same time as Stanley's new edition. The amateur version amounts to a paraphrase, not to say a new poem; the original being 'altered and added to,' to square it with 'the cause of religion and morality.' Blake's illustrations are engraved by a man named Perry, and are three in number. One is a frontispiece, – Lenore clasping her ghostly bridegroom on their earth-scorning charger; groups of imps and spectres from hell hovering above and dancing below; a composition full of grace in the principal figures, wild horror and *diablerie* in the accessories. Another – a vignette – is an idealized procession of Prussian soldiers, escorted by their friends; Lenore and her mother vainly gazing into the crowd in quest of their missing William. It is a charmingly composed group, characterized by more than Stothard's grace and statuesque beauty. The third illustration, also a vignette, is the awakening of Lenore from her terrible dream, William rushing into her arms in the presence of the old St Anna-like mother, – for such is the turn the catastrophe takes under Mr Stanley's hands. This again is a composition of much daring and grace; its principal female figure, one of those spiritual, soul-startled forms Blake alone of men could draw. To Stanley's translation the publisher added the original German poem, with two engravings after Chodowiecki, 'the German Hogarth,' as he has been called, which, though clever, look, as here executed, prosaic compared with Blake.

Edwards, of New Bond Street, at that day a leading bookseller, engaged Blake, in 1796, to illustrate an expensive edition, emulating Boydell's Shakspere and Milton, of Young's *Night Thoughts*. The *Night Thoughts* was then, as it had been for more than half a century, a living classic, which rival booksellers delighted to re-publish. Edwards paid his designer and engraver 'a despicably low sum,' says Smith, which means, I believe, a guinea a plate. And yet, the prefatory *Advertisement*, dated December 22, 1796, tells us that the enterprise had been undertaken by the publisher 'not as a speculation of advantage, but as an indulgence of inclination, in which fondness and partiality would not permit him to be curiously accurate in adjusting the estimate of profit and loss' undertaken also from the wish 'to make the arts in their most honourable agency subservient to the purposes of religion.' In the same preface, written with Johnsonian swing, by Fuseli probably – the usual literary help of fine-art publishers in those days – and who I suspect had something to do with Edwards' choice of artist, 'the merit of Mr Blake' is spoken of in terms which show it to have been not wholly ignored then: 'to the eyes of the discerning it need not be pointed out; and while a taste for the arts of design shall continue to exist, the original conception, and the bold and masterly execution of this artist cannot be unnoticed or unadmired.' The edition, which was to have been issued in parts, never got beyond the first; public encouragement proving inadequate. This part extends to ninety-five images, – to the end of *Night the Fourth*, – and includes forty-three designs. It appeared in the autumn of 1797.

These forty-three plates occupied Blake a year. A complete set of drawings for them had been made, which were afterwards sold by Edwards for twenty guineas, and passed ultimately, I am told, into one of the royal collections. At this very time was preparing and in 1802 was published by Vernor and Hood, and the trade, an octavo edition of *Young*, illustrated by Stothard, which did prove successful.

Edwards' edition was as much a book of design as of type, splendidly printed in folio on thick paper, with an ample margin to each page. Around every alternate leaf Blake engraved wild, allegorical figures; designs little adapted to the apprehension of his public. He so engraved them as to make a picture of the whole page, as in his own illustrated poems; but not with an equally felicitous result, when combined with formal print. To each of the four *Nights* was prefixed an introductory design or title. The illustrations have one very acceptable aid, and that is, a written 'explanation of the engravings' at the end; drawn up or put into shape by another hand than Blake's, – the same possibly which had penned the *Advertisement*. It would be well if all his designs had this help. For at once literal in his translation of word into line, daring and unhacknied in his manner of indicating his pregnant allegories, Blake's conceptions do not always explain themselves at a glance, and without their meaning, half their beauty too must needs be lost.

Looked at merely as marginal book illustrations, the engravings are *not* strikingly successful. The space to be filled in these folio pages is of itself too large, and the size of the outlines is æsthetically anything but a gain. For such meanings as Blake's, not helped by the thousand charms of the painter's language, can be advantageously compressed into small space. The oft-repeated, colossal limbs of Death and Time sprawling across the page, – figures too large for the margin of the book, and necessarily always alike, – become somewhat uninteresting. How little Blake was adapted to ingratiate himself with the public, the whole series exemplifies. The general spectator will find these designs, all harping on life, death, and immortality, far from attractive; austere themes, austerely treated, if also sweetly and grandly; without even the relief of so much admixture of worldly topic and image as is introduced in the text of the epigrammatic poet. There is monotony of subject, of treatment, of handling the graver even. Blake's art, never imitative, but the expression of *ideas* pure and simple, ideas similar to those literature is commonly employed to convey, yet transcending words, is at the very opposite pole to that of the great mass of modern painters. There is little or no individuality in his faces, if more in his forms. Typical forms and faces, abstract impersonations, are used to express his meaning. Everything, – figures, landscape, costume, accessory, – is reduced to its elemental shape, its simplest guise – 'bare earth, bare sky, and ocean bare.'

The absence of colour, the use of which Blake so well understood, to relieve his simple design and heighten its significance, is a grave loss. I have seen one copy of the *Young*, originally coloured for Mr Butts, now in the hands of Mr Monckton Milnes, much improved by the addition; forming a book of great beauty.

Many of these designs, taken by themselves, are however surpassingly imaginative and noble. As the first – 'Death, in the character of an old man, having swept away with one hand part of a family, is presenting with the other their spirits to immortality;' in which, as often happens with Blake, separate parts are even more beautiful compositions than the whole. And again, the literal translation into outline of a passage few other artists would have selected, to render closely:

> 'What though my soul fantastic measures trod
> O'er fairy fields; or mourn'd along the gloom
> Of pathless woods; or down the craggy steep
> Hurl'd headlong; swam with pain the mantled pool
> Or scaled the cliff, or danced on hollow winds,
> With antic shapes, wild natives of the brain.'

Again, the illustration to the line

> ''Tis greatly wise to talk with our past hours,'

in which 'the hours are drawn as aërial and shadowy beings some of whom are bringing their scrolls to the inquirer, while others are carrying their records to heaven.' Again, 'the author, encircled by thorns emblematical of grief, laments the loss of his friend to the midnight hours,' here also represented as aërial shadowy beings. A grand embodiment is that of the *Vale of Death* where 'the power of darkness broods over his victims as they are borne down to the grave by the torrent of a sinful life;' the life stream showing imploring, upturned faces rising to the surface, of infancy, youth, age; while the pure, lovely figure of Narcissa wanders in the shade beside.

Of a higher order still, are some illustrations in which the designer chooses themes of his own, parallel to, or even independent of the text, not mere translations of it. As to the line

> 'Its favours here are trials not rewards,'

where in exemplification of the 'frailty of the blessings of this life, the happiness of a little family is suddenly destroyed by the accident of the husband's death from the bite of a serpent.' The father is writhing in the serpent's sudden coil, while beside him his beautiful wife, as yet unconscious of his fate, is bending over, and holding back her infant, who stretches out eager little hands to grasp a bird on the wing. A truly pregnant allegory, nobly designed, and of Raffaelesque grace. On so slight a hint as the line

'Oft burst my song beyond the bounds of life,'

a lovely and spiritual 'figure holding a lyre, and springing into the air, but confined by a chain to the earth,' typifies 'the struggling of the soul for immortality.' The line

'We censure nature for a span too short,'

waywardly suggests a naïve but fine composition of 'a man measuring an infant with his span, in allusion to the shortness of life.' To the words

'Know like the Median, fate is in thy walls,'

we have of course the story of Belshazzar. Illustrative of the axiom 'teaching we learn,' is introduced an unaffected and beautiful group, an aged father instructing his children.

Some of the designs trench on those afterwards more matured in Blair's *Grave:* as 'Angels attending the death-bed of the righteous,' and 'Angels conveying the spirit of the good man to heaven,' both of aërial tenderness and grace. 'A skeleton discovering the first symptoms of re-animation on the sounding of the archangel's trump,' is precisely the same composition as one introduced in *The Grave*, except that in the earlier design the foreshortened figure of the archangel is different and finer.

Throughout, the familiar abstractions Death and Time are originally conceived, as they had need be, recurring so frequently. They are personified by grand, colossal figures. Instead of the hacknied convention of a skeleton, Death appears as a solemn, draped, visionary figure. So, too, the conventional wings of angel and spirit are dispensed with. The literalness with which the poet's metaphors are occasionally embodied, is a startling and not always felicitous invasion of the province of words. As when Death summons the living 'from sleep to his kingdom the grave,' with a handbell; or 'plucks the sun from his sphere.' Or again, when a personification of the Sun hides his face at the crucifixion; or another of Thunder, directs the poet to admiration of God; all which difficulties are fearlessly handled. Any less daring man would have fared worse. In Blake's conceptions it is hit or miss, and the miss is a wide one: witness the 'Resurrection of our Saviour,' and 'Our Saviour in the furnace of affliction;' large, soulless figures, quite destitute of Blake's genius.

Excepting one or two such as I have last named, familiarity does much to help the influence of these, as of all Blake's designs; to deepen the significance of our artist's high spiritual commentary on the poet; to modify the monotony of the appeal. The first unpleasant effect wears off, of the conventional mannikins which here represent humanity, wherewith gigantic Time and Death disport on the page. Art hath her tropes as well as poetry.

Blake's *Young* compares advantageously, I may add, with Stothard's, whose designs, with some few exceptions, display a very awkward attempt to reconcile the insignia of the matter-of-fact world with those of the spiritual. Better Blake's nude figures (in which great sacrifices are made to preserve decorum), better his favourite, simple draperies of close-fitting garments, and his typical impersonation of 'the author,' than Stothard's clerical gentleman, in full canonicals, looking, with round-eyed wonder, at the unusual phenomenon of winged angels fluttering above.

Returning to Blake's career, I find him, in 1799, exhibiting a picture at the Academy, *The Last Supper*. 'Verily I say unto you

155

that one of you shall betray me.' Among the engravings of the same year are some slight ones after the designs of Flaxman for a projected colossal statue of the allegoric sort for Greenwich Hill, to commemorate Great Britain's naval triumphs. They illustrate the sculptor's *Letter* or quarto pamphlet, addressed to the committee which had started the scheme of such a monument. It is a curious pamphlet to look at now. Flaxman's design, rigidly classical of course, is not without recommendations, on paper. There is an idea in it, a freshness, purity, grand simplicity we vainly look for in the Argand-lamp style of the Trafalgar Square column, or in any other monument erected of late by the English, so unhappy in their public works.

SIXTEEN

A New Life 1799–1800
[ÆT. 42–43]

About this time (1800) the ever-friendly Flaxman gave Blake an introduction which had important consequences; involving a sudden change of residence and mode of life. This was in recommending him to Hayley, 'poet,' country gentleman, friend and future biographer of Cowper; in which last capacity the world alone remembers him. *Then*, though few went to see his plays, or read his laboured *Life of Milton*, he retained a traditional reputation on the strength of almost his first poem, – still his *magnum opus*, after nearly twenty years had passed since its appearance, – the *Triumphs of Temper*. He held, in fact, an honoured place in contemporary literature: his society eagerly sought and obtained, by lovers of letters; to mere ordinary squires and neighbours sparingly accorded; to the majority point-blank refused. His name continued to be held in esteem among a slow-going portion of the world, long after his literary ware had ceased to be marketable. People of distinction and 'position in society,' princesses of the blood, and others, when visiting Bognor, would, even many years later, go out of their way to see him, as if he had been a Wordsworth.

Between Flaxman and the Hermit of Eartham, as the book-loving squire delighted to subscribe himself, friendly relations had, for some twenty years, subsisted. During three of these,

Hayley's acknowledged son (he had no legitimate children), Thomas Alphonso, had been an articled pupil of the sculptor's. Early in 1798, beginnings of curvature of the spine had necessitated a return from Flaxman's roof into Sussex. There, after two years' more suffering, he died of the accumulated maladies engendered in a weakly constitution by sedentary habits; a victim of *forcing*, I suspect.

In 1799, the author of the *Triumphs of Temper* was seeing through the press one of his long *Poetical Essays*, as smooth and tedious as the rest, on *Sculpture*; in the form of 'Epistles to Flaxman.' It was published in 1800, with three trivial illustrations. Two of these are engraved by Blake: *The Death of Demosthenes*, after a bald outline by Hayley junior, whom the father easily persuaded himself into believing, as well as styling, his 'youthful Phidias;' and a portrait of the 'young sculptor,' after a medallion by his master, Flaxman, the drawing of which was furnished Blake by Howard; the combined result being indifferent.

On April 25th, 1800, the long intermittent tragedy of Cowper's life came to an end, amid dark and heavy clouds: the last years of suffering having been smoothed by a pension obtained through Hayley's intercession. A week later died Hayley's hapless son. And our poor bard had to solace himself in his own way, by inditing sonnets to his child's memory, 'on his pillow,' at four o'clock in the morning; a daily sonnet or two soon swelling into MS. volumes.

As further consolation, Hayley resolved on ample memoirs of son and friend. To the biography of Cowper he was ultimately urged by Lady Hesketh herself. During one of his frequent flying visits to town, and his friends the Meyers, at Kew, in June, 1800, and while he, nothing loth, was being coaxed to the task of writing Cowper's life, the idea was mooted of helping a deserving artist, by the employment of Blake to engrave the illustrations of the projected quarto. And in the same breath followed the proposal for the artist to come and live at Felpham, that, during the book's progress, he might be near 'that highly respected hermit,' as Smith styles the squire; a generous, if hot-headed hermit, who thought to push Blake's fortunes by introducing him to his numerous well-connected friends. All Hayley's projects were hurried into execution in the very hey-day of conception, or as speedily abandoned. Blake at once fell in with this scheme, encouraged perhaps by the prospect of a patron. And his friend, Mr Butts, rejoiced aloud, deeming his *protégé's* fortune made.

A copy of the *Triumphs of Temper* (tenth edition), illustrated by Stothard, which had belonged to the poet's son, and was now given to Blake, contains evidence, – in verse of course, – of Hayley's esteem for him. Perhaps the fact can palliate our insertion of rhymes so guiltless of sense otherwise. It is Smith who is answerable for having preserved them:

> Accept, my gentle visionary Blake,
>   Whose thoughts are fanciful and kindly mild;
> Accept, and fondly keep for friendship's sake,
>   This favoured vision, my poetic child!
>
> Rich in more grace than fancy ever won,
>   To thy most tender mind this book will be,
> For it belonged to my departed son;
>   So from an angel it descends to thee.

W. H. July, 1800.

After seven productive years in Lambeth, the modest house in Hercules Buildings was exchanged for a cottage by the sea, where Blake spent four years; the only portion of his life passed in the country. He was now in his forty-third year, Hayley in his fifty-seventh. In August, Blake went down to Felpham to look at his future home, and secure a house; which he did at an annual rent of twenty pounds: not being provided with one rent-free by Hayley, as some supposed, – a kind of patronage which would have ill suited the artist's independent spirit. The poet was not even his landlord, owning, in fact, no property in the village beyond what he had bought to build his house on. Blake's cottage belonged to one Archdeacon Webber, Vicar of Boxgrove.

Hayley, whose forte was not economy nor prudent conduct of any kind, had, by ill-judged generosities and lavish expenditure, seriously incumbered the handsome estate inherited from his father. Felpham, his present retreat, lay some six miles off the patrimonial 'paradise,' as he, for once, not hyperbolically styled it, – romantic Eartham, a peaceful, sequestered spot among the wooded hills stretching southward from the Sussex Downs; a hamlet made up of some dozen widely-scattered cottages, a farm-house or two, a primitive little antique church, and the comfortable modern 'great house,' lying high, in the centre of lovely sheltered gardens and grounds, commanding wide, varied views of purple vale and gleaming sea. At Felpham, during the latter years of his son's life, he had built a marine cottage, planned to his own fancy, whither to retire and retrench, while he let his place at Eartham. It was a cottage with an embattled turret; with a library fitted up with busts and pictures; 'a covered way for equestrian exercise,' and a well laid-out garden; all as a first step in the new plans of economy. His son passed the painful close of his ill-starred existence in it; and here Hayley himself had now definitely taken up his abode. He continued there till his death in 1820; long before which he had sold Eartham to Huskisson, the statesman; whose widow inhabited it until five years ago.

On the eve of removing from Lambeth, in the middle of September, was written the following characteristic letter from Mrs Blake to Mrs Flaxman, – the 'dear Nancy' of the sculptor. I am indebted for a copy of it to the courtesy of Mrs Flaxman's sister, the late Miss Denman. Characteristic, I mean, of Blake; for though the wife be the nominal inditer, the husband is obviously the author. The very handwriting can hardly be distinguished from his. The verses with which it concludes may, in their artless spiritual simplicity, almost rank with the *Songs of Innocence and Experience*.

From Mrs Blake to Mrs Flaxman.

'MY DEAREST FRIEND,

'I hope you will not think we could forget your services to us, or any way neglect to love and remember with affection even the hem of your garment. We indeed presume on your kindness in neglecting to have called on you since my husband's first return from Felpham. We have been incessantly busy in our great removal; but can never think of going without first paying our proper duty to you and Mr Flaxman. We intend to call on Sunday afternoon in Hampstead, to take farewell; all things being now nearly completed for our setting forth on Tuesday morning. It is only sixty miles and Lambeth one hundred; for the terrible desert of London was between. My husband has been obliged to finish several things necessary to be finished before our migration. The swallows call us, fleeting past our window at this moment. O! how we delight in talking of the pleasure we shall have in preparing you a summer bower at Felpham. And we not only talk, but behold! the angels of our journey have inspired a song to you:

To my dear Friend, Mrs Anna Flaxman.

This song to the flower of Flaxman's joy;
To the blossom of hope, for a sweet decoy;
Do all that you can or all that you may,
To entice him to Felpham and far away.

Away to sweet Felpham, for Heaven is there;
The Ladder of Angels descends through the air,
On the turret its spiral does softly descend,
Through the village then winds, at my cot it does end.

You stand in the village and look up to heaven;
The precious stones glitter on flight seventy-seven;
And my brother is there; and *my* friend and thine
Descend and ascend with the bread and the wine.

The bread of sweet thought and the wine of delight
Feed the village of Felpham by day and by night;
And at his own door the bless'd hermit does stand,
Dispensing unceasing to all the wide land.

W. BLAKE

'Receive my and my husband's love and affection, and believe me to be yours affectionately,

CATHERINE BLAKE

'H. B. Lambeth, 14 Sept. 1800.'

A letter from Blake's own hand to Flaxman, penned immediately after arrival in Sussex, has been put into print by our excellent friend Smith. This very physiognomic composition, lucid enough to all who *know* Blake, needlessly puzzled Allan Cunningham. It does not, to my mind, separate, as he maintains, into two distinct parts of strongly contrasted spirit; nor does it

162

betoken that irreconcilable discord of faculties he imagines. The mingling of sound sagacity with the utmost licence of imagination showed itself at every hour of Blake's life. He would, at any moment, speak as he here writes, and was not a mere sensible mortal in the morning and a wild visionary in the evening. Visionary glories floated before his eyes even while he stooped over the toilsome copper-plate. There was no pause or hiatus in the lifelong wedding of spiritual and earthly things in his daily course; no giving the reins to imagination at one time more than another.

And if immortality, if eternity *mean* something, if they imply a pre-existence as well as a post-mortal one, that which startles the practical mind in this letter is not so wholly mad; especially if we make due allowance for the *dialect*, the unwonted phraseology (most very original men have their phraseology), which long custom had made familiar and anything but extravagant to him, or to those who have read themselves into Blake's writing and design; a dialect so full of trope and metaphor, dealt with as if they were literal, not symbolic facts.

DEAR SCULPTOR OF ETERNITY,

We are safe arrived at our cottage, which is more beautiful than I thought it, and more convenient. It is a perfect model for cottages, and I think for palaces of magnificence, only enlarging not altering its proportions, and adding ornaments and not principles. Nothing can be more grand than its simplicity and usefulness. Simple without intricacy, it seems to be the spontaneous expression of humanity, congenial to the wants of man. No other formed house can ever please me so well, nor shall I ever be persuaded, I believe, that it can be improved either in beauty or use.

'Mr Hayley received us with his usual brotherly affection. I have begun to work. Felpham is a sweet place for study, because it is more spiritual than London. Heaven opens here on all sides her golden gates: her windows are not obstructed by vapours; voices of celestial inhabitants are more distinctly heard, and their forms more distinctly seen; and my cottage is also a shadow of their houses. My wife and sister are both well, courting Neptune for an embrace.

'Our journey was very pleasant; and though we had a great deal of luggage, no grumbling. All was cheerfulness and good humour on the road, and yet we could not arrive at our cottage before half-past eleven at night, owing to the necessary shifting of our luggage from one chaise to another; for we had seven different chaises, and as many different drivers. We set out between six and seven in the morning of Thursday, with sixteen heavy boxes and portfolios full of prints.

'And now begins a new life, because another covering of earth is shaken off. I am more famed in Heaven for my works than I could well conceive. In my brain are studies and chambers filled with books and pictures of old, which I wrote and painted in ages of eternity before my mortal life; and those works are the delight and study of archangels. Why then should I be anxious about the riches or fame of mortality? The Lord our Father will do for us and with us according to his Divine will, for our good.

'You, O dear Flaxman! are a sublime archangel, – my friend and companion from eternity. In the Divine bosom is our dwelling place. I look back into the regions of reminiscence, and behold our ancient days before this earth appeared in its vegetated mortality to my mortal vegetated eyes. I see our houses of eternity which can never be separated, though our mortal vehicles should stand at the remotest corners of heaven from each other.

'Farewell, my best friend! Remember me and my wife in love and friendship to our dear Mrs Flaxman, whom we ardently desire to entertain beneath our thatched roof of rusted gold. And believe me for ever to remain your grateful and affectionate

'WILLIAM BLAKE'

'Felpham, Sept. 21st, 1800.
  Sunday morning.'

164

From this letter it appears the squire's method of travelling by post-chaise was adopted by the painter. His sister, nearly seven years younger than himself, made one in the party and in Blake's family during his residence at Felpham.

'I have begun to work,' Blake writes; on the plates to a ballad of Hayley's, that is: *Little Tom the Sailor*, written and printed for a charitable purpose. The project had been set going in Hayley's fervid head by an account his friend Rose the barrister gave of the boy's heroism and the mother's misfortunes, as celebrated in the poem. Hayley was at once to write a ballad, Blake to illustrate and engrave it, and the broadsheet to be sold for the widow's benefit to the poet's friends, or any who would join in helping the 'necessities of a meritorious woman;' in which the brochure, says Hayley's *Memoirs*, proved successful.

The poem, like some others of Hayley's, has simplicity, and perhaps even a touch of sweetness. At any rate, it is brief. If its author had not been cursed with the fatal facility of words and numbers, he might have done better things. A tinge of Blake-like feeling seems to have passed for once into the smooth verse of the poet of Eartham. The ballad was written 22d September, 1800; Blake's broadsheet bears date October 5th. Both verse and designs, of which there are two, one at the head, the other at the foot of the page, are executed on metal – pewter, it is said – the designs being graver work, in the same manner as on wood, the ballad and imprint bitten in with acid. The impressions were printed off by himself and Mrs Blake: 'Printed for and sold by the Widow Spicer of Folkstone, for the benefit of her orphans.' The sheet is now exceedingly scarce, as broadsheets always become, even when far more widely circulated than this could ever have been. I have come across but two or three copies.

The engravings are vigorous and effective, in an unpretending, rude style. The designs have all Blake's characteristic directness and *naiveté*. At the foot we see the future widow leaving her humble cottage to seek her sick husband, and turning her head wistfully round as she steps forth on her way; her little son rocking the cradle within. Around stretches a landscape in the typical style of Poussin, – wood, and winding path, and solemn distant downs. It is a grand and simple composition. The engraving at the head of the sheet represents the sailor-boy aloft on the shrouds, climbing to the top-mast, the embodied spirit of his father bursting with extending arms from the midst of the storm-cloud and forked lightnings. This picture also is full of high feeling.

To those disposed to judge a work of art vulgarly by what the eye merely can see, instead of by the emotions aroused, it may look like gross exaggeration to speak of grandeur in so rude and slight a work. But the kindled imagination of the artist can speak eloquently through few and simple strokes, and with them kindle imagination in others. This is more than the most skilful piece of mere artistic handicraft can do, which as it does not come from, neither can it appeal to, the mind. Hence we venture to claim for these designs, a place among the genuinely great, in kind though not in degree of excellence. In truth, there are very few works by Blake for which thus much, at least, cannot be claimed.

SEVENTEEN

Poet Hayley and Felpham 1800–1801
[ÆT. 43–44]

Blake's life at Felpham was a happy one. In Hayley he had a kind and friendly neighbour; notwithstanding disparity of social position and wider discrepancies of training and mental character. Hayley, the valued friend of Gibbon in one generation, of Cowper in the next, whose reputation, like many another reputation then and since, was for a time in excess of his literary deservings, has since been, even from a literary point of view, just as disproportionately despised, – sneered at with excess of rigour. By Allan Cunningham he is never mentioned, in connexion with Blake or Romney, but to be injuriously spoken of, and the worst construction put upon his motives. This he does, swayed by the gratuitous assertions of Romney's too acrimonious son, and giving the rein to one of those unmeasured dislikes the stalwart Scot was prone to take into his head; witness his distorted portrait of the amiable, urbane Sir Joshua.

As a poet, Hayley was no worse, if little better, than his compeers; Cowper and Burns standing of course apart. One must judge him not as a literary man, but as a literary country gentleman; an amateur, whose words flowed a thousand times faster than his thoughts. His *Life of Cowper* was one of the earliest and best examples in that modern school of biography wherein authentic letters form the basis, and the hero draws his own portrait. Mason's *Life of Gray* was the first, but not an unexceptionable one; Mason being at the pains of mutilating and otherwise doctoring Gray's lively scholarly gossip. Hayley's own part in the *Life of Cowper* is well and gracefully written, in the smooth style, – in *a* style, which is something.

If Hayley was always romancing, as it were, which his position in life allowed; always living in a fool's paradise of ever-dispelled, ever-renewed self-deceptions about the commonest trifles; seeing all men and things athwart a fog of amiability; it was not in the main a worse world than common, and sometimes it was a useful life to others. The pension his bustling energy obtained for Cowper outweighs many an absurdity and inanity. He was surely an endurable specimen, for variety's sake, among corn-law and game-preserving squires. A sincere, if conventional love of literature, independence of the great world, and indifference to worldly distinctions, are, after all, not criminal foibles. Pertinacious, wrongheaded, and often foolish in his actions; weakly greedy of applause, as ready to lavish it; prone to exaggeration of word and thought; without reticence: he was also an agreeable companion, really kind-hearted and generous; though vanity mixed itself with all he did; for ever going out of his way to befriend some one, to set in motion some well-intended, ill-considered scheme. For Blake, – let us remember, to the hermit's honour, – Hayley continued to entertain unfeigned respect. And the self-tutored, wilful visionary must have been a startling phenomenon to so conventional a mind. During the artist's residence at Felpham his literary friend was constantly on the alert to advance his fortunes.

Another source of happiness for Blake at Felpham was the natural beauty which surrounded him, and which the transplanted Londoner keenly enjoyed. 'A cottage which is more beautiful than I had thought it, and more convenient; a perfect model for cottages,' Blake had written of his new home on his first arrival. It is still standing, and is on the southern or seaward side of the village. It is really a cottage; a long, shallow, white-faced house, one room deep, containing but six in all, – small and cosy; three on the ground-floor, opening one into another, and three above. Its latticed windows look to the front; at back the thatched roof comes sweeping down almost to the ground. A thatched wooden verandah, which runs the whole length of the house, forming a covered way, paved with red brick, shelters the lower rooms from a southern sun; a little too much so at times, as the present tenant (a gardener) complains. The entrance is at the end of this verandah, out of the narrow lane leading from the village to the sea. In front lies the slip of garden (there is none at back), inclosed by a low, flint wall. In front of that again is a private way, shaded with evergreens, to the neighbour-ing large red brick mansion, surrounded by ample gardens, in which Cyril Jackson, Dean of Christ Church and Tutor to George IV. once lived. Beyond, corn-fields stretch down to the sea, which is but a few furlongs distant, and almost on the same level, – the coast here being low and crumbling. To the right are scattered one or two labourers' humble cottages, with their gardens and patches of corn-field. Further seaward are two windmills standing conspicuously on a tongue of land which shuts off adjacent Bognor from sight. The hideous buildings now to be descried in that direction were not extant in Blake's time. His upper or bedroom windows commanded a glorious view of the far-stretching sea, with many a white sail gleaming at sunset in the distance, on its way betwixt the Downs and the chops of the Channel. The wide and gentle bay is terminated westward by Selsea Bill, above which the cloud-like Isle of Wight is commonly visible; eastward by Worthing and the high cliff of Beechy Head beyond. Often, in after years, Blake would speak with enthusiasm of the shifting lights on the sea he had watched from those windows. In fine weather the waves come rippling in to the gently shelving, sandy beach, but when rough, with so much force as to eat away huge mouthfuls of the low, fertile coast. Middleton Church and signal-house, on a point of land a mile or so eastward, have disappeared bodily since Blake's time. The village, a large but compact one, spreading along two or three winding roads, still wears much the same aspect it must have done then; rustic, pleasant, and (as yet) unspoiled by the close vicinity of a 'genteel' watering-place. It includes a few tolerably commodious marine residences of the last century, and several picturesque old thatched cottages. The church has within the last few years been restored, all but its fine western tower of perpendicular date. Excellent in proportion, strikingly pictur-esque in hue and outline, this tower is at once well preserved and in good state for the artist. It is a landmark for many miles, rising above the thick foliage which in the distance hides yet distinguishes the village from the surrounding flats. Several epit-aphs of Hayley's, – in the composition of which species of poetry, it may perhaps be still conceded, he was happy, – are to be met with in the church and adjoining graveyard.

A few steps up the winding lane, by the old Fox Inn, brought Blake to the postern-like gate of his patron's house, in the centre of the village; a plain white house, of little architectural pretension (but for its turret) and less beauty. It stands at one corner of the garden which Hayley had carefully inclosed with high walls for privacy's sake. The lofty turret commanded some remarkable views, of the sea in one direction, of the adjacent levels and great part of the South Downs in another. For walks,

Blake had the pleasant sands which stretch below the shingle, or an upper path along the coast on one hand; the Downs eight or nine miles distant rising in undulating solemn clouds on the other. These were the great natural features, ever the same, yet ever varying with shifting lights and tones and hues. The walks inland, within a range of five or six miles, are tame and monotonous, though in summer pleasant, with corn and pasture, shady lane, fair old homestead, and humble early English village church. One especially pleasant summer-walk is that by footpath to the village of Walberton, some five miles northward. Bognor was not then ugly and repulsive as great part of it is now. At all events, there were none of those ghastly blocks of untenanted, unfinished houses, dreary monuments of building infatuation, which lower upon the traveller and put him out of heart as he approaches from Felpham, looking like so many builder's night-mares; erections that bespeak an almost brutish absence of natural instincts for the beautiful or expressive in construction. It was only some nine years previous to Blake's residence in Sussex that Sir Richard Hotham, the retired hatter, had set Bognor going as a fashionable watering-place. He had found it a sequestered hamlet of smugglers. The 'retired and beautiful village of Hothamton,' as it was for a time called, included then but fifty houses, Hothamton Place, viz. and those which form now the eastern section of Bognor, visited or tenanted only by a select and aristocratic few.

By the sounding shore, visionary conversations were held with many a majestic shadow from the Past – Moses and the Prophets, Homer, Dante, Milton: 'All,' said Blake, when questioned on these appearances, 'all majestic shadows, grey but luminous, and superior to the common height of men.' Sometimes his wife accompanied him, seeing and hearing nothing, but fully believing in what *he* saw. By the sea, or pacing the pretty slip of garden in front of his house, many fanciful sights were witnessed by the speculative eyes. The following highly imaginative little scene was transacted there. It is related by Allan Cunningham. 'Did you ever see a fairy's funeral, madam?' he once said to a lady who happened to sit by him in company. 'Never, sir,' was the answer. 'I have!' said Blake, 'but not before last night. I was walking alone in my garden; there was great stillness among the branches and flowers, and more than common sweetness in the air; I heard a low and pleasant sound, and I knew not whence it came. At last I saw the broad leaf of a flower move, and underneath I saw a procession of creatures, of the size and colour of green and grey grasshoppers, bearing a body laid out on a rose leaf, which they buried with songs, and then disappeared. It was a fairy funeral!'

Among the engravings executed by Blake's industrious hands during his first year at Felpham, I make note of a fine one of Michael Angelo at the end of the first edition (in quarto) of Fuseli's famous *Lectures on Painting*, – the first three, delivered at the Academy in March, 1801, published in May. It is an interesting and characteristic full-length portrait. The great Florentine is standing, looking out on the world with intent, searching gaze, the Coliseum in the background. The circular plate on the title-page of the same volume, well engraved by F. Legat, has no designer's name. Grand and suggestive, in a dim allegoric way, is this drooping female figure seated on the earth, her crossed arms flung down in expressive *abandon*; the face bowed between them and hidden by her streaming hair. This is a design I could swear to as Blake's, whether 'adopted' by Fuseli or not.

In the latter part of 1801 Hayley began spinning a series of *Ballads on Anecdotes relating to Animals*, of very different merit

172

from *Little Tom the Sailor* of the previous year; empty productions, long winded, bald, devoid of every poetic virtue save simplicity, – in the unhappy sense of utter insipidity. What must the author of the *Songs of Innocence* have thought of them? On these *Ballads* hung a project, as usual with Hayley. They were to be illustrated by Blake, printed by another *protégé*, Seagrave, a Chichester bookseller, and published for the artist's sole benefit; in realizing which they were fated to have but ill success. Our hermit sincerely believed in contributing verse of his he was giving money's worth, in that serene faith meaning as generously as when handing over tangible coin.

EIGHTEEN

Working Hours 1801–3
[ÆT. 44–46]

During the progress of the *Life of Cowper*, and of the *Ballads*, the letters of Hayley to the Rev. John Johnson supply glimpses, here and there, of Blake at his engraving, or in familiar intercourse with his patron; and they supply more than glimpses of the writer himself, in his accustomed undress of easy, slipshod vanity and amiability. This Johnson was Cowper's cousin, his right-hand man in latter years, and faithful guardian ultimately. The letters are entombed in Hayley's *Memoirs* of himself and his son, edited, or, at all events, seen through the press, by the amiable clergyman in 1823.

'Our Good Blake,' scribbles the artist's patron, one hot day in August, 1801, 'is actually *in labour with a young lion*. The newborn cub will probably kiss your hands in a week or two. *The Lion* is his third Ballad,' (none are yet printed) 'and we hope his plate to it will surpass its predecessors. *Apropos* of this good warm-hearted artist. He has a great wish that you should prevail on Cowper's dear Rose' (Mrs Anne Bodham, a cousin of the poet on the mother's side, and the correspondent who sent him that picture of his mother which elicited the poem we all know so well) 'to send her portrait of the beloved bard, by Abbott, to Felpham that Blake may engrave it for the Milton we meditate; which we devote (you know) to the sublime purpose of raising a monument suited to the dignity of the dear bard, in the metropolis; if the public show proper spirit (as I am persuaded it will) on that occasion – a point that we shall put to the end, in publishing the Life.'

A portrait of Cowper, by Abbott, the Academician, – a very prosaic one, – was not, I presume, sent to Felpham; for it was never engraved by Blake. A print of it, by one W. C. Edwards, forms the frontispiece to Vol. I. of *The Private Correspondence of Cowper*, edited by Johnson in 1824. The scheme here referred to was that of an edition of Cowper's unfinished Commentary on *Paradise Lost*, and MS. translations of Milton's Latin and Italian poetry, together with Hayley's previously published, lengthy *Life of Milton*. The whole was to be in three quarto volumes, 'decorated with engravings,' by Blake, after designs by Flaxman: the proceeds to go towards a London monument to Cowper, from Flaxman's chisel. The project, like so many from the same brain, had to be abandoned for one of later birth: a single quarto, illustrated by Flaxman, of Cowper's *Translations and Notes on Milton*, for the proposed 'benefit,' as usual, of somebody, – this time of 'an orphan godson of the poet,' which in 1808 actually did take shape; followed in 1810, by a 'neat pocket edition,' for the emolument of Cowper's kinsman, Johnson.

September 3, 1801: (Hayley to Johnson again) 'The good Blake is finishing, very happily, the plate of the poet's mother. He salutes you affectionately.' *October* 1, 1801: 'October, you see, is arrived, and you, my dear Johnny, will arrive, I trust, before half this pleasant month shall pass away; for we want you as a faithful coadjutor in the turret, more than I can express. I say *we*, for the warm-hearted indefatigable Blake works daily by my side, on the intended decorations of our biography. Engraving, of all human works, appears to require the largest portion of patience; and he happily possesses more of that inestimable virtue than I ever saw united before to an imagination so lively and so prolific. Come, and criticize what we have done! Come, and assist us to do more! I want you in a double capacity, as an excellent scribe, and as an infallible fountain of intelligence for all the latter days of our dear bard.'

Hayley, whose sight was often weak, availed himself of Blake's help too, as amanuensis, and in other ways, during the progress of the *Life*. Blake had thus opportunity to form a judgment of Hayley's mode of dealing with his material; he was not greatly impressed by its candour and fidelity.

November 8th, 1801: (Hayley again) 'And now let me congratulate you on having travelled so well through the Odyssey!' (an edition of Cowper's Homer, with the translator's final touches, which the clergyman was bringing out). 'Blake and I read every evening that copy of the Iliad which your namesake' (the bookseller) 'of St Paul's was so good as to send me; comparing it with the first edition, and with the Greek, as we proceed. We shall be glad to see the Odyssey also, *as soon as it is visible.*'

This and other passages in the correspondence show the familiar intimacy which had been established between the literary gentleman and the artist. The latter evidently spent much of his time, and most of his working hours, in Hayley's library, in free companionship with its owner; which, in the case of so proud and sensitive a man as Blake, can only have been due to much delicacy and genial courtesy on the part of his host; whose manners, indeed, were those of a polished gentleman of the old school. We can, for a moment, see the oddly assorted pair; both visionaries, but in how different a sense! the urbane amateur seeing nothing as it really was; the painter seeing only, so to speak, the unseen: the first with a mind full of literary conventions, swiftly writing without thought; the other, with a head just as full of originalities, – right or wrong, – patiently busying his hands at his irksome craft, while his spirit wandered through the invisible world.

November 18th, 1801. – Hayley writes to Johnson from the house of his friend Mrs Poole: 'Your warm-hearted letter (that has met me this instant in the apartments of our benevolent Paulina, at Lavant) has delighted us all so much (by *all*, I mean Paulina, Blake, and myself), that I seize a pen, while the coffee is coming to the table, to tell you with what cordial pleasure we shall expect you and your young pupil. If my Epitaph' (on Mrs Unwin) 'delighted you, believe me, your affectionate reception of it has afforded me equal delight. I have been a great scribbler of Epitaphs in the last month, and as you are so kindly partial to my monumental verses, I will transcribe for you, even in the bustle of this morning, a recent Epitaph on your humble old friend, my good William, who closed his height of cheerful and affectionate existence (near eighty) this day fortnight, in the great house at Eartham, where Blake and I had the mournful gratification of attending him (by accident) in the few last hours of his life.'

November 22d, 1801. 'Did I tell you that our excellent Blake has wished to have Lawrence's original drawing to copy, in his second engraving; and that our good Lady Hesketh is so gracious as to send it?'

The engravings to the *Life of Cowper* – the first issue in two volumes quarto (they were omitted in the subsequent octavo edition) – are not of that elaborate character the necessity of their being executed under the 'biographer's own eye' might have led us to expect. One is after that portrait of Cowper, by Romney, in crayons, made during the poet's own visit to Eartham in 1792; which drew forth the graceful, half sad, half sportive sonnet, concluding with so skilful an antithesis of friendly hyperbole in complimenting his painter and host. A correct copy as to likeness, the engraving gives no hint of the refinement of Romney's art. In so mannered, level a piece of workmanship, industry of hand is more visible than of mind. Another is after the stiff, Lely-like portrait of Cowper's mother, by D. Heins, which suggested the poet's beautiful lines. In Vol. II. we have a good rendering of young Lawrence's clever, characteristic sketch of Cowper; and, at the end, a group of pretty, pastoral designs from Blake's own hand. The subjects are that familiar household by 'the weather house,' described in *The Task*; and Cowper's tame hares. These vignettes are executed in a light, delicate style, very unusual with Blake.

In January, 1802, Cowper's cousin paid the promised visit, and brought with him the wished-for anecdotes of the poet's last days. Hayley, with friendly zeal, had urged Blake to attempt the only lucrative walk of art in those days – portraiture; and during Johnson's stay, the artist executed a miniature of him, which Hayley mentions as particularly successful. It would be an interesting one to see, for its painter's sake, and for the subject – the faithful kinsman and attendant with whom *The Letters* of Cowper have put on friendly terms all lovers of that loveable poet, the fine-witted, heaven-stricken man.

Hayley, desiring the artist's worldly advancement, introduced him to many of the neighbouring gentry; among them Lord Egremont of Petworth, Lord Bathurst of Lavant, Mrs Poole; and obtained him commissions for miniatures. Some of which, reports Hayley, 'that singularly industrious man, who applied himself to various branches of the art,' and 'had wonderful talents for original design,' executed 'very happily.'

Besides bestirring himself to obtain Blake commissions, Hayley did what his means would allow to furnish employment himself. The interior of his new villa was fitted up in a manner bespeaking the cultivated man of letters and of taste, – thanks, in great part, to his friendly relations with such artists as Flaxman and Romney, – was adorned with busts, statues, and pictures. Among the latter were interesting portraits of distinguished contemporaries and friends, and of the Hermit himself; all from Romney's hand, and originally painted for the library at Eartham. There was one of Gibbon, sitting and conversing; there were others, in crayons, of Cowper, Charlotte Smith, Anna Seward, Madame de Genlis; above all, there were fine studies of Lady Hamilton in various fancy characters, as Cassandra, Andromeda, Cecilia, *Sensibility*, &c. When, twenty years earlier, Hayley had built himself at Eartham a large and handsome room, specially to contain his fine collection of books in many languages, Flaxman had superintended the sculptured ornaments, and had modelled for it busts of the poet and his friend Romney. The new library at Felpham, Blake, during his residence in Sussex, decorated with temperas: – eighteen heads of the poets, life size, some accompanied by appropriate subsidiary compositions. Among them were Shakespeare, Homer, Camöens, Sir Philip Sidney, Cowper, Hayley himself (encircled by cooing doves). Within twenty years after Hayley's death the marine villa passed by sale from the hands of his cousin and heir, Captain Godfrey, to strangers. The place was dismantled and the effects sold. Among other things, these temperas, so interesting in their original position, were dispersed. Five of them, including Homer, Cowper, Hayley, are now (1860) with Mr Toovey, the bookseller. Like most of Blake's 'temperas' and 'frescoes,' they are blistered and cracked, and have not been improved by varnish and exposure to dust and gas; but they bear the unmistakable Blake impress. The head of Cowper I remember as one of the most interesting, and the accompanying vignette, with its hint of landscape, in which appears Cowper's favourite dog, as being in Blake's best manner. I know not into whose hands the other five passed from Mr Toovey's. Booksellers are nervously afraid of giving one too much information.

Our next excerpts from Hayley's garrulous letters date after Johnson's visit to Felpham.

February 3d, 1802. [Hayley to Johnson, as before.] 'Here is instantaneously a title-page for thee' (for the new edition of Cowper's Homer), 'and a Greek motto, which I and Blake, who is just become a Grecian, and literally learning the language, consider as a happy hit! . . . The new Grecian greets you affectionately.'

Blake, who had a natural aptitude for acquiring knowledge, little cultivated in youth, was always willing to apply himself to the vocabulary of a language for the purpose of reading a great original author. He would declare that he learnt French, sufficient to read it, in a few weeks. By-and-by, at sixty years of age, he will set to learning Italian, in order to read Dante.

The references in our next extract to Cowper's monumental tablet at East Dereham, then under discussion, and Blake a party to it, are sufficiently amusing, surely, to warrant our staying to smile over the same. Consider what 'the Design' actually erected is. An oblong piece of marble, bearing an inscription, with a sculptured 'Holy Bible' on end at top; another marble volume, lettered. 'The Task,' leaning against it; and a palm leaf inclined over the whole, as the redeeming 'line of beauty.' Chaste and simple!

February 25th, 1802. 'I thank you heartily for your pleasant letter, and I am going to afford you, I hope, very high gratification in the prospect of our overcoming all the prejudices of our good Lady Hesketh against simple and graceful ornaments for the tomb of our beloved bard. I entreated her to suspend her decision till I had time to send for the simply elegant sketches that I expected from Flaxman. When these sketches reached me, I was not myself perfectly pleased with the shape of the lyre introduced by the sculptor, and presumptuously have tried myself to out-design my dear Flaxman himself, on this most animating occasion. I formed, therefore, a device of *the Bible upright* supporting *The Task*, with a laurel leaf and *Palms*, such as I send you, neatly copied by our kind Blake. I have sent other copies of the same to her ladyship and to Flaxman; requesting the latter to tell me frankly how he likes my design, and for what sum he can execute the said design, with the background, – a firm slab of dove-coloured marble, and the rest white. If her ladyship and Flaxman are as much pleased with my idea as the good Blake and Paulina of Lavant are, all our difficulties on this grand monumental contention will end most happily. Tell me how *you*, my dear Johnny, like my device. To enable you to judge fairly, even against myself, I desired the kind Blake to add for you, under the copy of my design, a copy of Flaxman's also, with the lyre whose shape displeases me.'

In the sequel the *Lyre* was eliminated, and the amateur's emendation, in the main, adhered to; *The Task*, however, being made to prop the Bible, instead of *vice versâ*, as at first the Hermit heedlessly suggests.

March 11th, 1802. 'The kind indefatigable Blake salutes you cordially, and begs a little fresh news from the spiritual world;' an allusion to some feeble joke of Hayley's on Johnson's timorous awe of the public, which the latter makes believe to think has slain the bashful parson.

The *Life of Cowper*, – commenced January, 1801, finished the following January, – was, this March, in the hands of Seagrave, whom the author had, 'for the credit of his native city,' induced reluctant Johnson to accept as printer. The four copper-plates were entirely printed off by Blake and his wife at his own press, a very good one for that day, having cost 40*l.* when new – a heavy sum for him. From March till December Hayley, after beginning the *Memoir* of his son, was busy getting his two quartos through the press.

The issue of *The Ballads* was not commenced till June; they were in quarto numbers, three engravings to each – a frontispiece and two vignettes. The first was *The Elephant. A Series of Ballods. Number 1. The Elephant. Ballad the First. Chichester: printed by J. Seagrave, and sold by him and P. Humphry; and by R. H. Evans, Pall Mall, London, for W. Blake, Felpham*, 1802. None of the plates to this ballad were republished in the subsequent duo-decimo edition.

In May we hear, through Hayley, of illness:

May 16*th*, 1802. 'You will feel anxious when I tell you that both my good Blakes have been confined to their bed a week by a severe fever. Thank heaven! they are both revived, and he is at this moment by my side, representing, on copper, an *Adam*, of his own, surrounded by animals, as a frontispiece to the projected ballads:' a frontispiece which appeared in the first number.

In June, healthfully restored, 'our alert Blake,' scribbles Hayley, one '*Monday afternoon*,' June 28*th*, 1802, 'is preparing, *con* *spirito*, to launch his *Eagle*, with a lively hope of seeing him superior to *The Elephant*, and

'Sailing with supreme dominion
Through the azure deep of air.

'Lady Hesketh has received and patronised his *Elephant* with the most obliging benignity, and we hope soon to hear that the gentle and noble beast arrived safe at Dereham, and finds favour with the good folks of your county. The ingenious maker of elephants and eagles, who is working at this instant on the latter, salutes you with kindest remembrance.'

A few days later, July 1st, 1802, *The Eagle* was published, forming No. II. of *The Ballads*. The frontispiece is one of the finest designs in the series. The frantic mother, kneeling on the topmost verge of the over-hanging crag amid the clouds, who stretches forth passionate, outspread arms over her smiling babe below, as he lies and sports with his dread comrade in this perilous nest, – the blood-stained cranny in the rocks, – is a noble and eloquent figure. It was subsequently reproduced in the duodecimo edition, but without either of the vignettes. In one of these, the eagle is swooping down on the child in its cradle outside the mother's cottage. In the other, the liberated little one is standing upon the dead eagle among the mountains. Both have a domestic simplicity of sentiment, and both are good in drawing.

Between September, 1802, and January, 1804, occurs an unlucky hiatus in the printed letters of Hayley to Johnson; and we catch no further glimpses of the artist by that flickering rushlight.

The third number of *The Ballads*, – *The Lion*, – appeared in 1802 after which they were discontinued; the encouragement being too slender to pay for mere printing, in so expensive a form. Though Phillips' name was added on the title-page, and copies, perhaps consigned to him, the book can hardly be said to have been published, as matters were managed down at Felpham and Chichester. Had it been efficiently made known, the illustrations ought to have commanded some favour with the public. The style of design and engraving, careful and finished, is, for once, not of a kind to repel the ordinary gazer; and the themes are quite within popular comprehension, though their treatment be unusually refined. I here speak of the quarto edition.

The whole fifteen windy ballads were, three years later, printed in duodecimo by Seagrave, for Phillips of London, the aim still being to benefit the artist, and still proving ineffectual. Hayley had not more power to help Blake with a public challenged now by Wordsworth, Coleridge, Lamb, won by Crabbe, Campbell, Scott, than Blake had by his archaic conceptions, caviare to the many, to recal roving readers to an obsolete style of unpoetic verse, – a tame instead of a rattling one, such as had come into vogue. The engravings to the incomplete quarto *Ballads* are infinitely superior to the reduced ones; being far more delicate and careful.

November 15th, 1802, died Hayley's old friend Romney, after a sad and lengthened twilight of his faculties; which solemn event set Hayley 'composing an epitaph before the dawn of day,' and revolving in his mind pious intent of further biographic toil, in which Blake was to help. This autumn, too, died Blake's old master, Basire.

Next year, in an extract from Hayley's *Diary*, we again get sight of Blake for a moment: *26th and 29th of March*, 1803 – 'Read the death of Klopstock in the newspaper of the day, and looked into his *Messiah*, both the original and the translation. Read Klopstock into English to Blake, and translated the opening of his third canto, where he speaks of his own death.' Hayley was at this time trying to learn German, finding that it contained a poem on the Four Ages of Woman, of which he, 'for some time, made it a rule to translate a few lines' daily; finding also, by the arrival of presentation copies in the alien tongue, that three of his own works had been translated into German: the *Essay on Old Maids*, the *Life of Milton*, and the *Triumphs of Temper*. O Time! eater of men and books, what has become of these translations?

At the latter end of 1803, Hayley, prompted by the unexpected success of Cowper's *Life*, began preparing a third volume of Additional Letters, with 'desultory remarks' of his own on letter-writing. The volume was finished and published by the spring of 1804, Blake executing for it two tame engravings of tame subjects. One is from a drawing by a Francis Stone, of the chancel of East Dereham Church, – Cowper's burial-place; the other an etching of the mural tablet in the same chancel, as designed by Flaxman and Hayley.

Among other journeywork at this date, I may mention engravings finished May, 1803, after six original designs by Maria Flaxman (the sculptor's wife), to the *Triumphs of Temper*, – the thirteenth edition, not published until 1807. These amateur designs, aiming at an idealized domesticity, are expressive and beautiful in the Flaxman-Stothard manner; abound in grace of line, elegance of composition, and other artist-like virtues of a now obsolete sort. The engravings are interesting to admirers of Blake, though monotonous and devoid of ordinary charms, smoothness, and finish.

Uncommissioned work must also have been in course of

production now. I mean the illustrated 'prophecies' in the old class, which will next year issue from Blake's private press: *Jerusalem, The Emanation of the Giant Albion*, very grandly designed, if very mistily written; also *Milton, a Poem in two Books*. Of these, more hereafter.

NINETEEN

Trial for High Treason 1803-4
[ÆT. 46-47]

High visions and patient industry, friendly intercourse with his neighbours, happy enjoyment of nature, were all interrupted for Blake in the autumn of 1803, by an incongruous event in a peaceful and innocent life. One day in August, a drunken soldier, – probably from the barracks at Aldwick or Chichester, – broke into the little slip of garden fronting the painter's sequestered cottage, and was there as violent and unruly as is the wont of drunken soldiers to be. He refused to go. The red-coat was a great hulking fellow, the artist of short stature, but robust, well knit, with plenty of courage, and capable of a supernatural energy, as it were, on occasions. In his exasperation, he laid hold of the intrusive blackguard, and turned him out neck and crop, in a kind of inspired frenzy, which took the man aback, and fairly frightened him; such volcanic wrath being a novelty in his experience. 'I do not know *how* I did it, but I did it,' said Blake, afterwards; and was himself disposed to attribute his success to that demoniac or spiritual *will* by stress of which, he believed, a man might achieve anything physical.

In the course of the scuffle, while blows were being exchanged, angry words passed of course; the red-coated bully vapouring that 'he was the king's soldier,' and so forth. 'Damn the king, and you too,' said Blake, with pardonable emphasis – a not unnatural reply, perhaps. But the event proved it to be an imprudent outburst, even as late as 1803. The soldier, bent on revenge, out of Blake's hasty words, made up a story, and got a comrade to bear him out, that his rough host had been guilty of seditious language. The sequel forcibly reminds us we are here in the times of 'the good old king,' not in those of Victoria. The soldier and 'his mate' made their charge on oath before a magistrate, and Blake had to stand his trial for high treason at the next Quarter Sessions.

Hayley, full of zeal for the artist, whose extraordinary entanglement 'pressed not a little on his mind and heart,' engaged, as defendant's counsel, his friend, Samuel Rose, another name familiar to the reader of Cowper's correspondence, as that of the enthusiastic young Scotchman, who, at twenty-two, had introduced himself to the shy recluse, winning a large share of the poet's regard and favour. Now in his thirtieth year, he had been about eight years at the bar, practising with fair success on the home circuit. Prospects of a brilliant future were only dashed by wavering health, – a constitution unequal to the strain of his profession. On *that* sunken rock, how many struggling in the same arduous career, – often those of brightest promise, of finest nature, – have been wrecked, almost at the outset, not great and famous, but nameless and unremembered.

A few days before the impending trial, Hayley met with an accident, which very nearly prevented his attending to give evidence in his *protégé's* favour. It was of a kind, however, to which he was pretty well accustomed. A persevering and fearless rider, he was in the eccentric habit of using an umbrella on horseback, to shade his eyes; the abrupt unfurling of which was commonly followed, naturally enough, by the rider's being forthwith pitched on his head. He had on this occasion lighted on a flint with more than usual violence, owing his life, indeed, to the opportune shield of a strong, new hat. 'Living or dying,' however, he declares to his doctor, 'he *must* make a public appearance, within a few days, at the trial of our friend Blake.' And on the appointed day he did appear in Court, to speak to the character and habits of the accused.

The trial came off at Chichester, 11th January, 1804, at the Quarter Sessions; the Duke of Richmond (the radical, not the corn-law duke) being the presiding magistrate. The sessions were held, in those days, in the Guildhall, which is the shell of a Gothic building, having been formerly the chancel, of early English date, in the old church of the Grey Friars convent. The fragmentary chancel and the Friary grounds are still extant, just within what used to be the city walls, at the north-east corner of the cheerful old cathedral town.

Reference obligingly made for me by the present editor, to the file of the *Sussex Advertiser*, at that date the only Sussex newspaper, discovers a report (16th Jan. 1804) of this singular trial, one its inditer little thought would ever become curious and interesting. The report is after the curt fashion of local journals in those backward days. 'William Blake, an engraver at Felpham, was tried on a charge exhibited against him by two soldiers, for having uttered seditious and treasonable expressions, such as "D—n the king, d—n all his subjects, d—n his soldiers, they are all slaves; when Bonaparte comes, it will be cut-throat for cut-throat, and the weakest must go to the wall; I will help him; &c. &c.'

Mrs Blake used afterwards to tell how, in the middle of the trial, when the soldier invented something to support his case, her husband called out '*False!*' with characteristic vehemence, and in a tone which electrified the whole court, and carried conviction with it. Rose greatly exerted himself for the defence. In his cross-examination of the accuser, he 'most happily exposed,' says Hayley, the falsehood and malignity of the charge, and also spoke very 'eloquently for his client,' though, in the midst of his speech, seized with illness, and concluding it with difficulty. Blake's neighbours joined Hayley in giving him the same character of habitual gentleness and peaceableness; which must have a little astonished the soldier, after his peculiar experiences of those qualities. A good deal of the two soldiers' evidence being plainly false, the whole was received with suspicion. It became clear that whatever the words uttered, they were extorted in the irritation of the moment by the soldier's offensive conduct.

'After a very long and patient hearing,' the *Sussex Advertiser* continues, 'he was by the jury acquitted; which so gratified the auditory that the court was, in defiance of all decency, thrown into an uproar by their noisy exultations. The business of the aforegoing Sessions,' it is added, 'owing to the great length of time taken up by the above trials' (Blake's and others), 'was extended to a late hour on the second day, a circumstance that but rarely happens in the western division' of the county. 'The Duke of Richmond sat the first day from ten in the morning till eight at night, without quitting the court, or taking any refreshment.'

Great was Hayley's satisfaction. 'It was late in the evening,' writes he to Johnson, and 'I was eager to present the delivered artist to our very kind and anxious friend, the lady of Lavant, Mrs Poole.' The friendly welcome and social evening meal which followed all this frivolous vexation and even peril, the pleasant meeting in the cheerful hospitable house of the venerable lady, we can picture. Her house, in which Blake often was, yet stands, somewhat altered, by the wayside to the right as you enter the hamlet of Mid Lavant, ten minutes' drive from Chichester; at the back, pleasant grounds slope down to the babbling Lavant brook, with a winding road beside it, across which rise other pleasant wooded slopes, and beyond, the solemn, rounded Downs, – in this part bare of trees; among them, to the right, Goodwood, and that specially conspicuous hill, the Trundle (or St Roche's). The 'peerless villa,' Hayley used to call it; everything of his, or of his friends, being more or less extraordinary and romantic. The lady herself was a woman respected far and wide, sociable, cheerful, and benevolent. She is still remembered in those parts, though none of her kin remain there. 'Ah! good creature!' exclaimed an infirm old labourer but the other day, on hearing mention of her name; he had worked for her. She died at a ripe age, suddenly, while dining among her friends at the Bishop's palace, a little more than three years after Blake's trial.

Poor Rose, – defendant's counsel, – never rallied from the illness which attacked him on that day. The 'severe cold' proved the commencement of a rapid consumption, of which he died at the close of the same year; sorrowful Hayley effervescing into an 'epitaph in the middle of the night.'

Not ten years before, quiet literary men and shoemakers, theoretic enthusiasts such as Horne Tooke the learned and witty, Holcroft, Thelwall, Hardy, members of a corresponding society – society corresponding with 'the friends of liberty' abroad that is – had been vindictively prosecuted by the Crown for (constructive) high treason, and almost convicted. At this very time, men were being hung in Ireland on such trivial charges. Blake's previous intimacy with Paine, Holcroft, and the rest, was doubtless unknown to an unlettered soldier, and probably at Chichester also. But as a very disadvantageous antecedent, in a political sense, of which counsel for the prosecution might have made good use, it was, in connexion with this vamped-up charge, a curious coincidence. Friend Hayley himself was not a very orthodox man in politics or religion, a Whig at the least, a quondam intimate of Gibbon's, admirer of Voltaire and Rousseau; holding, in short, views of his own. He was a confirmed absentee, moreover, from church, though an exemplary reader, to his household, of Church-service, and sermon, and family prayer, winding up with devotional hymns of his own composition.

Blake used to declare the Government, or some high person, knowing him to have been of the Paine set, 'sent the soldier to entrap him;' which we must take the liberty of regarding as a purely visionary notion.

TWENTY

Adieu to Felpham 1804
[ÆT. 47]

By the 25th of March following Blake's trial, the two slight engravings to the supplementary third volume of Cowper's *Life and Letters* were finished, as the engraved dates on the plates tell us. Hayley, at the end of 1803, had made a beginning of his *Life of Romney*. And now must have been executed Blake's only engraving for the often deferred quarto, not finished until four years after, nor published till 1807. Unnoticed when it did appear, the book is now scarce and, for its illustrations, interesting. Blake's contribution is after Romney's *Sketch of a Shipwreck*; a fine and characteristic bit of engraving. Of the remaining eleven, all save one after pictures by Romney, most were engraved by Caroline Watson, in her very fascinating style – bold and masterly, yet graceful. The *Infant Shakespeare, Sensibility, Cassandra, Miranda*, are well known to the collector. One of the engravings, a poor *Head of Christ*, is by Raimbach, afterwards famous as Wilkie's engraver. Another, from a curious early effort of Romney's in the comic vein, – *The Introduction of Slop into the Parlour of Shandy*, – is by W. Haines, a Sussex man, then an engraver, subsequently a painter of repute.

Blake, indefatigable in toil, – that 'singularly industrious man,' as Hayley and all who knew him pronounced, – would, at his craft of engraving, honestly execute for bread whatever was set him, good or bad. Humble as the task was, for so imaginative a man, of tracing servilely, line by line, other men's conceptions, he would patiently and imperturbably work at a design, however inferior to his own, though with an obvious and natural absence of enthusiasm. Blake's docility, however, had a limit. He was wont to say he had refused but one commission in his life, – to paint a set of hand-screens for a lady of quality, one of the great people to whom Hayley had introduced him. *That* he declined! For Lady Bathurst it was, I think. The Bathursts had then a seat near Lavant, which subsequently, like most other estates in the neighbourhood, was absorbed by the Duke of Richmond. Blake taught for a time in her family, and was admired by them. The proposal was, I believe, that he should be engaged at a regular annual salary, for tuition and services such as the above; as painter in ordinary, in fact, to this noble family.

In his art, in truth, Blake would not barter independence, or the exercise of his imaginative faculty, for patronage or money. This residence at Felpham, under poet Hayley's protection, might have proved a turning-point in his life. Had he complied with Hayley's evident wishes, and set himself, as a miniature painter, to please patrons, he *might* have climbed to fortune and fame. It was a 'choice of Hercules' for him once again. But he had made *his* choice in boyhood, and adhered to it in age. Few are so perseveringly brave. Many who, in early life, elect as he had done, falter and waver in after years: perchance too late to win that worldly success for which they have learned to hanker.

The failure of the *Ballads*, though illustrated in so poetic a spirit, and in a more popular style than anything previous from the same hand, – a failure not in pecuniary respects alone, but in commanding even a moderate share of public attention, – had been as complete, despite Hayley's poetry, and Seagrave's printing, as that of any in the long list of Blake's privately printed books. This had been a heavy disappointment. The vexatious squabble with a common soldier, and its vexatious results, had broken the flow of Blake's previously serene life at Felpham. The last volume of Cowper's *Life*, the original cause of his change of abode, was finished, and Blake felt it was time to return to familiar London.

His leaving would seem to have been as abrupt as his coming. He saw there was presented to him that choice of paths I have alluded to, and that longer stay was perilous to the imaginative faculty he prized above all earthly good. He feared being tempted to sell his birthright for a mess of pottage; feared to become a trader in art; and that the Visions would forsake him. He even began to think they *were* forsaking him. 'The Visions were angry with me at Felpham,' he would afterwards say.

Aversion to being any man's dependent may also have contributed to his determination. I fear the friendly connexion with Hayley ceased with this otherwise amiable episode in the life of each; honourable to each, especially to Hayley, considering how little nature had fitted him to enter into the spiritual meanings of Blake's art. Smooth, clever execution was an excellence far more within *his* critical ken. Hayley's sanguine temperament and pertinacity of disposition, to use a mild term, would lead him in the end to take offence at a *protégé* so perverse as to follow his own counsels, a friend who would not be befriended, and who could be as obstinate as himself. Not that any quarrel occurred, or even that any ill humour was betrayed on either side. But, as sometimes ensues in the case of far more congenial minds, many things which failed, amid the amenities of personal intercourse, to disturb good understanding at the time, rankled, or were felt resentfully afterwards. If direct proofs were wanting, indeed, that Hayley's society became irksome, and his sentiments distasteful to Blake, however it may have fared with the hermit himself, the MS. volume, before alluded to, furnishes us with an abundance. In his spleenful as well as in his elevated moods, this book appears to have generally lain at the artist's elbow. Intermingled with more serious matter, are to be found many sarcastic and biting reflections, in an epigrammatic form, on those against whom he had, or fancied he had, cause of offence. The following evidently belong to this period; they were probably written just before or just after Blake's leaving Felpham:

To Hayley.

You think Fuseli is not a great painter? I'm glad;
This is one of the best compliments he ever had.

To the same.

Thy friendship oft has made my heart to ache:
Do be my enemy, for friendship's sake!

In the next, it is poor Flaxman's turn as well as Hayley's:

My title as a genius thus is proved,–
Not praised by Hayley, nor by Flaxman loved.

On H. [Hayley], the Pickthank.

I write the rascal thanks; till he and I
With thanks and compliments are quite drawn dry.

The following is of more general application, though probably a result of Felpham experiences:

Friends were quite hard to find, old authors say,
But now they stand in everybody's way.

Certain it is, the Felpham episode in Blake's life once over, there is no further influence of Hayley on the artist's fortunes. And with the duodecimo edition of the *Ballads* of next year, an after result of Felpham activities, – with that last nugatory enterprise, mortifying doubtless on both sides, will finally close relations with Hayley. Amid the estrangement of distance and years, I no longer find them even alluding to one another, except on Blake's part, in the manner just displayed. Other engravers are employed for Hayley's subsequent publications. As early as the close of the next year, Caroline Watson executed the frontispiece (Cowper's Oak) of the *Supplementary Pages* to the *Life of Cowper*, which appeared with the octavo edition. She and Raimbach succeeded Blake as Hayley's *protégés*. The former amiable lady stayed some weeks at Felpham in 1806, making drawings after Romney's pictures, for her engravings to the *Life*. Their attractive merit was cordially appreciated by Hayley.

Blake's residence at Felpham terminated after nearly four years duration. Early in 1804 he bade adieu to Hayley; left the literary hermit producing his daily occasional poem, epitaph, or song, on waking in the morning; extempore sonnet while shaving; and facile labours during the day, at an extensive composition on the *Triumphs of Music*, 'with devotional sonnets and hymns interspersed.' Two days sufficed for a whole canto. This composition the English public has hitherto declined to trouble its head about, despite the confident prediction of an amiable female friend, 'that it would gradually become a favourite with readers' of a turn 'for simplicity and tenderness.' After the *Life of Cowper*, no book of Hayley's again won an audience.

TWENTY-ONE

South Molton Street 1804
[ÆT. 47]

The friendly haven of sweet Felpham was exchanged for the deeper seclusion of the brick-and-mortar desert, in the hope, as I hinted, of more perfect converse there with the Visions, undistracted by appeals from the beauty of the visible world, or by temptations from well-meaning patrons; above all, undisturbed by daily contact with so essentially material and eighteenth century a mind as Hayley's, which *must* have had its benumbing influence on the visionary or imaginative faculty, though perhaps unrecognized. Blake did not return to a cottage at Lambeth, but to lodgings in South Molton Street, within a mile of the spot where he was born. There neither garden nor tree reminded him of what he had left behind. South Molton Street, less shabby then than now, runs diagonally from Oxford Street into Brook Street. At No. 17 he took a first-floor, in which he remained for nearly seventeen years.

The first works issued from South Molton Street were the two engraved books, last mentioned, *Jerusalem* and *Milton*. The *Jerusalem* is prefaced by an 'Address' to the public, in a style to which the public is little accustomed:

Sheep   Goats

To the Public

After my three years' slumber on the banks of Ocean, I again display my giant forms to the public: my former giants and fairies having received the highest reward possible; the ... and ... of those with whom to be connected is to be ... I cannot doubt that this more consolidated and extended work will be ... as kindly received ... &c. * * * Reader, what you do not approve, &c ... me for this energetic exertion of my talents.

Jerusalem: the Emanation of the Giant Albion, 1804, *Printed by W. Blake, South Molton Street*, is a large quarto volume, of a hundred engraved pages, writing and design, only one side of each leaf being engraved. Most copies are printed in plain black and white, some with blue ink, some red; a few are tinted. For a tinted copy the price was twenty guineas.

The poem, since poem we are to call it, is mostly written in prose; occasionally in metrical prose; more rarely still it breaks forth into verse. Here is the author's own account of the matter:

When this verse was first dictated to me, I considered a monotonous cadence, like that used by Milton, Shakespeare and all writers of English blank verse, derived from the modern bondage of rhyming, to be a necessary and indispensable part of the verse. But I soon found that, in the mouth of a true orator, such monotony was not only awkward, but as much a bondage as rhyme itself. I, therefore, have produced a variety in every line, both in cadence and number of syllables. Every word and every letter is studied, and put into its place. The terrific numbers are reserved for the terrific parts, the mild and gentle for the mild and gentle parts, and the prosaic for inferior parts: all are necessary to each other.

199

The *Jerusalem* bears little resemblance to the 'prophetic books' of earlier date. We hear no longer of the wars, the labours, the sufferings, the laments of Orc, Rintrah, Urizen, or Enitharmon; though some of these names are casually mentioned once or twice. What we *do* hear of, the reader shall gather for himself, from a few extracts. The following lines instance in brief, the devout and earnest spirit in which Blake wrote; the high aims he set before him; and afford also a glimpse of the most strange and unhappy result: dark oracles, words empty of meaning to all but him who uttered them:

> Trembling I sit, day and night. My friends are astonisht at me:
> Yet they forgive my wand'rings. I rest not from my great task:
> To open the eternal worlds! To open the immortal eyes
> Of man inwards; into the worlds of thought: into eternity
> Ever expanding in the bosom of God, the human imagination.
> O Saviour! pour upon me thy spirit of meekness and love.
> Annihilate selfhood in me! Be thou all my life!
> Guide thou my hand, which trembles exceedingly, upon the Rock
>   of Ages!
> While I write of the building of Golgonooza and of the terrors of
>   Entuthon:
> Of Hand and Hyle, and Coban; of Kwantok, Peachey, Brereton,
>   Slayd, and Hutton:
> Of the terrible sons and daughters of Albion and their
>   generations.
> Scofield, Kox, Kotope and Bowen revolve most mightily upon
> The furnace of Los, before the eastern gate bending their fury.
> They war to destroy the furnaces; to desolate Golgonooza,
> And to devour the sleeping humanity of Albion in rage and
>   hunger.

Of these names, many never occur again throughout the book; and to the remainder we, to the last, fail to attach any idea whatever. Their owners cannot even be spoken of as shadows, for a shadow has a certain definiteness of form. But these continue *mere* names. Perhaps abstract qualities, of some kind or other, may be the things signified; for the *Jerusalem*, so far as I can understand it, is an allegory in which the lapse of the human race from a higher spiritual state, and its struggles towards a return to such, are the main topics. 'Jerusalem' is once spoken of as 'Liberty;' she is also apostrophized as 'mild shade of man,' and must perhaps, on the whole, be taken to symbolize this ideal state.

There is sometimes a quaint felicity in the choice of homely, familiar things as symbols, which calls John Bunyan to mind; as in this description of Golgonooza, the 'spiritual, fourfold London' (or so it is afterwards called in the *Milton*):

<blockquote>
Lo!
The stones are pity, and the bricks well-wrought affections,
Enamelled with love and kindness; and the tiles, engraven gold,
Labour of merciful hands: the beams and rafters are forgiveness;
The mortar and cement of the work, tears of honesty: the nails
And the screws and iron braces are well-wrought blandishments,
And well-contrived words; firm fixing never forgotten,
Always comforting the remembrance: the floors humility:
The ceilings devotion: the hearths thanksgiving.
</blockquote>

Far more curious is the following song, which let who can interpret. It occurs in a portion of the *Jerusalem* that is addressed

<blockquote>
To the Jews

The fields from Islington to Marybone,
  To Primrose Hill and Saint John's Wood,
Were builded over with pillars of gold;
  And there Jerusalem's pillars stood.
</blockquote>

Her little ones ran on the fields,
  The Lamb of God among them seen;
And fair Jerusalem, his Bride,
  Among the little meadows green.

Pancras and Kentish Town repose
  Among her golden pillars high,
Among her golden arches which
  Shine upon the starry sky.

The Jews'-Harp House and the Green Man,
  The Ponds where boys to bathe delight,
The fields of cows by Welling's farm,
  Shine in Jerusalem's pleasant sight.

She walks upon our meadows green,
  The Lamb of God walks by her side,
And every English child is seen,
  Children of Jesus and His Bride:

Forgiving trespasses and sins,
  Lest Babylon, with cruel Og,
With moral and self-righteous Law,
  Should crucify in Satan's synagogue.

What are those golden builders doing
  Near mournful, ever-weeping Paddington?
Standing above that mighty ruin
  Where Satan the first victory won?

Where Albion slept beneath the fatal tree,
And the Druid's golden knife
Rioted in human gore,
  In offerings of human life?

They groaned aloud on London Stone,
  They groaned aloud on Tyburn's brook:
Albion gave his deadly groan,
  And all the Atlantic mountains shook.

Albion's spectre from his loins
  Tore forth in all the pomp of war,
Satan his name: in flames of fire,
  He stretched his Druid pillars far.

Jerusalem fell from Lambeth's vale.
  Down through Poplar and old Bow,
Through Malden, and across the sea,
  In war and howling, death and woe.

The Rhine was red with human blood,
  The Danube roll'd a purple tide,
On the Euphrates Satan stood
  And over Asia stretch'd his pride.

He wither'd up sweet Zion's hill
  From every nation of the earth,
He wither'd up Jerusalem's gates,
  And in a dark land gave her birth.

He wither'd up the human form
  By laws of sacrifice for sin,
Till it became a mortal worm,
  But, O! translucent all within!

The Divine Vision still was seen,
  Still was the human form divine;
Weeping, in weak and mortal clay,
  O Jesus! still the form was Thine!

And Thine the human face; and Thine
  The human hands, and feet, and breath,
Entering through the gates of birth
  And passing through the gates of death.

And, O! Thou Lamb of God! whom I
  Slew in my dark, self-righteous pride,
Art Thou return'd to Albion's land?
  And is Jerusalem Thy Bride?

Come to my arms, and never more
  Depart, but dwell for ever here;
Create my spirit to Thy love,
  Subdue my spectre to Thy fear.

Spectre of Albion! warlike fiend!
  In clouds of blood and ruin roll'd,
I here reclaim Thee as my own,
  My selfhood; Satan arm'd in gold.

Is this thy soft family love?
  Thy cruel patriarchal pride?
Planting thy family alone,
  Destroying all the world beside?

A man's worst enemies are those
  Of his own house and family:
And he who makes his law a curse
  By his own law shall surely die.

In my exchanges every land
  Shall walk, and mine in every land,
Mutual, shall build Jerusalem,
  Both heart in heart and hand in hand.

Many of Blake's favourite metaphysical and theological tenets
are enlarged upon. As, for instance, the antagonism of Reason
to Faith:

And this is the manner of the sons of Albion in their strength:
They take two contraries, which are called qualities, with which
Every substance is clothed: they name them Good and Evil.
From these they make an abstract, which is a negation,
Not only of the substance from which it is derived, –
A murderer of its own body: but also a murderer
Of every divine member: – it is the Reasoning Power,
An abstract, objecting Power, that negatives everything.
This is the spectre of man, – the holy Reasoning Power;

And in its holiness is closed the abomination of desolation.

And again:

> He who would do good to another, must do it in minute
>   particulars:
> General good is the plea of the scoundrel, hypocrite, and flatterer.
> For Art and Science cannot exist but in minutely organized
>   particulars,
> And not in generalizing demonstrations of the Rational Power.
> The Infinite alone resides in definite and determinate identity.

Here is another theme he loved to dwell on:

> All that has existed in the space of six thousand years
> Permanent and not lost: not lost nor vanish'd; and every little act,
> Word, work, and wish that have existed, – all remaining still
> In those churches, ever consuming and ever building by the
>   spectres
> Of all the inhabitants of earth waiting to be created;
> Shadowy to those who dwell not in them – mere possibilities;
> But, to those who enter into them, they seem the only realities.
> For everything exists; and not one sigh, nor smile, nor tear,
> One hair, nor particle of dust – not one can pass away.

*   *   *

> All things acted on earth are seen in the bright sculptures of
>   Los's Hall. And every age renews its powers from these works;
> With every pathetic story possible to happen from Hate or
> Wayward Love. And every sorrow and distress is carved here;
> Every affinity of parents, marriages and friendships are here
> In all their various combinations; wrought with wondrous art,
> All that can happen to man in his pilgrimage of seventy years.

Interesting fragments, surely, if only as being so eminently
characteristic of the man. A few more such – mere fragments

– I will add before proceeding to speak of the decorative designs
with which every page of the original is enriched:

> Imagination [is] the real and eternal world, of which this veg-
> etable universe is but a faint shadow: and in which we shall live,
> in our eternal or imaginative bodies, when these vegetable mortal
> bodies are no more.

> It is easier to forgive an enemy than to forgive a friend.

> Without forgiveness of sin, Love itself is eternal Death.

> O Albion! why didst thou a female will create?

> Negations are not contraries. Contraries mutually exist,
> But negations exist not; exceptions, objections, unbelief,
> Exist not; nor shall they ever be organized for ever and ever.

> If I were pure, never could I taste the sweets of the forgiveness of
>   sins.
> If I were holy, I never could behold the tears of love:
> Of Him who loves me in the midst of His anger.

> I heard His voice in my sleep, and His angel in my dream
> Saying, Doth Jehovah forgive a debt, only on condition that it
>   shall
> Be paid? Doth He forgive pollution only on condition of purity?
> That debt is not forgiven! that pollution is not forgiven!
> Such is the forgiveness of the gods; the moral virtues of the
> Heathen, whose tender mercies are cruelty. But Jehovah's
>   salvation
> Is without money and without price in the continual forgiveness
>   of sins.

> The vegetative universe opens like a flower from the earth's
>   centre,
> In which is Eternity. It expands in stars to the mundane shell,
> And there it meets Eternity again, both within and without.
> What may man be? Who can tell? But what may woman be
> To have power over man from cradle to corruptible grave?

He who was an Infant, and whose cradle was a manger,
Knoweth the Infant Sorrow, whence it came and where it goeth,
And who weave it a cradle of the grass that withereth away.
This world is all a cradle for the erred, wandering Phantom,
Rock'd by year, month, day, and hour. And every two moments
Between, dwells a daughter of Beulah, to feed the human
  vegetable.

Rock the cradle, ah me! of that eternal man!

The magic influences of one of these mysterious 'daughters of Beulah' are thus described:

She creates at her will a little moony night and silence,
With spaces of sweet gardens and a tent of elegant beauty
Closed in by sandy deserts, and a night of stars shining;
A little tender moon, and hovering angels on the wing.
And the male gives a time and revolution to her space
Till the time of love is passed in ever-varying delights:
For all things exist in the human imagination.

This last line contains what deserves to be called the cornerstone of Blake's philosophy. For his philosophy *had* corner-stone and foundation, and was not miraculously suspended in the air, as his readers might sometimes feel tempted to believe. Amid all contradictions, incoherences, wild assertions, this principle, – that the conceptions of the mind are the realities of realities, that the human imagination is an eternal world, 'ever expanding in the bosom of God,' – shines steadily forth: and to readers of a speculative turn, who will be at the pains to examine by its light these erratic writings, the chaos will resolve itself into *substance*, though not into form and order. It is needless to tell such thinkers that Bishop Berkeley was one on the list of Blake's favourite authors. But with his fervid, dauntless imagination, the artist seized hold of the metaphysician's theory of Idealism, and quickened it into a grand poetic reality.

There is another 'Song' in the *Jerusalem*, addressed *To the Deists*, beginning

> I saw a monk of Charlemaine,

which follows soon after the one already quoted *To the Jews*. As it is far less singular and characteristic than its predecessor, however, the concluding beautiful stanza is all that shall here detain us:

> For a tear is an intellectual thing,
> And a sigh is the sword of an angel king,
> And the bitter groan of a martyr's woe
> Is an arrow from the Almighty's bow.

It were scarcely honest to call these extracts, *specimens* of the *Jerusalem*. They are exceptions, rather than specimens; and occur, for the most part, in the midst of such a chaos of words, names, and images, that, as the eye wanders, hopeless and dispirited, up and down the large closely-written pages, the mind cannot choose but busy itself with the question, how a man of Blake's high gifts ever came to produce such; nay, to consider this, as he really did, his greatest work. It must have been that, conscious of the deaf ear so resolutely turned towards him by the public, 'charmed he never so wisely,' he cared no longer to address it; but, casting away all idea of ordering and shaping his thoughts and imaginations in such wise that other minds could lay hold upon them, he followed the less laborious and more exciting pleasure of pouring his conceptions freely forth, all crude and inchoate, in words so vaguely and arbitrarily expressive of his meaning, that to himself alone could they suggest it.

Of the pictorial part of the *Jerusalem* much might be said

which would merely be applicable to all Blake's works alike. One point, perhaps, somewhat distinctive about it, is an extreme largeness and decorative character in the style of the drawings, which are mostly made up of a few massive forms, thrown together on a grand, equal scale. The beauty of the drawings varies much, according to the colour in which they are printed. One copy, possessed by Mr Monckton Milnes, is so incomparably superior, from this cause, to any other I have seen, that no one could know the work properly without having examined this copy. It is printed in a warm, reddish brown, the exact colour of a very fine photograph; and the broken blending of the deeper tones with the more tender shadows, – all sanded over with a sort of golden mist peculiar to Blake's mode of execution, – makes still more striking the resemblance to the then undiscovered 'handling' of Nature herself. The extreme breadth of the forms throughout, when seen through the medium of this colour, shows sometimes, united with its grandeur, a suavity of line which is almost Venetian.

The subjects are vague and mystic as the poem itself. Female figures lie among waves full of reflected stars: a strange human image, with a swan's head and wings, floats on water in a kneeling attitude, and drinks: lovers embrace in an open water-lily: an eagle-headed creature sits and contemplates the sun: serpent-women are coiled with serpents: Assyrian-looking human-visaged bulls are seen yoked to the plough or the chariot: rocks swallow or vomit forth human forms, or appear to amalgamate with them: angels cross each other over wheels of flame: and flames and hurrying figures writhe and wind among the lines. Even such slight things as these rough intersecting circles, each containing some hint of an angel; even these are made the unmistakable exponents of genius. Here and there some more familiar theme meets us, − the creation of Eve, or the Crucifixion; and then the thread is lost again. The whole spirit of the designs might seem well symbolized in one of the finest among them, where we see a triple-headed and triple-crowned figure embedded in rocks, from whose breast is bursting a string of youths, each in turn born from the other's breast in one sinuous throe of mingled life, while the life of suns and planets dies and is born and rushes together around them.

Milton: a Poem in Two Books. The Author and Printer, W. Blake, 1804, is a small quarto of forty-five engraved pages, coloured by hand in the usual manner. In the frontispiece of the *Jerusalem*, a man enters at a dark door, carrying a planet. Would we might follow him through those dim passages, and see them by his light! Nor would his company be less serviceable among the mazes of the *Milton*. As this latter work has no perceptible affinity with its title, so the designs it contains seem unconnected with the text. This principle of independence is carried even into Blake's own portrait of his cottage at Felpham, which bears no accurate resemblance to the real place. In beauty, the drawings do not rank with Blake's most notable works; the copy at the Museum (as seen by the water-mark of its paper − 1808) is not one of the earliest, and others might, probably, be found, surpassing it in point of colour. Two of the designs chiefly arrest attention; each of which shows us a figure falling as if struck by Heaven; one bearing the inscription *Robert*, and the other *William*. They embody the sweet remembrance which Blake preserved of his lost brother, throughout the dying life of every day. Of the two figures, Robert, the already dead, is wrapped in the deeper shadow; but, in other respects, they are almost the same.

The poem is very like the *Jerusalem* in style: it would seem, in fact, to be a sort of continuation; an idea that is borne out by the verses with which its singular Preface concludes:

> And did those feet in ancient time
>   Walk upon England's mountain green?
> And was the holy Lamb of God
>   On England's pleasant pastures seen?
>
> And did the countenance Divine
>   Shine forth upon our clouded hills?
> And was Jerusalem builded here
>   Among these dark Satanic mills?
>
> Bring me my bow of burning gold!
>   Bring me my arrows of desire!
> Bring me my spear: O clouds, unfold!
>   Bring me my chariot of fire!
>
> I will not cease from mental fight,
>   Nor shall my sword sleep in my hand,
> Till we have built Jerusalem
>   In England's green and pleasant land.

'Would to God that all the Lord's people were prophets!'

NUMBERS xi. 29.

The *Milton*, as I have hinted, equals its predecessor in obscurity; few are the readers who will ever penetrate beyond the first page or two. There is also the same religious fervour, the same high, devout aim:

> I touch the heavens as an instrument to glorify the Lord!

exclaims Blake in one place; and the reader is, with impassioned earnestness, besought to give heed unto him in the following line, which recurs incessantly:

> Mark well my words; they are of your eternal salvation!

About Milton we hear very little, but his name *is* occasionally mentioned; as in the opening invocation:

> Daughters of Beulah! muses who inspire the poet's song!
> Record the journey of immortal Milton through your realms
> Of terror and mild moony lustre!

And afterwards we are told:

> First Milton saw Albion upon the rock of ages,
> Deadly pale outstretch'd and snowy cold, storm-cover'd:
> A giant form of perfect beauty outstretch'd on the rock
> In solemn death: the Sea of Time and Space thunder'd aloud
> Against the rock which was inwrapp'd with the weeds of death
> Hovering over the cold bosom. In its vortex Milton bent down
> To the bosom of death. What was underneath soon seem'd
> above,
> A cloudy heaven mingled with stormy seas in loudest ruin.
> But as a wintry globe descends precipitant through Beulah,
> bursting
> With thunders loud and terrible, so Milton's shadow fell
> Precipitant, loud thund'ring into the sea of Time and Space.

Whither we will not attempt to follow him, but conclude our gleanings from the 'Prophetic Books' with the following sweet reminiscence of life at Felpham which occurs in the Second Book of *Milton*; and with the quaint and pretty lines *àpropos* of which Blake introduces the idealized view of his cottage.

> Thou hearest the nightingale begin the song of spring;
> The lark, sitting upon his earthy bed, just as the morn
> Appears, listens silent; then, springing from the waving
> corn-field, loud
> He leads the choir of day: trill – trill – trill – trill –
> Mounting upon the wings of light into the great expanse,
> Re-echoing against the lovely blue and shining heavenly shell.
> His little throat labours with inspiration; every feather

On throat, and breast, and wing, vibrate with the effluence
   divine.
All nature listens to him silent; and the awful Sun
Stands still upon the mountains, looking on this little bird
With eyes of soft humility, and wonder, love, and awe.
Then loud, from their green covert, all the birds begin their
   song, –
The thrush, the linnet and the goldfinch, robin and the wren,
Awake the Sun from his sweet reverie upon the mountains;
The nightingale again essays his song, and through the day
And through the night warbles luxuriant; every bird of song
Attending his loud harmony with admiration and love.

(This is a vision of the lamentation of Beulah over Ololon.)

Thou perceivest the flowers put forth their precious odours,
And none can tell how from so small a centre come such sweets,
Forgetting that within that centre Eternity expands.
* When Los join'd with me, he took me in his fiery whirlwind;
My vegetated portion was hurried from Lambeth's shades;
He set me down in Felpham's vale, and prepared a beautiful
  Cottage for me, that, in three years, I might write all these
   visions;
To display Nature's cruel holiness; the deceits of Natural
   Religion.
Walking in my cottage garden, sudden I beheld
The virgin Ololon, and address'd her as a daughter of Beulah:
'Virgin of Providence! fear not to enter into my cottage!'

TWENTY-TWO

A Keen Employer 1805-7
[ÆT. 48-50]

June 18th, 1805, is the engraver's date on the plates to the duodecimo edition, already mentioned, of Hayley's *Ballads on Animals*: an edition planned during the Felpham stay; printed by Seagrave, of Chichester, for Richard Phillips, and, as I said, for Blake's benefit; which, I fear, proved *nil*. The book fell still-born from the press, though now in some degree of request, on account of Blake's plates. These, however, are unfair examples of his skill and imperfect versions of his design. They have more than Blake's ordinary hardness of manner. Two – *The Eagle* and *The Lion* – are repetitions from the quarto. *The Dog, The Hermit's Dog,* and *The Horse,* are new. The last-named is, perhaps, the finest in the series. Even though the horse's hind leg be in an impossible position, and though there be the usual lack of correct local detail, very striking and soulful is the general effect; especially so is that serene, majestic, feminine figure, standing before her terrified child and bravely facing the frenzied animal, which, by mere spiritual force, she subdues into motionless awe.

To Hayley succeeded a patron who will give even less pecuniary help, but a more efficient introduction to the public. This was R. H. Cromek, hitherto an engraver, now turning print-jobber and book-maker, who at this period *discovered* Blake. The slighted artist sorely needed a discoverer; he and his wife being now, according to Cromek, 'reduced so low as to be obliged to live on half a guinea a week.' 'Living' must here mean board; for weekly rent alone would amount to that sum. Thus interpreted, the statement is not an exaggerated one of Blake's straitened resources at this and other periods of his life.

During 1804 to 1805 had been produced that series of Drawings illustrative of Blair's *Grave*, by which, from the accident of their having been afterwards really *published* and pushed in the regular way, Blake is most widely known – known at all, I may say – to the public at large. It is the only volume, with his name on its title-page, which is *not* 'scarce.' These drawings Blake had intended engraving and publishing himself. They were seen, however, admired and purchased, by engraver Cromek – 'engraver, printseller, publisher, author – and Yorkshireman.' He gave, according to Smith, 'the insignificant sum of one guinea each for them,' but, in fact, a guinea and a half; 'on the express understanding,' adds Smith, 'that the artist was to engrave them for a projected edition of *The Grave*.' This, involving a far more considerable remuneration, would have made the total payment for the designs tolerably adequate.

Robert Hartley Cromek, a native of Hull, now a man of five-and-thirty, had been a pupil of Bartolozzi, and, during the past ten years, had engraved, with credit, many book plates after Stothard. He was one in the numerous band whom that graceful artist's active fingers kept employed; for, as may well be believed, it is vastly quicker work the making of designs than the engraving them. Among Cromek's doing are some of the plates to an edition of *The Spectator* (1803), to Du Roveray's edition of Pope (1804), and one in an early edition of Rogers' *Pleasures of Memory*. With a nervous temperament and an indifferent constitution, the painful confinement of his original profession ill agreed.

An active, scheming disposition, combined with some taste for literature and superficial acquaintance with it, tempted him to exchange, as many second-rate engravers have done, the steady drudgery of engraving for the more profitable, though speculative, trade of print-publisher and dealer, or farmer of the talents of others. He had little or no capital. This edition of Blair's *Grave*, with illustrations by Blake, was his first venture. And twenty guineas for twelve of the most original designs of the century, and not unintelligible designs, though from Blake's mystic hand, was no bad beginning. Even in this safe investment, however, the tasteful Yorkshireman showed bolder discernment of unvalued genius than the stolid trade ever hazarded.

In 1805 the *Prospectus* was issued; from which it appears, it was then intended for Blake to engrave the illustrations. The *Prospectus* was helped by an elaborate opinion in favour of the Designs from Fuseli's friendly pen, whose word then carried almost judicial weight. As collateral guarantee was added an authorized statement of their cordial approval by President West, and ten other academicians; among them Cosway, Flaxman, Lawrence, Nollekens, Stothard. These were credentials by which the practical Cromek set some store. He had submitted the drawings to those academic dons, disinterestedly anxious to be assured 'how far he was warranted in calling the attention of connoisseurs to what he himself imagined to be a high and original effort of genius;' not, of course, with any eye to the value of such testimonials with the public. Accomplished Thomas Hope – *Anastasius* Hope – and virtuoso Mr Locke, of Norbury, also 'pledged their character as connoisseurs' (according to Malkin) in their favour, 'by approving and patronizing these designs.'

Blake was looking 'forward with anxious delight' to the congenial task of engraving his 'Inventions,' and did engrave one or two. A print in his peculiar, vigorous manner, from his favourite design – *Death's Door* – I have seen. But shrewd Cromek's eye had been educated in the school of graceful Bartolozzi. By him, Blake's old-fashioned, austere style was quickly perceived to be not in unison with public taste, and far less likely to draw subscribers than a lucid version of his wild grandeur by some competent hand. To the initiated, an artist's rendering of his own conception – that, say, of an Albert Dürer, a Lucas von Leyden, a Hogarth – has always the infinitely superior claim, in its first-hand vigour, freshness, and air as of an original. Such engravings *are*, in fact, originals.

Cromek selected for his purpose Lewis Schiavonetti, a native of Bassano, in Venetia, who, on coming to England, had put himself under Bartolozzi, Cromek's master. In that studio, probably, the two became acquainted. Schiavonetti rose above all Bartolozzi's other pupils; above the master too; developing an individual style, which united grandeur with grace, boldness, draughtsman-like power, and intelligence with executive delicacy and finish. It was a happy choice of engraver on Cromek's part, and with his views. The large outlay requisite to secure the Italian's services was pretty sure of ultimate return, with good interest. Cromek's sagacity cannot, indeed, be denied. It resulted in the wedding of remarkable powers of engraving to high design, worthy of them. In his brief course, Schiavonetti was generally most unfortunate in having subjects to engrave not deserving of his skill. A previous engraving from Leonardo's noble Cartoon of Pisa, the plates to *The Grave*, and a subsequent etching from Stothard's *Canterbury Pilgrims*, are the only examples of a fitly-directed exercise of his powers. By them alone can they now be estimated. On another ground, Cromek's decision can hardly be blamed. Schiavonetti introduced Blake's designs to a wider public than himself could ever have done.

On the other hand, the purchaser of the designs having made a certain engagement, it was not open to him, in honour or common honesty, because it was an unwritten one, to depart from it for his own advantage, without Blake's consent, or without making compensation to the artist for his pecuniary loss. In point of fact, Cromek jockeyed Blake out of his copyright. And Blake was naturally mortified and incensed at the loss of profitable and happy employment to which the new arrangement sentenced him, and at becoming a mere conduit for the enrichment of two fellow-engravers.

Allan Cunningham, who also had had relations with Cromek, and had kindly reasons for judging him leniently, tells us the speculator, in paying Blake twenty guineas for the twelve designs, gave a price which, 'though small, was more than what he usually received for such productions.' This is what Cromek, or his widow, told Cunningham; but the statement is incorrect. True, Blake's gains were always small. A guinea to a guinea and a half each was his price for the water-colour drawings sold to Mr Butts and others. But then he did not lose his copyright; he was always at liberty to make duplicates and to engrave them. Clearly he did make more by those; more, also, by the *Songs of Innocence and of Experience*, and the other series of designs which he kept in his own hands, and sold engraved copies of, for sums varying from five to twenty guineas.

While Schiavonetti was at work on his etchings from the Designs to Blair, hungry Cromek would call every now and then on Blake, to see what he was doing. One day, he caught sight of a pencil drawing from a hitherto virgin subject – the *Procession* of Chaucer's *Canterbury Pilgrims;* Chaucer being a poet read by fewer then than now. Cromek 'appeared highly delighted' with Blake's sketch, says Smith, as being an original treatment of an original subject. In point of fact, he wanted to secure a finished drawing from it, for the purpose of having it engraved, and *without* employing Blake, just as he had served him over the Designs to *The Grave;* as I learn from other sources, on sifting the matter. However, Blake was not to be taken in a second time. Negotiations on that basis failed; but, as Blake understood the matter, he received a commission, tacit or express, from Cromek, to execute the design. The Yorkshireman, nevertheless, went to Stothard, suggested the subject as a novelty, and, in fine, commissioned of that artist an oil-picture for sixty guineas, to be engraved by Bromley; for whom Schiavonetti was eventually substituted. Whether Stothard knew of Blake's design I can hardly pronounce; possibly not; certainly he did not, I should say, of Cromek's previous overtures to Blake, nor of the fact that a subscription paper for an engraving of the *Canterbury Pilgrims* had been circulated by Blake's friends.

This was in 1806, two years before publication of *The Grave.* One day, while Stothard was painting his picture, Blake called on his friend and saw it, ignorant, evidently, that it was to supersede his own, and that slippery Cromek was at the bottom of its having existed at all; nay, was making it his next speculation with the public. For the two artists to design from the same poets and subjects was no new thing, as a comparison of their works will show. Take, for instance, the *Night Thoughts* of Young, illustrated by Blake in 1797, by Stothard in 1802. Such coincidences naturally happen to all painters of history and poetry. According to Stothard, Blake praised his picture, and expressed much pleasure at seeing it. Stothard, on his side, talked of introducing Blake (a good subject, by the way) into the Procession, 'as a mark of esteem for him and his works.' From these he candidly confessed to have long derived pleasure and profit.

When Blake came to know how the case really stood, his indignation was vehement against Cromek, at whom his grudge was yet fresh for having robbed him of the engraving his designs to Blair. Indignation, too, he long cherished towards Stothard, whom he took to have been privy to Cromek's previous dealings with himself for his design from Chaucer. My own induction from all the evidence coincides with Flaxman's opinion, viz., that Stothard's act was not a wilful one, in being made a party to an engraving of a picture by himself, on a subject previously taken by Blake. Certain it is, indeed, that the general composition of his Procession has a suspicious resemblance to Blake's. This, however, may be due to hints given by the unscrupulous go-between.

By May 1807 Stothard's 'Cabinet Picture' was publicly exhibited; and, what with its own merits and novelty, and what with Cromek's judicious puffing, drew several thousand gazers and admirers. Hoppner, at the end of May, wrote an encomiastic descriptive 'Letter' to Cumberland, printed in Prince Hoare's *Artist*, and turned to good account in Cromek's *Prospectus* for the engraving. Connoisseur, picture-dealing Carey, – afterwards as 'Ridolfi,' Etty's panegyrist, – always too happy to get his verbiage set up in type free of cost, penned a still longer *Critical Description* the following year, which wily Cromek had well circulated as a bait to subscribers.

During this May was scribbled a letter from Cromek to Blake, bearing incidentally on this matter, but mainly on the designs to *The Grave*, and the differences which had arisen between the two. The letter sets forcibly before us Blake's circumstances at the time; is an example of the spurns he from the unworthy took; and throws a flood of light on the character of the writer. It subsequently fell into Allan Cunningham's hands, thence into his son, Mr Peter Cunningham's, and has been printed in the *Gentleman's Magazine* (Feb. 1852):

64, Newman Street, May, 1807.

SIR,

I rec'd, not with^t great surprise, your letter demanding four guineas for the *sketched* vignette ded^n to the Queen. I have returned the drawing with this note, and I will briefly state my reasons for so doing. In the first place, I do not think it merits the price you affix to it, *under any circumstances.* In the next place, I never had the remotest suspicion that you^d for a moment entertain the idea of writing *me* to supply money to create an honour in w^h I cannot possibly participate. The Queen allowed *you*, not *me*, to dedicate the work to *her!* The honour w^d have been yours exclus^y, but that you might not be deprived of any advantage likely to contribute to your reputation, I was willing to pay Mr Schiavonetti *ten* guineas for etching a plate from the drawing in question.

Another reason for returning the sketch is, that I *can do without it*, having already engaged to give a greater number of etchings than the price of the book will warrant; and I neither have, nor ever had, any encouragement from *you* to place you before the public in a more favourable point of view than that which I have already chosen. You charge me w^h *imposing upon you.* Upon my honour, I have no recollection of anything of the kind. If the world and I were to settle accounts to-morrow, I do assure you the balance w^d be considerably in my favour. In this respect I am more sinned against than sinning! But if I cannot recollect any instances wherein I have imposed upon *you*, several present themselves in w^h I have imposed upon myself. Take two or three that press upon me.

When I first called on you, I found you without reputation;

I *imposed* on myself the labour, and an herculean one it has been, to create and establish a reputation for you. I say the labour was herculean, because I had not only to contend with, but I had to battle with a man who had pre-determined not to be served. What public reputation you have, the reputation of eccentricity excepted, I have acquired for you; and I can honestly and conscientiously assert, that if you had laboured through life for yourself as zealously and as earnestly as I have done for you, your reputation as an artist w^d not only have been enviable, but it would have put it out of the power of an individual as obscure as myself either to add to or take from it. *I also imposed on myself,* when I believed what you so often have told me, that your works were equal, nay superior, to a Raphael, or to a Michael Angelo! Unfortunately for me as a publisher, the public awoke me from this state of stupor, this mental delusion. That public is willing to give you credit for what real talent is to be found in your productions, *and for no more.*

I have imposed on myself yet more grossly in believing you to be one altogether abstracted from this world, holding converse with the world of spirits! simple, unoffending, a combination of the *serpent* and the *dove.* I really blush when I reflect how I have been cheated in this respect. The most effectual way of benefiting a designer whose aim is general patronage, is to bring his designs before the public through the medium of engraving. Your drawings have had the *good fortune* to be engraved by one of the first artists in Europe, and the specimens already shown have already produced you orders that I verily believe you otherwise w^d not have rec^d. Herein I have been gratified, for I was determined to bring you food as well as reputation, though, from your late conduct, I have some reason to embrace your wild opinion, that to manage genius, and to cause it to produce good things, it is absolutely necessary to starve it; indeed, this opinion is considerably heightened by the recollection that your best work, the illustrations of 'The Grave,' was produced when you and Mrs Blake were reduced so low as to be obliged to live on half a guinea a week!

Before I conclude this letter, it will be necessary to remark, when I gave you the order for the drawings from the poem of 'The Grave,' I paid you for them more than I could then afford; more in proportion than you were in the habit of receiving, and what you were perfectly satisfied with; though I must do you the justice to confess much less than I think is their real value. Perhaps you have friends and admirers who can appreciate their merit and worth as much as I do. I am decidedly of opinion that the twelve for 'The Grave' should sell at the least for sixty guineas. If you can meet with any gentleman who will give you this sum for them, I will deliver them into his hands on the publication of the poem. I will deduct the twenty guineas I have paid you from that sum, and the remainder forty ditto shall be at your disposal.

I will not detain you more than one minute. Why did you so *furiously rage* at the success of the little picture of 'The Pilgrimage?' Three thousand people have now *seen it and have approved of it*. Believe me, yours is '*the voice of one crying in the wilderness!*'

You say the subject is *low*, and *contemptibly treated*. For his excellent mode of treating the subject, the poet has been admired for the last 400 years! The poor painter has not yet the advantage of antiquity on his side, therefore w^h some people an apology may be necessary for him. The conclusion of one of Squire Timkin's letters to his mother in the Bath Guide will afford one. He speaks greatly to the purpose:

'I very well know,
Both my subject and verse is exceedingly low;
But if any *great critic* finds fault with my letter,
He has nothing to do but to send you a better.'

With much respect for your talents,

I remain, Sir,

Your real friend and well-wisher,

R. H. CROMEK.

It is one thing to read such a letter fifty years after it was written, though one can hardly do so without indignation; another to have had to receive and digest its low affronts. A poet had need have a world of visions to retire to when exposed to these 'slings and arrows of outrageous fortune.' Blake might well get irascible, might well give vent to his contempt and scorn in epigrams such as the following, which I find in that same MS. note-book wherein poor Hayley figures so ignominiously:

> Cromek loves artists as he loves his meat;
> He loves the art, but 'tis the art to cheat!

And again:

> A petty sneaking knave I knew;
> Oh, Mr Cromek! how do you do?

Here is a taste of 'Cromek's opinions put into rhyme.'

* * *

> I always take my judgments from a fool,
> Because his judgment is so very cool;
> Not prejudiced by feelings great and small.
> Amiable state! he cannot feel at all.

And yet is not a needy publisher to make that profit out of a needy painter he cannot for himself? May not the purchaser of twelve drawings at twenty pounds do what he likes with his own? That Cromek had no answer to the charge of 'imposition,' and of having tricked Blake, is obvious from his preferring to open up irrelevant questions: he defends by attacking. The artist's discouragement of Cromek's herculean labours in behalf of Blake's fame, refers to his infatuated preference for being his own engraver, according to agreement. Through Cromek's reluctance to part with four guineas, the Blair lost a crowning grace in the vignette or *setting*, as in Blake's hands it would have been, of the *Dedication to the Queen*.

Poor Blake, in asking four guineas instead of one, for a single sketch, had evidently felt entitled to some insignificant atonement for previous under-pay. Perhaps, on the hint at the close of Cromek's letter

'He has nothing to do but to send you a better,'

the indignant painter acted in executing, hereafter, his projected 'fresco' from the *Canterbury Pilgrimage*, and exhibiting and engraving it.

TWENTY-THREE

Gleams of Patronage 1806–1808
[ÆT. 49–51]

Another 'discoverer' of Blake's singular and ignored genius was Dr Malkin, Head-Master of Bury Grammar School, to whose account of the artist's early years we were indebted at the outset. It was, probably, after the return from Felpham, and through Cromek, they were made known to one another. Dr Malkin was the author of various now all but forgotten works, – *Essays on Subjects connected with Civilization*, 1795: *Scenery, Antiquities, and Biography of South Wales*, 1804, which was his most popular effort, reaching, in 1807, to a second edition: also, *Almahide and Hamet, a Tragedy*, 1804. His name may likewise be found to a current revision of Smollett's Translation of *Gil Blas*, the earlier editions of which contain illustrations by Smirke.

Blake designed, and originally engraved, the 'ornamental device' to the frontispiece for Malkin's *Father's Memoirs of his Child*, but it was erased before the appearance of the work, and the same design re-engraved by Cromek. The book was published February 1806; in which month, by the way, died Barry, whom Blake knew and admired. The frontispiece consists of a portrait of the precocious infant, when two years old, from a miniature by Page, surrounded by an emblematic design of great beauty. An Angel is conducting the child heavenward; he takes leave, with consoling gesture, of his kneeling mother, who, in a half-resigned, half-deprecating attitude, stretches towards him her wistful, unavailing arms, from the edge of a cliff – typifying Earth's verge. It is in a rambling introductory Letter to Johnes of Hafod, translator of Froissart, the account in question of the designer of the frontispiece is given, with extracts from his Poems: a well-meant, if not very successful, attempt of the kindly pedagogue to serve the 'untutored proficient,' as he terms Blake. The poor little defunct prodigy who is the subject of the *Memoir*, and who died in 1802, after little more than a six years' lease of life, was not only an expert linguist, a general reader, something of a poet, the historian and topographer of an imaginary kingdom, of which he drew an 'accurate map;' but was also a designer, producing 'copies from some of Raphael's heads so much in unison with the style and sentiment of the originals, as induced our late excellent and ingenious friend, Mr Banks, the sculptor, to predict, "that if he were to pursue the arts as a profession, he would one day rank among the more distinguished of their votaries."'

He was also an original inventor of 'little landscapes; accustomed to cut every piece of waste paper within his reach into squares' an inch or two in size, and to fill them with 'temples, bridges, trees, broken ground, or any other fanciful and picturesque materials which suggested themselves to his imagination.' The father gives tracings from six of these as 'specimens of his talent in composition;' himself descrying a decisive idea attached to each, and that 'the buildings are placed firm on the ground;' not to mention a taste and variety, the 'result of a mind gifted with just feeling and fertile resources.'

The 'testimony of Mr Blake' is added, who, being a man of imagination, can decipher more in these pre-Claudite jottings of pillar and post, arch and scrub, than his humble biographer can. What he says is, in its general tenor, interesting and true enough. But surely Mr Blake saw double on the occasion, – for his sincerity never admits of doubt.

'They are all,' writes he, 'firm determinate outline, or identical form. Had the hand which executed these little ideas been that of a plagiary, who works only from the memory, we should have seen blots, called masses,' (Blake is girding at his own opposites in Art) 'blots without form, and therefore without meaning. These blots of light and dark, as being the result of labour, are always clumsy and indefinite; the effect of rubbing out and putting in; like the progress of a blind man, or one in the dark, who feels his way but does not see it. These are not so. Even the copy from Raphael's cartoon of *St Paul preaching*' (from Dorigny's plate of the same) 'is a firm determinate outline, struck at once, as Protogenes struck his line, when he meant to make himself known to Apelles. The map of Allestone has the same character of the firm and determinate. All his efforts prove this little boy to have had that greatest of blessings, a strong imagination, a clear idea, and a determinate vision of things in his own mind.'

Cromek, in the letter of May 1807, quoted in the previous chapter, tells Blake incidentally, 'The specimens' (in proof) 'of Schiavonetti's etchings have already produced you orders that, I verily believe, you would not otherwise have received.' One commission, the credit whereof Cromek may here be assuming to himself, was that which occupied Blake during 1807, for the Countess of Egremont, to whom he had already been made known by Hayley. It was for a repetition, or enlargement rather, of the most elaborate of the Blair drawings – *The Last Judgment*. In reality, however, the commission was obtained through his staunch friend Ozias Humphrey, the miniature painter. A letter to him from Blake (18th February 1808), descriptive of this composition, is, in its commencement, applicable to that in the Blair, but shows the new picture to have contained many more figures and considerable variations from the previous treatment. Smith got hold of this letter from Upcott, Humphrey's godson, or, as some say, son in a less spiritual sense. The original is now in the possession of Mr Anderdon, and, thanks to his courtesy, has been here followed; Smith's version being a slightly inaccurate one. To those familiar with Blake's works, a very extraordinary and imaginative composition is indicated.

To Ozias Humphrey, Esq.

The design of *The Last Judgment*, which I have completed by your recommendation for the Countess of Egremont, it is necessary to give some account of; and its various parts ought to be described, for the accommodation of those who give it the honour of their attention.

Christ seated on the Throne of Judgment: before His feet and around Him the Heavens in clouds are rolling like a scroll, ready to be consumed in the fires of Angels who descend with the four trumpets sounding to the four winds.

Beneath, the earth is convulsed with the labours of the Resurrection. In the caverns of the earth is the Dragon with seven heads and ten horns, chained by two Angels; and above his cavern, on the earth's surface, is the Harlot, seized and bound by two Angels with chains, while her palaces are falling into ruins, and her counsellors and warriors are descending into the abyss, in wailing and despair.

Hell opens beneath the Harlot's seat on the left hand, into which the wicked are descending.

The right hand of the design is appropriated to the Resurrection of the just: the left hand of the design is appropriated to the Resurrection and Fall of the Wicked.

Immediately before the Throne of Christ are Adam and Eve, kneeling in humiliation, as representatives of the whole human race; Abraham and Moses kneel on each side beneath them; from the cloud on which Eve kneels, is seen Satan wound round by the Serpent, and falling headlong; the Pharisees appear on the left hand pleading their own Righteousness before the Throne of Christ and before the Book of Death, which is opened on clouds by two Angels; many groups of figures are falling from before the throne, and from the sea of fire, which flows before the steps of the throne; on which are seen the seven Lamps of the Almighty, burning before the throne. Many figures chained and bound together, and in various attitudes of despair and horror, fall through the air, and some are scourged by Spirits with flames of fire into the abyss of Hell, which opens beneath, on the left hand of the Harlot's seat; where others are howling and descending into the flames, and in the act of dragging each other into Hell, and of contending and fighting with each other on the brink of perdition.

Before the Throne of Christ on the right hand, the Just, in humiliation and in exultation, rise through the air, with their children and families; some of whom are bowing before the Book of Life, which is opened on clouds by two Angels: many groups arise in exultation; among them is a figure crowned with stars, and the moon beneath her feet, with six infants around her, – she represents the Christian Church. Green hills appear beneath with the graves of the blessed, which are seen bursting with their births of immortality; parents and children, wives and husbands, embrace and arise together, and, in exulting attitudes, tell each other that the New Jerusalem is ready to descend upon earth; they arise upon the air rejoicing; others, newly awaked from the grave, stand upon the earth embracing and shouting to the Lamb, who cometh in the clouds with power and great glory.

The whole upper part of the design is a view of Heaven opened, around the Throne of Christ. In the clouds which roll away are the four living creatures filled with eyes, attended by

230

seven Angels with seven vials of the wrath of God and, above these, seven Angels with the seven trumpets; these compose the cloud, which, by its rolling away, displays the opening seats of the Blessed; on the right and the left of which are seen the four-and-twenty Elders seated on thrones to judge the Dead.

Behind the seat and Throne of Christ appears the Tabernacle with its veil opened, the Candlestick on the right, the Table with Shew-bread on the left, and, in the midst, the Cross in place of the Ark, the Cherubim bowing over it.

On the right hand of the Throne of Christ is Baptism, on His left is the Lord's Supper – the two introducers into Eternal Life. Women with infants approach the figure of an Apostle, which represents Baptism, and on the left hand the Lord's Supper is administered by Angels, from the hands of another aged Apostle; these kneel on each side of the Throne, which is surrounded by a glory: in the glory many infants appear, representing Eternal Creation flowing from the Divine Humanity in Jesus; who opens the Scroll of Judgment upon his knees before the Living and the Dead.

Such is the design which you, my dear Sir, have been the cause of my producing, and which, but for you, might have slept till the Last Judgment.

WILLIAM BLAKE.

February 18, 1808.

The Last Judgment was, in the final years of Blake's life, once more repeated as a 'fresco,' into which he introduced some thousand figures, bestowing much finish and splendour of tint on it.

The reader will find a very curious paper by Blake, concerning the Last Judgment, appearing to be partly descriptive of his picture, partly, as usual with him, running off into vision, and speculation about vision, and explanations of what a last judgment is and is not. This paper is a piecing together of many scattered paragraphs or pages in the MS. Book by Blake, belonging to Mr Rossetti, elsewhere already referred to; most of the fragments certainly, and all of them very likely, forming a continuous whole. The descriptive portion of the paper is valuable in proportion to the interest appertaining to the fresco, one of the most important of the culminating productions of Blake's life. One would give a good deal to have a similar sort of explanation by Orcagna, Michael Angelo, or Rubens, of the Last Judgment, as conceived and painted by those painters respectively; and none of them certainly was more capable of *conceiving* the subject than Blake, whatever may be the connoisseur's verdict as to the relative powers for executing it. How close, in many respects, the affinity of treatment, of framework and detail of incident, in all these paintings: yet how immense the divergence of the feeling, of the minds embodied in the works, of the aspects under which the subject, the *Dies illa* presented itself within the inner precincts of the painters' intellects! As regards the visionary or speculative portion of the paper referred to, a remarkable resemblance to Swedenborg may be observed in it here and there, as in the 'Doctrine of Concordances' which it implies – the principle that spiritual conditions are *represented* by material objects, properties, and events.

Ozias Humphrey, a miniature painter of rare excellence, whose works have a peculiar sweetness of painting and refined simplicity in a now old-fashioned style, was himself a patron as well as friend, for whom Blake had expressly coloured many of his illustrated books. Humphrey had passed three years of his life, 1785–88, in India, and had reaped a golden harvest in Oude by painting miniatures of the native princes. What has become of these, I wonder? 1858 may have brought some of them across seas as the work of native artists! His sketches and note-books during that period are in the British Museum. When, in 1790, his sight first became imperfect, he took to crayons and oils with ill success. His eyes failed him altogether in 1799, after which he lived at Knightsbridge.

At the Academy's Exhibition in Somerset House for 1808, Blake, after nine years' intermission, exhibited two works, hung, as usual, in the Drawing and Miniature room. Both were subjects eminently suited to show, in his enemies' despite, what he could do: *Christ in the Sepulchre guarded by Angels*, and *Jacob's Dream*. *Jacob's Dream*, a tempera, now in the possession of Mr Monckton Milnes, is a poetic and beautiful composition, of far deeper imaginative feeling than the much-praised landscape effect of Allston, the American, or the gracefully designed scene of Stothard, whose forte, by the way, did not lie in bringing angels from the skies, though he did much to raise mortals thither. In Blake's tempera, angelic figures, some winged, others wingless, but all truly angelic in suggestion, make radiant the mysterious spiral stairs heavenward; and some among them lead children – a very Blake-like touch.

This was the last time Blake exhibited at the Royal Academy: he had done so but five times in all. No wonder that his name was little known to an exhibition-going public. And in truth, dreams so devout as his, and brought from very different worlds, were ill suited to jostle in the miscellaneous crowd. Solitude and silence are needed to enter into their sequestered spirit.

TWENTY-FOUR

The Designs to Blair 1804–8
[ÆT. 47–51]

From July 1805 to May 1808, the twelve admirable etchings after Blake's designs had been in progress under the skilful and conscientious hands of the Italian workman, – etchings which have not a line too much nor too little. They were, as I have said, a really favourable medium for introducing Blake to the many; although admirers might prefer the artist's own characteristic expression of himself with the graver. There were no such thorough-paced admirers then, perhaps there are not above half a dozen now. Schiavonetti's version is, in fact, a graceful translation, and, as most would think, an improvement.

The boldly-engraved portrait of Blake after Phillips' fine drawing, prefixed to *The Grave*, was considered like. We in it recognise the high visionary brow, the speculative eyes, characteristic of William Blake. But the aspect is a too idealized and *made-up* one, too studiously *inspired*, and does not therefore convey a wholly reliable impression. You would hardly, for instance, suspect its original to have been short in stature, as he really was.

In the autumn of 1808, the book was published by Cromek, in alliance with Cadell and Davies, Johnson, Payne, and other leaders in the trade. It was beautifully printed in quarto by Bensley, the best printer of his day, and was indorsed with

Fuseli's testimonial, and the credentials from the R.A.'s again.
Cromek had certainly worked hard for his own profit and Blake's
fame, in obtaining subscriptions. His list comprises no less than
five hundred and eighty-nine names, from London and the
chief provincial towns, – Liverpool, Manchester, Birmingham,
Bristol, Edinburgh, Newcastle. Native Yorkshire, – Leeds,
Wakefield, Halifax, – contributes a large contingent. There are,
however, only one or two titled subscribers. The artists, always
best appreciators of one another, muster in strength as supporters
of the enterprise, not without importunity on busy Cromek's
part. We particularize with interest the names of Bewick, from
far Newcastle, and 'Mr Green, landscape draughtsman, Amble-
side.' A few literary men came forward; among them Holcroft
and Hayley, bringing with him Mrs Poole, of Lavant, and printer
Seagrave. Vigilant Cromek had at the outset taken care not to
neglect these old friends of the designer's. The subscriptions at
two and a half guineas amount to above £1,800; besides proof
copies at four guineas, and a margin of unsubscribed-for copies
on sale. This makes Cromek pretty sure of a good profit by his
protégé's genius and his own activities, after all outlay to designer
(twenty guineas), engraver (perhaps £500), printing, advertising,
puffing, travelling expenses, and allowances to the trade.

While the engravings were in progress, the name of the Queen
as a subscriber had been somehow obtained, and permission to
dedicate the designs to her; of which Blake availed himself in
the following simple and earnest stanzas, – a mere enigma, I
should fancy, to 'old Queen Charlotte.' The vignette which was
to have accompanied it Cromek, as we saw, returned on his
hands:

> The door of death is made of gold,
> That mortal eyes cannot behold

But when the mortal eyes are clos'd,
And cold and pale the limbs repos'd,
The soul awakes, and, wond'ring, sees
In her mild hand the golden keys.
The grave is heaven's golden gate,
And rich and poor around it wait:
O Shepherdess of England's fold,
Behold this gate of pearl and gold!

To dedicate to England's Queen
The visions that my soul has seen,
And, by her kind permission, bring
What I have borne on solemn wing
From the vast regions of the grave,
Before her throne my wings I wave,
Bowing before my sov'reign's feet:
The Grave produced these blossoms sweet,
In mild repose from earthly strife;
The blossoms of eternal life!

WILLIAM BLAKE.

When Blake speaks of

The visions that my soul has seen,

*   *   *

borne on solemn wing
From the vast regions of the grave,

it is no metaphorical flourish, but plain fact he means and feels.
This is cultivating 'the Arts' in a high spirit indeed.

The simple beauty and grandeur of the *Illustrations to Blair's
Grave* are within the comprehension of most who possess any
feeling for what is elevated in art. Fuseli's evidence in their
favour, despite turgid Johnsonianism, which, as usual with him,

fails to conceal the uneasy gait of a man not at home in our language, is, in part, lucid and to the purpose.

'The author of the moral series before us,' he writes, after some preliminary generalizing on the triteness of the ordinary types employed in art, 'endeavoured to awake sensibility by touching our sympathies with nearer, less ambiguous, and less ludicrous imagery than what mythology, Gothic superstition, or symbols as far-fetched as inadequate, could supply. His invention has been chiefly employed to spread a familiar and domestic atmosphere round the most important of all subjects; to connect the visible and the invisible world, without provoking probability; and to lead the eye from the milder light of time to the radiations of eternity.

'Such is the plan and the moral part of the author's invention The technic part and the execution of the artist, though to be examined by other principles, and addressed to a narrower circle, equally claim approbation, sometimes excite our wonder, and not unseldom our fears, when we see him play on the very verge of legitimate invention. But wildness so picturesque in itself, so often redeemed by taste, simplicity, and elegance, what child of fancy, what artist would wish to discharge? The groups and single figures, on their own basis, abstracted from the general composition and considered without attention to the plan, frequently exhibit those genuine, unaffected attitudes, those simple graces, which nature and the heart alone can dictate, and only an eye inspired by both discover. Every class of artists, in every stage of their progress or attainments, from the student to the finished master, and from the contriver of ornament to the painter of history, will find here materials of art and hints of improvement.'

The designs to *Blair* are in the same key as those to *The Night*

Thoughts of eight years previous; but are more mature, purer, and less extravagant. Both sets of designs occupy, to some extent, the same ground. And thus similar *motives* occur, and even compositions, as already noticed. Blake's previous etching, by the way, of the *Skeleton Re-animated*, compares favourably with the present one by Schiavonetti, showing, as do all the etchings to *Young*, that he *could* have executed his own designs to *The Grave*. The chief want of those etchings was what engravers call *colour*.

Blair's *Grave*, a poem written before the *Night Thoughts*, though published the same year (1743), was, sixty-two years later, still a popular English classic. Blake's designs form a strangely spiritual commentary on the somewhat matter-of-fact homily of the dry, old Scottish divine: they belong to a more heavenly latitude. Running parallel to the poem rather than springing out of it, they have, in some cases, little foundation in the text, in others absolutely none; as, for instance, the emblematic '*Soul exploring the recesses of the Tomb*.' The Series in itself forms a poem, simple, beautiful, and exalted: what tender eloquence in '*The Soul hovering over the Body*;' in the passionate ecstasy of '*The Re-union of Soul and Body*;' the rapt felicity of mutual recognition in '*The Meeting of a Family in Heaven*.' There meet husband and wife, little brothers and sisters; two angels spread a canopy of loving wings over the group, one remarkable for surpassing sculpturesque beauty. Such designs are, in motive, spirit, manner of embodiment, without parallel, and enlarge the boundaries of art. Equally high meaning has the oft-mentioned allegory, *Death's Door*, into which 'Age on crutches is hurried by a tempest,' while above sits a youthful figure, 'the renovated man in light and glory,' looking upwards in joyful adoration and awe. And again, the *Death of the Strong Wicked Man:* the still-

238

fond wife hanging over the convulsed body, in wild, horror-struck sympathy, the terrified daughter standing beside, with one hand shutting out the scene from her eyes; while the wicked soul is hurried amid flames through the casement. What unearthly surprise and awe expressed in that terrible face, those uplifted deprecating hands! *The Last Judgment*, unlike the other designs, is a subject on which great artists had already lavished imagination and executive skill. But Blake's conception of it is an original and homogeneous one, worthy of the best times of art. What other painter since Michael Angelo *could* have really designed anew that tremendous scene?

These are not mere *exercises* of art, to be coldly measured by the foot-rule of criticism, but truly inventions to be read and entered into with something of the spirit which conceived them. The oftener I have looked into them, the more meaning and eloquence I have discovered, and the more freshness. Never, surely, were the difficulties of human speech (whether with word or outline) more fearlessly encountered. A poor designer moves in shackles, when handling such topics; has, for instance, but the same tangible flesh and blood wherewith to express material body and immaterial soul. And that anomaly alone leads many a practical person to dismiss the designs at once, as absurd and puerile. But if we stay to consider how this allegorical mode is a necessary convention to symbolize a meaning beyond the reach of art, we are soon reconciled to the discrepancy, and begin to value aright the daring and the suggestive beauty with which these meanings are indicated. That shuddering awe of the Strong Wicked Man's naked soul (even though a material form express it), as he enters the unknown world; the living grace of the draped feminine figure, emblem of a purer human soul, which lingers a moment yearningly over the stiffening mortal frame it has forsaken, its mute eloquence so strangely enhanced by that utterly lonely mountain landscape into which it is about to vanish, seen through the open casement: I say such art ranks with that of the greatest eras; is of the same sublime reach and pure quality. What signifies it that these drawings cover but a few inches, and are executed in water-colours instead of oils or fresco?

Now, in maturity, as when in youth producing the *Songs of Innocence*, or in age the *Inventions to Job*, we see Blake striking always the same mystic chord. The bridge thrown across from the visible to the invisible world was ever firm and sure to him. The unwavering hold (of which his 'Visions' were a result) upon an unseen world, such as in other ways poetry and even science assure us of, and whose revelation is the meaning underlying all religions, – this habitual hold is surely an authentic attainment, *not* an hallucination; whether the particular form in which the faith clothes itself, the *language* of Blake's mind, – souls entering and departing from material forms, angels hovering near poor human creatures, and the like emblems, – be adequate or not. In such intensity as Blake's, it was truly a blissful possession; it proved enchanted armour against the world, the flesh, and the devil, and all their sordid influences.

I have still a word to say *àpropos* of one of these twelve designs, and a water-colour drawing formerly in Mr Butts' collection, illustrative of the verse –

> 'But Hope rekindled only to illume
> The shades of death, and light her to the tomb.'

It is a duplicate, probably, of one of the unengraved designs from *Young*. The main feature, a descending precipice broken into dark recesses, is the same as in that grand and eloquent tableau in the *Blair*, of the *Descent of Man into the Vale of Death*. The figures are different, but the same motive pervades both designs.

Of the composition in the *Blair*, an intelligible summary occurs in Cromek's Descriptive List at the end of the volume. 'The pious daughter, weeping and conducting her sire onward; age, creeping carefully on hands and knees; an elder, without friend or kindred; a miser; a bachelor, blindly proceeding, no one knows whither, ready to drop into the dark abyss; frantic youth, rashly devoted to vice and passion, rushing past the diseased and old who totter on crutches; the wan declining virgin; the miserable and distracted widow; the hale country youth; and the mother and her numerous progeny, already arrived in this valley, are among the groups which, &c. – are, in fact, *all* the groups.'

The fate of the original copper-plates has been somewhat singular. After being used by Ackermann to illustrate a Spanish Poem, *Meditaciones Poeticas por Jose Janquin de Mora: Londres: asimismo in Colombia, Buenos Ayres, Chili, Pero y Guatemala*, 1826, they, at a more recent period, I have been told, found their way across the Atlantic, serving for an American edition – not of Blair's poem, but of Martin Tupper's *Proverbial Philosophy*.

In the unengraved drawing I have referred to, we have the *Soul departing from the dying Narcissa*, over whose lifeless form her lover, with lamenting outstretched arms, is bending; the bright figure of Hope, with lighted lamp, beckons to the shades below; down the rocky stairs leading to which old and young are wending, as in the *Blair* design: the timid, hesitating girl, the strong man hurrying, age creeping, the tender mother (a very beautiful figure) leading her infant children. In the recesses of the tomb below, we again encounter emblematic, sorrowful deathbeds. On the hills in the background above, are faintly seen the dim populations of the earth, all journeying to the same bourne. The principal figures are of exceeding grace and loveliness; as, in particular, the heavenly one of Hope, and that of the little girl who accompanies her youthful brothers, with reluctant step, with drooping head and face hidden in her hand, shuddering and sad to exchange the fair daylight for the gloomy tomb – a figure which, for its expressive beauty, Raphael himself might have sketched.

TWENTY-FIVE

Appeal to the Public 1808–10
[ÆT. 51–53]

Schiavonetti was, by 1808, engaged on the plate from Stothard's *Canterbury Pilgrimage*. At the end of the *Blair*, published, as we saw, in the autumn of 1808, appeared, to indignant Blake's unspeakable disgust doubtless, a flowery Prospectus of Cromek's, for publishing by subscription and 'under the immediate patronage of H.R.H. the Prince of Wales,' a line engraving after the now 'well-known Cabinet Picture;' which, in fact, Cromek had exhibited throughout the three kingdoms, at a shilling a head.

It was now Blake finished *his* 'fresco' of the *Canterbury Pilgrimage*, with the view of 'appealing to the public,' – the wrong kind of tribunal for him. To this end, also, he painted or finished some other 'frescos' and drawings. The completion of the *Pilgrimage* was attended by adverse influences of the supernatural kind – as Blake construed them. He had hung his original design over a door in his sitting-room, where, for a year perhaps it remained. When, on the appearance of Stothard's picture, he went to take down his drawing, he found it nearly effaced: the result of some malignant spell of Stothard's, he would, in telling the story, assure his friends. But as one of them (Flaxman) mildly expostulated, 'Why! my dear sir! as if, after having left a pencil drawing so long exposed to air and dust, you could have

243

expected otherwise!' The *fresco* was ultimately bought by a customer who seldom failed – Mr Butts; and is now in the possession of Mr Stirling, of Keir.

Thinking to take a leaf out of Cromek's book, Blake determined to *show* his work, and 'shame the fools' who preferred Stothard; to show it under more advantageous conditions than were to be had in the Academy Exhibitions. In May, 1809, – the year in which our old friend Hayley brought out his *Life of Romney*, and made a second marriage even more ill-advised than the first; – in May, Blake opened an Exhibition of his own, on the first floor of his brother the hosier's house, at the corner of Broad Street. The plan had the merit of cheapness, at any rate, involving little outlay or risk; the artist, in fact, not having money to venture. The Exhibition comprised sixteen 'Poetical and Historical Inventions,' as he designated them, – eleven 'frescos,' seven drawings: a collection singularly remote from ordinary sympathies, or even ordinary apprehension. Bent on a violent effort towards justifying his ways to men and critics, he drew up and had printed a *Descriptive Catalogue* of these works, in which he interprets them, and expounds at large his own canons of art. Of which more anon. The price of this Catalogue, which included admission to the Exhibition, was half a crown.

A singular enterprise, for unpractised Blake, was this of vying with adroit, experienced Cromek! As if a simple-minded visionary could advertise, puff, and round the due preparatory paragraphs for newspaper and magazine, of 'latest fine arts intelligence.' An exhibition set going under such auspices was likely to remain a profound secret to the world at large. A few, however, among the initiated were attracted by curiosity to see a picture which was the subject of a notorious quarrel between two friendly artists, and which had been painted in rivalry of

Stothard's already famous work. A gentleman still among us, of singularly wide intercourse with the distinguished men of two generations, a friend of Wordsworth and of Lamb, – Mr Henry Crabb Robinson, – has related to me the visit some such motives as these induced him to pay. On entering the room, he found himself alone. With a wise prescience of the inevitable future scarcity of that remarkable *brochure*, the *Descriptive Catalogue*, he purchased four copies for himself and friends – Charles Lamb among them. When, after that wholesale purchase, he inquired of James Blake, the custodian of the unique gallery, whether he could not come again free? – 'Oh! yes; *free as long as you live!*' was the reply of the humble hosier, overjoyed at having so munificent a visitor, or a visitor at all.

This James Blake is characterized, by those who remember him, as an honest, unpretending shopkeeper in an old-world style, ill calculated for great prosperity in the hosiery, or any other line. In his dress he is described to me as adhering to knee-breeches, worsted stockings, and buckles. As primitive as his brother he was, though very unlike: his head not in the clouds amid radiant visions, but bent downwards, and studying the pence of this world – how to get them, which he found no easy task, and how to keep. He looked upon his erratic brother with pity and blame, as a wilful, misguided man, wholly in a wrong track; while the latter despised him for his grovelling, worldly mind, – as he reckoned it. Time widened the breach. In after years, when James had retired on a scanty independence and lived in Cirencester Street, becoming a near neighbour of Mr Linnell, at whose house Blake was then a frequent visitor, they did not even speak. At James's shop, ladies yet living, friends of Blake's, remember to have made their little purchases of gloves and haberdashery.

Lamb preferred Blake's *Canterbury Pilgrimage* to Stothard's. 'A work of wonderful power and spirit, hard and dry, yet with grace,' he says of it, on one occasion. That rare critic was delighted also with the *Descriptive Catalogue*. The analysis of the characters in the Prologue – the Knight, the Prioress, the Friar, &c. – he pronounced the finest criticism of Chaucer's poem he had ever read.

In Southey's *Doctor*, special allusion is made to one of the pictures in this exhibition. 'That painter of great but insane genius, William Blake, of whom Allan Cunningham has written so interesting a memoir, took this *Triad* (the story of the three who escaped from the battle of Camlan, where Arthur fell – 'the strongest man, the beautifullest man, and the ugliest man') – 'for the subject of a picture, which he called the Ancient Britons. It was one of his worst pictures, which is saying much; and he has illustrated it with one of the most curious commentaries in his very curious and very rare *Descriptive Catalogue* of his own pictures.'

The Catalogue *is* excessively rare. I have seen but three copies; heard of, perhaps, three more. Here is the title: '*A Descriptive Catalogue of Pictures; Poetical and Historical Inventions; Painted by William Blake in Water-colours, being the ancient method of Fresco Painting resumed: and Drawings, for Public Inspection and for Sale by Private Contract. London: printed by D. N. Shury, 7, Berwick Street, Soho, for J. Blake, 28, Broad Street, Golden Square.* 1809.' It is reprinted entire in Part II.

In treacherous Cromek's despite, Blake had resolved to engrave, as well as exhibit, the *Pilgrimage*. On opening his exhibition, he issued a printed prospectus of his intended engraving, almost as curious as the Catalogue. It is a literary composition which halts between the monologue of a self-taught enthusiast and the circular of a competing tradesman. Observe how he girds, parenthetically, at Cromek and Schiavonetti. *Date, May 15th*, 1809.

BLAKE'S CHAUCER,
THE CANTERBURY PILGRIMS.
THE FRESCO PICTURE,
Representing CHAUCER'S Characters, painted by
WILLIAM BLAKE,
As it is now submitted to the Public.

'The Designer proposes to engrave [it] in a correct and finished line manner of engraving, similar to those original copper-plates of Albert Durer, Lucas, Hisben, Aldegrave, and the old original engravers, who were great masters in painting and designing; whose method, alone, can delineate Character as it is in this Picture, where all the lineaments are distinct.

'It is hoped that the Painter will be allowed by the public (notwithstanding artfully disseminated insinuations to the contrary) to be better able than any other to keep his own characters and expressions; having had sufficient evidence in the works of our own Hogarth, that no other artist can reach the original spirit so well as the Painter himself, especially as Mr B. is an old well-known and acknowledged engraver.

'The size of the engraving will be three feet one inch long, by one foot high. The artist engages to deliver it, finished, in one year from September next. No work of art can take longer than a year: it may be worked backwards and forwards without end, and last a man's whole life; but he will, at length, only be forced to bring it back to what it was, and it will be worse than it was at the end of the first twelve months. The value of this [the?] artist's year is the criterion of Society; and as it is valued, so does Society flourish or decay.

'The price to Subscribers, FOUR GUINEAS; two to be paid at the time of subscribing, the other two, on delivery of the print.

'Subscriptions received at No. 28, corner of BROAD STREET, GOLDEN SQUARE, where the Picture is now exhibiting, among other works, by the same artist.

'The price will be considerably raised to non-subscribers.'

Singularly artful announcement, – surely a suggestion of brother James'! The swan *walks* very ungracefully. Cromek had little cause for alarm at such naïve self-assertion; so innocent an attempt to divide the public favour. In reading this, and similar effusions of Blake's, allowances must be made for a want of early familiarity with the conventions of printed speech, parallel to his want of dexterity with those of the painter's language; which explains a good deal of the crudeness and eccentricity.

It was a favourite dogma of Blake's not, certainly, learned of the political economists, that the true power of Society depends on its recognition of the arts. Which is his meaning when, pardonably regarding himself as a representative of high art, he mysteriously announces, 'The value of this artist's year is the criterion of Society, and as *it* is valued, so does society flourish or decay.' Society had little to congratulate itself upon in its recognition of '*this* artist's year.' Miserably did she undervalue it, to her discredit and our loss. This artist's fresh and daring conceptions it would have been well to have embodied in happier, maturer, more lucid shape, than 'society' ever vouchsafed him the slenderest help towards realizing. As it is, one of his archaic-looking drawings is often more *matterful* and suggestive, imprisons more thought and imagination than are commonly beaten out thin over the walls of an entire exhibition.

In September or October 1809, the engraving of his *Canterbury Pilgrimage* was commenced. And, fulfilling the voluntary engagement recorded in the prospectus, the print, – somewhat smaller in size than the picture, – was issued on the 8th of the following October; a year or two before the plate after Stothard's picture emerged from the difficulties which befell it. Blake thus forestalled his forestaller, to the indignation of Stothard in his turn; the print being of the same size as Cromek's intended one, and having inevitable resemblances to it in general composition.

It was launched without the slightest help from the elaborate machinery usually put in motion to secure a welcome for an important engraving, and, by energetic Cromek, worked on so unprecedented a scale. As may readily be believed, the subscribers might almost have been counted on the hand. Blake's work, indeed, lacks all the alluring grace of Stothard's felicitous composition, in which a wide range of previous art is indirectly laid under contribution, or, to speak plainly, cribbed from, after the fashion of most well-educated historical painters; whereas Blake boldly and obstinately draws on his own resources. Bare where Stothard's composition is opulent, yet challenging comparison as to the very qualities in which Blake was most deficient, his design creates an unfavourable impression before the superficial spectator has time to recognise its essential merits. A good notion of the work may be obtained from our reduced outline with the series of heads, on the same scale as the original, engraved below it. 'Hard and dry,' as Lamb observes, it is, – uncouth compared with Stothard's; but, tested by the poetry and spirit of Chaucer, it is in all points of character and arrangement, undoubtedly superior. There is, too, a mediæval look about Blake's which does not distinguish Stothard's version.

I have heard that Blake retouched the plate of the *Canterbury Pilgrimage*, and did not improve it. There are impressions, rather black and heavy in effect, which would seem to confirm this rumour.

To judicious counsel from a friend Blake was always amenable, but was stiffened in error by hostile criticism. Unaided by the former while at work on his fresco and engraving, he had been in the very worst mood for realizing success, or even the harmonious exercise of his powers. He was in the temper to exaggerate his eccentricities, rather than to modify them. If Cromek, instead of throwing up Blake's drawing when he could not dictate terms, had gone on and gently persuaded the designer to soften his peculiarities; or if Blake had suffered his design to be engraved by Schiavonetti, and doctored (as that engraver so well knew how) by correct, smooth touches, some of Blake's favourite hard, 'determinate outline' being sacrificed a little, a different fortune would have awaited the composition. It *might* have become almost as well known and admired as Stothard's, certainly as the *Blair*, instead of being a curiosity sought only by collectors of scarce things.

Blake was at no pains, throughout this business or afterwards, to conceal his feelings towards Stothard. To the end of his life he would, to strangers, abuse the popular favourite, with a vehemence to them unaccountable. With friends and sympathizers, he was silent on the topic. Such was the mingled waywardness and unworldliness of the man; exaggerating his prejudices to the uncongenial, waiving them with the few who could interpret them aright. He was blind to the fact that his motives for decrying Stothard were liable to misconstruction; and would have been equally unguarded could he have perceived it. For Stothard's art – in his eyes far too glib, smooth, and mundane in its graces – he entertained a sincere aversion; though, as in the case of Reynolds, some degree of soreness may have aggravated the dislike. And the epithets he in familiar conversation applied to it, would, repeated in cold blood, sound extravagant and puerile.

On his part, too, the ordinarily serene Stothard, the innocent instrument of shifty Cromek's schemes, considered himself just as much aggrieved by Blake. Up to 1806 they had been friends, if not always warm ones; friends of nearly thirty years' standing. The present breach was never healed. Once, many years later, they met at a gathering of artists – of the Artists' Benevolent, I think. Before going in to dinner, Blake, placable as he was irascible, went up to Stothard and offered to shake hands; an overture the frigid, exemplary man declined, as Mr Linnell, an eye-witness, tells me. Another time, Stothard was ill: Blake called and wished to see him and be reconciled, but was refused. There is something of the kingdom of heaven in this – on the one side. Such men are not to be judged by wayward words. Warm hearts generally spend their worst violence in *them*.

This squabble with Cromek was a discordant episode in Blake's life. The competition with Stothard it induced, placed him in a false position, and, in most people's eyes, a wrong one. In Blake's own mind, where all should have been, and for the most part was, peace, the sordid conflict left a scar. It left him more tetchy than ever; more disposed to wilful exaggeration of individualities already too prominent, more prone to unmeasured violence of expression. The extremes he again gave way to in his design and writings – mere ravings to such as had no key to them – did him no good with that portion of the public the illustrated *Blair* had introduced him to. Those designs most people thought wild enough; yet they were really a modified version of his style. Such demand as had existed for his works, never considerable, declined.

Now, too, was established for him the damaging reputation 'Mad,' by which the world has since agreed to recognise William

Blake. And yet it is one – and let the reader note this – which none who knew the visionary man personally, at any period of his life, thought of applying to him. And, in his time, he was known to, and valued by, many shrewd, clear-headed men; of whom suffice it to mention Fuseli, Flaxman, Linnell. More on this point hereafter.

TWENTY-SIX

Engraver Cromek 1807–1812
[ÆT. 50–55]

While Blake had been nursing his wrath against Cromek and Stothard, and making ineffectual reprisals by exhibition and engraving, the course of Cromek's speculation had not run smoothly. As intimately, if indirectly, bearing on Blake's life of struggles, this matter ought, perhaps, to be glanced at here. We must first go back a little, and track Cromek in his versatile career. The retrospect will, here and there, throw a vivid ray of light on the real character of the man, and so enable us to construe Blake aright in the critical relation in which the two, for a time, stood to one another. It may help the reader to a conclusion as to the rights of that difficult case – for so Smith and Cunningham seemed to find it – *Blake v. Stothard and Another*.

During the progress, under the engraver, of his first publishing scheme, the active Yorkshireman had been turning his literary tastes to account. He had made a tour in Dumfriesshire, in quest of unpublished fugitive pieces of Robert Burns; a tour undertaken, according to his own statement, from pure interest in the poet. He discovered many previously unknown; others rejected 'on principle' by the great man's posthumous patron, prim Currie, of now seldom blessed memory. The visit was well timed. Burns had been dead ten years; but everything by him,

253

everything about him, was already carefully treasured by those privileged enough to have aught to keep or remember. His mother, and others of his family and friends, were still living. Cromek returned with well-filled wallet; though he too, squeamish as Currie, must needs keep back *The Jolly Beggars* and *Holy Willie's Prayer*. Of these gleanings he made an octavo volume, supplementary to Currie's four, entitling it *The Reliques of Burns*. It was published by Cadell and Davies in 1808, – the year in which the *Blair* came out, – and is a volume on which subsequent editors and biographers of Burns have freely drawn. It had the peculiar fortune of calling forth memorable manifestations of bad feeling towards the poet, of tepid taste and supercilious vulgarity, from two persons high in the world of letters, – the articles of Jeffrey in the *Edinburgh*, of Walter Scott in the *Quarterly*.

Here, again, Cromek's well-directed industry bore off, I fear, the profits, to part of which, another – Burns' widow – was entitled. Cromek might, indeed, plead in self-defence, the lapse of ten years during which no one else had had the pious zeal to glean the open field.

The following summer, which was that of Blake's exhibition, Cromek, encouraged by the success of his first literary venture, revisited Dumfries, with Stothard as a companion, and with new schemes in his head. One was an enlarged and illustrated edition of Burns' works, for which materials and drawing were now to be got together; an enterprise which, in the sequel, failing health prevented his carrying out. The other was a *Collection of Old Scottish Songs*, such, especially, as had been the favourites of Burns, together with the poet's notes already printed in the *Reliques*, and any other interesting scraps that could be picked up, could be begged, borrowed, or filched from various contributors. Two duodecimo volumes *were* got together, and, in the summer of 1810, published under the above title, with three vignettes after Stothard, characteristically cut on wood by clever, hapless Luke Clennell, hereafter the tenant of a madhouse.

During this visit of 1809, the bookmaker fell an easy victim to the hoax devised by a stalwart young stone-mason, afterwards known to fame as poet, novelist, biographer, and art critic. This was Allan Cunningham, then in his twenty-fifth year, earning eighteen shillings a week as a working mason. Cromek, we learn from Mr Peter Cunningham's interesting introduction to his father's collected *Poems and Songs* (1847), looked coldly on the mason's acknowledged verses, but caught eagerly at the idea of discoveries of old Songs, to be made among the Nithsdale peasantry. He greedily swallowed Allan's happy imitations, and ever 'called out for more!' On quitting Dumfries for Newman Street, he put a MS. book into Allan's hands with the modest written injunction, '*to be filled* with old unpublished songs and ballads, with remarks on them, historical and critical.' Another milch-cow has turned up!

Under pretence of collecting a world of previously unknown local song from the well-gleaned land of Burns and Scott, the young man, finding in Cromek (who had more natural taste than reading or acumen) a good subject for the cheat, and a willing one, palmed off, as undoubted originals, a whole deskful of his own verse in slightly antique mould. Verse, it proved, bold, energetic, and stirring, or tender, sentimental, and graceful; the best of modern Scottish songs and ballads since those of the Ayrshire peasant, though wide the interval! Cromek, who reminds one of Burns's Johnson, of *Musical Museum* memory, a man of the same type, was, as usual, only too happy to avail himself of another's genius and labours; too ready a recipient to be over-curious as to authenticity. But his letters to Cunningham reveal often pertinent doubts as to any high antiquity, even while he and the eager domestic circle in Newman Street, whom a northern raven was feeding, were receiving the poems with delighted wonder. 'I have read these verses,' he writes of one song (*She's gone to dwell in Heaven*), 'to my old mother, my wife, sister, and family, *till all our hearts ache*.' Cromek spared neither urging nor vague hints of a future 'kind return,' for all services, to extract from his young friend an original and striking volume of verse, and even copious prose notes illustrative of local traditions. The poet was lured to London, to help push the volume through the press. Cromek gave him free quarters the while, and then left him to hire himself as a sculptor's mason, at six-and-twenty shillings a week. Subsequently Cromek spoke a good word for his *protégé* to Chantrey, young then, and with little to employ a second pair of hands, but who some years later took Allan as a workman. The engagement, as Chantrey's fortunes rose, transformed itself into a higher one, which lasted to the end of the sculptor's life.

The volume was swelled to due dimensions by a few poems collected from other sources, and by plausible, loose-spun letterpress of Cromek's own, – an 'Introduction' and critical 'Notices' of the poems; including grave details of how one had been taken down from the recitation of such and such 'a young girl,' or 'worthy old man.' The *Remains of Nithsdale and Galloway Song*, printed by Bensley, was published by Cadell and Davies, at the latter end of 1810, with a spirited woodcut vignette by Clennell, after Stothard. It is now scarce.

Some general expressions of 'obligation to Mr Allan Cunningham' for 'guidance and interesting conversation,' was the sole acknowledgment accorded the gratis contributor (as author and collector) of the bulk, and all the value of the volume. To which add a presentation copy, accompanied by the candid assurance, 'It has been a costly work, and I have made nothing by it, but it is 'd—d good, let the critics say what they will, and *when it goes to a second edition, I will give you something handsome!'* The book was well received, and sold well, but never went to a second edition; our publishers having taken care to make the first a large one. None of Cromek's clients grew sleek on his bounty. Nine years later, Cunningham's true share in the volume became known. And further cultivation of the profession (or trade sometimes) of literature, while he was still clerk of the works to Chantrey, was rendered easy to him on the strength of that volume alone.

On this, as on other occasions of the kind, Cromek fulfilled to admiration his legitimate part as publisher. While he picked the brains of his *protégés* – Blake, Stothard, Cunningham – and stopped the pay, he could not help doing them incidental good service, in dragging them forward a stage with the public; a service which genial Allan Cunningham seems always to have remembered with a kind of tenderness.

One more illustrative anecdote. 'Cromek,' as Mr Peter Cunningham mildly puts it, 'had rather lax ideas about *meum et tuum* when valuable autographs were laid before him. I remember an instance of this, which I have heard my father relate. Sir Walter Scott was talking to him of some of the chief curiosities he possessed at Abbotsford. "I had once (I am sorry to say *once*) an original letter from Ben Jonson to Drummond of Hawthornden, all in Ben's own beautiful handwriting: I never heard of another." My father mentioned one he had seen in London *in Cromek's hands*. Scott used some strong expression, and added, "The last person I showed that letter to was Cromek, and I have never seen it since."' Cromek had favoured Scott with a visit during his Dumfries tour of 1809.

After this unexpectedly vivid ray of evidence as to character, Mr Cromek's bare word cannot be taken, when he contradicts the positive assertion of simple, upright, if visionary Blake, that Cromek had actually commissioned him to paint the *Pilgrimage* before 'Stothard thought of *his*.' We doubt the jocose turn given the denial − 'that the order had been given in a vision, for he never gave it,' will not serve. The order was a *vivâ voce* one. And that, like a previous *vivâ voce* agreement, is even easier to forget than the ownership of an autograph worth, perhaps, ten pounds in the market. Mr Blake was not aware of the desirableness of getting a man's hand to a bargain. There is no palming off a signature as visionary.

During these three years of bookmaking, Cromek had, as print-seller, published engraved portraits of Currie and of Walter Scott, after Raeburn. Meanwhile, the grand speculation of all, Schiavonetti's engraving of Stothard's best picture, − a subject new to art, as freshly and gracefully handled, − had been going on slowly, though not unprosperously. Ingenious Cromek made it pay its own expenses: in this way.

Besides the stinted sixty pounds, the original price of the picture, Cromek, while it was in progress, and assuming daily new importance, had engaged to add another forty, in consideration of unforeseen labour and research, and of extra finish: this to be paid as soon as collections from the subscribers came in. But when the time for payment arrived, came excuses instead, on the score of heavy expenses incurred for advertising, exhibiting, &c. The picture itself the dexterous man sold for £300, some say £500; but still excused himself, to quiet Stothard, on the old grounds. The poor artist never handled solid cash again from that quarter; though, through his own exertions, he realized another hundred or two by repetitions of his masterpiece for various patrons.

In June 1810, just as Cromek had issued his *Select Scottish Songs*, the enterprise received its first check. The fine *etching* for the engraving was completed, but further progress was stayed by the failing health (in a consumption) of the gifted Italian, to whose hands it had been committed. On the 7th of that month, Schiavonetti, who had entered on life at beautiful Bassano, quitted it at Brompton, at the premature age of forty-five. Schiavonetti was to have had £840 for his engraving, but only lived to receive, or entitle himself to, £275. In the following autumn, – the same in which Blake's print of *his* Canterbury Pilgrimage, and Cromek's *Nithsdale and Galloway Song* appeared, – the plate was confided to Engleheart, who worked on it from the 20th of September to the end of December, receiving some £44. But heavier troubles now involved both print and proprietor. On Cromek, too, consumption laid its hand, arresting all his ingenious and innocent schemes, or, as Smith calls it, the long 'endeavour to live by speculating on the talents of others.' Lengthened visits to native Yorkshire failed to stay the inevitable course of his malady, and he returned to Newman Street, there to linger another year of forced inaction, during which poor Cromek and family, – comprising a wife, two young children, and a dependent sister, – were reduced to great straits. Doubtless, many a valuable autograph and Design had then to be changed into cash. So that we have to pity the predacious Yorkshireman after all. On the 12th March 1812, at the age of forty-two, he went where he could jockey no more men nor artists.

The widow had her fresh difficulties in realizing the property her husband's scheming brain had created; had first to raise money for the engraver to proceed with the *Pilgrimage*. The engraver then in view was Lewis Schiavonetti's brother, Niccolò, who had worked in Lewis's studio, and caught his manner. To finish the plate, he wanted three hundred and thirty guineas, in three instalments, and fifteen months' time. To raise the first instalment, Mrs Cromek parted with a good property, – sold the remainder and copyright of Blake's *Blair*, for £120, to the Ackermanns, who re-issued the book in 1813, with biographic notices of Blair, Cromek, and Schiavonetti. Then Niccolò followed in his brother's steps to an early grave. This last in the chain of sorrowful casualties caused further delays. The plate, – Mrs Cromek borrowing the necessary money with difficulty from her father, – was at last, after having passed under the hands of three distinct engravers, finished by James Heath, or in his manufactory rather. Thence it eventually issued, a very much worse one for all these changes than when poor Lewis Schiavonetti's failing hand had left it a brilliant, masterly etching. It had an extraordinary sale, as everybody knows, and proved exceedingly profitable to the widow. The long-cherished venture turned out no despicable dower for a needy man, living by his wits, to leave her. As for the producer of the picture, who, artist-like, had forborne to press the adventurer in his straits, or the widow in hers, his share in this great success was a certain number of copies of the print (commercially useless to him), as an equivalent for the long deferred £40. Such I gather from Mrs Bray's *Life of Stothard*, and other sources, to have been the fluctuating fortunes of the most popular of modern prints; of an enterprise which, thanks to Cromek's indirect courses, excited, first and last, so much bitterness in the mind of Blake.

TWENTY-SEVEN

Years of Deepening Neglect 1810–17
[ÆT. 53–60]

I have mentioned that Blake's *Canterbury Pilgrimage* (the *fresco*) was bought by Mr Butts. Among the drawings executed, at this period, for the same constant patron, was a grandly-conceived scene from the apocalyptic vision, the *Whore of Babylon:* a colossal, sitting figure, around whose head a wreath of figures issues from the golden cup of Abominations; below, is gathered a group of kings and other arch offenders. This drawing (dated 1809) formed one in the numerous collection of Blake's works sold at Sotheby's by Mr Butts' son, in 1852, and is now in the British Museum Print-room. There, also, a few other drawings and a large, though not complete, collection of Blake's illustrated books, are now accessible to the public; thanks to the well-directed zeal of the present Keeper, Mr Carpenter.

In these years, more than one of Blake's old friends had dropped away. In December 1809 died, of asthma, Fuseli's ancient crony, Johnson, who had more than once extended to Blake what little countenance his hampered position, as a book-seller who must live to please, allowed. In March 1810 the friendly miniature painter, Ozias Humphrey, died. Hayley, as we foretold, lost sight of Blake. Mr Butts, steady customer as he was, had already a house-full of his works.

December 26, 1811, is the engraver's date affixed to a small

261

reduction, by Blake, of a portion of the *Canterbury Pilgrimage*, – including eight of the principal figures in the left-hand corner, – which forms the frontispiece to a duodecimo volume, published at Newberry's famous shop in St Paul's Churchyard. The little book, with its small specimen or *taste*, as it were, of the original composition, was evidently intended to spread a knowledge of the larger engraving. The title runs thus: 'The Prologue and Characters of Chaucer's Pilgrims, selected from the Canterbury Tales, intended to illustrate a particular design of Mr William Blake, which is engraved by himself, and may be seen at Mr Colnaghi's, Cockspur Street; at Mr [James] Blake's, No. 28, Broad Street, Golden Square; and at the publisher's, Mr Harris, Bookseller, St Paul's Churchyard. Price two shillings and sixpence. 1812.' The brief introductory preface is not from Blake's hand; possibly from that of the friendly pedagogue, Malkin. 'To the genius and fancy of that celebrated man, Mr Blake,' writes the editor, after a notice of Southwark and the Tabard Inn, 'it occurred, that though the names and habits of men altered by time, yet their characters remained the same; and as Chaucer had drawn them four hundred years past, he might as justly delineate them at the present period, and, by a pleasant picture, bring to our imagination the merry company setting out upon their journey. As the *Canterbury Tales* may be too long a story for modern amusement, I have selected the Prologue and the characters' (the whole Introduction, in short) 'that the heads as represented by Mr Blake may be compared with the lineaments drawn by Chaucer, and I think the merit of the artist will be acknowledged.' A double text is given on opposite pages: the original from Speght's edition of 1687, and a modernized version, or free translation, from Mr Ogle's edition of 1741. The frontispiece is well engraved in Blake's style, with necessary and skilful variations from the large engraving; the distribution of light being different, and some of the details improved, – the towers and spires in the background, for example. Towards the end of the volume, a pretty and characteristic, but *very* generalised little etching by Blake occurs, of a Gothic cathedral, among trees, meant probably for that of Canterbury.

Few new patrons arose to fill the gaps I have recapitulated in the chosen circle of the old. All, it may be observed, were in the middle rank of life. There was nothing in William Blake's high and spiritual genius to command sympathy from a fastidious, *pococurante* aristocracy, still less from Majesty, in those days. 'Take them away! take them away!' was the testy mandate of disquieted Royalty, on some drawings of Blake's being once shown to George the Third.

Among present friends may be mentioned Mr George Cumberland of Bristol. This gentleman did an important service to Blake, when he introduced him, about 1813, to a young artist named John Linnell, who was to become the kindest friend and stay of the neglected man's declining years, and afterwards to be famous as one of our great landscape-painters. He was then, and till many a year later, industriously toiling at *Portrait*, as a bread profession; at miniatures, engraving – whatever, in short, he could get to do; while he painted *Landscape* as an unremunerative luxury. The present brisk, not to say eager, demand for good modern pictures was not, in those years, even beginning. The intimacy between the two arose from the younger artist applying to the elder to help him over engravings then in hand, from portraits of his own. Such as were jointly undertaken in this way, Blake commenced, Linnell finished.

Of the half-dozen years of Blake's life succeeding the exhibition in Broad Street, and the engraving of his *Pilgrimage*,

I find little or no remaining trace, except that he was still living in South Molton Street, in his accustomed poverty, and, if possible, more than accustomed neglect.

He was no longer at the pains or trivial cost, to him not trivial, of being even his own publisher; of throwing off from his copper-plate press Books of 'Prophetic' poetry and design, such as we saw him busied with, year by year, in Hercules Buildings. The *Milton* and the *Jerusalem* were the only ones thus issued from South Molton Street, and his last in that class. Sibylline leaves of engraved writing were, however, now and then put forth: such as that *On Homer's Poetry*, the *Laocoon*, the *Death of Abel*. As I have hinted, funds failed for the mere copper requisite to engrave lengthy productions like the *Jerusalem*; perhaps also, amid entire discouragement, the spirit for such weighty, bootless toil. He continued *writing* in the old strain till the end of his life, – wrote more, he declared himself, than Shakespeare and Milton put together. Scores of MSS. were produced, which never got beyond MS., and have since been scattered, most of them destroyed or lost. He could find no publisher here for writing or design. Many an unsuccessful application to the trade, as to undertaking some book of his he, in his time, had to make. 'Well, it is published elsewhere,' he, after such an one, would quietly say, 'and beautifully bound.' Let the reader construe such words with candour. Blake, by the way, talked little about 'posterity,' an emptier vision far than those on which his abstracted gaze was oftimes fixed. The invisible world, present to him even here, it was that to which his soul turned; in it found refuge amid the slights of the outward vulgar throng.

Many of the almost numberless host of Blake's water-colour drawings, on high scriptural and poetic themes, or *frescos*, as he called those (even on *paper*) more richly coloured, and with more impasto than the rest, continued to be produced; some for Mr Butts, some to lie on hand; all now widely dispersed, nearly all undated, unhappily, though mostly *signed*. If men would but realize the possible value of a *date!* Still more numerous rough sketches were thrown off; for Blake's hand was ceaselessly at work. His was indefatigable industry. He thought nothing of entering on such a task as writing out, with ornamental letters, a MS. Bible as a basis for illustration; and actually commenced one, in later years, for Mr Linnell, getting as far as *Genesis*, chap. iv. verse 15. He cared not for recreation. Writing and design were *his* recreation from the task-work of engraving. 'I don't understand what you mean by the want of a holiday,' he would tell his friends. Art was recreation enough for him. Work itself was pleasure, and *any* work, engraving, whilst he was at it, almost as much as design, – nay even what, to another, would have been the irksome task of engraving bad pictures. He was an early riser, and worked steadily on through health and sickness. Once, a young artist called, and complained of being very ill: 'What was he to do?' 'Oh!' said Blake, 'I never stop for anything; I work on, whether ill or not.' Throughout life, he was always, as Mrs Blake truly described him, either reading, writing, or designing. For it was a tenet of his, that the inner world is the all-important; that each man has a world within, greater than the external. Even while he engraved, he read, – as the plate-marks on his books testify. He never took walks for mere walking's sake, or for pleasure; and could not sympathize with those who did. During one period, he, for two years together, never went out at all, except to the corner of the Court to fetch his porter. That in-doors 'recreation' of his held him spell-bound. So wholly did the topics on which he thought, or dreamed, absorb his mind, that 'often,' Smith tells us, 'in the middle of the night he would, after thinking deeply upon a particular subject, leap from his bed and write for two hours or more.'

Through his friend Linnell, Blake became acquainted with a new and sympathizing circle of artists, which hereafter will include some very enthusiastic younger men. They, in part, filled the place of the old circle, now thinned by death and (in Stothard's case) by dissension. Of which, however, Flaxman and Fuseli remained; men friendly to him personally, and just to his genius, though, as respects the former, Blake did not always choose to think so. Once in these, or later, years, Cary (Lamb's Cary, translator of Dante) was talking with his friend Flaxman of the few Englishmen who followed historical painting, enumerating Stothard, Howard, and others. Flaxman mentioned a few more, and among them Blake. 'But Blake is a wild enthusiast, isn't he?' Ever loyal to his friend, the sculptor drew himself up, half offended, saying, 'Some think me an enthusiast.'

Among Blake's new intimates were John Varley, Richter, and Holmes, the water-colour painters. From the works of the last two, Blake learned to add greater fulness and depth of colour to his drawings, such, indeed, as he, bred in the old school of slight tints, had hardly thought *could* have been developed in this branch of art. The painters in water-colours had, by this time, laid the foundation of that excellence, which has become an English speciality. An adventurous little band of now mostly forgotten men, whom their great successors, Turner, Copley, Fielding, De Wint, Prout, David Cox, have pushed from their stools, had, in 1805 (tired of the Academy's cold shade) started their first separate Exhibition in Pall Mall, as a daring experiment.

Buyers for coloured copies of the *Songs of Innocence and Experience* would generally be found by Blake's artist friends, when no other encouragement could. Task-work as an engraver, Flaxman, still wishful to serve as of old, obtained him, in 1816, from the Longmans: a kind office Blake did not take quite in good part. He would so far rather have been recommended as a designer! So long ago as 1793, the author of the *Songs of Innocence* had engraved Flaxman's outlines to the *Odyssey*, as Piroli's substitute. Piroli's engravings of the sculptor's *Æschylus* and *Iliad* appeared in 1795 and 1796. And now, twenty-four years later, Blake, not a whit more prosperous with the world, had thankfully to engrave his friend's compositions from the *Works and Days of Hesiod*, published in 1817. January 1st, Blake dates his plates. They are sweet and graceful compositions, harmonious and contenting so far as they go, but deficient in *force*, as Blake himself thought Flaxman to have always been, and as many now think. Some touch of natural sorrow Blake might well feel at having to copy, where he could have invented with far more power and originality. For Blake was as full of *ideas* as Flaxman of *manner*, a tender and eloquent, but borrowed idiom. And while Flaxman relied on the extraneous help (or impediment?) of a conventional, and in fact *dead* language or manner in art, and on archæological niceties, Blake could address us, in his rude, unpolished way, in an universal one and appeal to the Imagination direct.

During this period Blake engraved some plates for Rees' *Encyclopædia*, illustrative of the articles on Armour and Sculpture, the latter written by Flaxman, I believe. One example selected was the Laocoon, which carried our artist to the Royal Academy's antique school, for the purpose of making a drawing from the cast of that group. 'What! you here, *Meesther Blake?*' said

Keeper Fuseli, 'we ought to come and learn of you, not you of us!' Blake took his place with the students, and exulted over his work, says Mr Tatham, like a young disciple; meeting his old friend Fuseli's congratulations and kind remarks with cheerful, simple joy.

TWENTY-EIGHT

John Varley and the Visionary Heads, 1818–20
[ÆT. 61–63.]

I have mentioned John Varley as one in the new circle to which Mr Linnell introduced Blake. Under Varley's roof, Linnell had lived for a year as pupil; with William Hunt, a since famous name, as a comrade.

John Varley, one of the founders of the New School of Water-Colour Painting, a landscape designer of much delicacy and grace, was otherwise a remarkable man, of very pronounced character and eccentricities; a professional Astrologer in the nineteenth century, among other things, and a sincere one; earnestly practising judicial Astrology as an Art, and taking his regular fees of those who consulted him. He was the author of more than one memorable nativity and prediction; memorable, that is, for having come true in the sequel. And strange stories are told on this head; such as that of Collins the artist, whose death came, to the day, as the stars had appointed. One man, to avoid his fate, lay in bed the whole day on which an accident had been foretold by Varley. Thinking himself safe by the evening, he came downstairs, stumbled over a coal-scuttle, sprained his ankle, and fulfilled the prediction. Scriven, the engraver, was wont to declare, that certain facts of a personal nature, which *could* be only known to himself, were nevertheless confided to his ear by Varley with every particular. Varley cast the nativities of James Ward, the famous animal-painter's children. So many of his predictions came true, their father, a man of strong though peculiar religions opinions, – for he, too, was 'a character,' – began to think the whole affair a sinful forestalling of God's will, and destroyed the nativities. Varley was a genial, kind-hearted man; a disposition the grand dimensions of his person – which, when in a stooping posture, suggested to beholders the rear view of an elephant – well accorded with. Superstitious and credulous, he cultivated his own credulity, cherished a passion for the marvellous, and loved to have the evidence of his senses contradicted. Take an instance. – Strange, ghostly noises had been heard at a friend's, to Varley's huge satisfaction. But interest and delight were exchanged for utter chagrin and disappointment, when on calling one day, eager to learn how the mystery progressed, he was met by the unwelcome tidings: 'Oh, we have discovered the cause – the cowl of the chimney!'

To such a man, Blake's habitual intercourse with the visionary world had special attractions. In his friend's stories of spiritual appearances, sight of which Varley could never share however wishful, he placed implicit and literal credence. A particularly close intimacy arose between the two; and, during the last nine years of Blake's life, they became constant companions.

At Varley's house, and under his own eye, were drawn those Visionary Heads, or Spiritual Portraits of remarkable characters, whereof all who have heard of Blake have heard something. Varley it was who encouraged Blake to take authentic sketches of certain among his most frequent spiritual visitants. The Visionary faculty was so much under control, that, at the wish of a friend, he could summon before his abstracted gaze any of the familiar forms and faces he was asked for. This was during the favourable and befitting hours of night; from nine or ten in the evening, until one or two, or perhaps three and four o'clock, in the morning; Varley sitting by, 'sometimes slumbering, and sometimes waking.' Varley would say, 'Draw me Moses,' or David; or would call for a likeness of Julius Cæsar, or Cassibellaunus, or Edward the Third, or some other great historical personage. Blake would answer, 'There he is!' and paper and pencil being at hand, he would begin drawing with the utmost alacrity and composure, looking up from time to time as though he had a real sitter before him; ingenuous Varley, meanwhile, straining wistful eyes into vacancy and seeing nothing, though he tried hard, and at first expected his faith and patience to be rewarded by a genuine apparition. A 'vision' had a very different signification with Blake to that it had in literal Varley's mind.

Sometimes Blake had to wait for the Vision's appearance; sometimes it would come at call. At others, in the midst of his portrait, he would suddenly leave off, and, in his ordinary quiet tones and with the same matter-of-fact air another might say 'It rains,' would remark, 'I can't go on, – it is gone! I must wait till it returns;' or, 'It has moved. The mouth is gone;' or, 'He frowns; he is displeased with my portrait of him:' which seemed as if the Vision were looking over the artist's shoulder as well as sitting *vis-à-vis* for his likeness. The devil himself would politely sit in a chair to Blake, and innocently disappear; which obliging conduct one would hardly have anticipated from the spirit of evil, with his well-known character for love of wanton mischief.

In sober daylight, criticisms were hazarded by the profane on the character or drawing of these or any of his visions. 'Oh, it's all right!' Blake would calmly reply; 'it *must* be right: I saw it so.' It did not signify what you said; nothing could put him out: so assured was he that he, or rather his imagination, was right,

271

and that what the latter revealed was implicitly to be relied on, – and this without any appearance of conceit or intrusiveness on his part. Yet critical friends would trace in all these heads the Blake mind and hand, – his *receipt* for a face: every artist has his own, his favourite idea, from which he may depart in the proportions, but seldom substantially. John Varley, however, could not be persuaded to look at them from this merely rationalistic point of view.

At these singular nocturnal sittings, Blake thus executed for Varley, in the latter's presence, some forty or fifty slight pencil sketches, of small size, of historical, nay, fabulous and even typical personages, summoned from the vasty deep of time, and 'seen in vision by Mr Blake.' Varley, who accepted all Blake said of them, added in writing the names, and in a few instances the day and hour they were seen. Thus: *'Wat Tyler, by Blake, from his spectre, as in the act of striking the tax-gatherer*, drawn Oct. 30, 1819, 1 h. P.M.' On another we read: *'The Man who built the Pyramids, Oct.* 18, 1819, *fifteen degrees of* 1, *Cancer ascending.'* Another sketch is indorsed as *'Richard Cœur de Lion, drawn from his spectre. W. Blake fecit, Oct.* 14, 1819, *at quarter-past twelve, midnight.'* In fact, two are inscribed *'Richard Cœur de Lion,'* and each is different. Which looks as if Varley misconstrued the seer at times, or as if the spirits were lying spirits, assuming different forms at will. Such would doubtless have been De Foe's reading, had *he* been gravely recording the fact.

Most of the other Visionary Heads bear date August, 1820. Nearly all subsequently fell into Mr Linnell's hands, and have remained there. Remarkable performances these slight pencil drawings are, intrinsically, as well as for the circumstances of their production: truly original and often sublime. All are marked by a decisive, portrait-like character, and are in fact evidently literal portraits of what Blake's imaginative eye beheld. They are not seldom strikingly in unison with one's notions of the characters of the men they purport to represent. Some are very fine, as the *Bathsheba* and the *David*. Of these two beauty is, of course, the special attribute. *William Wallace* and *King Edward the First* have much force, and even grandeur. A remarkable one is that of '*King Edward the Third as he now exists in the other world, according to his appearance to Mr Blake*:' his skull enlarged in the semblance of a crown, – swelling into a crown in fact, – for type and punishment of earthly tyranny, I suppose. Remarkable too, are *The Assassin lying dead at the feet of Edward the First in the Holy Land*, and the *Portrait of a Man who instructed Mr Blake in Painting and in his Dreams*.

Among the heads which Blake drew was one of King Saul, who as the artist related, appeared to him in armour, and wearing a helmet of peculiar form and construction, which he could not, owing to the position of the spectre, see to delineate satisfactorily. The portrait was therefore left unfinished, till some months after, when King Saul vouchsafed a second sitting, and enabled Blake to complete his helmet; which, with the armour, was pronounced, by those to whom the drawing was shown, sufficiently extraordinary.

The ideal embodiment of supernatural things (even things so wild and mystic as some of these) by such a man – a man of mind and sense as well as of mere fancy – could not but be worth attention. And truly they have a strange coherence and meaning of their own. This is especially exemplified in one which is the *most* curious of all these Visionary Heads, and which has also been the most talked of, viz. the *Ghost of a Flea*, or *Personified Flea*. Of it, John Varley, in that singular and now very scarce book, *A Treatise on Zodiacal Physiognomy*, published in 1828, gave the first and best account; one which Southey, connoisseur in singularities and scarce books, thought worth quoting in *The Doctor:*

'This spirit visited his (Blake's) imagination in such a figure as he never anticipated in an insect. As I was anxious to make the most correct investigation in my power of the truth of these visions, on hearing of this spiritual apparition of a Flea, I asked him if he could draw for me the resemblance of what he saw. He instantly said, "I see him now before me." I therefore gave him paper and a pencil, with which he drew the portrait of which a fac-simile is given in this number. I felt convinced, by his mode of proceeding, that he had a real image before him; for he left off, and began on another part of the paper to make a separate drawing of the mouth of the Flea, which the spirit having opened, he was prevented from proceeding with the first sketch till he had closed it. During the time occupied in completing the drawing, the Flea told him that all fleas were inhabited by the souls of such men as were by nature blood-thirsty to excess, and were therefore providentially confined to the size and form of insects; otherwise, were he himself, for instance, the size of a horse, he would depopulate a great portion of the country.'

An engraved outline of the *Ghost of a Flea* was given in the *Zodiacal Physiognomy*, and also of one other Visionary Head – that of the *Constellation Cancer*. The engraving of *The Flea* has been repeated in the *Art Journal* for August, 1858, among the illustrations to a brief notice of Blake. The original pencil drawing is in Mr Linnell's possession. Coloured copies of three of the Visionary Heads – *Wallace, Edward the First*, and the *Ghost of a Flea* – were made for Varley, by Mr Linnell.

TWENTY-NINE

Opinions: Notes on Reynolds 1820
[ÆT. 63]

From internal evidence I judge 1820, or thereabout, to have been the date of the Notes to Reynolds' *Discourses*, already referred to. The present, therefore, is a fit place to give the reader a taste of them, eminently characteristic as they are of the vehement, one-sided enthusiast. In the same indignant strain as that in which the Notes began, commenting on the patronage of his day, is written on the fly-leaf the following curious doggrel:

Advice of the Popes who succeeded the Age of Raphael
Degrade first the Arts if you would mankind degrade;
Hire idiots to paint with cold light and hot shade;
Give high price for the worst, leave the best in disgrace,
And with labour of idleness fill every place.

In plain prose he asks, 'Who will dare to say that "polite Art" is encouraged, or either wished or tolerated, in a nation where the Society of Arts suffered Barry to give them his labour for nothing? A Society composed of the flower of the English nobility and gentry, suffering an artist to starve, while he really supported what they, under pretence of encouraging, were endeavouring to depress! Barry told me that while he did that,' – painted, namely, the pictures in the Society's Great Room at the Adelphi, – 'he lived on bread and apples.

275

'O! Society for the Encouragement of Art! King and Nobility of England, where have you hid Fuseli's *Milton*? Is Satan troubled at his exposure?' alluding to Fuseli's *Satan building the Bridge*. At the words in Reynolds' *Dedication to the King* – 'royal liberality,' he exclaims, 'Liberality! we want no liberality! we want a fair price and proportionate value, and a general demand for Art. Let not that nation where less than nobility is the "reward" pretend that Art is encouraged by that nation. Art is first in intellect, and ought to be first in nations.'

At page 120, Blake tells the following anecdote, bearing on orator Burke's vaunted patronage of Barry: 'Barry painted a picture for Burke equal to Raphael or Michael Angelo, or any of the Italians (!). Burke used to show this picture to his friends, and to say, "I gave twenty guineas for this horrible daub, and if anyone would give me **"' The remainder of the sentence has been cut off by the binder, but may easily be guessed, – 'Such was Burke's patronage of Art and Science.' A little further on Blake declares 'the neglect of Fuseli's *Milton*, in a country pretending to the encouragement of Art, is a sufficient apology for my vigorous indignation: if, indeed, the neglect of my own powers had not been. Ought not the employers of fools to be execrated in future ages? They *will* and SHALL! Foolish men! your own real greatness depends on the encouragement of the Arts; and your fall will depend on their neglect and depression. What you fear is your own interest. Leo the Tenth was advised *not* to encourage the Arts. He was too wise to take this advice. The rich men of England form themselves into a Society,' (alluding to the British Institution, founded in 1805,) 'a Society to *sell*, and not to buy, pictures. The artist who does not throw his contempt on such trading Exhibitions does not know either his own interest or his own duty –

276

When nations grow old
The Arts grow cold,
And Commerce settles on every tree;
And the poor and the old
Can live upon gold,
For all are born poor.

Aged sixty-three.'

Which concluding enigmatical line indicates, I presume, the age of the annotator at the date of writing.

Again, still alluding to his own case: 'The inquiry in England is, not whether a man has talents and genius, but whether he is passive and polite, and a virtuous ass, and obedient to noblemen's opinions in art and science. If he is, he is a good man; if not, he must be starved.'

In a highly personal strain of sarcastic allusion to the favoured portrait-painters of his era, Blake scribbles in verse –

Some look to see the sweet outlines
And beauteous forms that Love does wear;
Some look to find out patches, paint,
Bracelets and stays and powdered hair.

And in even more eccentric vein:

When Sir Joshua Reynolds died,
All nature was degraded;
The king dropped a tear
Into the queen's ear,
And all his pictures faded. (!)

Angels of light make sorry wits – handle mere terrestrial weapons of sarcasm and humorous assault in a very clumsy, ineffectual manner.

'I consider Reynolds' *Discourses* to the Royal Academy,' our

277

annotator in plainer, if still startling words announces, 'as the simulation of the hypocrite who smiles particularly when he means to betray. His praise of Raphael is like the hysteric smile of revenge; his softness and candour the hidden trap and the poisoned feast. He praises Michael Angelo for qualities which Michael Angelo abhorred; and he blames Raphael for the only qualities which Raphael valued. Whether Reynolds knew what he was doing is nothing to me. The mischief is the same whether a man does it ignorantly or knowingly. I always considered true art and true artists to be particularly insulted and degraded by the reputation of these *Discourses;* as much as they were degraded by the reputation of Reynolds' paintings; and that such artists as Reynolds are, at all times, hired by Satan for the depression of art: a pretence of art to destroy art.' A sufficiently decided opinion.

At page 20, we read – 'Mem. That I make a note on "sudden and irresistible approbation."' This threat is in reference to Sir Joshua's observations respecting the kindling effect of the great examples of Art on the student's mind. 'How grossly inconsistent with what he says somewhere on the Vatican!' At page 17 of the *First Discourse*, where, after cautioning the student against following his 'vague and uncertain ideas of beauty,' and drawing the figure, not as it is, but as he fancies it ought to be, Reynolds adds that the habit of drawing correctly what we see gives the power of drawing correctly what we imagine: – 'Excellent!' is Blake's comment; and further on, 'This is admirably said! Why does he not always allow as much?' Instances of praise seldom elicited. Once, indeed, he finds a passage wholly after his own heart: 'A firm and determined outline is one of the characteristics of the great style in painting.' Against which is written: 'Here is a noble sentence: a sentence which overthrows all his book.'

On Sir Joshua's singular inconsistency in condemning generalization in one place, while approving and recommending it in a hundred, he remarks: 'The contradictions in Reynolds' *Discourses* are strong presumption that they are the work of several hands; but this is no proof that Reynolds did not write them. The man, either painter or philosopher, who learns or acquires all he knows from others, must be full of contradictions.' And elsewhere, more definitely, on this subject of generalization he says: 'Real effect is making out the parts, and it is nothing else but that.'

Expressive of the special creed of Blake, to whom invention and meaning were all in all, and of his low estimate of the great rhetoricians in painting, – Correggio, the Venetians, Rubens, and those whom we weak mortals have been wont to admire as great colourists, – is such a note as this, at the beginning of the *Second Discourse*: 'The laboured works of journeymen employed by Correggio, Titian, Veronese, and all the Venetians, ought not to be shown to the young artist as the works of original conception, any more than the works of Strange, Bartolozzi, or Woollett. They are works of manual labour.'

Blake cherished his visionary tendency as an essential function of imagination. 'Mere enthusiasm,' he here declares, 'is the all in all.' And again, – 'The man who asserts that there is no such thing as *softness* in art, and that everything is definite and determinate' (which is what Blake was ever asserting), 'has not been told this by practice, but by inspiration and vision; because vision is determinate and perfect and he copies *that* without fatigue. Everything *seen* is definite and determinate. Softness is produced by comparative strength and weakness, alone, in the marking of the forms. I say these principles would never be found out by the study of nature, without con- or in- nate science.'

With no more than justice he remarks on 'the very weakest feature' in Sir Joshua's system: 'Reynolds' opinion was, that genius may be taught, and that all pretence to inspiration is a lie or deceit, to say the least of it. If it *is* deceit, the whole Bible is madness. This opinion' (of Sir Joshua's) 'originates in the Greeks calling the Muses daughters of Memory.' In the same spirit, and with truth too, he of the *Third Discourse* energetically avers: 'The following *Discourse* is particularly interesting to blockheads, as it endeavours to prove that there is no such thing as inspiration, and that any man of a plain understanding may, by thieving from others, become a Michael Angelo.'

So, too, when Reynolds tells his hearers that 'enthusiastic admiration seldom promotes knowledge;' and proceeds to encourage the student who perceives in his mind 'nothing of that divine inspiration with which he is told so many others have been favoured;' who 'never travelled to heaven to gather new ideas,' &c. Blake answers: 'And such is the coldness with which Reynolds speaks! and such is his enmity! Enthusiastic admiration is the first principle of knowledge, and its last. How he begins to degrade, to deny, and to mock! The man who on examining his own mind finds nothing of inspiration, ought not to dare to be an artist: he is a fool, and a cunning knave suited to the purposes of evil demons. The man who never in his mind and thought travelled to heaven, is no artist. It is evident that Reynolds wished none but fools to be in the arts; and in order to this, he calls all others vague enthusiasts or madmen. What has reasoning to do with the art of painting?'

Characteristic opinions are the following:

'Knowledge of ideal beauty is not to be acquired. It is born with us. Innate ideas are in every man, born with him; they are truly himself. The man who says that we have no innate ideas must be a fool and knave; having no con-science, or *innate* science.' And yet it is a question metaphysicians have been discussing since metaphysics began.

Again: 'One central form composed of all other forms being granted, it does not therefore follow that all other forms are deformity. All forms are perfect in the poet's mind: but these are not abstracted or compounded from nature; they are from imagination.'

On some of the more technical points respecting art, Blake observes: 'No one can ever design till he has learned the language of Art by making many finished copies both of Nature and Art, and of whatever comes in his way, from earliest childhood. The difference between a bad artist and a good is, that the bad artist *seems* to copy a great deal, the good one *does* copy a great deal.'

'To generalize is to be an idiot. To particularize is the great distinction of merit.'

'*Servile* copying is the great merit of copying.'

'Execution is the Chariot of Genius.'

'Invention depends altogether upon execution or *organization*. As that is right or wrong, so is the invention perfect or imperfect. Michael Angelo's art depends on Michael Angelo's execution altogether.'

'Grandeur of ideas is founded on precision of ideas.'

'Passion and expression are beauty itself. The face that is incapable of passion and expression is deformity itself, let it be painted and patched and praised and advertised for ever. It will be admired only by fools.'

With strong reprobation our annotator breaks forth when Sir Joshua quotes Vasari to the effect that Albert Dürer 'would have been one of the finest painters of his age, if,' &c. 'Albert Dürer is not "would have been!" Besides, let them look at Gothic figures and Gothic buildings, and not talk of "Dark Ages," or of any "Ages!" Ages are all equal, but genius is always above its age.'

'A sly dog!' 'He makes little concessions that he may take great advantages,' says Blake, *àpropos* of the remark that the Venetians, notwithstanding their surpassing excellence as colourists, did not attain to the 'great style,' but, with 'splendour' of manner, concealed poverty of meaning. 'If the Venetian's outline *were* right, his shadows would destroy it,' persists Blake. And finally, unable to give vent to the full measure of his contempt in plain prose, he breaks out into an epigram:

On the Venetian Painter

He makes the lame to walk, we all agree;
But then he strives to blind all who can see!

Many readers of the present day, who have learned to almost worship the transcendant Venetian painters – Giorgione, Titian, Tintoret, Veronese, not to speak of the Bellini, Carpaccio, &c. – may be startled to note Blake's pertinacious scorn of them. Such readers will do well to remember that Blake, who had never been abroad, must have formed his idea of the Venetians almost wholly from engravings, and from what writers like Reynolds say of the characteristics of the school. 'He had picked up his notions of Titian,' says Mr Palmer, 'from picture-dealers' "Titians!"'

When Reynolds speaks of *Fresco* as 'a mode of painting which excludes attention to minute elegancies,' Blake observes, 'This is false. *Fresco*-painting is the most minute. It is like miniature painting. A wall is a large ivory.'

In the *Fifth Discourse* we are told that Raphael 'was never able' (in his easel-pictures) 'to conquer perfectly that dryness, or even littleness of manner, which he inherited from his master.' Upon which, Blake: 'He who does not admire Raphael's execution does not even *see* Raphael!' And the assertion that Raphael owes the grandeur of his style, and much else, to Michael Angelo, is met by a favourite simile of Blake's: 'I believe this no more than I believe that the rose teaches the lily how to grow, or that the apple teaches the pear tree how to bear fruit.'

Prefatory to the same *Discourse* Blake writes, 'Gainsborough told a gentleman of rank and fortune that the worst painters always chose the grandest subjects. I desired the gentleman to set Gainsborough about one of Raphael's grandest subjects, namely, *Christ delivering the Keys to St Peter*; and he would find that in Gainsborough's hands it would be a vulgar subject of poor fishermen and a journeyman carpenter. The following *Discourse* is written with the same end in view Gainsborough had in making the above assertion; namely, to represent vulgar artists as the models of executive merit.'

And again: 'Real effect is making out the parts. Why are we to be told that masters, who could think, had not the judgment to perform the inferior parts of art? (as Reynolds artfully calls them); that we are to learn to *think* from great masters, and to perform from underlings – to learn to design from Raphael, and to execute from Rubens?'

Blake had, in truth, just personal grounds for speaking with indignant emphasis on this topic. 'The lavish praise I have received from all quarters, for invention and drawing,' says he elsewhere, 'has generally been accompanied by this: "He can conceive, but he cannot execute." This absurd assertion has done, and may still do me the greatest mischief.'

In the MS. note-book are some stray verses, manifestly the overflowings of the same mood as these notes. We shall be best able to appreciate their vigour of meaning, and tolerate the occasional hobbling of the verse, by taking them in connexion with the foregoing:

> Raphael, sublime, majestic, graceful, wise, –
> His executive power must I despise?
> Rubens, low, vulgar, stupid, ignorant, –
> His power of execution I must grant!
>
> The cripple every step drudges and labours,
> And says, 'Come, learn to walk of me, good neighbours!'
> Sir Joshua, in astonishment, cries out,
> 'See what great labour springs from modest doubt!'

On Colourists

> Call that the public voice which is their error?
> Like as a monkey, peeping in a mirror,
> Admireth all his colours brown and warm,
> And never once perceives his ugly form.

On Sir Joshua again:

> No real style of colouring now appears,
> Save thro' advertisements in the newspapers;
> Look there – you'll see Sir Joshua's colouring:
> Look at his pictures – all has taken wing!

I think it may not be superfluous to take into account here, as we did when first alluding to these notes on Reynolds, all the sources of Blake's hostility towards the universally admired and extolled Prince of English Portrait-painting. The deepest of these was the honest contempt of a man with high spiritual aims for one whose goal, though honourable, and far above the common attainment, was at as widely different an altitude from

Blake's as the mere earthly hill-top from the star which shines down upon it. Hence the entire antagonism of their views; for such different ends must be reached by wholly different means. It is no invalidation of this high claim for Blake to add that the vivid contrast of their respective lots was another source; for *recognition* is dear to every gifted man, however unworldly, however sincere his indifference to those goods of fortune which ordinarily accompany recognition, but are the mere accidents of which that is the precious substance.

There was also, I am bound to confess (and it is not much to confess either), some personal antipathy in the case which added, doubtless, an extra dash of sharpness to the flavour of these pungent notes, and would seem to have originated in an interview (probably anterior to the one already described), at which Blake's experiences were not wholly of Sir Joshua's 'blandness.' 'Once I remember his talking to me of Reynolds,' writes a surviving friend: 'he became furious at what the latter had dared to say of his early works. When a very young man he had called on Reynolds to show him some designs, and had been recommended to work with less extravagance and more simplicity, and to correct his drawing. This Blake seemed to regard as an affront never to be forgotten. He was very indignant when he spoke of it.'

At page 61 of the Notes we are introduced to another of Blake's antipathies: 'The "great Bacon," as he is called (I call him the little Bacon), says that everything must be done by experiment. His first principle is unbelief, and yet here he says that art must be produced without such method. He is like Sir Joshua, full of self-contradiction and knavery.' Bacon, known to Blake by his *Essays*, was also Antichrist in his eyes. The high worldly wisdom and courtier-like sagacity, not unmingled with politic craft, of those Essays, were alien to the sympathies of the republican spiritualist, despite the imaginative form with which those qualities are clothed in Bacon's grand speech, – his stately, organ-like eloquence.

The artist's copy of the *Essays*, a duodecimo, published by Edwards, in 1798, is roughly annotated in pencil in a very characteristic if very unreasonable fashion; marginal notes dating, I should say, during the latter years of Blake's life. We have frequent indignant comment and execration. The epithets 'fool,' 'liar,' 'villain,' 'atheist,' nay, 'Satan,' and even (most singular of all) 'stupid,' are freely indulged in. There is in these notes, however, none of that leaven of real sense and acumen which tempers the violence of those on Reynolds. Bound by the interests of faithful biography, we will borrow a few characteristic sentences; but only a few.

'Good advice for Satan's kingdom,' is the inscription on the title-page. 'Is it true or is it false,' asks the annotator, 'that the wisdom of the world is foolishness with God? This is certain if what Bacon says is true, what Christ says is false. If Cæsar is right, Christ is wrong, both in politics and religion, since they will divide themselves in two.' 'Everybody knows,' he writes again, 'that this is epicurism and libertinism, and yet everybody says that it is Christian philosophy. How is this possible? Everybody must be a liar and deceiver? No! "Everybody" does not do this; but the hirelings of Kings and Courts, who made themselves "everybody," and knowingly propagate falsehood. It was a common opinion in the Court of Queen Elizabeth that knavery is wisdom. Cunning plotters were considered as wise Machiavels.'

Whatever Bacon may say, his singular annotator refuses to be pleased. When the former innocently enough tells us, 'It is great blasphemy to personate God, and bring him in saying, "I will demand," &c.' Blake answers: 'Did not Jesus descend and become a servant? The Prince of Darkness is a gentleman and not a man: he is a Lord Chancellor.'

Characteristic comment on the *Essay on Virtue* is this: 'What do these knaves mean by virtue? Do they mean war and its horrors, and its heroic villains?' 'Good thoughts,' says Bacon, are little better than good dreams.' 'Thought *is* act,' replies Blake: 'Christ's acts were nothing to Cæsar's, if this is not so.' When Bacon, after the fashion of his age, says, 'The increase of any State must be upon the foreigner,' the artist, innocent of political economy though he be, has for once what would be generally considered now-a-days in part a just retort: 'The increase of a State, as of a man, is from internal improvement or intellectual acquirement. Man is not improved by the hurt of another. States are not improved at the expense of foreigners.' Again: 'Bacon calls intellectual arts unmanly: and so they are for kings and wars, and shall in the end annihilate them.' 'What is fortune but an outward accident? for a few years, sixty at the most, and then gone!'

'King James was Bacon's *primum mobile*,' exclaims the scornful Blake. And elsewhere his political prejudices explode in an amusing way. The philosopher speaks of 'mighty Princes:' – the 'Powers of Darkness,' responds Blake. Again: 'A tyrant is the worst disease, and the cause of all others!' And in the same spirit: 'Everybody hates a king! David was afraid to say that the envy was upon a king: but is this envy or indignation?'

And here let the singular dialogue at cross-purposes end.

THIRTY

Designs to Phillips' Pastorals 1820–21
[ÆT. 63–64]

Blake was in 1820–21 employed by Dr Thornton for some illustrations to the Doctor's School *Virgil* – Virgil's *Pastorals*, that is. The result of the commission was a series of designs, among the most beautiful and original of Blake's performance. These are the small woodcuts to Ambrose Phillips' imitation of Virgil's first *Eclogue:* designs simple, quaint, poetic, charged with the very spirit of pastoral.

Dr Thornton, son of Bonnell Thornton of humorous memory, colleague with Colman in *The Connoisseur*, was a physician and botanist of note in his day. He was the author of several very expensively illustrated folios and quartos on botany: *A New Illustration of the Sexual System of Linnæus*, 1797; *The Temple of Flora, or Garden of the Poet, Painter, and Philosopher*, and other similar productions about botany in its picturesque aspect; costly books, illustrated in colours, which impoverished their amiable projector.

More successful in its generation was the Doctor's edition of the *Pastorals* of Virgil, 'with a course of English reading adapted for schools,' and other explanatory helps. All which was designed to enable youth 'to acquire ideas as well as words' with 'ease to the master and delight to the scholar.' One means to this end was ultimately added in a series of illustrative woodcuts. The first edition of 1812 had none: illustrations were issued as a

288

supplementary volume in 1814. In the second edition of 1819 the two were incorporated. In this third edition of 1821 the illustrations were increased to as many as two hundred and thirty, including these from Blake's hand.

And hereby hangs a tale. Blake made twenty drawings to illustrate the Pastorals of Phillips, introduced by Thornton into his 'course' of Virgil reading. From these he executed seventeen wood blocks, the first he had ever cut, and, as they will prove, the last. The rough, unconventional work of a mere 'prentice hand to the art of wood engraving, they are in effect vigorous and artist-like, recalling the doings of Albert Dürer and the early masters, whose aim was to give ideas, not pretty language. When he sent in these seventeen, the publishers, unused to so daring a style, were taken aback, and declared 'this man must do no more;' nay, were for having all he *had* done re-cut by one of their regular hands. The very engravers received them with derision, crying out in the words of the critic, 'This will never do.' Blake's merits, seldom wholly hidden from his artist contemporaries, were always impenetrably dark to the book and print selling genus.

Dr Thornton had, in his various undertakings, been munificent to artists to an extent which, as we have said, brought him to poverty. But he had himself no knowledge of art, and, despite kind intentions, was disposed to take his publishers' view. However, it fortunately happened that meeting one day several artists at Mr Aders' table, – Lawrence, James Ward, Linnell, and others, – conversation fell on the Virgil. All present expressed warm admiration of Blake's art, and of those designs and woodcuts in particular. By such competent authority reassured, if also puzzled, the good Doctor began to think there must be more in them than he and his publishers could discern. The contemplated sacrifice of the blocks already cut was averted. The three other designs, however, had been engraved by another, nameless hand: those illustrative of the three 'comparisons' in the last stanza but one of Phillips' Pastoral. Wretched, jejune caricatures of the beautiful originals they proved, scarce any trace of Blake being left.

To conciliate the outraged arts, Dr Thornton introduced the designs with an apology. 'The illustrations of this English Pastoral are by the famous BLAKE, the illustrator of Young's *Night Thoughts*, and Blair's *Grave*; who designed and engraved them himself. This is mentioned as they display less of art than of genius, and are much admired by some eminent painters.'

One of the designs engraved by Blake was re-cut among the engravers, who scrupled not, by way of showing what it ought to have been, to smooth down and conventionalize the design itself; reducing a poetic, typical composition to mere commonplace, 'to meet the public taste.' This as an earnest of what had been contemplated for the whole series. The amendment was not adopted by Thornton. Both versions may be seen in the *Athenæum* for January 21st, 1843; where, in the course of a very intelligent article on the true principles of wood engraving, they are introduced, with other cuts from Holbein, &c. to illustrate the writer's just argument: that 'amid all drawbacks there exists a power in the work of the man of genius which no one but himself can utter fully;' and that 'there is an authentic manifestation of feeling in an author's own work, which endears it to all who can sympathize with art, and reconciles all its defects. Blake's rude work,' adds the critic, 'utterly without pretension, too, as an engraving, the merest attempt of a fresh apprentice, is a work of genius; whilst the latter' – the doctored cut – 'is but a piece of smooth, tame mechanism.'

The more these remarkable designs are seen, the more power do they exert over the mind. With few lines, and the simplest, rudest hints of natural objects, they appeal to the imagination direct, not the memory; setting before us condensed, typical ideas. Strange to think of Blake, shut up in dingy, gardenless South Molton Street, designing such pastorals! His mind must have been impregnated with rural images, enabling him, without immediate reference to Nature, to throw off these beautiful suggestions, so pastoral in feeling, of Arcadian shepherds and their flocks, under the broad setting sun or tranquil moon. As Thornton's purpose was to give his young readers pictured images of his author's words, the designs accompany the poem literally, and line for line. Thenot addresses Colinet, who leans lonesome against a tree, crook in hand, and sheep beside, and so on.

The original designs, in sepia, are of much delicacy and grace. Their expression and drawing are a little distorted in the transference to wood, even under Blake's own hands. The blocks, moreover, proved in the first instance too wide for the page and were, irrespective of the composition, summarily cut down to the requisite size by the publishers. They are now, together with the drawings, in the possession of Mr Linnell, who has kindly permitted impressions from three of them to be taken for the present work.

Dr Thornton found further employment for Blake in etchings, scattered through the two volumes of 1821, from antique busts: Theocritus, Virgil, Augustus, Agrippa, Julius Cæsar, Epicurus; task-work Blake well and honestly performed. A drawing of his, from Poussin's *Polypheme*, was put into Byfield's hands to engrave; which the latter did, poorly enough. As for the rest of the two hundred and thirty cuts, though executed by some of the best wood engravers of the time, they are, with the exception of one or two by Bewick and Thurston, of singularly laughable calibre. The designers obviously thought they could not be too puerile in addressing boys. The old, rude woodcuts to Croxall's *Æsop* are respectable works of art, compared with these. It is a curious practical satire on the opinion of Blake the engravers had, that the book, which has become scarce, is seldom looked at now but for Blake's slight share in it.

THIRTY-ONE

Fountain Court, 1821–25
[ÆT. 64–68]

After seventeen years in South Molton Street, Blake, in 1821, migrated to No. 3, Fountain Court, Strand, – a house kept by a brother-in-law named Baines. It was his final change of residence. Here, as in South Molton Street, his lodgings were not a 'garret,' as Allan Cunningham, with metaphorical flourish, describes them, but now, as before, in the best part – the first floor – of a respectable house. Fountain Court, unknown by name, perhaps, to many who yet often pass it on their way through a great London artery, is a court lying a little out of the Strand, between it and the river, and approached by a dark narrow opening, or inclined plane, at the corner of Simpson's Tavern, and nearly opposite Exeter Hall. At one corner of the court, nearest the Strand, stands the Coal Hole Tavern, once the haunt of Edmund Kean and his 'Wolf Club' of *claquers*, still in Blake's time a resort of the Thespian race; not then promoted to the less admirable notoriety it has, in our days, enjoyed. Now the shrill tinkle of a dilapidated piano, accompaniment to a series of tawdry *poses plastiques*, wakes the nocturnal echoes, making night hideous in the quiet court where the poet and visionary once lived and designed the *Inventions to Job*.

An old-fashioned respectable court in 1821, as other similar streets in that neighbourhood still are – its red-brick houses with overhanging cornices, dating from the end of the seventeenth and beginning of the eighteenth century – it is silent and sordid now; having, like all Blake's abodes, suffered a decline of fortune. No. 3, then a clean red-brick house, is now a dirty stuccoed one, let out, as are all in the court, in single rooms to the labouring poor. That which was Blake's front room was lately in the market at four and sixpence a week, as an assiduous inquirer found. The whole place wears that inexpressibly forlorn, squalid look houses used for a lower purpose than the one for which they were built always assume. There is an ancient timber and brick gateway under a lofty old house hard by; and a few traces yet linger here and there, in bits of wall, &c. of the old Savoy Palace, destroyed to make way for the approaches to Waterloo Bridge, which had been opened just four years when Blake first came to the court.

Those capable of feeling the beauty of Blake's design were, if anything, fewer at this period than they had ever been. Among these few numbered a man who was hereafter to acquire a sombre and terrible notoriety, – Thomas Griffiths Wainwright; the lively magazine writer, fine-art critic, artist, man of pleasure, companion of poets and philosophers, and future murderer, secret poisoner of confidential friend and trustful sister. This was the Janus' Weathercock of *The London Magazine*; the 'light-hearted Janus' of Charles Lamb. To the other anomalies of this unhappy man's career may be added the fact of his intimacy with William Blake, whom he assisted by buying two or three of his expensive illustrated books. One among the best of the *Songs of Innocence and Experience* I have seen formerly belonged to Wainwright. Blake entertained, as did Lamb, Procter, and others of *The London* coterie, a kindness for him and his works.

For this spiritual voluptuary, with the greedy senses, soft coat, and tiger heart, painted and exhibited as well as wrote. I trace him at the Academy in 1821, – *Subject from Undine, ch.* 6; in 1822 (year of Wilkie's *Chelsea Pensioners*), *Paris in the Chamber of Helen*; and in 1825, *First Idea of a Scene from Der Freyschütz*, and a *Sketch from Gerusalemme Liberata* – both sketches, it is worth notice, as indicating uncertain application to the practice of art. He was then living at 44, Great Marlborough Street. Mr Palmer, one of Blake's young disciples in those days, well remembers a visit to the Academy in Blake's company, during which the latter pointed to a picture near the ceiling, by Wainwright, and spoke of it as 'very fine.' It was a scene from *Walton's Angler*, exhibited in 1823 or 4. 'While so many moments better worthy to remain are fled,' writes Mr Palmer to me, 'the caprice of memory presents me with the image of Blake looking up at Wainwright's picture; Blake in his plain black suit and *rather* broad-brimmed, but not quakerish hat, standing so quietly among all the dressed-up, rustling, swelling people, and myself thinking "How little you know *who* is among you!"'

During the first years of *The London Magazine*, 1820–23, Wainwright was a contributor, under various pseudonyms, of articles, not, as Talfourd mistakenly describes them, 'of mere flashy assumption,' full of 'disdainful notices of living artists;' but articles of real literary merit and originality; in a vein of partly feigned coxcombry and flippant impertinence, of wholly genuine sympathy with art (within orthodox limits), and recognition of the real excellencies of the moderns, – of Retsch, of Stothard, for example, and of Etty, then a young man. They are articles by no means obsolete yet, even in their opinions; in matter and style still fresh and readable; standing out in vivid contrast to the heavy common-place of the Editor's, *now* so stale and flat, in the same department of art-criticism. They attracted the notice and admiration of Lamb, whose personal regard he retained for many years; of De Quincey and of Procter – no mean judges.

In one of these smart, harum-scarum articles (Sept. 1820), entitled 'Mr Janus Weathercock's Private Correspondence,' – a letter on topics so miscellaneous as Recent Engravings, Pugilism, and Chapman's Homer, – occurs incidental reference to Blake, the only one I have found in the series. 'Talking of articles, my learned friend Dr Tobias Ruddicombe, M.D. is, at my earnest entreaty, casting a tremendous piece of ordnance, *an eighty-eight pounder!* which he proposeth to fire off in your next. It is an account of an ancient, newly discovered, illuminated manuscript, which has to name "𝔍𝔢𝔯𝔲𝔰𝔞𝔩𝔢𝔪 𝔱𝔥𝔢 𝔈𝔪𝔞𝔫𝔞𝔱𝔦𝔬𝔫 𝔬𝔣 𝔱𝔥𝔢 𝔊𝔦𝔞𝔫𝔱 𝔄𝔩𝔟𝔦𝔬𝔫"!!! It contains a good deal anent one *"Los,"* who, it appears, is now, and hath been from the Creation, the *sole* and four-fold dominator of the celebrated city of *Golgonooza!* The doctor assures me that the redemption of mankind hangs on the universal diffusion of the doctrines broached in this MS. But, however, that isn't the subject of this *scrinium,* scroll, or scrawl, or whatever you may call it.'

This was probably a feeler of Wainwright's, to try Editor Scott's pulse as to a paper on Blake; which, however, if written never appeared. Scott, who had originally encouraged Wainwright to use the pen, was rather discomposed by his systematic impertinences and flightiness, and now began 'rapping him over the knuckles,' cutting his articles down, and even refusing them admission; as is related in a subsequent contribution, one of Wainwright's last (Jan. 1823). After Scott's tragic end in a preposterous duel with one of the rancorous Blackwood set, Wainwright had been put on the staff again, at the urgent representations of Lamb and Procter. The paper in question, entitled *Janus Weatherbound*, contains some singularly interesting reminiscences – when we call to mind the man's subsequent history – of the writer's own previous career; of John Scott himself and his sudden death-bed, of Lamb and his sister, and of other fellow-contributors to *The London*.

Talfourd, in his *Final Memorials* of Lamb, has told the after story of Wainwright's life; Bulwer, in his *Lucretia*, has worked it up into fiction; and De Quincey, in his *Autobiographic Sketches*, has thrown over it a gleam from the fitful torchlight of his vivifying imagination. From them we learn how expensive tastes for fine prints, rare books, articles of *virtù*, on the one hand; for mere elegant living on the other; for combining, in short, the man about town and the man of refined taste and high sympathies, led him into inevitable money difficulties, into shifts of all kinds, and convulsive efforts to raise the wind. How, in 1830, about half a dozen years subsequent to his connexion with *The London* and familiar intercourse with some of the most original men of that generation, he began insuring the life of a young and beautiful sister-in-law, for a short term, in various offices, to the amount of 18,000*l.* in all. How he contrived that the poor girl, after having made a will in his favour, *should* die before the two years' term was out, without any appearance of foul play, – he using the then little known vegetable poison, *strychnine*, now so familiar to newspaper readers. How the assurance offices instinctively disputed his claims; and, after five years of 'the law's delay' in Chancery and two trials at common law, succeeded in their resistance on the technical point – that the insurance was not a *bonâ fide* one of the deceased's own effecting: the graver ground of objection being waived for want of conclusive evidence, though sufficient daylight was let in to warrant the darkest construction of Wainwright's real character. How, after skulking about France a few years, with a bottle of strychnine in his pocket, and, it is suspected, using the same on a confiding friend or two, Wainwright was, in 1836, apprehended for forgery of his wife's trustee's signature (he had a wife and child); was tried, pleaded guilty, and sentenced to transportation for life: finally made base revelations to the offices, enabling them to defeat the claims of his surviving sister-in-law, in the craven hope of mitigation of punishment; in which hope he was deceived. In the extremity of infamy and wretchedness, the somewhile associate of Coleridge, Blake, Lamb, still piqued himself on being the gentleman, though under a cloud; still claimed a soul sympathizing with poetry, philosophy, and all high things, showing no remorse. In Australia ended the ghastly motley of his life, a few years ago.

Complete oblivion seems already to have overtaken all that Wainwright painted; though we cannot doubt, from Blake's testimony, as reported by Mr Palmer, that his works belonged, in whatever degree, to the class showing individual power. He seems to have practised painting as a means of subsistence in Australia during his last years, as well as at an earlier, and not yet hopeless, time in England. Of the first period of his painting, there is said to be some evidence in designs to an edition of Chamberlayne's poems, which I have sought for, but failed to find, at the British Museum; and in the preface to which he is spoken of, I am told, as a young man of high hopes. To the last period belongs a portrait of the Hon. Miss Power, painted in Australia, which also is known to me by report, not by eyesight. Into any of the works of such a life it is difficult to search without feeling as if every step were taken among things dead and doomed. But the truth about Wainwright's essays on art is, that they display a real knowledge, insight, and power of language, which remained unequalled, in their own walk of criticism, from that day till the splendid advent and immediate influence of Ruskin. This being thus in fact, though sometimes otherwise stated, it would be interesting, even highly so, to discover what has become of Wainwright's pictures, and what were the practical artistic gifts of one whose nature presents such strange and hideous contrasts.

I trust that the decision with which I have spoken of this man's great talents will not be taken as implying any bluntness of repugnance for the great criminality which, I fear, stands substantially, though never explicitly, proved against him. But art has its own truth, as absolute as that of life itself, and demanding a wholly independent verdict, not to be appealed against on any ground of good deeds, and which not even the sternest personal censure can annul.

THIRTY-TWO

Inventions to the Book of Job 1823–25
[ÆT. 66–68]

As we have often to repeat, Blake was even more a neglected man in these days of Lawrence and Wilkie than he had been in those of Reynolds and Gainsborough. The majority of connoisseurs, a set of men who, to tell the truth, know little more about art, the vital part of it, have no quicker perception or deeper insight into its poetic and spiritual qualities than the mob of educated men, though they prate more: these were, as they still are, blind to his beauties. And this being so, the publishing class deserves no special blame for its blindness and timidity.

Even his old friend Mr Butts, a friend of more than thirty years' standing, the possessor of his best *temperas* and watercolour drawings, and of copies of all his engraved books, grew cool. The patron had often found it a hard matter *not* to offend the independent, wilful painter, ever the prouder for his poverty and neglect, always impracticable and extreme when ruffled or stroked the wrong way. The patron had himself begun to take offence at Blake's quick resentment of well-meant, if blunt, advice and at the unmeasured violence of his speech when provoked by opposition. The wealthy merchant employed him but little now, and during the few remaining years of Blake's life they seldom met.

One of the last, if not the very last, works bought by Mr Butts of Blake, was the original series of twenty-one watercolour drawings or *Inventions* from the *Book of Job*, the longest and most important series executed since *The Grave*, in 1805; still loftier in theme, nobler in achievement, most original and characteristic of all his productions. *This* set of drawings to *Job* has passed from Mr Butts' son into the possession of Mr Monckton Milnes.

It is to the credit of the Royal Academy that, at this conjuncture, Blake, in the year 1822, received from its funds a donation of 25*l*. Collins and Abraham Cooper recommended him for the grant; Baily and Rd. Bone were the movers and seconders of the vote according it. The Forty of that day, as the testimonial in favour of the *Grave* showed, numbered many who could recognize Blake's high artistic genius.

With no remaining patrons for his design, few to employ him as an engraver, Blake, in age, was on the verge of want. Grim poverty had throughout life stared him in the face. Throughout life he had calmly looked back into *her* eyes. For him she had no terrors. He would have been in actual want but for one friend, himself an artist, himself not overburthened at that time with the gifts of Fortune; who had, as other rising artists have – but in 1823 it was a still tougher struggle than in 1860 – to toil hard for himself and family at often ungenial task-work. The drawings to *Job* had been borrowed from Mr Butts to be shown to such as might seem likely to prove employers. From Mr Linnell alone they drew a commission. He engaged Blake to execute and engrave a duplicate set. The agreement, recorded in writing in a business-like way, bears date 25th March, 1823. It was such an one as Blake had never set hand to before, nor could have obtained in any other quarter. Blake was to receive 100*l*. for the designs and copyright, to be paid from time to time; and another 100*l*. out of the profits. No profits were realized by the engravings, their sale hardly covering expenses. But as the designs and stock of engravings remained with the purchaser, Mr Linnell subsequently paid over, from time to time, 50*l*. more, making a total of 150*l*., – the largest sum Blake had ever received for any one series. The drawings, the remainder of engravings and plates, are still in the hands of this liberal friend, who discounted, as it were, Blake's bill on posterity, when none else would. While the *Job* was in progress, Blake received his money in the way handiest to him, – instalments of 2*l*. to 3*l*. a week; sums amply sufficient for all his ordinary wants, thanks to his modest *ménage* and simple habits. More he would hardly have spent, if he had had it.

The set of drawings made for Mr Linnell varies much in detail from that for Mr Butts, and is often finer. The engravings were still further altered; faces in profile in the drawings are given full view in the prints, and so on. Both sets of designs are very finely drawn, and pure in colour; necessarily very much finer than the prints. No artist can quite reproduce even his own drawings. Much must be lost by the way.

The engravings are the best Blake ever did: vigorous, decisive, and, above all, in a style of expression in keeping with the designs, which the work of no other hand could have been in the case of conceptions so austere and primeval as these. Blake's manner of handling the graver had been advantageously modified since his acquaintance with Mr Linnell. The latter had called his attention to the works of Albert Dürer, Marc Antonio, and the Italian's contemporary and disciple Bonosoni, a more elegant and facile, if less robust, Marc Antonio. From Bonosoni especially Blake gleaned much, and was led, on first becoming familiar with his work, to express a regret that he had been trained in the Basire school, wherein he had learned to work as a mere engraver, cross-hatching freely. He now became an artist, making every line tell. The results of this change of style are manifest in the engraved *Inventions to Job*. In them, too, Bonosoni's plan was adopted, of working wholly with the graver and etching nothing; so that the plates lose little by having a few hundred impressions taken off.

These *Inventions to the Book of Job*, which may be regarded as the works of Blake's own hand, in which he most unreservedly competes with others – belonging as they do in style to the accepted category of engraved designs – consist of twenty-one subjects on a considerably smaller scale than those in the *Grave*, each highly wrought in light and shade, and each surrounded by a border of allusive design and inscription, executed in a slighter style than the subject itself. Perhaps this may fairly be pronounced, on the whole, the most remarkable series of etchings on a scriptural theme which has appeared since the days of Albert Dürer and Rembrandt, widely differing, too, from either.

Except the *Grave*, these designs must be known to a larger circle than any other series by Blake.

The first among them shows us the patriarch Job worshipping among his family under a mighty oak, surrounded by feeding flocks, range behind range, as far as the distant homestead, in a landscape glorified by setting sun and rising moon. 'Thus did Job continually,' the leading motto tells us. In the second plate we see the same persons grouped, still full of happiness and thanksgiving. But this is that day when the sons of God came to present themselves before the Lord, and Satan came also among them; and above the happy group we see what they do not see, and know that power is given to Satan over all that Job has. Then in the two next subjects come the workings of that power; the house falling on the slain feasters, and the messengers hurrying one after another to the lonely parents, still with fresh tidings of ruin. The fifth is a wonderful design. Job and his wife still sit side by side, the closer for their misery, and still out of the little left to them give alms to those poorer than themselves. The angels of their love and resignation are ever with them on either side; but above, again, the unseen Heaven lies open. There sits throned that Almighty figure, filled now with inexpressible pity, almost with compunction. Around Him His angels shrink away in horror; for now the fires which clothe them – the very fires of God – are compressed in the hand of Satan into a phial for the devoted head of Job himself. Job is to be tried to the utmost; only his life is withheld from the tormentor. How this is wrought, and how Job's friends come to visit him in his desolation, are the subjects which follow; and then, in the eighth design, Job at last lifts up his voice, with arms uplifted too, among his crouching shuddering friends, and curses the day when he was born. The next, again, is among the grandest of the series. Eliphaz the Temanite is telling Job of the thing which was secretly brought to him in the visions of the night; and above we are shown the matter of his words, the spirit which passed before his face; all blended in a wondrous partition of light, cloud, and mist of light. After this Job kneels up, and prays his reproachful friends to have pity on him, for the hand of God has touched him. And next – most terrible of all – we see embodied the accusations of torment which Job brings against his Maker: a theme hard to dwell upon, and which needs to be viewed in the awful spirit in which Blake conceived it. But in the following subject there comes at last some sign of soothing change. The sky, till now full of sunset and surging cloud, in which the stones of the ruined home looked as if they were still burning, has here given birth to the large peaceful stars, and under them the young Elihu begins to speak: 'Lo! all these things worketh God oftentimes with man, to bring forth his soul from the pit.' The expression of Job, as he sits with folded arms, beginning to be reconciled, is full of delicate familiar nature; while the look of the three unmerciful friends, in their turn reproved, has something in it almost humorous. And then the Lord answers Job out of the whirlwind, dreadful in its resistless force, but full also of awakening life, and rich with lovely clinging spray. Under its influence, Job and his wife kneel and listen, with faces to which the blessing of thankfulness has almost returned. In the next subject it shines forth fully present again, for now God Himself is speaking of His own omnipotence and right of judgment – of that day of creation 'when the morning stars sang together, and all the sons of God shouted for joy.' All that He says is brought before us, surrounding his own glorified Image; while below, the hearers kneel rapt and ecstatic. This is a design which never has been surpassed in the whole range of Christian art. Very grand, too, is the next, where we see Behemoth, chief of the ways of God, and Leviathan, king over the children of pride. The sixteenth plate, to which we now come, is a proof of the clear dramatic sense with which Blake conceived the series as a whole. It is introduced in order to show us the defeat of Satan in his contest against Job's uprightness. Here, again, is the throned Creator among His angels, and beneath Him the Evil One falls with tremendous plummet-force; Hell naked before his face, and Destruction without a covering. Job with his friends are present as awestruck witnesses. In the design which follows, He who has chastened and consoled Job and his wife is seen to bestow His blessing on them; while the three friends, against whom 'His wrath is kindled,' cover their faces in fear and trembling. And now comes the acceptance of Job, who prays for his friends before an altar, from which a heart-shaped body of flame shoots upward into the sun itself; the background showing a distant evening light through broad tree-stems – the most peaceful sight in the world. Then Job's kindred return to him, 'every one also gave him a piece of money, and every one an earring of gold.' Next he is seen relating his trials and mercies to the new daughters who were born to him – no women so fair in the land. And, lastly, the series culminates in a scene of music and rapturous joy, which, contrasted with the calm thanksgiving of the opening design, gloriously embodies the words of its text, 'So the Lord blessed the latter end of Job more than the beginning.'

In these three last designs, I would specially direct attention to the exquisite beauty of the female figures. Nothing proves more thoroughly how free was the spiritualism of Blake's art from any ascetic tinge. These women are given to us no less noble in body than in soul; large-eyed, and large-armed also; such as a man may love with all his life.

The angels (and especially those in plate 14, 'When the morning stars sang together,') may be equally cited as proofs of the same great distinctive quality. These are no flimsy, filmy creatures, drowsing on feather-bed wings, or smothered in draperies. Here the utmost amount of vital power is the heavenly glory they display; faces, bodies, and wings, all living and springing fire. And that the ascetic tendency, here happily absent, is not the inseparable penalty to be paid for a love of the Gothic forms of beauty, is evident enough, when we see those forms everywhere rightly mingling with the artist's conceptions, as the natural breath of sacred art. With the true daring of genius, he has even introduced a Gothic cathedral in the background of the worshipping group in plate 1, as the shape in which the very soul of worship is now for ever embodied for us. It is probably with the fine intention of symbolizing the unshaken piety of Job under heavy affliction, that a similar building is still seen pointing its spires heavenward in the fourth plate, where the messengers of ruin follow close at one another's heels. We may, perhaps, even conjecture that the shapeless buildings, like rude pagan cairns, which are scattered over those scenes of the drama which refer to the gradual darkening of Job's soul, have been introduced as forms suggestive of error and the shutting out of hope. Everywhere throughout the series we meet with evidences of Gothic feeling. Such are the recessed settle and screen of trees in plate 2, much in the spirit of Orcagna; the decorative character of the stars in plate 12; the Leviathan and Behemoth in plate 15, grouped so as to recall a mediæval medallion or wood-carving; the trees, drawn always as they might be carved in the woodwork of an old church. Further instances of the same kind may be found in the curious sort of painted chamber, showing the themes of his discourse, in which Job addresses his daughters in plate 20; and in the soaring trumpets of plate 21, which might well be one of the rich conceptions of Luca della Robbia.

Nothing has yet been said of the borders of illustrative design and inscription which surround each subject in the *Job*. These are slight in manner, but always thoughtful and appropriate, and often very beautiful. Where Satan obtains power over Job, we see a terrible serpent twined round tree-stems among winding fires, while angels weep, but may not quench them. Fungi spring under baleful dews, while Job prays that the night may be solitary, and the day perish wherein he was born. Trees stand and bow like ghosts, with bristling hair of branches, round the spirit which passes before the face of Eliphaz. Fine examples also are the prostrate rain-beaten tree in plate 13; and, in the next plate, the map of the days of creation. In plate 18 (the sacrifice and acceptance of Job), Blake's palette and brushes are expressively introduced in the border, lying, as it were, on an altar-step beside the signature of his name. That which possesses the greatest charm is, perhaps, the border to plate 2. Here, at the base, are sheepfolds watched by shepherds; up the sides is a trellis, on whose lower rings birds sit upon their nests, while angels, on the higher ones, worship round flame and cloud, till it arches at the summit into a sky full of the written words of God.

Such defects as exist in these designs are of the kind usual with Blake, but far less frequent than in his more wilful works; indeed, many among them are entirely free from any damaging peculiarities. Intensely muscular figures, who surprise us by a sort of line round the throat, wrists, and ankles, but show no other sign of being draped, are certainly to be sometimes found here as elsewhere, but not many of them. The lifted arms and pointing arms in plates 7 and 10 are pieces of mannerism to be regretted, the latter even seeming a reminiscence of Macbeth's Witches by Fuseli; and a few other slight instances might, perhaps, be cited. But, on the whole, these are designs no less well and clearly considered, however highly imaginative, than the others in the small highest class of original engraved inventions, which comprises the works of Albert Dürer, of Rembrandt, of Hogarth, of Turner, of Cruikshank in his best time, and some few others. Like all these they are incisive and richly toned to a degree which can only be attained in engraving by the original inventor, and have equally a style of execution all their own. In spirit and character they are no less independent, having more real affinity, perhaps, with Orcagna than with any other of the greatest men. In their unison of natural study with imagination, they remind one decidedly of him; and also of Giotto, himself the author of a now almost destroyed series of frescos from Job, in the Campo Santo at Pisa, which it would be interesting to compare, as far as possible, with these inventions of Blake.

To the high artistic value of this series Mr Ruskin has borne witness. In his *Elements of Drawing for Beginners* (1857), it is specified among the 'Things to be Studied.' 'The *Book of Job*, engraved by himself' (by Blake, that is), it is there said, 'is of the highest rank in certain characters of imagination and expression; in the mode of obtaining certain effects of light, it will also be a very useful example to you. In expressing conditions of glaring and flickering light, Blake is greater than Rembrandt.'

March 8th, 1825, was the publishing date on the plates; the date by which Blake had expected to have finished them. But, March, 1826, is the date given on the cover, and the correct one. The publishing price was three guineas; proofs, five; India paper proofs, six. The circulation was limited; the mode of publication, for one thing, being a very quiet one.

In April, 1825, another lingerer in the small knot of Blake's earliest friends was summoned away by Death: Fuseli, whose health and bodily strength had, for the last year or two, been failing but not his faculties. He died in his eighty-fourth year; neglected by picture-buyers, honoured by all in his own profession, by men of letters, by some among 'the great,' and not without a fair share of the goods of fortune. Of Fuseli, Blake had always been a warm and generous admirer, and was wont to declare, 'This country must advance two centuries in civilization before it can appreciate him.' Let us hope a few of that remarkable man's original, if mannered and undisciplined, works will survive the extraordinary and disproportioned neglect which has exiled them to the cellar and the garret.

THIRTY-THREE

Hampstead; and Youthful Disciples, 1825–27
[ÆT. 68–70]

The following letter is the first in a brief series preserved by Mr Linnell, interesting as among the very small number of Blake's writing extant. I think he, throughout life, wrote comparatively few. It is to 'Mrs Linnell, Collins's Farm, North End, Hampstead,' and is dated *Tuesday, 11th October,* 1825:

'DEAR MADAM,

'I have had the pleasure to see Mr Linnell set off safe in a very comfortable coach. And I may say I accompanied him part of the way on his journey in the coach. For we both got in, together with another passenger, and entered into conversation, when at length we found that we were all three proceeding on our journey. But as I had not paid, and did not wish to pay for or take so long a ride, we, with some difficulty, made the coachman understand that one of his passengers was unwilling to go, when he obligingly permitted me to get out – to my great joy. Hence, I am now enabled to tell you that I hope to see you on Sunday morning, as usual, which I could not have done if they had taken me to Gloucester.

'I am, dear Madam,

'Yours sincerely,

'WILLIAM BLAKE'

Blake was, at this period, in the habit, when well, of spending frequent happy Sundays at his friend's Hampstead Cottage,

311

where he was received by host and hostess with the most cordial affection. Mr Linnell's manner was as that of a son; Mrs Linnell was hospitable and kind, as ladies well know how to be to a valued friend. The children, whenever he was expected, were on the *qui vive* to catch the first glimpse of him from afar. One of them, who has now children of her own, but still cherishes the old reverence for 'Mr Blake,' remembers thus watching for him when a little girl of five or six; and how, as he walked over the brow of the hill and came within sight of the young ones, he would make a particular signal; how Dr Thornton, another friend and frequent visitor, would make a different one, – the Doctor taking off his hat and raising it on his stick. She remembers how Blake would take her on his knee, and recite children's stories to them all: recollects his kind manner; his putting her in the way of drawing, training her from his own doings. One day he brought up to Hampstead an early sketch-book, full of most singular things, as it seemed to the children. But, in the midst of them, they came upon a finished, pre-Raphaelite-like drawing of a grasshopper, with which they were delighted.

Mr Linnell had first taken lodgings at Hampstead in June, 1822; and in March, 1824, moved his family to a farm-house there, part of which was let off as a separate habitation, as it is to this day. For Collins's Farm yet stands, altered by the erection of new out-buildings, and the loss of some of its trees, but not so much altered as most things in Hampstead. It is on the north, or countryward side, beyond the Heath, between North End and the 'Spaniards.' North End, as every cockney knows, lies in a hollow over the Heath, – a cluster of villa residences, amid gardens and pleasure-grounds, their roofs embosomed in trees. As you walk from it towards the 'Spaniards,' a winding lane to the left brings you back into the same high road. A little off this, there is another winding way, in the middle of which stands Collins's Farm, at the bottom of another hollow. The house, an old one, looks out in front upon the heathery hill-side; at back, upon meadows and hedgerows, in summer one monotonous tint of heavy green. From the hill-side, the well-pitched red roof of the farm-house picturesquely peeps out among the trees below. To London children the place must have been a little Paradise. Blake, too, notwithstanding a theoretic dislike to Hampstead, practically enjoyed his visits. Mr Linnell's part of the house, – a later erection than the rest, and of lower height, with a separate entrance through the garden which stretches beside, – was small and humble, containing only five rooms. In front it commanded a pleasant southern aspect. Blake, it is still remembered, would often stand at the door, gazing in tranquil reverie across the garden toward the gorse-clad hill. He liked sitting in the arbour, at the bottom of the long garden, or walking up and down the same at dusk, while the cows, munching their evening meal, were audible from the farmyard on the other side the hedge. He was very fond of hearing Mrs Linnell sing Scottish songs, and would sit by the pianoforte, tears falling from his eyes, while he listened to the Border Melody, to which the song is set, commencing

> 'O Nancy's hair is yellow as gowd,
> And her een as the lift are blue.'

To simple national melodies Blake was very impressionable, though not so to music of more complicated structure. He himself still sang, in a voice tremulous with age, sometimes old ballads, sometimes his own songs, to melodies of his own.

The modest interior of the rustic cottage was rendered delightful, as artists can generally render their houses, by tasteful fitting up and by fine prints and pictures hanging on the walls.

Many an interesting friendly gathering took place there, comprising often a complete circle of what are vulgarly called 'characters.' Sometimes, for instance, it would be, besides Blake and Mr Linnell, Dr Thornton, John Varley, and his brother Cornelius, the latter living still, well known in the scientific world and a man devoted to the ingenious arts; all, as one of them confessed to me, men 'who did not propose to themselves to be as others,' but to follow out views of their own. Sometimes Mulready would be of the company: Richter also – a name familiar to frequenters of the old Water-colour Society's exhibitions – who was a fervent disciple of Emanuel Kant, and very fond of iterating the metaphysical dogma of the non-existence of matter. Of Richter's, by the way, still survives, in odd corners of the world, a curious thin octavo, published by Ackermann, in 1817. I can here only quote the characteristic title of this (mentally) very physiognomic *brochure*, which runs thus: '*Daylight. A recent Discovery in the Art of Painting. With Hints on the Philosophy of the Fine Arts, and on that of the Human Mind, as first dissected by Emanuel Kant.*' A meeting at twilight, in the British Institution, of the Old Masters' Ghosts is the artifice for enunciating, in dialogue, the author's views as to representing on canvas the true 'perpendicular light from the sky.' This dialogue occupies thirteen octavo pages; besides which there are fifty-two pages of notes, discourse at large on the same subject, and 'on the human mind, as first dissected by Kant.' Such hobbies as these offer a piquant contrast to those smooth, Book of Beauty faces exhibition-goers may remember as the staple of the old man's doings in later years.

More often the circle at Hampstead would be Blake, Linnell, and John Varley. A curiously contrasted trio – as an eye-witness reports – to look upon in animated converse: Blake, with his quiet manner, his fine head – broad above, small below; Varley's the reverse: Varley, stout and heavy, yet active, and in exuberant spirits – ingenious, diffuse, poetical, eager, talking as fast as possible: Linnell, original, brilliant, with strongly marked character, and filial manner towards Blake, assuming nothing of the patron, forbearing to contradict his stories of his visions, &c. but trying to make reason out of them. Varley found them explicable astrologically – 'Sagittarius crossing Taurus' – and the like; while Blake, on his part, believed in his friend's astrology, to a certain extent. *He* thought you could oppose and conquer the stars. A stranger, hearing the three talk of spirits and astrology in this matter-of-fact way, would have been mystified. Varley was a terrible assertor, bearing down all before him by mere force of loquacity; though not learned or deeply grounded or even very original in his astrology, which he had caught up at second hand. But there was stuff in him. His conversation was powerful, and by it he exerted a strong influence on ingenuous minds – a power he lost in his books. Writing was an art he had not mastered. Strange books they are: his *Treatise on Zodiacal Physiognomy* (8vo. 1828), *Observations on Colouring and Sketching from Nature* (8vo. 1830), and *Practical Treatise on Perspective* (folio). All are dry and barren, wholly lacking the piquancy which belonged to his character and conversation. Varley was twenty years younger than Blake; like him was born in humble circumstances, and in humble circumstances died (in 1842). For though, at one time, his professions, as artist, teacher, and astrologer, procured him a handsome income, his former helpmate had dissipated as fast as he could earn. Thrice in his life, too, he was 'burnt out.' The portfolio of drawings he used latterly to carry about yielded anything but affluence. Delicate transcripts of closing day, – bars of purple cloud crossing the light being his favourite effect, – these drawings often had a peculiar fascination, though they became very mannered at last; conventional reminiscences of Varley himself rather than of nature.

In those days stage coaches started for Hampstead in the morning, and returned to London in the evening. Blake, however, used to walk up from town by a road which was not, as now, one continuous line of houses. Generally, too, he walked back at night; his host sending a servant with a lantern to guide him through the darkness to 'the village.' On his way from Fountain Court to North End, he would often call on a young artist, also a frequent visitor of Mr Linnell's, – one day to be more nearly related, – and the two would walk up together. This was Mr Samuel Palmer, now an accomplished Painter of poetic landscape, well known to visitors of the (old) Water-colour Society's Exhibitions; then a stripling and an enthusiastic disciple of Blake's. To him we are already indebted for many a reminiscence; that picture of Blake standing before a canvas of murderer Wainwright's, for one. The acquaintance commenced, when Blake was about midway in the task of engraving his *Job*. 'At my never-to-be-forgotten first interview,' says Mr Palmer, 'the copper of the first plate – "Thus did Job continually" – was lying on the table where he had been working at it. How lovely it looked by the lamplight, strained through the tissue paper!'

Among the young painters attracted at this period towards Blake was Frederick Tatham, to whose father, the architect, Mr Linnell had introduced his friend. Mr Richmond, the now distingushed portrait-painter, was another. As a lad of sixteen, he met Blake one day at the elder Tatham's, and was allowed to walk home with him. To the boy, it was 'as if he were walking with the prophet Isaiah;' for he had heard much of Blake, greatly admired all he had heard, and all he had seen of his designs.

The prophet talked fully and kindly, freely opening his mind, as was his wont with the young – with men of eighteen or twenty say – even more freely and favourably, perhaps, than with their elders. There was more community of sentiment, – a bond of sympathy. He was not provoked by them to utter extravagances and extreme opinions. On this occasion he talked of his own youth, and of his visions. Just as Mr Palmer speaks of Blake's tolerant kindness towards young men, Mr Richmond relates that, in their intercourse, he would himself, as young men are prone to do, boldly argue and disagree, as though they were equals in years and wisdom, and Blake would take it all good-humouredly. 'Never,' adds Mr Richmond, 'have I known an artist so spiritual, so devoted, so single-minded, or cherishing imagination as he did.' Once, the young artist, finding his invention flag during a whole fortnight, went to Blake, as was his wont, for some advice or comfort. He found him sitting at tea with his wife. He related his distress; how he felt deserted by the power of invention. To his astonishment, Blake turned to his wife suddenly and said: 'It is just so with us, is it not, for weeks together, when the visions forsake us? What do we do then, Kate?' 'We kneel down and pray, Mr Blake.'

Another young artist to seek out Blake and sit at his feet was Mr Finch, for many years a member of the (old) Society of Water-colour Painters.* As a boy, he had heard again and again

---

* NOTE. – Since the above was written, this good man has been called away. His early connexion with Blake, through which the present biography is indebted to him for many an interesting recollection, seems to invite us to pause a moment here over a brief record of the life and character of one whom, apart even from his artistic claims, it is a gain to the world to hold in affection-ate remembrance. To Mr Samuel Palmer we owe the following sketch of his friend, which the genial reader will thank me for the opportunity of perusing. – ED.

FRANCIS OLIVER FINCH
IN MEMORIAM

On the twenty-seventh of August, 1862, the old Society of Painters in Water Colours lost, in Mr Finch, one of their earliest members, who had long enjoyed, in the highest degree, their confidence and esteem, and the warm affection of such as had the pleasure of knowing him intimately.

He was the last representative of the old school of landscape-painting in water-colours, – a school which had given pleasure to the public for half a century, and contributed to obtain for Englishmen in that department of art an European reputation.

When he left school, he was articled as a pupil to Mr John Varley, from whose studio came also two of our most eminent living artists, one of whom has engraved, *con amore*, Varley's *Burial of Saul* and from such a work we may estimate the value of his influence and instruction. It led to the study of refined models, and pointed to sentiment, as the aim of art. It will probably be acknowledged, that the aim was essentially right, and that, if the old school did not arrest and detain the eye by intricate imitation, yet that it was massive and manly, and that its tendency was to elevate and refine. It is difficult to call to mind a single work by Mr Finch, that did not suggest happy and beautiful lands, where the poet would love to muse: the moonlit glade, the pastoral slope, the rocky stream, the stately terrace, and mouldering villas or casements opening on the foam –

'Of perilous seas in fairy lands forlorn.'

How the society estimated his works, was shown by their occupying some of the most conspicuous places on the walls.

He had imagination, that inner sense which receives impressions of beauty as simply and surely as we smell the sweetness of the rose and woodbine. When a boy, he chanced to light on the poetry of Keats, and a plaster figure-maker, seeing him hang with longing eye over a cast of the poet's head which lay in his shop, made him a present of it, and he bore it home in triumph. At this time Keats was known to the public only by the ridicule of a critique.

Those who were intimate with Mr Finch will find it difficult to name a man more evenly and usefully accomplished. Besides modern languages and scientific acquisition, he had large general knowledge. His conversation was never obtrusive, and it never flagged; it was solemn, playful, or instructive, always at the right time and in the right place. An eminent friend, a sagacious observer of men, said that he never thought a friendly dinner party complete, unless Finch were at the table: 'It was like forgetting the bread.'

He had read much, and was familiar with the great poets and satirists; knew the philosophy of the mind, and had observed men and manners. Of those departments of knowledge which lay apart, his good sense enabled him to take at least the relative dimensions. Knowledge apprehends things in themselves; wisdom sees them in their relations. He taught his young friends that goodness was better even than wisdom, and the philosophy which is conversant with the unseen than any ingenuities of technical science. He said he thought we ought not to claim a monopoly of wisdom, because we had discovered that steam would turn a wheel.

It is difficult to convey a notion of his musical genius, because the skill of amateurs, after all the time which is lavished to acquire it, so seldom amounts to more than the doing indifferently what professors do well; but it was not so with him: it seemed to be his natural language – an expression of that melody within, which is more charming than any modulation of strings or voices. The writer has felt more pleasure in sitting by his piano-forte, listening to fragments of Tallis, Croft, or Purcell, with the interlude, perhaps, of an Irish melody, than from many displays of concerted music. To music his friend resorted at the right time; after his temperate dinner, as Milton directs in his 'Tractate.'

Nor was his pen unused, and he could use it well. 'His endeavour,' says one who knew him best, 'to benefit his young friends, will be long and affectionately remembered, nor is it probable that those of maturer age will easily forget his gentle influence and wise counsel.'

Of his social and moral excellence it is difficult to speak in so short a notice, for the heart overflows with memories of his active kindness, and the skill is lacking to condense a life into a paragraph.

In all the domestic relations, he was exemplary; throughout his single and married life his good mother never left his house but for her grave, to which the unremitting kindness of her new relative had smoothed the passage. He did not work alone: were another resting by his side, it might be told that, with one will and purpose, there were two hearts equally busy in 'devising liberal things.' His hospitality was not adjusted to his interest, nor his table spread for those who could repay beef with venison; but for old friends who were in the shade; for merit and virtue in distress or exile; for pale faces which brought the recommendation of sorrow. Let us bear with his simplicity! Perhaps, when *he* 'made a feast,' he consulted a very old fashioned BOOK as to the selection of his guests.

The writer willingly incurs the ridicule of those who believe goodness to be only a refined selfishness, when he looks back, as far as boyhood, to recal some single piece of slight or rudeness, some hard unkindness or cold neglect, some evil influence or moral flaw in his old friend's character, and cannot find it. Were there many such, sarcasm might break her shafts.

Our great satirist said that, if his wide experience had shown him twelve men like Arbuthnot, he never would have written the 'Travels.'

A symmetrical soul is a thing very beautiful and very rare. Who does not find about him and within him grotesque mixtures, or unbalanced faculties, or inconsistent desires; the understanding and the will at feud, the very will in vacillation; opinions shifting with the mode, and smaller impertinencies which he forgives, if they are not his own, for the amusement they afford him?

Let those who knew Francis Finch be thankful: they have seen a disciplined and a just man – 'a city at unity with itself.'

S. P.

319

of Blake from John Varley, whose pupil he was for five years, and his imagination had been much excited by what he had heard. For once, expectation was fulfilled. In Mr Finch's own felicitous words, Blake 'struck him as *a new kind of man*, wholly original, and in all things. Whereas most men are at the pains of softening down their extreme opinions, not to shock those of others, it was the contrary with him.' Yes! he *was* a new kind of man; and hence his was a new kind of art, and a new kind of poetry.

Edward Calvert was another attached friend of this period. He introduced himself to Blake, was received most kindly, as if he had been an old friend; and thereafter enjoyed the privilege of calling on and walking with him. It is a touching sight to summon before one's mental eyes this of the grey-haired visionary, opening his soul to these fresh-hearted youths. They all came to know one another, and would often meet and talk over their views on art; other views than were commonly current in that era of Lawrence, Shee, and the rest. Blake and his house used to be familiarly spoken of among them as 'The House of the Interpreter.' I can still trace something of the mystic Poet's influence, surviving the lapse of more than thirty years, in all who ever knew and loved Blake; as of men who once in their lives had, as it were, entertained an angel *not* unawares.

Let us pause and listen to the reminiscences of one of these friends of Blake's later years. They are embodied in a *Letter on Blake*, kindly addressed by Mr Samuel Palmer to the present writer when first commencing the collection of materials for this biography, some years before they began to take shape:

'Kensington, Aug. 23d, 1855.

'My Dear Sir,

'I regret that the lapse of time has made it difficult to recal many interesting particulars respecting Mr Blake, of whom I can give you no connected account; nothing more, in fact, than the fragments of memory; but the general impression of what is great remains with us, although its details may be confused; and Blake, once known, could never be forgotten.

'His knowledge was various and extensive, and his conversation so nervous and brilliant, that, if recorded at the time, it would now have thrown much light upon his character, and in no way lessened him in the estimation of those who know him only by his works.

'In him you saw at once the Maker, the Inventor; one of the few in any age: a fitting companion for Dante. He was energy itself, and shed around him a kindling influence; an atmosphere of life, full of the ideal. To walk with him in the country was to perceive the soul of beauty through the forms of matter; and the high gloomy buildings between which, from his study window, a glimpse was caught of the Thames and the Surrey shore, assumed a kind of grandeur from the man dwelling near them. Those may laugh at this who never knew such an one as Blake; but of him it is the simple truth.

'He was a man without a mask; his aim single, his path straightforwards, and his wants few; so he was free, noble, and happy. 'His voice and manner were quiet, yet all awake with intellect. Above the tricks of littleness, or the least taint of affectation, with a natural dignity which few would have dared to affront, he was gentle and affectionate, loving to be with little children, and to talk about them. 'That is heaven,' he said to a friend, leading him to the window, and pointing to a group of them at play.

'Declining, like Socrates, whom in many respects he resembled, the common objects of ambition, and pitying the scuffle to obtain them, he thought that no one could be truly great who had not humbled himself "ever as a little child." This was a subject he loved to dwell upon, and to illustrate.

'His eye was the finest I ever saw: brilliant, but not roving, clear and intent, yet susceptible; it flashed with genius, or melted in tenderness. It could also be terrible. Cunning and falsehood quailed under it, but it was never busy with them. It pierced them, and turned away. Nor was the mouth less expressive; the lips flexible and quivering with feeling. I can yet recal it when, on one occasion, dwelling upon the exquisite beauty of the parable of the Prodigal, he began to repeat a part of it; but at the words, "When he was yet a great way off, his father saw him," could go no further; his voice faltered, and he was in tears.

'I can never forget the evening when Mr Linnell took me to Blake's house, nor the quiet hours passed with him in the examination of antique gems, choice pictures, and Italian prints of the sixteenth century. Those who may have read some strange passages in his *Catalogue*, written in irritation, and probably in haste, will be surprised to hear, that in conversation he was anything but sectarian or exclusive, finding sources of delight throughout the whole range of art; while, as a critic, he was judicious and discriminating.

'No man more admired Albert Dürer; yet, after looking over a number of his designs, he would become a little angry with some of the draperies, as not governed by the forms of the limbs, nor assisting to express their action; contrasting them in this respect with the draped antique, in which it was hard to tell whether he was more delighted with the general design, or with the exquisite finish and the depth of the chiselling; in works of the highest class, no mere adjuncts, but the last development of the design itself.

'He united freedom of judgment with reverence for all that is great. He did not look out for the works of the purest ages, but for the purest works of every age and country – Athens or Rhodes, Tuscany or Britain; but no authority or popular consent could influence him against his deliberate judgment. Thus he thought with Fuseli and Flaxman that the Elgin Theseus, however full of antique savour, could not, as ideal form, rank with the very finest relics of antiquity. Nor, on the other hand, did the universal neglect of Fuseli in any degree lessen his admiration of his best works.

'He fervently loved the early Christian art, and dwelt with peculiar affection on the memory of Fra Angelico, often speaking of him as an inspired inventor and as a saint; but when he approached Michael Angelo, the Last Supper of Da Vinci, the Torso Belvidere, and some of the inventions preserved in the Antique Gems, all his powers were concentrated in admiration.

'When looking at the heads of the apostles in the copy of the *Last Supper* at the Royal Academy, he remarked of all but Judas, "Every one looks as if he had conquered the natural man." He was equally ready to admire a contemporary and a rival. Fuseli's picture of *Satan building the Bridge over Chaos* he ranked with the grandest efforts of imaginative art, and said that we were two centuries behind the civilization which would enable us to estimate his *Ægisthus*.

'He was fond of the works of St Theresa, and often quoted them with other writers on the interior life. Among his eccentricities will, no doubt, be numbered his preference for ecclesiastical governments. He used to ask how it was that we heard so much of priestcraft, and so little of soldiercraft and lawyercraft. The Bible, he said, was the book of liberty and Christianity the sole regenerator of nations. In politics a Platonist, he put no trust in demagogues. His ideal home was with Fra Angelico: a little later he might have been a reformer, but after the fashion of Savanarola.

'He loved to speak of the years spent by Michael Angelo, without earthly reward, and solely for the love of God, in the building of St Peter's, and of the wondrous architects of our cathedrals. In Westminster Abbey were his earliest and most sacred recollections. I asked him how he would like to paint on glass, for the great west window, his "Sons of God shouting for

Joy," from his designs in the *Job*. He said, after a pause, "I could do it!" kindling at the thought.

'Centuries could not separate him in spirit from the artists who went about our land, pitching their tents by the morass or the forest side, to build those sanctuaries that now lie ruined amidst the fertility which they called into being.

'His mind was large enough to contain, along with these things, stores of classic imagery. He delighted in Ovid, and, as a labour of love, had executed a finished picture from the *Metamorphoses*, after Giulio Romano. This design hung in his room, and, close by his engraving table, Albert Dürer's *Melancholy the Mother of Invention*, memorable as probably having been seen by Milton, and used in his *Penseroso*. There are living a few artists, then boys, who may remember the smile of welcome with which he used to rise from that table to receive them.

'His poems were variously estimated. They tested rather severely the imaginative capacity of their readers. Flaxman said they were as grand as his designs, and Wordsworth delighted in his *Songs of Innocence*. To the multitude they were unintelligible. In many parts full of pastoral sweetness, and often flashing with noble thoughts or terrible imagery, we must regret that he should sometimes have suffered fancy to trespass within sacred precincts.

'Thrown early among the authors who resorted to Johnson, the book-seller, he rebuked the profanity of Paine, and was no disciple of Priestley, but, too undisciplined and cast upon times and circumstances which yielded him neither guidance nor sympathy, he wanted that balance of the faculties which might have assisted him in matters extraneous to his profession. He saw everything through art, and, in matters beyond its range, exalted it from a witness into a judge.

'He had great powers of argument, and on general subjects was a very patient and good-tempered disputant; but materialism was his abhorrence and if some unhappy man called in question the world of spirits, he would answer him "according to his folly," by putting forth his own views in their most extravagant and startling aspect. This might amuse those who were in the secret, but it left his opponent angry and bewildered.

'Such was Blake, as I remember him. He was one of the few to be met with in our passage through life, who are not, in some way or other, "double minded" and inconsistent with themselves; one of the very few who cannot be depressed by neglect, and to whose name rank and station could add no lustre. Moving apart, in a sphere above the attraction of worldly honours, he did not accept greatness, but confer it. He ennobled poverty, and, by his conversation and the influence of his genius, made two small rooms in Fountain Court more attractive than the threshold of princes.

'I remain, my dear Sir,
'Yours very faithfully,
'SAMUEL PALMER

To Alexander Gilchrist, Esq.'

THIRTY-FOUR

Personal Details

The intelligent sympathy and candour animating the life-like portraiture of the *Letter* which concludes the foregoing chapter need no comment on my part. I will here simply add a few additional details, characteristic of Blake personally, and of his manner of life in Fountain Court, gleaned from the recollections of others who knew him there.

Blake's two rooms on the first floor were approached by a wainscoted staircase, with handsome balustrades, such as we find in houses of Queen Anne's date, and lit by a window to the left, looking out on the well-like back yard below. Having ascended, two doors faced you, opening into the back and front rooms. That in front, with the windows looking out on Fountain Court, its panelled walls hung with *frescos, temperas*, and drawings of Blake's, was used as a reception room. From it a door opened into the smaller back room, the window of which (a side one) looked down a deep gap between the houses of Fountain Court and the parallel street; in this way commanding a peep of the Thames with its muddy banks, and of distant Surrey hills beyond. This was, at once, sleeping and living room, kitchen and studio. In one corner was the bed; in another, the fire at which Mrs Blake cooked. On one side stood the table serving for meals, and by the window, the table at which Blake always

326

sat (facing the light), designing or engraving. There was an air of poverty as of an artisan's room; but everything was clean and neat; nothing sordid. Blake himself, with his serene, cheerful, dignified presence and manner, made all seem natural and of course. Conversing with him, you saw or felt nothing of his poverty, though he took no pains to conceal it; if he had, you would have been effectually reminded of it. What in description sounds mean and miserable wore, to Blake's intimates, a delightful aspect. Such an expression as his 'wretched rooms,' as by some they have been described, is to them quite unintelligible. 'I should only like to go in this afternoon!' declared one friend, while talking of them to me. 'And, ah! that divine window!' exclaimed another. Charming and poetic the view from it seemed to those accustomed to associate Blake's person and conversation with it. While a third with brisk emphasis affirms, 'There was no "misery" in Blake's rooms, for men who love art, a good table' (not, of course, in the epicure's sense), 'and warmth.' 'I never look upon him as an unfortunate man of genius. He knew every great man of his day, and had enough.'

Happening to read to the author of the letter lately quoted a passage from a MS. in which the word 'squalor' was used in connexion with Blake's home, the following quaint remonstrance was elicited:

'*May 3d*, 1860.

'My Dear Sir,

Late as we parted last night, I awaked at dawn with the question in my ear, Squalor? – squalor?

'Crush it; it is a roc's egg to your fabric.

'I have met with this perverse mistake elsewhere. It gives a notion altogether false of the man, his house, and his habits.

'No, certainly; – whatever was in Blake's house, there was no squalor. Himself, his wife, and his rooms, were clean and orderly; everything was in its place. His delightful working corner had its implements ready – tempting to the hand. The millionaire's upholsterer can furnish no enrichments like those of Blake's enchanted rooms.

'Believe me, dear Sir,

'Yours most truly,

'S. PALMER.'

Simplicity and natural dignity such as Blake's can confer refinement on any environment. External discordances vanished before the spiritual concords of the man. 'There was a strange expansion,' says one of his friends, 'and sensation of FREEDOM in those two rooms *very* seldom felt elsewhere.' Another who, as a little girl, visited the rooms with her father, can only remember the beautiful things she saw on the walls, and Blake's kind manner to herself. Had there been anything sordid or poverty-stricken to remember, she would have done so, for children are keenly sensitive to such impressions. Blake, I may here mention, was especially fond of children, and very kind to them; his habitual quiet gentleness assuming a new beauty towards them. He was kind to the young generally; and, as a lady (Miss Maria Denman), to whom in youth this fostering behaviour had been, in slight ways, shown, observed to me with some emotion, 'One remembers even in age the kindness of such a man.'

'Blake knew nothing,' writes the valued correspondent whom I have so frequent occasion to quote, 'of dignified reserve, polite *hauteur*, "bowings out, or condescension to inferiors," nor had he dressed himself for masquerade in "unassuming manners." Somewhere in his writings occur these lines, droll, but full of meaning:

'"The fox, the owl, the spider, and the bat,
By *sweet reserve* and modesty grow fat."'

328

The courtly and politic were denied Blake. But he was not among those who fancy genius raises them above the courtesies and humanities of life. Competent judges describe him as essentially 'the politest of men.' To this gentlemanliness, and to what I may call the originality of his manners or mental dress, observers of various habits agree in speaking. 'Very courteous,' 'very polite;' and 'withal there was great meekness and retirement of manner, such as belong to the true gentleman and commanded respect,' says one. In society he was more urbane than many of greater pretension, and in the face often of uncourteous opposition. At Hampstead, one day, Collins the painter, – after having said very rude things such as people of the world, under the consciousness of superior sense and sanity, will indulge in towards those they call 'enthusiasts,' – was obliged to confess Blake had made a very gentlemanly and temperate return. Nobody, to look at or listen to him in society, would have taken him for the knock-me-down assertor he was in his writings. Crudities *there* may, in fact, be set down to his never having won real ease or freedom in that mode of expression. In more intimate relations again, his own goodness and sweetness of nature spoke still more eloquently. And if he had received a kindness, the tender heart was so sensitive, he could hardly do enough to show his consciousness of it.

Nor was Blake one of that numerous class who reserve their civility for their social superiors or mental equals, the distinguished and celebrated, – those recommended, in short, by the suffrages of others. 'He was *equally* polite (and that is rare indeed) to men of every age and rank; honouring all men.' In which he resembled Flaxman, who addressed his carvers and workmen as 'friends,' and *made* them such by his kindness. Of this spontaneous courtesy to all, the following is an instance: Once, while his young friend Calvert was with him in Fountain Court, a man brought up a sack of coals, knocked at the door, and asked, 'Are these coals for here?' 'No, Sir,' answered Blake, in quiet, courteous tones, as to an equal; 'but I'll ask whose they are.' Blake's fellow-lodgers were humble but respectable. The court did not, in those days, present, as now, its idle groups of women, hanging about outside the doors, with free and easy, not to say unfinished, toilets. There was no excessive noise of children in the court. Children at play there doubtless often were, as one of Mr Palmer's anecdotes would indicate.

Vehement and outrageous as Blake could at times be (in words), his ordinary habit of mind was – at all events in these latter years – one of equable gentleness. He was no longer angry with the world and its often unworthy favourites, or rebellious against its awards; jostled though he were in his quiet course by thousands of coarse, eager men, 'famous' and prosperous in their day. 'I live in a hole here,' he would say, 'but God has a beautiful mansion for me elsewhere.' 'Poor, dear man,' exclaimed one of his friends to me, 'to think how ill he was used, and yet he took it all so quietly.' Surely 'the world,' if it had a conscience to be pricked, might blush at a few of its awards. 'The public,' say some, 'may be compared to a reigning beauty, whose favour is hard to win, and who often gives it to a fool in the end.'

Blake, however, was rich in poverty. 'They pity me,' he would say of Lawrence and other prosperous artists, who condescended to visit him; 'but 'tis they are the just objects of pity: I possess my visions and peace. They have bartered their birthright for a mess of pottage.' For he felt that he could have had fame and fortune, if he had chosen; if he had not voluntarily, and with his eyes open, cleaved to the imaginative life. 'If asked,' writes Mr Palmer, 'whether I ever knew among the intellectual a happy man, Blake would be the only one who would immediately occur to me.' And this feeling of happiness communicated itself as a serene, beneficent influence to others. His disciples would often wonder thereat, and wish they had within themselves the faculty, unhelped by him, to feel as he did.

There is a short poem in the MS. note-book which speaks eloquently on this head of unworldliness with its resultant calm elevated joy. Let us listen to it:

> I rose up at the dawn of day:
> 'Get thee away! get thee away!
> Prayest thou for riches? away! away!
> This is the throne of Mammon grey!'

> Said I: 'This, sure, is very odd;
> I took it to be the throne of God.
> Everything besides I have:
> It's only riches that I *can* crave.

> 'I have mental joys and mental health,
> Mental friends and mental wealth;
> I've a wife that I love, and that loves me,
> I've all but riches bodily.

> 'Then if for riches I must not pray,
> God knows, it's little prayers I need say.
> I am in God's presence night and day;
> He never turns His face away.

> 'The accuser of sins by my side doth stand,
> And he holds my money bag in his hand;
> For my worldly things God makes him pay;
> And he'd pay for more, if to him I would pray.

> 'He says, if I worship not him for a god,
> I shall eat coarser food, and go worse shod;
> But as I don't value such things as these,
> You must do, Mr Devil, just as God please.'

A lady tells a pretty and very characteristic story of her first and only interview with the spiritual man, which illustrates, in another way, how he came by this happiness. The lady was thought extremely beautiful when a child, and was taken to an evening party and there presented to Blake. He looked at her very kindly for a long while, without speaking; and then, stroking her head and long ringlets, said: 'May God make this world to you, my child, as beautiful as it has been to me!' She thought it strange, at the time – vain little darling of Fortune! – that such a poor old man, dressed in shabby clothes, could imagine that the world had ever been so beautiful to him as it must be to her, nursed in all the elegancies and luxuries of wealth. But, in after years, she understood plainly enough what he meant, and treasured the few words he had spoken to her. Well might he sweetly and touchingly say of himself (I draw from the note-book again):

> The Angel who presided at my birth
> Said: 'Little creature formed of joy and mirth,
> Go, love without the help of anything on earth.'

Blake's mind was so sensitively strung, as in intercourse with others to give immediate response to the right appeals. All speak of his conversation as most interesting, nay enchanting, to hear. Copious and varied, the fruit of great, but not morbid, intellectual activity; it was, in its ordinary course, full of mind, sagacity, and varied information. Above all, it was something quite different from that of other men: conversation which carried you 'from earth to heaven and back again, before you knew where you were.' Even a young girl would feel the fascination, though sometimes finding his words wild and hard to follow. To conventional minds, it often seemed a mixture of divinity, blasphemy, and licence; but a mixture not even by them to be quickly forgotten. In a walk with a sympathetic listener, it seldom flagged. He would have something pertinent to say about most objects they chanced to pass, were it but a bit of old wall. And such as had the privilege of accompanying him in a country walk felt their perception of natural beauty greatly enhanced. Nature herself seemed strangely more spiritual. Blake's mind warmed his listener's, kindled his imagination; almost creating in him a new sense. Nor was his enjoyment of all that is great in Art, of whatever school or time, less genuine and vivid: notwithstanding an appearance to the contrary in some passages of his writings, where, in doing battle energetically for certain great principles, random blows not a few, on either side the mark, come down on unoffending heads; or where, in the consciousness that a foolish world had insisted on raising the less great above the greatest, he delighted to make matters even by thrusting them as much too far below. 'I think I hear him say,' writes one of those friends whose congeniality ensured serene, wise moods on Blake's part, 'As fine as possible, Sir. It is not given to man to do better;' (this when talking of the great examples of Art, whether antique or modern). 'He delighted to think of Raphael, Giulio Romano, Polidoro, and others, working together in the chambers of the Vatican, engaged, without jealousy, as he imagined, in the carrying out of one great common object; and he used to compare it (without any intentional irreverence) to the co-labours of the holy Apostles. He dwelt on this subject very fondly . . . Among spurious old pictures, he had met with many "Claudes," but spoke of a few which he had seen really untouched and unscrubbed, with the greatest delight; and mentioned, as a peculiar charm, that in these, when minutely examined, there were, upon the focal lights of the foliage, small specks

333

of pure white which made them appear to be glittering with dew which the morning sun had not yet dried up . . . His description of these genuine Claudes, I shall never forget. He warmed with his subject, and it continued through an evening walk. The sun was set; but Blake's Claudes made sunshine in that shady place.' . . . 'Of Albert Dürer, he remarked that his most finished woodcuts, when closely examined, seemed to consist principally of outline; – that they were "everything and yet nothing" . . . None but the finest of the antiques, he held, equalled Michael Angelo.'

As we have seen, Blake's was no 'poetic poverty,' of a kind to excite the pensive interest of sentimental people without shocking their nerves; but real, prosaic poverty. Such 'appearances' as I have described tasked his whole income to maintain. And his was an honourable code: he was never, amid all his poverty, in debt. 'Money,' says Mr Palmer, 'he used with careful frugality, but never loved it; and believed that he should be always supplied with it as it was wanted: in which he was not disappointed. And he worked on with serenity when there was only a shilling in the house. Once (he told me) he spent part of one of these last shillings on a camel's hair brush . . . He would have laughed very much at the word *status*, which has been naturalized into our language of late years.' Last shillings were, at all periods of Blake's life, a frequent incident of his household economy. For, while engrossed in designing, he had often an aversion to resuming his graver, or to being troubled about money matters. It put him out very much when Mrs Blake referred to the financial topic, or found herself constrained to announce, 'The money is going, Mr Blake.' 'Oh, d— the money!' he would shout; 'it's always the money!' Her method of hinting at the odious subject became, in consequence, a very quiet and expressive one. She would set before him at dinner just what there was in the house, without any comment until, finally, the empty platter had to make its appearance: which hard fact effectually reminded him it was time to go to his engraving for awhile. At that, when fully embarked again, he was not unhappy; work being his natural element.

Allan Cunningham has talked of Blake's living on a crust. But, in these latter years he, for the most part, lived on good, though simple fare. His wife was an excellent cook – a talent which helped to fill out Blake's waistcoat a little, as he grew old. She could even prepare a made dish, when need be. As there was no servant, he fetched the porter for dinner himself, from the house at the corner of the Strand. Once, pot of porter in hand, he espied coming along a dignitary of Art – that highly respectable man, William Collins, R.A., whom he had met in society a few evenings before. The Academician was about to shake hands, but seeing the porter, drew up, and did not know him. Blake would tell the story very quietly, and without sarcasm. Another time, Fuseli came in, and found Blake with a little cold mutton before him for dinner; who, far from being disconcerted, asked his friend to join him. 'Ah! by G—!' exclaimed Fuseli, 'this is the reason you can do as you like. *Now I can't do this.*' His habits were very temperate. It was only in later years he took porter regularly. He then fancied it soothed him, and would sit and muse over his pint after a one o'clock dinner. When he drank wine, which, at home, of course, was seldom, he professed a liking to drink off good draughts from a tumbler, and thought the wine glass system absurd: a very heretical opinion in the eyes of your true wine drinkers. Frugal and abstemious on principle, and for pecuniary reasons, he was sometimes rather imprudent, and would take anything that came in his way. A nobleman once sent him some oil of walnuts he had had expressed purposely for an artistic experiment. Blake tasted it, and went on tasting, till he had drunk the whole. When his lordship called to ask how the experiment had prospered, the artist had to confess what had become of the ingredients. It was ever after a standing joke against him.

In his dress, there was a similar triumph of the man over his poverty, to that which struck one in his rooms. In-doors, he was careful, for economy's sake, but not slovenly: his clothes were threadbare, and his grey trousers had worn black and shiny in front, like a mechanic's. Out of doors, he was more particular, so that his dress did not, in the streets of London, challenge attention either way. He wore black knee breeches and buckles, black worsted stockings, shoes which tied, and a broad-brimmed hat. It was something like an old-fashioned tradesman's dress. But the general impression he made on you was that of a gentleman, in a way of his own.

In person, there was much in Blake which answered to the remarkable man he was. Though low in stature, not quite five feet and a half, and broad shouldered, he was well made, and did not strike people as short. For he had an upright carriage and a good presence; he bore himself with dignity, as not unconscious of his natural claims. The head and face were strongly stamped with the power and character of the man. There was great volume of brain in that square, massive head, that piled up brow very full and rounded at the temples, where, according to phrenologists, ideality or imagination resides. His eyes were fine – 'wonderful eyes,' some one calls them; prominently set, but bright, spiritual, visionary; – not restless or wild, but with 'a look of clear heavenly exaltation.' The eyes of some of the old men in his *Job*, recall his own to surviving friends. His nose was insignificant as to size, but had that peculiarity which gives to a face an expression of fiery energy, as of a high-mettled steed, – a little *clenched* nostril; a nostril that opened as far as it could, 'but was tied down at one end.' His mouth was wide, the lips not full, but tremulous, and expressive of the great sensibility which characterized him. He was short-sighted, as the prominence of his eyes indicated; a prominence in keeping with his faculty for languages, according to the phrenologists again. He wore glasses only occasionally.

Mrs Blake, the artist's companion at almost every hour of the twenty-four, now, as of old, cheerfully accepted the lot of a poor man's wife as few gifted men's wives are prepared to do. 'Rigid, punctual, firm, precise,' and, as I have said, a good housewife, she extracted the utmost possible amount of domestic comfort out of their slender means, which she, like her husband, was scrupulously careful never to exceed. She shared his destiny and softened it, ministering to his daily wants. Not that he put off everything menial upon her, willing though she were. 'For many years,' writes J. T. Smith, who knew both well, 'he made a constant practice of lighting the fire, and putting on the kettle for breakfast before his Kate awoke.' Smith speaks of the uninterrupted harmony in which Blake and 'his beloved Kate' lived. Such harmony there really was; but, as we saw, it had not always been unruffled. There *had* been stormy times in years long past, when both were young; discord by no means trifling while it lasted. But with the cause (jealousy on her side, not wholly unprovoked,) the strife had ceased also. In age and affliction each grasped the reward of so wise a reconciliation, in an even, calm state of companionship and mutual helpfulness. And 'his Kate' was capable of sharing to some extent, at all events, the inner life too, and of yielding true sympathy. 'Having never been

337

a mother,' says the same cordially appreciative friend, who saw much of her in later years, and whose words I have already often borrowed, 'to this devoted wife Blake was at once lover, husband, child. She would get up in the night, when he was under his very fierce inspirations, which were as if they would tear him asunder, while he was yielding himself to the Muse, or whatever else it could be called, sketching and writing. And so terrible a task did this seem to be, that she had to sit motionless and silent; only to stay him mentally, without moving hand or foot: this for hours, and night after night. Judge of the obedient, unassuming devotion of her dear soul to him!'

Mrs Blake's spirit, in truth, was influenced magnetically, if one may so speak, by her husband's. She appears to have had the same *literal* belief in his visions as John Varley; and when he, in his wild way, would tell his friends that King Alfred, or any great historical personage, had sat to him, Mrs Blake would look at her husband with an awe-struck countenance, and then at his listener to confirm the fact. Not only was she wont to echo what he said, to talk as he talked, on religion and other matters – this may be accounted for by the fact that he had educated her; but she, too, learned to have visions; – to see processions of figures wending along the river, in broad daylight; and would give a start when they disappeared in the water. As Blake truly maintained, the faculty for seeing such airy phantoms can be cultivated. I have mentioned that she coloured Blake's designs under his direction, and successfully. One drawing, undoubtedly *designed* as well as executed by herself, is now in Mr Linnell's possession. It is so like a work of Blake's, that one can hardly believe it to have been the production of another hand. Captain Butts has also one, of small size, in pen and ink: a seated figure of a woman, which I would not hesitate, at first sight, to call a Blake; and even on inspection it proves a very fair drawing. I have no doubt of this too being *bonâ fide* Mrs Blake's. Some of the characteristics of an originally uneducated mind had clung to her, despite the late culture received from her husband: an exaggerated suspiciousness, for instance, and even jealousy of his friends. But vulgarity there was none. In person, the once beautiful brunette had, with years, grown – as we have elsewhere observed – common and coarse-looking, except 'in so far,' says one who knew her, 'as love made her otherwise, and spoke through her gleaming black eyes.' This appearance was enhanced by the common dirty dress, poverty, and perhaps age, had rendered habitual. In such cases, the traces of past beauty do but heighten the melancholy of its utter ruin. Amid so much that was beautiful in her affectionate, wifely spirit, these externals were little noticed. To friends who remember Blake in Fountain Court, those calm, patriarchal figures of Job and his Wife in the artist's own designs, still recall the two, as they used to sit together in that humble room.

ALL I have met, who at any period of the poet-artist's life knew much of Blake, speak with affection of him. A sweet, gentle, lovable creature, say all; courageous too, yet not bitter. Of course, casual acquaintances were more startled than pleased by his extravagancies and vehemences of speech. To men of the world, his was a mind which, whether judged by his writings or his talk, inevitably seemed scarcely a sane, still less a trustworthy one. The impression he made on others varied in proportion to the community of sentiment which existed; and, as I said, he showed his best self only to such as had this bond of sympathy; namely, a certain innocence and even humility of heart, a certain virgin freshness of mind. In society he was often brought into contact with men, superior and intellectual, but occupying widely different spheres of thought to his own; who, if they admired, marvelled still more and could not accept him and his strange, novel individuality in the frank, confiding spirit of those to whom we have been lately hearkening. We shall have evidence of this in a later chapter.

THIRTY-FIVE

Mad or Not Mad

In his familiar conversations with Mr Palmer and other disciples, Blake would speak in the most matter-of-fact way of recent spiritual visitors. Much of their talk was of the spirits he had been discoursing with, and, to a third person, would have sounded oddly enough. 'Milton the other day was saying to me,' so and so. 'I tried to convince him he was wrong, but I could not succeed.' 'His tastes are Pagan; his house is Palladian, not Gothic.' Ingenuous listeners hardly knew sometimes whether to believe Blake saw these spirits or not; but could not go so far as utterly to deny that he did. It often struck them, however, that the spirits came under false pretences, and were not what they represented themselves; inasmuch as they spoke false doctrine, broached unsound opinions.

In society, again, Blake would give accounts of romantic appearances which had shown themselves to him. At one of Mr Aders' parties – at which Flaxman, Lawrence, and other leading artists were present – Blake was talking to a little group gathered round him, within hearing of a lady whose children had just come home from boarding school for the holidays. 'The other evening,' said Blake, in his usual quiet way, 'taking a walk, I came to a meadow, and at the farther corner of it I saw a fold of lambs. Coming nearer, the ground blushed with flowers; and the wattled cote and its woolly tenants were of an exquisite pastoral beauty. But I looked again, and it proved to be no living flock, but beautiful sculpture.' The lady, thinking this a capital holiday-show for her children, eagerly interposed, 'I beg pardon, Mr Blake, but *may* I ask *where* you saw this?' '*Here*, madam,' answered Blake, touching his forehead. The reply brings us to the point of view from which Blake himself regarded his visions. It was by no means the mad view those ignorant of the man have fancied. He would candidly confess they were not literal matters of fact; but phenomena seen by his imagination: *realities* none the less for that, but transacted within the realm of mind. A distinction which widely separates such visions from the hallucinations of madness, or of the victims of ghostly or table-turning delusions; and indicates that wild habit of talk (and of writing) which startled outsiders, to have been the fruit of an excessive culture of the imagination, combined with daring licence of speech. No man, by the way, would have been more indifferent or averse than he (wide and tolerant as was his faith in supernatural revelations) towards the table-turning, wainscot-knocking, bosh-propounding 'Spiritualism' of the present hour; the gross and puerile materialism which tries to pass itself off for its eternal opposite. He might not have disbelieved in the 'communications' in question; but they would not, in *his* eyes, have seemed worth attending to, or as proceeding from a higher world at all: only, perhaps, as the witless pranks of very ignoble spirits from a lower one.

According to his own explanation, Blake saw spiritual appearances by the exercise of a special faculty – that of imagination – using the word in the then unusual, but true sense, of a faculty which busies itself with the subtler realities, *not* with fictions. He, on this ground, objected even to Shakspeare's expression –

And gives to airy *nothing*
A local habitation and a name.

He said the things imagination saw were as much realities as were gross and tangible facts. He would tell his artist friends, 'You have the same faculty as I (the visionary), only you do not trust or cultivate it. You can see what I do, *if you choose*.' In a similar spirit was his advice to a young painter: 'You have only to work up imagination to the state of vision, and the thing is done.' After all, he did but use the word vision in precisely the same sense in which Wordsworth uses it to designate the poet's special endowment; as when he speaks of Chaucer as one

– whose spirit often dwelt
In the clear land of vision.

The only difference is, that Blake was for applying the word boldly in detail, instead of merely as a general term. And why not? What word could more happily express the truth? In short, his belief in what he himself 'saw in vision,' was not as in a material, but a spiritual fact – to his mind a more real kind of fact. The greater importance of the latter was one of his leading canons. He was, moreover, inclined, metaphysically, to be a follower of Bishop Berkeley, – a disbeliever in matter, as I have already said.

Extravagant and apocryphal stories have passed current about Blake. One – which I believe Leigh Hunt used to tell – bears internal evidence, to those who understand Blake, of having been a fabrication. Once, it is said, the visionary man was walking down Cheapside with a friend. Suddenly he took off his hat and bowed low. 'What did you do that for?' 'Oh! that was the Apostle Paul.' A story quite out of keeping with the artist's ordinary demeanour towards his spiritual visitants, though quite in unison with the accepted notions as to ghosts and other apparitions with whom the ghost-seer is traditionally supposed to have tangible personal relations. Blake's was not that kind of vision. The spirits which appeared to him did not reveal themselves in palpable, hand-shaking guise, nor were they mistaken by him for bodily facts. He did not claim for them an external, or (in German slang) an *objective* existence.

In Blake, imagination was by nature so strong, by himself had been so much fostered and, amid the solitude in which he lived, had been so little interfered with by the ideas of others, that it had grown to a disproportionate height so as to overshadow every other faculty. He relied on it as on a revelation of the Invisible. The appearances thus summoned before his mental eye were implicitly trusted in, not dismissed as idle phantoms as an ordinary – even an imaginative – man dismisses them. Hence his *bonâ fide* 'portraits' of visionary characters, such as those drawn for John Varley. And to this genuine faith is due the singular difference *in kind* between his imaginative work and that of nearly every other painter who has left a record of himself. Such is the explanation which all who knew the man personally give of what seemed mere madness to the world.

And here let us finally dispose of this vexed question of Blake's 'madness;' the stigma which, in its haste to arrive at some decision on an unusual phenomenon, the world has fastened on him, as on many other notable men before. Was he a 'glorious madman,' according to the assumption of those who knew nothing of him personally, little of his works, nothing of the genesis of them – of the deep though wayward spiritual currents of which they were the unvarying exponent?

To Blake's surviving friends – all who knew more of his character than a few casual interviews could supply – the proposition is (I find) simply unintelligible; thinking of him, as they do, under the strong influence of happy, fruitful, personal intercourse remembered in the past; swayed by the general tenor of his life, rather than by isolated extravagancies of speech, or wild passages in his writings. All are unanimous on the point. And I have taken the opinions of many independent witnesses. 'I saw nothing but sanity,' declares one (Mr Calvert); 'saw nothing mad in his conduct, actions, or character.' Mr Linnell and Mr Palmer express themselves in the same sense, and almost in the same words. Another very unbiassed and intelligent acquaintance – Mr Finch – summed up his recollections thus: 'He was not mad, but perverse and wilful; he reasoned correctly from arbitrary, and often false premises.' This, however, is what madmen have been sometimes defined to do; grant them their premises, and their conclusions are right. Nor can I quite concur in it as characteristic of Blake, who was no reasoner, but pre-eminently a man of intuitions; and therefore more often right as to his premises than his deductions. But, at all events, a madman's *actions* are not consonant with sound premises: Blake's always were. He could throw aside his visionary mood and his paradoxes when he liked. Mad people try to conceal *their* crazes, and in the long run cannot succeed.

'There was nothing mad about him,' emphatically exclaimed to me Mr Cornelius Varley; 'people set down for mad anything different from themselves.' That vigorous veteran, the late James Ward, who had often met Blake in society and talked with him, would never hear him called mad. If mad he were, it was a madness which infected everybody who came near him; the wife who all but worshipped him, for one – whose sanity I never heard doubted; sensible, practical Mr Butts, his almost life-long friend and patron, for another – who, I have reason to know, reckoned him eccentric but nothing worse. The high respect which Flaxman and Fuseli always entertained for him, I have already referred to. Even so well-balanced a mind as Cary's (the translator of Dante) abandoned, after he came to know him, the notion he had taken up of his 'madness,' and simply pronounced him an 'enthusiast.' Evidently this was the light in which he was regarded, throughout life, by all who had personal relations with him; Paine at one time, Cromek at another, Hayley at another; the first two, men of sufficiently *un*-visionary, the last of sufficiently commonplace, intellect. So, too, by honest, prosaic John Thomas Smith, who had known Blake as a young man. He commences his notice of Blake with the declaration *à propos* of what he calls this 'stigma of eccentricity.' 'I believe it has been invariably the custom of every age, whenever a man has been found to depart from the usual mode of thinking, to consider him of deranged intellect, and not unfrequently, stark, staring mad.' And he quotes Cowper's words, when writing to Lady Hesketh, speaking of a dancing master's advertisement: 'The author of it had the good hap to be crazed, or he had never produced anything half so clever; for you will ever observe that they who are said to have lost their wits, have more than other people.' 'I could see in Blake's wild enthusiasm and extravagance,' writes another of his personal friends, 'only the struggle of an ardent mind to deliver itself of the bigness and sublimity of its own conceptions.' Even shrewd Allan Cunningham, a man who lived in an atmosphere of common sense, had, it is evident, spontaneously adopted a similar conclusion, and writes of Blake in a manner that tacitly assumes his sanity. 'Blake's misfortune,' says he, 'was that of possessing this precious gift (imagination) in excess. His fancy overmastered him, until he at length confounded "the mind's eye" with the corporeal organ, and dreamed

346

himself out of the sympathies of actual life.' And again: 'Painting, like poetry, has followers, the body of whose genius is light compared to the length of its wings, and who, rising above the ordinary sympathies of our nature, are, like Napoleon, betrayed by a star which no eye can see save their own. To this rare class belonged William Blake.'

That the present writer shares the view of his predecessors and of Blake's personal intimates, is doubtless already apparent. And, perhaps, the deliberate opinion, on such a point, of a biographer who has necessarily devoted a *bonâ fide* slice of his life to deciphering the character of him he writes of, is entitled to *some* weight, – to more, say, than the rough and ready decisions, which are based on an isolated anecdote or two, or on certain incoherent passages in a series of professedly mystical writings. So far as I am concerned, I would infinitely rather be mad with William Blake than sane with nine-tenths of the world. When, indeed, such men are nicknamed 'mad,' one is brought in contact with the difficult problem 'What is madness?' Who is *not* mad – in some other person's sense, himself, perhaps, not the *noblest* of created mortals? Who, in certain abstruse cases, is to be the judge? Does not prophet or hero always seem 'mad' to the respectable mob, and to polished men of the world, the motives of feeling and action being so alien and incomprehensible?

In a letter respecting Blake, addressed by the late James Ward, in June, 1855, to his son, George Raphael, the engraver, the venerable artist gave expression to an interesting view of his own – itself, some may think, tinged by eccentricity. 'There can be no doubt,' he writes, 'of his having been what the world calls a man of genius. But his genius was of a peculiar character, sometimes above, sometimes below the comprehension of his fellow-men ... I have considered him as amongst the many proofs I have witnessed, of men being possessed of different orders of spirits *now*, as well as in the time when the Saviour Christ was upon the earth, – although our Established Church (to their shame) set themselves against it – some good, some evil, in their different degrees. It is evident Blake's was not an evil one, for he was a good man, the most harmless and free from guile. But men, and even our Church, set down everyone who is eccentric as mad. Alas! how many, now in Bedlam, are there for disorders of soul (spirit), and not of the body?' A similar suspicion to this Blake himself would sometimes hazard, viz. that 'there are probably men shut up as mad in Bedlam, who are not so: that possibly the madmen outside have shut up the sane people.' Which, by the way, is not the kind of talk a madman, or a man conscious of lying under such a suspicion among his friends, would indulge in. Madmen, and those sus-pected of madness, do not make common cause with the mad; they rather shun, or take side against them, as animals treat a diseased or wounded comrade. Above all, a madman, with his uneasy sense of his own true condition, has a sensitive horror of so personal a topic and cunningly avoids it.

One ground of the exaggerated misconception of Blake's eccentricities prevalent among those who had *heard* about Blake rather than sat at his feet, – those strange 'visions' of his, we have accounted for quite consistently with sanity. As we said, he, in conversation with his friends, admitted so much, – viz. the inchoate power of others to see the same things he saw, – as to eliminate any outrageous extravagance from his pretensions as a soothsayer. Bearing on this point, it is to be remarked that a madman insists on others seeing as he sees. But Blake did not expect his companion of the moment, John Varley, or Mrs Blake, to behold the visionary spectres summoned from the void before *his* eyes, of prophet, king, and poet.

One curious but indubitable historical fact is worth remembrance here. It is full of suggestion in connexion with our present subject. For Blake was, in spirit, a denizen of other and earlier ages of the world than the present mechanical one to which chance had rudely transplanted him. It is within the last century or so, that 'the heavens have gone further off,' as Hazlitt put it. The supernatural world has during that period removed itself further from civilized, cultivated humanity than it was ever before – in all time, heathen or Christian. There is, at this moment, infinitely less practical belief in an invisible world, or even apprehension of it, than at any previous historical era, whether Egyptian, classic, or mediæval. It is *only* within the last century and a half, the faculty of seeing visions could have been one to bring a man's sanity into question. Ever before, by simple, believing Romanist, by reverent awe-struck pagan, or in the fervent East, the exceptional power had been accepted as a matter of course in gifted men, and had been turned to serious account in the cause of religion. Even so late a manifestation of this abiding tendency (the visionary) in all spiritual persons, as that in the case of Jacob Boehmen in Lutheran time, excited, not sceptical disbelief, but pedantic hostility, as presumably a delusive gift from the Father of Evil rather than from the Author of all Good.

Another source of the false estimate formed of Blake by many, is traceable to the 'wild and hurling words' he would utter in conversation, – especially when provoked. In society, people would disbelieve and exasperate him, would set upon the gentle yet fiery-hearted mystic, and stir him up into being extravagant, out of a mere spirit of opposition. Then he would say things on purpose to startle, and make people stare. In the excitement of conversation he would exaggerate his peculiarities of opinion and doctrine, would express a floating notion or fancy in an extreme way, without the explanation or qualification he was, in reality, well aware it needed; taking a secret pleasure in the surprise and opposition such views aroused. 'Often,' – to this effect writes Mr Linnell, – 'he said things on purpose to puzzle and provoke those who teased him in order to bring out his strongest peculiarities. With the froward, he showed himself froward, but with the gentle, he was as amiable as a child ... His eccentricities have been enlarged upon beyond the truth. He was so far from being so absurd in his opinions, or so nearly mad as has been represented, that he always defended Christian truth against the attacks of infidels, and its abuse by the super-stitious ... It must be confessed, however, he uttered occasion-ally sentiments sadly at variance with sound doctrine.'

Some persons of a scientific turn were once discoursing pomp-ously and, to him, distastefully, about the incredible distance of the planets, the length of time light takes to travel to the earth, &c., when he burst out, ''Tis false! I was walking down a lane the other day, and at the end of it I touched the sky with my stick;' perhaps with a little covert sophistry, meaning that he thrust his stick out into space, and that, had he stood upon the remotest star, he could do no more; the blue sky itself being but the limit of our bodily perceptions of the Infinite which encompasses us. Scientific individuals would generally make him come out with something outrageous and unreasonable. For he had an indestructible animosity towards what, to his devout old-world imagination, seemed the keen polar atmosphere of modern science. In society, once, a cultivated stranger, as a mark of polite attention, was showing him the first number of *The*

Mechanic's Magazine. 'Ah, sir,' remarked Blake, with bland emphasis, 'these things we artists HATE!' The latter years of Blake's life were an era when universal homage was challenged for mechanical science, – as for some new Evangel; with a triumphant clamour on the part of superficial enthusiasts, which has since subsided.

But, after all, no candid person would, even in society, have taken Blake for mad. Nor did he really believe his own vaunt, say his friends, when he uttered such things as the above, or as, 'I can reach the sun with my hand, if I stretch it out,' &c. He believed them only in a *non-natural* sense. If it gave him pleasure to think of the welkin, as the old Hebrews did, as a smooth surface which he *might* feel with his hand, he *would* believe it as well as he *could*; contending (among friends) that the idea had a spiritual reality. For, to recur to the explanation of his character I lately quoted, he was 'not mad, but perverse and wilful;' believing a thing because he chose to do so. His reasoning powers were far inferior, as are, more or less, those of all artists, to his perceptive, above all to his perceptions of beauty. He elected his opinions because they seemed beautiful to him, and fulfilled 'the desires of his mind.' Then he would find reasons for them. Thus, Christianity was beautiful to him, and was accepted even more because it satisfied his love of spiritual beauty, than because it satisfied his religious and moral sense. Again, the notion was attractive and beautiful to him that 'Christianity is Art,' and conversely, that 'Art is Christianity:' *therefore* he believed it. And it became one of his standing theological canons, which, in his sybilline writings, he is for ever reiterating.

Both in his books, and in conversation, Blake was a vehement *assertor*; very decisive and very obstinate in his opinions, when he had once taken them up. And he was impatient of control, or of a law in anything, – in his Art, in his opinions on morals, religion, or what not. If artists be divided into the disciplined and undisciplined, he must fall under the latter category. To this, as well as to entire want of discipline in the literary art, was due much of the incoherence in his books and design; incoherence and wildness, which is another source of the general inference embodied by Wordsworth and Southey, who knew him only in his poems, when they described him as a man 'of great, but undoubtedly insane genius.' If for *insane* we read *undisciplined*, or ill-balanced, I think we shall hit the truth.

I have spoken of Blake's daring heterodoxy on religious topics. He not only believed in a pre-existent state, but had adopted, or thought out for himself, many of the ideas of the early Gnostics; and was otherwise so erratic in his religious opinions as to shock orthodox Churchmen. Once, in later years, a disputant got up and left his company. 'Ah,' said Blake, 'we could not get on at all: he wanted to teach me, and I to teach him.' A transcendental Christian rather than a literal one, he would often hazard wild assertions about the Sacred Person. Yet he would consider that a believer only in the historical character of Christ in reality denied Christ. 'I have unspeakable pleasure,' says Smith, 'in being able to state, that though I admit he did not, for the last forty years, attend any place of Divine worship, yet he was not a Free-thinker, as some invidious detractors have thought proper to assert, nor was he ever in any degree irreligious. Through life, his Bible was everything with him.' And, to the same effect, another friend of Blake's writes to me: 'If it *must* be told, that he did not go to church, it should also be told that he was no scoffer at sacred mysteries; and, although thus isolated from the communion of the faithful, ever professed his preference of the Church to any sort of sectarianism. On one occasion, he expressed the uneasiness he should have felt (had he been a parent) at a child of his dying unbaptized. One day, rather in an opposing mood, I think, he declared that the Romish Church was the only one which taught the forgiveness of sins.' 'Forgiveness of sins' was the corner-stone of Christianity to Blake's mind. He was for ever inscribing the tenet over his *Gates of Paradise* and elsewhere. The English Church, as he thought, too little inculcated it. He had a sentimental liking for the Romish Church, and, among other paradoxes, would often try to make out that priestly despotism was better than kingly. 'He believed no subjects of monarchies were so happy as the Pope's;' which sounds still more absurd now, than in times nearer those of the First Napoleon, when the poor Pope had, for a while, seemed the victim of military force, and an object of legitimate sympathy. Blake's friend may well add: 'I fancy this was one of his *wilful* sayings, and meant that he believed priests to be more favourable to liberty than kings: which he certainly did. He loved liberty, and had no affection for statecraft or standing armies, yet no man less resembled the vulgar radical. His sympathies were rather with Milton, Harrington, and Marvel – not with Milton as to his puritanism, but his love of a grand ideal scheme of republicanism; though I never remember him speaking of the American institutions: I suppose Blake's republic would always have been ideal.' We must assuredly number among his more 'wilful' assertions the curious hypothesis, 'that the Bonaparte of Italy was killed, and that another was somehow substituted from the exigent want of the name, who was the Bonaparte of the Empire! He referred to the different physiognomies (as he thought) in the earlier and later portraits. But, stranger still, he gave me the (forgotten) name of some public man – ambassador, or something of the sort '– who

353

assured him such was the case; and a very plausible story he made of it,' says the same friend.

Similar latitude of speculation was, as we have seen, cultivated on ethics. Practically obedient to moral law, a faithful husband, and temperate in all his habits, Blake is for ever, in his writings, girding at the '*mere* moral law,' as being the letter which killeth. His conversation on social topics, his writings, his designs, were equally marked by theoretic licence and virtual guilelessness; for he frankly said, described, and drew everything as it arose to his mind. 'Do you think,' he once said in familiar conversation, and in the spirit of controversy, 'if I came home, and discovered my wife to be unfaithful, I should be so foolish as to take it ill?' Mrs Blake was a most exemplary wife, yet was so much in the habit of echoing and thinking right whatever he said that, had she been present, adds my informant, he is sure she would have innocently responded, '*Of course not!*' 'But,' continues Blake's friend, 'I am inclined to think (despite the philosophic boast) it would have gone ill with the offenders.'

354

THIRTY-SIX

Declining Health: Designs to Dante 1824–1827
[ÆT. 67–70]

While the *Job* was in progress, Blake had, among other work, assisted, from August to December, 1824, in engraving a portrait from his friend Linnell's hand, of Mr Lowry, and perhaps in some other plates. It was during this period, also, Mr Linnell introduced him to the knowledge of Dante, and commissioned a series of drawings from the *Divina Commedia*, to be hereafter engraved; justly thinking Blake 'the very man and the only' to illustrate the great mediæval master of supernatural awe and terror. While still engaged over the engravings to *Job*, Blake set to work full of energy, sketching, while confined to bed by a sprained foot, the first outlines of the whole, or nearly the whole, of this new series, in a folio volume of a hundred pages, which Mr Linnell had given him for the purpose. This was during the years 1824 to 1826. With characteristic fervour and activity of intellect, he, at sixty-seven years of age, applied himself to learning Italian, in order to read his author in the original. Helped by such command of Latin as he had, he taught himself the language in a few weeks; sufficiently, that is, to comprehend that difficult author substantially, if not grammatically: just as, earlier in life, he had taught himself something of Latin, French, and even Greek.

The drawings after Dante, at first dividing Blake's time with the engravings of the *Job*, engrossed nearly the whole of it during the brief remnant of his life. They amount to a hundred in all, many unfinished; presenting his conceptions in all stages, in fact, from the bare outline to high finish.

These designs (which will be found catalogued, with a few remarks, in List No. 1, of the Appendix) form the largest series ever undertaken by Blake, except the one from Gray, which numbers 118 subjects; and, from the profound interest and the variety and special nature of the subject, not to speak of the merits of the designs themselves, they maintain a high rank among his performances. It was a great labour for a man of 'threescore years and ten' to undertake; and a labour which, in its result, exhibits no symptom of age or feebleness. The designs, it is true, are scarcely ever carried to full completion, and are often extremely slight; but the power of mind, eye, hand – the power of grappling with a new subject matter, and making all its parts, so to speak, organic – is in no wise dimmed. The conception is not always such as most students of Dante will be willing to admit as Dantesque, though certainly much more Dantesque than the refined performance of Flaxman, or than any other known to me; it is, at any rate, the highly creative mind of Dante filtered through the highly creative, sympathetic mind of Blake.

Blake lived to engrave only seven, published in 1827. These seven, all from the *Hell*, are –

1. The Circle of the Lustful – Paolo and Francesca.

2. The Circle of the Corrupt Officials – The Devils tormenting Ciampolo.

3. Same Circle – The Devils mauling each other.

4. The Circle of the Thieves – Agnolo Brunnelleschi attacked by the serpent.

5. Same Circle – Buoso Donati attacked by the serpent.

6. The Circle of the Falsifiers.

7. The Circle of the Traitors – Dante's foot striking Bocca degli Abati.

These engravings are, like the designs, uncompleted works. They are executed in Blake's strict, sharp-lined manner; and, though they are more than outlines, do not aim at entire finish of light and shade, or at any strong effects. It will be observed, in the list of engravings, that the two circles of the Corrupt Officials and of the Thieves receive a more than proportionate share of illustration, and the same is still more strikingly apparent in the list of the complete series of designs. Blake flapped, like a moth round a candle, time after time at the grotesqueness of the pitchforked devils, and the horror of the transforming serpents.

The agreement between the two friends as to the *Dante* was, that Mr Linnell should go on paying Blake $2l$. or $3l$. a week, as he wanted money, Blake doing as little or as much as he liked in return. The payments on account amounted in the end to $150l$. By this truly genial and friendly arrangement, the ease and comfort of Blake's declining years were placed on a sure footing; which was the object Mr Linnell had at heart.

These drawings are unique, no duplicates having been executed: two of them (as shown in the Appendix), are known in a preparatory stage also. They still remain in the congenial keeping of their first owner, and have never been engraved, except the seven just mentioned, nor otherwise made use of.

While, in 1825, the designs from Dante were progressing, I find Mr Linnell a purchaser also of twelve drawings from Milton's *Paradise Regained*, a sequel to those from the *Paradise Lost*, executed for Mr Butts, which are now scattered in various hands. Mr Linnell had unsuccessfully endeavoured to persuade the jovial, affluent Chantrey, to buy the *Paradise Regained* for $20l$.

They are of great beauty, refined in execution, especially tender and pure in colour, and pervading feeling. Like all Mr Linnell's other purchases from Blake, they have been retained by him.

A letter from Blake, in November, 1825, shows him still adding final touches to the plates of the *Job*. It is addressed John Linnell, Esq. Cirencester Place, Fitzroy Square, and is dated *Thursday Evening, 10th Nov.* 1825, from *Fountain Court, Strand:*

> 'DEAR SIR,
>
> 'I have, I believe, done nearly all that we agreed on. And if you should put on your considering cap, just as you did last time we met, I have no doubt that the plates would be all the better for it. I cannot get well, and am now in bed, but seem as if I should be better to-morrow. Rest does me good. Pray take care of your health this wet weather; and though I write, do not venture out on such days as to-day has been. I hope a few more days will bring us to a conclusion.
>
> 'I am, dear Sir,
> 'Yours sincerely,
> 'WILLIAM BLAKE.'

Among the new friends to whom Mr Linnell had introduced Blake, was Mr Aders, a wealthy merchant of an old German family; a liberal and art-loving man, whose doors were always open to literary men and artists. To his house came Coleridge and Lamb, and, as we saw, Lawrence, James Ward, Stothard, Linnell; finally Blake, with whom, I think, Coleridge here became acquainted. Of Blake, Mr Aders bought copies of the *Songs of Innocence and Experience*, and a few others of the illustrated books. His house in Euston Square was filled with pictures, chosen with excellent judgment, of a class not commonly selected in those days, viz. examples of the early Italian and, above all, early Flemish and German schools. It was as much a picture gallery as a house. The walls of drawing-room, bed-rooms, and even staircase, were all closely covered; with gallery railings in front to protect the pictures from injury. The collection was a remarkable and celebrated one, and has left lasting traces of itself in the history of picture-collecting. It comprised many works deeply interesting in the annals of painting. Among these was a fine old copy of the famous *Adoration of the Lamb*, of Hubert and Jan Van Eyck; one of the chief landmarks in the history of Art (Hubert's sole surviving composition). In this copy – formerly in the Hôtel de Ville, Ghent – could be alone seen the effect of the altar-piece as a whole; for the various compartments, both of the original and of Coxcie's copy, are widely scattered. There were several other precious and authentic pictures of the school of the Van Eycks: a very interesting small altar-piece, attributed to Margaretta Van Eyck, but since assigned to Quintin Matsys; the *Portrait of an Artist*, by Hans Memling, or, as some say, Dierick Stuerbout, afterwards in Mr Rogers's collection; one or two undoubted small pieces from the hand of Hans Memling, some in the school of Roger Vander Weyden, and one of the dozen (or fewer) certain examples of Martin Schön known to exist.

The collection was visited by Passavant, the biographer of Raphael, during his visit to England in 1831, and the Flemish and German portion of it is described at length in his *Tour of a German Artist*. It is characteristic of our National Gallery management, that not one of these often invaluable examples of rare masters was secured for the nation (it was the *régime* of Seguier, of liquorice-brown varnish fame), when the opportunity arose. For, in a subsequent year, – 1836, – a terrible reverse in trade shattered the fabric of the munificent merchant's prosperity, and involved the dispersion of this interesting collection.

Mrs Aders, a daughter of Raphael Smith, the engraver and painter, was herself an amateur artist, sufficiently mistress of painting to execute clever copies after the old masters, and original pictures, which extorted the praise of Blake – always candid to amateur merit. She was a beautiful and accomplished lady, of much conversational power, able to hold her own with the gifted men who were in the habit of frequenting her house. It is to her Coleridge's poem of *The Two Founts* was addressed.

After the ruin of her husband's fortunes, she withdrew from society, dying only a few years since. She remembered Blake with especial interest, and to the last delighted to talk of him.

At Mr Aders' house the German painter, Gotzenberger, met Blake. On his return to Germany, he declared: 'I saw in England many men of talent, but only three men of genius – Coleridge, Flaxman, and Blake; and of these Blake was the greatest.' There, too, a gentleman first saw Blake, whom, so long ago as 1809, we beheld a solitary visitor to the abortive exhibition in Broad Street; and, in 1810, writing an account of the memorable man for the *Patriotische Annalen* of good Dr Perthes, of Hamburgh. Mr Crabb Robinson, a gentleman who began life as a barrister, but who, throughout his career, has cultivated the acquaintance of distinguished men of letters, had, during twenty years, heard much of Blake from Flaxman. The sculptor, if he did not go so far as to speak of him as an actual seer, was still further from joining in the ordinary derision of him as a madman. But it was not till 1825 that Mr Crabb Robinson met the visionary man, at Mr Aders' table, in the company of Mr Linnell. 'This was on the 10th December,' writes Mr Robinson, in the very interesting *Reminiscences* (based on his *Journals*), with the sight of a portion of which I have been kindly favoured. His account of Blake is from a point of view widely different from those of the artist's enthusiastic young disciples, yet, in all essentials, corroborates them. Many of the extravagances and incoherences recorded as falling from Blake's lips at these interviews indicate, to one familiar with his habits of mind, that he was often, in the course of them, ruffled by his friendly but very logical and cool-headed interlocutor, into extreme statements. He allowed himself to be drawn out pretty considerably, but not with closed eyes.

> '. . . I was aware of his idiosyncrasies, and therefore I to a great degree prepared for the sort of conversation which took place at and after dinner: an altogether unmethodical rhapsody on art, poetry, religion; he saying the most strange things in the most unemphatic manner, speaking of his *visions* as any man would of the most ordinary occurrence. He was then sixty-eight years of age. He had a broad pale face, a large full eye, with a benignant expression, – at the same time a look of languor, except when excited; and then he had an air of inspiration; *but not such as, without previous acquaintance with him, or attending to what he said, would suggest the notion that he was insane.*'

The italics are mine. Mr Robinson, I should mention, is among those who think Blake to have been an 'insane man of genius,' or, at any rate, a victim of monomania; and is the only one to think so of all I have met who actually knew anything of him.

> 'There was nothing *wild* about his looks. Though very ready to be drawn out to the assertion of his favourite ideas, yet there was no warmth, as if he wanted to make proselytes. Indeed, one of the peculiar features of his scheme, as far as it was consistent, was indifference, and a very extraordinary degree of tolerance and satisfaction with what had taken place – a sort of pious and humble optimism; not the scornful optimism of *Candide*. But, at the same time that he was very ready to praise, he seemed incapable of envy, as he was of discontent. He warmly praised some compositions of Mrs Aders'; and having brought for A.

an engraving of his *Canterbury Pilgrims*, he remarked that one of the figures resembled a figure in one of the works then in Aders' room, and that he had been accused of having stolen from it. But he added that he had drawn the figure in question twenty years before he had seen the original picture. "However, there is no wonder in the resemblance, as in my youth I was always studying that class of paintings." I have forgotten what the figure was. But his taste was in close conformity with the old German school. This was somewhat at variance with what he said, both this day and afterwards, – implying that he copied his visions.

'It was at this first meeting that, in answer to a question from me he said, "The Spirits told me." This led me to say: "Socrates used pretty much the same language – he spoke of his Genius. Now, what affinity or resemblance do you suppose was there between the *Genius* which inspired Socrates and your *Spirits?*" He smiled, and for once it seemed to me as if he had a feeling of vanity gratified. "The same as in our countenances." He paused and added: "I was Socrates, or a sort of brother. I must have had conversations with him. So I had with Jesus Christ; I have an obscure recollection of having been with both of them." As I had for many years been familiar with the idea that an eternity *a parte post* was inconceivable without an eternity *a parte ante*, I was naturally led to express that thought on this occasion. His eye brightened on my saying this. He eagerly assented – "To be sure! We are all coexistent with God; members of the Divine Body, and partakers of the Divine Nature." . . .

'. . . From something Blake said, drawing the inference, – then there is no use in education, – he hastily rejoined: "There *is* no use in education – I hold it wrong – it is the great Sin; it is eating of the tree of knowledge of Good and Evil. That was the fault of Plato: he knew of nothing but the virtues and vices. There is nothing in all that. Everything is good in God's eyes." On my asking whether there is nothing absolutely evil in what man does, he answered: "I am no judge of that – perhaps not in God's eyes." Notwithstanding this, he, however, at the same time, spoke of error as being in Heaven; for on my asking whether Dante was pure in writing his Vision, – "Pure!" said Blake, "is there any purity in God's eyes? No! He chargeth His angels with folly." He even extended this liability to error to the Supreme Being. "Did He not repent Him that He had made Nineveh?" My *Journal* here has the remark, that it is easier to retail his personal remarks than to reconcile those which seemed to be in conformity with the most opposed abstract systems.'

Perhaps, indeed, the attempt to methodize them into a system was so much labour lost? The key to the wild and strange rhapsodies Blake would utter can be supplied by love, but not by the intellect. To *go with* Blake, it almost required that a man should have the mind of an artist – and an artist of a peculiar kind – or one strongly in unison with that class of mind.

'He spoke with seeming complacency of his own life in connexion with art. In becoming an artist he acted by command: the Spirits said to him, "Blake, be an artist!" His eye glistened while he spoke of the joy of devoting himself to *divine* art alone. "Art is inspiration. When Michael Angelo, or Raphael, in their day, or Mr Flaxman, does one of his fine things, he does them in the spirit." Of fame he said: "I should be sorry if I had any earthly fame, for whatever natural glory a man has is so much detracted from his spiritual glory. I wish to do nothing for profit; I want nothing; I am quite happy." This was confirmed to me on my subsequent interviews with him. His distinction between the natural and spiritual worlds was very confused. Incidentally, Swedenborg was mentioned: he declared him to be a divine teacher; he had done, and would do, much good: yet he did wrong in endeavouring to explain to the *Reason* what it could not comprehend. He seemed to consider – but that was not clear – the visions of Swedenborg and Dante as of the same kind. Dante was the greater poet. He, too, was wrong, – in occupying his mind about political objects. Yet this did not appear to affect his estimation of Dante's genius, or his opinion of the truth of Dante's visions. Indeed, when he even declared Dante to be an atheist, it was accompanied by expression of the highest admiration; "though," said he, "Dante saw devils where I saw none."

'I put down in my journal the following insulated remarks: Jacob Boehmen was placed among the divinely inspired men. He praised also the designs to Law's Translation of Boehmen. "Michael Angelo could not have surpassed them." – "Bacon, Locke, and Newton, are the three great teachers of atheism, or Satan's doctrine." – "Irving is a highly gifted man: he is a *sent* man; but they who are sent sometimes go further than they ought." "I saw nothing but good in Calvin's house; in Luther's there were harlots." . . . He declared his opinion that the earth is flat, not round, and just as I had objected, – the circumnavigation, – dinner was announced. Objections were seldom of any use. The wildest of his assertions was made with the veriest indifference of tone, as if altogether insignificant. It respected the natural and spiritual worlds. By way of example of the difference between them, he said: "You never saw the spiritual Sun? I have. I saw him on Primrose Hill. He said, Do you take me for the Greek Apollo? No! *That* (pointing to the sky), *that* is the Greek Apollo: he is Satan." Not everything was thus absurd. There were glimpses and flashes of truth and beauty: as when he compared moral with physical evil. – "Who shall say what God thinks evil? That is a wise tale of the Mahomedans, – of the angel of the Lord who murdered the Infant." (The *Hermit* of Parnell, I suppose.) "Is not every infant that dies a natural death in reality slain by an angel?" And when he joined to the assurance of his happiness that of his having suffered, and that it was necessary, he added: "There is suffering in Heaven; for where there is the capacity of enjoyment, there is the capacity of pain." I include among the glimpses of truth this assertion: "I know what is true by internal conviction; – a doctrine is stated; my heart tells me it must be true." I remarked, in confirmation of it, that, to an unlearned man, what are called the external evidence of religion can carry no conviction with them; and this he assented to.

'After my first evening with him at Aders', I made the remark in my *Journal*, that his observations, apart from his visions and references to the spiritual world, were sensible and acute. In the sweetness of his countenance and gentility of his manner, he added an indescribable grace to his conversation. I added my regret, which I must now repeat, at my inability to give more than incoherent thoughts – not altogether my fault, perhaps.

'On the 17th, I called on him at his house in Fountain Court in the Strand. The interview was a short one, and what I saw was more remarkable than what I heard. He was at work, engraving, in a small bedroom, – light, and looking out on a mean yard – everything in the room squalid and indicating poverty, except himself. There was a natural gentility about him, and an insensibility to the seeming poverty, which quite removed the impression. Besides, his linen was clean, his hand white, and his air quite unembarrassed when he begged me to sit down as if he were in a palace. There was but one chair in the room, besides that on which he sat. On my putting my hand to it, I found that it would have fallen to pieces if I had lifted it. So, as if I had been a Sybarite, I said, with a smile, "Will you let me indulge myself?" and sat on the bed near him. During my short stay there was nothing in him that betrayed that he was aware of what to other persons might have been even offensive, – not in his person, but in all about him. His wife I saw at this time, and she seemed to be the very woman to make him happy. She had been formed by him; indeed otherwise she could not have lived with him. Notwithstanding her dress, which was poor and dirty, she had a good expression in her countenance, and, with a dark eye, remains of beauty from her youth. She had an implicit reverence for her husband. It is quite certain that she believed in all his visions. On one occasion – not this day – speaking of his visions, she said: "You know, dear, the first time you saw God was when you were four years old, and He put His head to the window, and set you screaming." . . .

'He was making designs, or engraving – I forget which. Cary's Dante was before him. He showed me some of his designs from Dante of which I do not presume to speak. They were too much above me. But Gotzenberger, whom I afterwards took to see them, expressed the highest admiration . . . Dante was again the subject of our conversation. Blake declared him a mere politician and atheist, busied about this world's affairs; as Milton was till, in his old age, he returned back to the God he had abandoned in childhood. I in vain endeavoured to obtain from him a qualification of the term atheist, so as not to include him in the ordinary reproach. Yet he afterwards spoke of Dante's being then with God. I was more successful when he also called Locke an atheist, and imputed to him wilful deception. He seemed satisfied with my admission, that Locke's philosophy led to the atheism of the French school. He reiterated his former strange notions on morals – would allow of no other education than what lies in the cultivation of the fine arts and the imagination.

'As he spoke of frequently seeing Milton, I ventured to ask, half ashamed at the time, which of the three or four portraits in Hollis's *Memoirs* was the most like? He answered: "They are all like, at different ages. I have seen him as a youth, and as an old man, with long flowing beard. He came lately as an old man. He came to ask a favour of me; said he had committed an error in his *Paradise Lost*, which he wanted me to correct in a poem or picture. But I declined; I said I had my own duties to perform." "It is a presumptuous question," I replied, "but might I venture to ask what that could be?" "He wished me to expose the falsehood of his doctrine taught in the *Paradise Lost*, that sexual intercourse arose out of the Fall." . . . At the time that he asserted his own possession of the gift of vision, he did not boast of it as peculiar to himself: "All men might have it if they would."

'On the 24th December I called a second time on him. On this occasion it was that I read to him Wordsworth's *Ode* on the supposed pre-existent state (*Intimations of Immortality*). The subject of Wordsworth's religious character was discussed when

366

we met on the 18th of February, and the 12th of May (1826). I
will here bring together Blake's declarations concerning Wordsworth. I had been in the habit, when reading this marvellous
Ode to friends, of omitting one or two passages, especially that –

> – "But there's a Tree, of many, one,
> A single Field which I have looked upon,
> Both of them speak of something that is gone:
>> The Pansy at my feet
>> Doth the same tale repeat:
> Whither is fled the visionary gleam?
> Where is it now, the glory and the dream?"

lest I should be rendered ridiculous, being unable to explain
precisely what I admired. Not that I acknowledged this to be a
fair test. But with Blake I could fear nothing of the kind. And
it was this very stanza which threw him almost into an hysterical
rapture. His delight in Wordsworth's poetry was intense. Nor
did it seem less, notwithstanding the reproaches he continually
cast on his worship of nature; which, in the mind of Blake,
constituted atheism. The combination of the warmest praise with
imputations which, from another, would assume the most serious
character, and the liberty he took to interpret as he pleased,
rendered it as difficult to be offended as to reason with him.
The eloquent descriptions of nature in Wordsworth's poems were
conclusive proofs of atheism: "For whoever believes in nature,"
said B., "disbelieves in God; for *Nature* is the work of the devil."
On my obtaining from him the declaration that the Bible was
the Word of God, I referred to the commencement of *Genesis*,
"In the beginning God created the heavens and the earth." But
I gained nothing by this; for I was triumphantly told that this
God was not Jehovah, but the Elohim; and the doctrine of the
Gnostics was repeated with sufficient consistency to silence one
so unlearned as myself. The *Preface* to *The Excursion*, especially
the verses quoted from *Book I.* of *The Recluse*, so troubled him
as to bring on a fit of illness. These lines he singled out:

"Jehovah – with His thunder, and the choir
Of shouting angels, and the empyreal thrones –
I pass them unalarmed."

'"Does Mr W. think he can surpass Jehovah?" There was a copy of the whole passage in his own hand in the volume of Wordsworth's poems returned to my chambers after his death. There was this note at the end – "Solomon, when he married Pharaoh's daughter, and became a convert to the heathen mythology, talked exactly in this way of Jehovah – as a very inferior object of man's contemplations: he also passed Him 'unalarmed,' and was permitted. Jehovah dropped a tear and followed him by His spirit into the abstract void. It is called the Divine mercy. Sarah dwells in it, but mercy does not dwell in him." Some of the poems he maintained were from the Holy Ghost, others from the Devil. I lent him the 8vo edition, in two vols. (1815), of W.'s poems, which he had in his possession at the time of his death. They were returned to me then. I did not recognise the pencil notes he had made in them to be his for some time, and was on the point of rubbing them out when I made the discovery; and they were preserved.'

Mr Crabb Robinson was not only a friend and admirer of Wordsworth, but among the believers, – fewer *then* than now, – in the new poetic revelation to be found in his works. The edition of 1815 was the first in which Wordsworth's poems were arranged into classes; and contained the celebrated new *Preface* on the various distinctive characteristics of poetry, as well as the celebrated *Preface* and *Supplementary Essay*, first printed in the *second* edition of the *Lyrical Ballads*. Blake's notes extend over the first volume only: they are characteristic iterations, according to his wont, of favourite dogmas.

In the *Preface* to the edition of 1815, Wordsworth writes, 'The powers requisite for the production of poetry are, first, those of observation and description.' 'One power alone makes a poet,' answers Blake, – 'Imagination; the Divine Vision.' On the line –

'Bound each to each by natural piety,'

Blake comments – 'There is no such thing as natural piety, because the natural man is at enmity with God.' And again, on the fly-leaf, under the heading, – *Poems referring to the Period of Childhood*, – 'I see in Wordsworth the natural man rising up against the spiritual man continually; and then he is no poet, but a heathen philosopher, at enmity with all true poetry or inspiration.' At the end of the divine poem *To H. C. Six Years Old*, he exclaims: 'This is all in the highest degree imaginative, and equal to any poet, but not superior. I cannot think that real poets have any competition. None are greatest in the kingdom of heaven. It is so in poetry.' Against the heading, 'On the Influence of Natural Objects,' – to the frost scene from the then unpublished *Prelude*, we have the singular, yet (to one who has the key to Blake's peculiar temperament) not unintelligible avowal: 'Natural objects always did, and now do, weaken, deaden, and obliterate imagination in me. Wordsworth must know that what he writes valuable is *not* to be found in nature. Read Michael Angelo's *Sonnet*, Vol. ii. page 179' (of this edition).

> 'No mortal object did these eyes behold
> When first they met the placid light of thine,
> And my Soul felt her destiny divine,
> And hope of endless peace in me grew bold:
> Heaven-born, the Soul a heavenward course must hold;
> Beyond the visible world she soars to seek
> (For what delights the sense is false and weak)
> Ideal Form, the universal mould.
> The wise man, I affirm, can find no rest
> In that which perishes: nor will he lend

His heart to aught which doth on time depend.
'Tis sense, unbridled will, and not true love,
That kills the soul: love betters what is best,
Even here below, but more in heaven above.'

In the margin of the *Essay Supplementary to the Preface*, against the words, 'By this time I trust the judicious reader,' Blake audaciously writes, 'I do not know who wrote these Prefaces: they are very mischievous, and direct contrary to Wordsworth's own practice.' At p. 341: 'This is not the defence of his own style in opposition to what is called poetic diction, but a sort of historic vindication of the unpopular poets.' Blake's disparaging view of the Prefaces is not shared by myself; but no less a critic than Shelley, one of Wordsworth's warmest contemporary admirers – though outraged by the poet's political and other delinquencies – in his wicked, random skit of *Peter Bell the Third* (1819), also disrespectfully describes Wordsworth, as in these Prefaces,

'Writing some sad stuff in prose:
It is a dangerous invasion
When poets criticise; their station
Is to delight, not pose.'

At the end of the *Supplementary Essay*, Blake again breaks out: 'It appears to me as if the last paragraph, beginning with "Is it the result of the whole that, in the opinion of the writer, the judgment of the people is not to be respected?" was writ by another hand and mind from the rest of these Prefaces. Perhaps they are the opinion of a landscape-painter. Imagination is the divine vision, not of the world, nor of man, nor *from* man, – as he is a natural man. Imagination has nothing to do with memory.'

In these years Blake's health was rapidly failing. He was a perpetual sufferer from intermittent attacks of cold and dysentery (evidently), as his letters to Mr Linnell show. The letters would never, in fact, have been written, but for illness on his part, and Mr Linnell's residence at Hampstead. So long as their writer was well, and Mr Linnell always in Cirencester Place, there had been no occasion for letters. They are characteristic, and explain what he suffered from. Here is one:

'February 1st, 1826.

'DEAR SIR,

'I am forced to write, because I cannot come to you. And this on two accounts. *First*, I omitted to desire you would come and take a mutton chop with us the day you go to Cheltenham, and I will go with you to the coach. Also, I will go to Hampstead to see Mrs Linnell on Sunday, but will return before dinner (I mean if you set off before that). And *second*, I wish to have a copy of *Job* to show to Mr Chantrey.

'For I am again laid up by a cold in my stomach. The Hampstead air, as it always did, so I fear it always will do this, except it be the morning air: and that, in my cousin's time, I found I could bear with safety, and perhaps benefit. I believe my constitution to be a good one, but it has many peculiarities that no one but myself can know. When I was young, Hampstead, Highgate, Hornsey, Muswell Hill, and even Islington, and all places north of London, always laid me up the day after, and sometimes two or three days, with precisely the same complaint, and the same torment of the stomach; easily removed, but excruciating while it lasts, and enfeebling for some time after. Sir Francis Bacon would say, it is want of discipline in mountainous places. Sir Francis Bacon is a liar: no discipline will turn one man into another, even in the least particle; and such discipline I call presumption and folly. I have tried it too much not to know this, and am very sorry for all those who may be led to such ostentatious exertions against their eternal existence itself; because it is a mental rebellion against the Holy Spirit, and fit only for a soldier of Satan to perform.

'Though I hope in a morning or two to call on you in Cirencester Place, I feared you might be gone, or I might be too ill
to let you know how I am, and what I wish.

'I am, dear Sir,
'Yours sincerely,
'WILLIAM BLAKE.'

Let us look over Mr Crabb Robinson's shoulder again, and
(with his courteous permission) glance at a few more entries:

'*Feb.* 19, 1826. – It was this day, in connexion with the assertion
that "the Bible is the Word of God, and all truth is to be
found in it," – he using language concerning men's reason being
opposed to grace, very like that used by the orthodox Christian,
that he qualified, and as the same orthodox would say, utterly
nullified all he said, by declaring that he understood the Bible
in a spiritual sense. As to the natural sense, "Voltaire was commissioned by God to expose *that*. I have had," he said, "much
intercourse with Voltaire, and he said to me: *I blasphemed the
Son of Man, and it shall be forgiven me, but they* (the enemies of
Voltaire) *blasphemed the Holy Ghost in me, and it shall not be
forgiven them.*"'

All the Spirits, it is worth notice, talk in the Blake manner.
To resume:

'I asked in what language Voltaire spoke. His answer was
ingenious, and gave no encouragement to cross-questioning: "To
my sensations it was English. It was like the touch of a musical
key: he touched it probably French, but to my ear it became
English." I also inquired, as I had before, about the form of the
persons who appeared to him, and asked why he did not *draw*
them? "It is not worth while. Besides, there are so many, the
labour would be too great; and there would be no use in it."'

Blake evidently began to feel himself a little badgered, and
not insensible that he was under the hands of a cross-examining,

372

though courteous, lawyer. For, as we know, he *did*, at times, make portraits of spiritual visitants.

'In answer to an inquiry about Shakspeare: "He is exactly like the old engraving – which is said to be a bad one; I think it very good." I inquired about his own writings. "I have written," he answered, "more than Rousseau or Voltaire; six or seven epic poems as long as Homer's, and twenty tragedies as long as *Macbeth*." He showed me his Version of *Genesis*, for so it may be called, as understood by a Christian Visionary. He read a wild passage in a sort of Biblical style. "I shall print no more," he said. "When I am commanded by the spirits, then I write; and the moment I have written, I see the words fly about the room in all directions. It is then published. The spirits can read, and my MS. is of no further use. I have been tempted to burn my MSS., but my wife won't let me." "She is right," I answered. "You wrote not from yourself, but from higher order. The MSS. are their property, not yours. You cannot tell what purpose they may answer." This was addressed *ad hominem*, and indeed amounted only to a deduction from his own premises. He incidentally denied causation: everything being the work of God or Devil. "Every man has a devil in himself; and the conflict between this Self and God perpetually carrying on." I ordered of him to-day a copy of his *Songs* for five guineas. My manner of receiving his mention of price pleased him. He spoke of his horror of money, and of turning pale when it was offered him. And this was certainly unfeigned.'

Blake's visitor made the purchase simply as a delicate means of assisting the artist. From the same motive, he bought some other books and drawings; but, though he had expressly asked for them, experienced the greatest difficulty in getting Blake to accept money. The latter wished to present them. Poor Blake! Next in order of date comes another letter to Mr Linnell:

'19th May, 1826.

'DEAR SIR,

'I have had another desperate shivering fit. It came on yesterday afternoon – after as good a morning as I ever experienced. It began by a gnawing pain in the stomach, and soon spread a deathly feel all over the limbs, which brings on the shivering fit; when I am forced to go to bed, where I contrive to get into a little perspiration, which takes it quite away. It was night when it left me; so I did not get up. But just as I was going to rise this morning, the shivering fit attacked me again, and the pain with the accompanying deathly feel. I got again into a perspiration, and was well again, but so much weakened that I am still in bed. This entirely prevents me from the pleasure of seeing you on Sunday at Hampstead, as I fear the attack again when I am away from home.

'I am, dear Sir,

'Yours sincerely,

'WILLIAM BLAKE.'

'Friday Evening.'

An entry in Mr Crabb Robinson's *Journal*, a few weeks later, refers to Blake –

'13th June, 1826.

'I saw him again. He was as wild as ever, says my *Journal*. But he was led to-day to make assertions more palpably mischievous, if capable of influencing other minds, and immoral, supposing them to express the will of a responsible agent, than anything he had said before.'

Which must be taken to signify that Blake and his visitor were at cross purposes, and the former not in a serene frame of mind; but in a mood to kick out, leaving his listener to make sense of his wild speech as best he could.

During the summer Mr Linnell, who showed a truly filial solicitude for his friend, proposed taking lodgings for him in the neighbourhood of his own cottage at Hampstead, which his growing family pretty well filled. To this project and its postponement, the three following letters refer:

'2d July, 1826.

'MY DEAREST FRIEND,

'This sudden cold weather has cut up all my hopes by the roots. Every one who knows of our intended flight into your delightful country concurs in saying, Do not venture till summer appears again. I also feel myself weaker than I was aware, being not able as yet to sit up longer than six hours at a time; and also feel the cold too much to dare venture beyond my present precincts. My heartiest thanks for your care in my accommodation, and the trouble you will yet have with me. But I get better and stronger every day, though weaker in muscle and bone than I supposed. As to pleasantness of prospect, it is all pleasant prospect at North End. Mrs Hurd's' [the lodgings of Mr Linnell before he went to Collins' Farm] 'I should like as well as any; but think of the expense, and how it may be spared, and never mind appearances.

'I intend to bring with me, besides our necessary change of apparel, only my book of drawings from Dante, and one plate shut up in the book. All will go very well in the coach, which at present would be a rumble I fear I could not go through. So that I conclude another week must pass before I dare venture upon what I ardently desire, – the seeing you with your happy family once again, and that for a longer period than I had ever hoped in my healthful hours.

'I am, dear Sir,
'Yours most gratefully,
'WILLIAM BLAKE.'

'5th July, 1826

'DEAR SIR, –

'I thank you for the receipt of five pounds this morning, and congratulate *you* on the receipt of another fine boy. Am glad to hear of Mrs Linnell's health and safety.

375

'I am getting better every hour. My plan is diet only; but if the machine is capable of it, shall make an old man yet. I go on just as if perfectly well, which indeed I am, except in those paroxysms which I now believe will never more return. Pray let your own health and convenience put all solicitude concerning me at rest. You have a family; I have none: there is no comparison between our necessary avocations.

'Believe me to remain, dear Sir,

'Yours sincerely,

'WILLIAM BLAKE.'

'16th July, 1826

'DEAR SIR, –

'I have been, ever since taking Dr Young's addition to Mr Fincham's prescription for me (the addition is dandelion), in a species of delirium, and in pain too much for thought. It is now past: as I hope. But the moment I got ease of body began pain of mind, and that not a small one. It is about the name of the child, which certainly ought to be Thomas, after Mrs Linnell's father. It will be brutal, not to say worse, in my opinion and on my part. Pray reconsider it, if it is not too late. It very much troubles me, as a crime in which I shall be the principal. Pray excuse this hearty expostulation, and believe me to be,

'Yours sincerely,

'WILLIAM BLAKE.

'Sunday Afternoon.

'P.S. – Fincham is a pupil of Abernethy's. This is what gives me great pleasure. I did not know it before yesterday, – from Mr Fincham.'

The child was to have been named after the artist as a mark of friendly respect; but was eventually called James, and the fulfilment of the intention postponed till the birth of the next boy, who did take Blake's name. Both brothers were destined to become famous in the picture-loving world. The art of landscape-painting will be indebted not only to the John Linnell whom two generations have delighted in and many more will delight to honour, but to the Linnell family collectively. Time after time, James and William Linnell have evinced capabilities which might carry them onward to almost any point of attainment in the art. In both we recognise keen, fresh, strong feeling, vivid perception, plenteous, expressive, sometimes startling realization; qualities which they are able to develop and combine in a form equally grateful to the ruralist and to the lover of art.

'1st August, 1826.

'DEAR SIR, –

'If this notice should be too short for your convenience, please to let me know. But finding myself well enough to come, I propose to set out from here as soon after ten as we can on Thursday morning. Our carriage will be a *cabriolet* [a vehicle now, – 1860, – like the hackney coach, extinct these twenty years, in which the driver sat on a sort of perch beside his fare]. 'For though getting better and stronger, I am still incapable of riding in the stage, and shall be, I fear, for some time; being only bones and sinews, all strings and bobbins like a weaver's loom. Walking to and from the stage would be to me impossible; though I seem well, being entirely free both from pain and from that sickness to which there is no name. Thank God! I feel no more of it, and have great hopes that the disease is gone.

'I am, dear Sir,

'Yours sincerely,

'WILLIAM BLAKE.'

The visit to Hampstead was paid, but with little of the anticipated benefit to Blake's health, who was then suffering from diarrhœa, or, perhaps, dysentery. As he had truly said, that bracing air ill agreed with his constitution. But he cherished a wilful dislike to Hampstead, and to all the northern suburbs of London, despite his affection for the family who made Hampstead a home for him, and the happy hours he had spent there. He, perhaps from early associations, could only tolerate the southern suburbs. They who are accustomed to the varied loveliness of Surrey, Sussex, and Kent, with their delightful mixture of arable, pasture, woodland, waste, and down, one shading off into the other, cannot but find the unvaried pastures and gentle hills of Middlesex and Hertfordshire wearisomely monotonous in their prevailing heavy tints and ever-recurring bounding lines; monotonous and unexhilarating, however agreeable they may be to the escaped Londoner. Mrs Collins, of the Farm, still remembers Blake as 'that most delightful gentleman!' His amiable qualities and ordinarily gentle manner left a lasting impression on the most humble. During this visit he was at work upon the *Dante*. A clump of trees on the skirts of the heath is still known to old friends as the 'Dante wood.'

At the close of this year died another associate in the circle of the gifted, with whom Mr and Mrs Blake had still, in Fountain Court, been in the habit of exchanging visits as of old: John Flaxman, whose always feeble frame had, for some time, been visibly affected for the worse. After a few days' illness from an inflammatory cold which gave his friends little warning of danger, he passed peacefully away, on the 7th December, 1826, in his seventy-second year: somewhat more than six years after the death of his devoted helpmate 'Nancy,' who had been his companion on equal terms; a woman of real gifts and acquirements, of classic accomplishments and sympathies like himself. Not till this biography was almost completed, in January, 1860, did the last member of Flaxman's refined, happy household, – Mrs Flaxman's sister, Maria Denman, – follow her beloved friends to the tomb. She also was a cultivated lady, of much energy and devotion of character, worshipping Flaxman's memory with a sisterly enthusiasm to the last. She had lived to fulfil one cherished object, – the housing a fine selection of Flaxman's original models in the safe keeping of London University College; to which institution she had presented them. My own obligations to her appear in more than one page of this volume. As a girl she had seen and reverenced Blake, so long ago as when he was living in Hercules Buildings.

Under the date of December occurs mention, by Mr Crabb Robinson, of another call on Blake:

'It was, I believe, on the 7th of December (1826) that I saw him. I had just heard of the death of Flaxman, a man whom he admired, and was curious how he would receive the intelligence. He had been ill during the summer, and he said with a smile, "I thought I should have gone first." He then added, "I cannot think of death as more than the going out of one room into another." He relapsed into his ordinary train of thinking . . . This day he said, "Men are born with an angel and a devil." This he himself interpreted as soul and body . . . He spoke of the Old Testament as if it were the evil element – "Christ took much after His mother." . . . He digressed into a condemnation of those who sit in judgment on others: "I have never known a very bad man who had not something very good about him." . . . I have no account of any other call; but this is probably an omission. I took Gotzenberger to see him, and he met the Masqueriers in my chambers. Masquerier was not the man to meet him. He could not humour B., nor understand the peculiar sense in which B. was to be received.'

One kind scheme of Mr Linnell's was the proposal that Blake should live in his town-house in Cirencester Place, now only used professionally. Blake and his wife were to take charge of the house and live rent free. To which proposal the following letter (Feb. 1827) refers:

'DEAR SIR,

I thank you for the five pounds received to-day. Am getting better every morning; but slowly, as I am still feeble and tottering; though all the symptoms of my complaint seem almost gone. The fine weather is very beneficial and comfortable to me. I go on, as I think, improving my engravings of *Dante* more and more; and shall soon get proofs of these four which I have; and beg the favour of you to send me the two plates of *Dante* which you have, that I may finish them sufficiently to make some show of colour and strength.

I have thought and thought of the removal. I cannot get my mind out of a state of terrible fear at such a step. The more I think, the more I feel terror at what I wished at first, and thought a thing of benefit and good hope. You will attribute it to its right cause – intellectual peculiarity that must be myself alone shut up in myself, or reduced to nothing. I could tell you of visions and dreams upon the subject. I have asked and entreated Divine help; but fear continues upon me, and I must relinquish the step that I had wished to take, and still wish, but in vain.

Your success in your profession is, above all things to me, most gratifying. May it go on to the perfection you wish, and more. So wishes also

'Yours sincerely,
'WILLIAM BLAKE.'

Our next letter is dated 15th March, 1827:

'DEAR SIR,

This is to thank you for two pounds, now by me received on account. I have received a letter from Mr Cumberland, in which he says he will take one copy of *Job* for himself, but cannot, as yet, find a customer for one; but hopes to do somewhat by perseverance in his endeavours. He tells me that it is too much finished, or overlaboured, for his Bristol friends, as they think. I saw Mr Tatham, senior, yesterday. He sat with me above one hour, and looked over the *Dante*. He expressed himself very much pleased with the designs as well as the engravings, and hopes soon to get proofs of what I am doing.

'I am, dear Sir,

'Yours sincerely,

'WILLIAM BLAKE.'

This Mr Cumberland, of Bristol, was one of the few buyers from Blake during these years. For him the artist now executed a slight, but interesting commission – an artistic card-plate; no infrequent thing in former days. Reynolds had such an one, and Hogarth also. Graceful little airy figures hover round the name and point to it. The inscription below is, *W. Blake inv. & sc. æt.* 70. 1827. The Mr Tatham, senior, was the architect I have already mentioned as father of a young sculptor then among Blake's most enthusiastic followers.

The little bundle of letters to Mr Linnell – too soon, alas! to be exhausted – will best continue to tell the story of Blake's fluctuating health, his sanguine hopes of recovery, and zealous devotion to his beloved task of finishing and engraving the Designs from Dante – task never to be completed by his faltering hands.

'25th April, 1827.

'DEAR SIR,

'I am going on better every day, as I think, both in health and in work. I thank you for the ten pounds which I received from you this day, which shall be put to the best use; as also for the prospect of Mr Ottley's advantageous acquaintance. I go on without daring to count on futurity, which I cannot do without doubt and fear that ruin activity, and are the greatest hurt to an artist such as I am. As to *Ugolino*, &c. I never supposed that I should sell them. My wife alone is answerable for their having

381

existed in any finished state. I am too much attached to Dante to think much of anything else. I have proved the six plates, and reduced the fighting devils ready for the copper. I count myself sufficiently paid if I live as I now do, and only fear that I may be unlucky to my friends, and especially that I may be so to you.

'I am, sincerely yours,
'WILLIAM BLAKE.'

The Mr Ottley, whose 'advantageous acquaintance' as a likely buyer, or recommender of buyers, is here anticipated, must have been the celebrated connoisseur of that day, author of an elaborate *History of Engraving*, somewhile Keeper, – and a very slovenly one, – of the British Museum Prints; a crony of Sir George Beaumont's. The reader of Constable's *Life* may remember how ill that original artist took Ottley's meddlesome condescension. The conventional, old-world connoisseur little had it in *his* trivial mind to apprehend the significance of Blake's works.

Mr Linnell still continued indefatigable in endeavours to obtain buyers for his friend's works, and recommended him to all he thought likely purchasers: Chantrey, who (as we said) declined the *Paradise Regained*, but took a highly finished copy of the *Songs of Innocence and Experience*, at 20*l.*; Lord Egremont, Sir Thomas Lawrence, Mr Tatham, and others. They considered it almost giving the money, even when they chose copies of the obviously beautiful *Songs*. Some of the last drawings executed, or at least finished by Blake, were two commissioned by Sir Thomas Lawrence, – 'that admirable judge of art,' as he was then considered, and, in a certain fastidious way, was; certainly the enthusiastic accumulator of a princely and matchless collection of drawings by the old masters. Sir Thomas gave fifteen guineas apiece for these designs of Blake's. One was *The Wise and Foolish Virgins*, the other *The Dream of Queen Katherine*;

both repetitions, though not literal ones, of careful drawings made for Mr Butts. The *Dream of Queen Katherine* is among Blake's most highly finished and elaborate water-colour drawings, and one of his most beautiful and imaginative.

During these last years, Blake lavished many finishing touches on his large *fresco* of the *Last Judgment*, of which subject we had to mention, twenty years back, two water-colour drawings – one for Blair's *Grave*, and the other for the Countess of Egremont. The *fresco* was a very different and much fuller composition than either, containing some thousand figures. It was an especial favourite with the artist, and, according to Smith, would have been exhibited at the Academy, had Blake lived another year. Nobody could be found to give twenty-five guineas for it then. I have been unable to discover in whose possession this singularly interesting and important work now is, and only know it from hearsay. Smith had seen the picture, and hands down a word or two on its executive peculiarities. 'The lights of this extraordinary performance,' writes he, 'have the appearance of silver and gold; but, upon Mrs Blake assuring me that there was no silver used, I found, upon a closer examination, that a blue wash had been passed over those parts of the gilding which receded; and the lights of the forward objects, which were also of gold, were heightened with a warm colour, to give the appearance of two metals.' Blake, on looking up one day at this *fresco* as it hung in his front room, candidly exclaimed, as one who was present tells me, 'I spoiled that – made it darker; it was much finer, but a Frenchwoman here (a fellow-lodger) didn't like it.' Ill advised indeed, to alter *colour* at a fellow-lodger and Frenchwoman's suggestion! Blake's alterations were seldom improvements.

THIRTY-SEVEN

Last Days, 1827
[ÆT. 69–70]

The last letter Mr Linnell received from Blake dates nearly three months after that which closed the previous chapter:

'3d July, 1827.

'DEAR SIR,

'I thank you for the ten pounds you are so kind as to send me at this time. My journey to Hampstead on Sunday brought on a relapse which has lasted till now. I find I am not so well as I thought; I must not go on in a youthful style. However, I am upon the mending hand to-day, and hope soon to look as I did; for I have been yellow accompanied by all the old symptoms.

'I am, dear Sir,
'Your sincerely,
'WILLIAM BLAKE.'

He was not to mend; though still, so long as breath lasted, to keep on at his life-long labours of love. This letter was written but six weeks before his death.

In the previous letter of the 25th April, Blake had said of himself, 'I am too much attached to Dante to think much of anything else.' In the course of his lingering illness, he was frequently bolstered up in his bed, that he might go on with these drawings. The younger Tatham had commissioned a coloured

384

impression of that grand conception in the *Europe*, the *Ancient of Days*, already noticed as a singular favourite with Blake and as one it was always a happiness to him to copy. Tatham gave three guineas and a half for this specimen; a higher rate of payment than Blake was accustomed to. This being so, of course Blake finished it to the utmost point, making it as beautiful in colour as already grand in design; patiently working on it till within a few days of his death. After he 'had frequently touched upon it,' says Tatham, as reported by Smith, 'and had frequently held it at a distance, he threw it from him, and with an air of exulting triumph exclaimed, "There! that will do! I cannot mend it."'

As he said these words, his glance fell on his loving Kate, no longer young or beautiful, but who had lived with him in these and like humble rooms, in hourly companionship, ever ready helpfulness, and reverent sympathy, for now forty-five years. August, forty-five years ago (back into a past century), they had wedded at Battersea Church, on the other side the river. August, 1827, he lies in failing strength in the quiet room looking out over the river, yet but a few yards' remove from the roaring Strand: she beside his bed, she alone. He has no other servant, nor nurse, and wants no other. As his eyes rested on the once graceful form, thought of all she had been to him in these years filled the poet-artist's mind. 'Stay!' he cried, 'keep as you are! *you* have been ever an angel to me: I will draw you!' And a portrait was struck off by a hand which approaching death – few days distant now – had not weakened nor benumbed. This drawing has been described to me by Mr Tatham, who once possessed it, as 'a phrenzied sketch of some power; highly interesting, but not like.'

Blake still went on designing as of old. One of the very last shillings spent was in sending out for a pencil. For his illness was not violent, but a gradual and gentle failure of physical powers, which no wise affected the mind. The speedy end was not foreseen by his friends.

The final leave-taking came he had so often seen in vision; so often, and with such child-like, simple faith, sung and designed. With the very same intense, high feeling he had depicted the *Death of the Righteous Man,* he enacted it – serenely, joyously. For life and design and song were with him all pitched in one key, different expressions of one reality. No dissonances there! It happened on a Sunday, the 12th of August, 1827, nearly three months before completion of his seventieth year. 'On the day of his death,' writes Smith, who had his account from the widow, 'he composed and uttered songs to his Maker, so sweetly to the ear of his Catherine, that when she stood to hear him, he, looking upon her most affectionately, said, "My beloved! they are *not mine. No!* they are *not* mine!" He told her they would not be parted; he should always be about her to take care of her.'

A little before his death, Mrs Blake asked where he would be buried, and whether a dissenting minister or a clergyman of the Church of England should read the service. To which he answered, that as far as his own feelings were concerned, she might bury him 'where she pleased.' But that as 'father, mother, aunt, and brother were buried in Bunhill Row, perhaps it would be better to lie *there.* As to service, he should wish for that of the Church of England.'

In that plain, back room, so dear to the memory of his friends, and to them beautiful from association with *him* – with his serene cheerful converse, his high personal influence, so spiritual and rare – he lay chaunting Songs to Melodies, both the inspir-

386

ation of the moment, but no longer as of old to be noted down. To the pious Songs followed, about six in the summer evening, a calm and painless withdrawal of breath; the exact moment almost unperceived by his wife, who sat by his side. A humble female neighbour, her only other companion, said afterwards: 'I have been at the death, not of a man, but of a blessed angel.'

A letter written a few days later to a mutual friend by a now distinguished painter, one of the most fervent in that enthusiastic little band I have so often mentioned, expresses their feelings better than words less fresh or authentic can.

'Wednesday Evening.

'MY DEAR FRIEND,

'Lest you should not have heard of the death of Mr Blake, I have written this to inform you. He died on Sunday night at six o'clock, in a most glorious manner. He said he was going to that country he had all his life wished to see, and expressed himself happy, hoping for salvation through Jesus Christ. Just before he died his countenance became fair, his eyes brightened, and he burst out into singing of the things he saw in heaven. In truth, he died like a saint, as a person who was standing by him observed. He is to be buried on Friday, at twelve in the morning. Should you like to go to the funeral? If you should, there will be room in the coach.

'Yours affectionately.'

THIRTY-EIGHT

Posthumous 1827–31

At noon on the following Friday, August 17th, the chosen knot of friends, – Richmond, Calvert, Tatham, and others, – attended the body of the beloved man to the grave, – saw it laid in Bunhill Fields burying-ground, Finsbury: Tatham, though ill, travelling ninety miles to do so. Bunhill Fields is known to us all as the burial-place of Bunyan and De Foe, among other illustrious nonconformists. Thither, seven years later, was brought Blake's old rival, Stothard, to be laid with his kin: a stone memorial marks his grave.

Among the 'five thousand head-stones' in Bunhill Fields, exists none to William Blake; nothing to indicate the spot where he was buried. Smith, with the best intentions (and Mr Fairholt, in the *Art Journal* for August, 1858, follows him), would identify the grave as one 'numbered 80, at the distance of about twenty-five feet from the north wall.' Unfortunately, that particular portion of the burying-ground was not added until 1836; in 1827 it was occupied by houses, then part of Bunhill Row. On reference to the register, now kept at Somerset House, I find the grave to be numbered '77, east and west; 32, north and south.' This, helped by the ex-sexton, we discover vaguely to be a spot somewhere about the middle of that division of the ground lying to the right as you enter. There is *no* identifying it further. As

388

it was an unpurchased 'common grave' (only a nineteen-shilling fee paid), it was doubtless – to adopt the official euphuism for the basest sacrilege – 'used again,' after the lapse of some fifteen years say: as must also have been the graves of those dear to him. For such had, of late years, become the uniform practice in regard to 'common graves,' the present custodian tells me, amid other melancholy detail of those good old times, which mortal sexton cannot but remember wistfully, – of some sixteen hundred burials in the year; until, in fact, the 'hallowed enclosure' and 'resting-place' was closed by authority in 1854. In 1827, indeed, the over-crowding had not reached its subsequent portentous dimensions. But only a few years later, viz. in 1831–32, when resurrection work was so active, a nightly guard of two watchmen had to be set on foot, and was continued till the closing of the ground. Their watch-box still lingered at the period of my visit in 1854.

To a neglected life, then, consistently followed a nameless and dishonoured grave. 'The *Campo Santo* of the Dissenters' these fields have been poetically styled. A truly *British* Campo Santo; bare of art, beauty, or symbol of human feeling: the very grave-stones of old nonconformist worthies now huddled into a corner, as by-past rubbish. Wandering lonely around that drear, sordid Golgotha, the continuous rumble of near omnibus traffic forming a running accompaniment of dismal sound in harmony with the ugliness which oppresses the eye: wandering dejected in that squalid Hades, it is, for the time, hard to realize the spiritual messages in song and design of the poet whose remains lie, or once lay there.

The year of Blake's death has been incorrectly given by Allan Cunningham as 1828; so, too, by Pilkington and the other dictionaries, and in *Knight's Cyclopædia*, all copying one another.

In the *Literary Gazette*, and in the *Gentleman's Magazine* appeared, at the time, brief notices of Blake, in substance the same. The year of Blake's death, it may be worth adding, was that of Beethoven's and of Jean Paul Richter's.

Blake left not a single debt behind; but a large stock of his works – Drawings, Engravings, Copper-Plates, and copies of Engraved Books – which will help ward off destitution from the widow. A month after her husband's death she, at Mr Linnell's invitation, took up her abode at his house in Cirencester Place, in part fulfilment of the old friendly scheme. There she remained some nine months; quitting in the summer of 1828, to take charge of Mr Tatham's chambers. Finally, she removed into humble lodgings at No. 17, Upper Charlotte Street, Fitzroy Square, in which she continued till her death; still under the wing, as it were, of this last-named friend. The occasional sale to such as had a regard for Blake's memory, or were recommended by staunch friends like Mr Richmond, Nollekens Smith and others, of single drawings, of the *Jerusalem*, of the *Songs of Innocence and Experience*, secured for her moderate wants a decent, if stinted and precarious competence. Perhaps we need hardly call it a *stinted* one, however; for, besides the friends just enumerated, one or two of her husband's old patrons, who had in later years fallen away, remembered their ancient kindness when tidings of his death reached them, and were glad to extend a helping hand to his widow. Nor did she live long enough to test their benevolence too severely; surviving her husband only four years. Among these Lord Egremont visited her and, recalling Blake's Felpham days, said regretfully, 'Why did he leave me?' The Earl subsequently purchased, for the handsome sum of eighty guineas, a large water-colour drawing containing 'The Characters of Spenser's *Faerie Queen*,' grouped together in a procession, as a companion picture to the *Canterbury Pilgrims*. Mr Haviland Burke, a nephew (or grand-nephew) of Edmund Burke, and a very warm appreciator of Blake's genius, not only bought of the widow himself, but urged others to do so. At his instance Dr Jebb, Bishop of Limerick, sent her twenty guineas intimating, at the same time, that, as he was not a collector of works of Art, he did not desire anything in return. To which Mrs Blake, with due pride as well as gratitude, replied by forwarding him a copy of the *Songs of Innocence and Experience*, which she described as, in her estimation, especially precious from having been 'Blake's own.' It is a very late example, the water-mark of the paper bearing date 1825; and certainly, as to harmony of colour and delicacy of execution, is not, throughout, equal to some of the early copies. But as the leaves were evidently numbered by Blake himself, the figures being in the same colour as the engraved writing.

Mr Cary, the translator of Dante, also purchased a drawing – *Oberon and Titania:* and a gentleman in the far north, Mr James Ferguson, an artist who writes from Tynemouth, took copies of three or four of the Engraved Books. Neither was Mrs Blake wanting in efforts to help herself, so far as it lay within her own power to do so. She was an excellent saleswoman, and never committed the mistake of showing too many things at one time. Aided by Mr Tatham she also filled in, within Blake's lines, the colour of the Engraved Books; and even finished some of the drawings – rather against Mr Linnell's judgment. Of her husband she would always speak with trembling voice and tearful eyes as 'that wonderful man,' whose spirit, she said, was still with her, as in death he had promised. Him she worshipped till the end. The manner of her own departure, which occurred somewhat suddenly, was characteristic, and in harmony with the tenor of her life. When told by the doctor that the severe attack of inflammation of the bowels which had seized her and which, always self-negligent, she had suffered to run to a height before calling in medical aid, would terminate in mortification, she sent for her friends, Mr and Mrs Tatham, and, with much composure, gave minute directions for the performance of the last sad details; requesting, among other things, that no one but themselves should see her after death, and that a bushel of slaked lime should be put in the coffin, to secure her from the dissecting knife. She then took leave of Miss Blake, and passed the remaining time – about five hours – calmly and cheerfully; 'repeating texts of Scripture, and calling continually to her William, as if he were only in the next room, to say that she was coming to him, and would not be long now.' This continued nearly till the end. She died in Mrs Tatham's arms, at four o'clock in the morning, on or about the 18th of October, 1831, at the age of sixty-five; and was buried beside her husband in Bunhill Fields. The remaining stock of his works, still considerable, she bequeathed to Mr Tatham, who administered her few effects – effects, in an artistic sense, so precious. They have since been widely dispersed; some destroyed.

Blake left no surviving blood relative, except his sister, concerning whom only the scantiest particulars are now to be gleaned. She had had in her youth, it is said, some pretensions to beauty, and even in age retained the traces of it; her eyes, in particular, being noticeably fine. She was decidedly a *lady* in demeanour, though somewhat shy and proud; with precise old-maidish ways. To this may be added that she survived her brother many years, and sank latterly, it is to be feared, into extreme indigence; at which point we lose sight of her altogether. Where or when she died, I have been unable to discover. Miss Blake has crossed our path but once casually during the course of this narrative, – during the Felpham days, when she made one in her brother's household.

APPENDIX

[The ten following *Letters* were written by Blake, during his residence at Felpham, to his friend and patron Mr Butts, whose grandson, Captain Butts, kindly permits their publication here. They did not come to hand until after the foregoing Biography was in type, and they could not, therefore, be inserted in their natural place, where they would have so incalculably enhanced the interest of the narrative: a narrative, – the reader will forgive me for pointing out, – which, drawn as it was from the scantiest materials, will yet be found to harmonize, both in letter and spirit, with the tenor of these new-found documents, though the broad daylight they let in upon the undercurrents of Blake's life at that period never greeted the eyes to which it would have been so precious. The first of these letters is almost word for word the same as one addressed to Flaxman, already quoted; but, being brief, to mar the completeness of the series by withdrawing it seemed a pity. – ED. *Life.*]

LETTERS TO THOMAS BUTTS

[Date of Post-mark, Sept. 23, 1800.]

DEAR FRIEND OF MY ANGELS,

We are safe arrived at our cottage, without accident or hindrance, though it was between eleven and twelve o'clock at night before we could get home, owing to the necessary shifting of our boxes and portfolios from one chaise to another. We had seven different chaises and as many different drivers. All upon the road was cheerfulness and welcome. Though our luggage was very heavy, there was no grumbling at all. We travelled through a most beautiful country on a most glorious day. Our cottage is more beautiful than I thought it, and also more convenient; for though small it is well proportioned, and if I should ever build a palace, it would be only my cottage enlarged. Please to tell Mrs Butts that we have dedicated a chamber to her service, and that it has a very fine view of the sea. Mr Hayley received us with his usual brotherly affection. My wife and sister are both very well, and courting Neptune for an embrace, whose terrors this morning made them afraid, but whose mildness is often equal to his terrors. The villagers of Felpham are not mere rustics; they are polite and modest. Meat is cheaper than in London; but the sweet air and the voices of winds, trees, and birds, and the odours of the happy ground, make it a dwelling for immortals. Work will go on here with God-speed. A roller and two harrows lie before my window. I met a plough on my first going out at my gate the first morning after my arrival, and the ploughboy said to the ploughman, 'Father, the gate is open.' I have begun to work, and find that I can work with greater pleasure than ever, hoping soon to give you a proof that Felpham is propitious to the arts.

God bless you! I shall wish for you on Tuesday evening as usual. Pray, give my and my wife and sister's love and respects to Mrs Butts. Accept them yourself, and believe me for ever

Your affectionate and obliged friend,

WILLIAM BLAKE.

My sister will be in town in a week, and bring with her your account, and whatever else I can finish.

Direct to me –

Blake, Felpham, near Chichester,

Sussex.

Felpham, Oct. 2, 1800.

FRIEND OF RELIGION AND ORDER,

I thank you for your very beautiful and encouraging verses, which I account a crown of laurels, and I also thank you for your reprehension of follies by me fostered. Your prediction will, I hope, be fulfilled in me, and in future I am the determined advocate of religion and humility – the two bands of society. Having been so full of the business of settling the sticks and feathers of my nest, I have not got any forwarder with the Three Maries, or with any other of your commissions; but hope, now I have commenced a new life of industry, to do credit to that new life by improved works. Receive from me a return of verses, such as Felpham produces by me, though not such as she produces by her eldest son. However, such as they are, I cannot resist the temptation to send them to you: –

To my friend Butts I write
My first vision of light,
On the yellow sands sitting.
The sun was emitting
His glorious beams
From Heaven's high streams.
Over sea, over land,
My eyes did expand
Into regions of air,
Away from all care;
Into regions of fire,
Remote from desire:
The light of the morning,
Heaven's mountains adorning.
In particles bright,
The jewels of light
Distinct shone and clear.
Amaz'd, and in fear,
I each particle gazed,
Astonish'd, amazed;
For each was a man
Human-formed. Swift I ran,
For they beckon'd to me,
Remote by the sea,
Saying: 'Each grain of sand,

Every stone on the land,
Each rock and each hill,
Each fountain and fill,
Each herb and each tree,
Mountain, hill, earth, and sea,
Cloud, meteor, and star,
Are men seen afar.'
I stood in the streams
Of heaven's bright beams,
And saw Felpham sweet
Beneath my bright feet,
In soft female charms;
And in her fair arms
My shadow I knew,
And my wife's shadow too,
And my sister and friend.
We like infants descend
In our shadows on earth,
Like a weak mortal birth.
My eyes more and more,
Like a sea without shore,
Continue expanding,
The heavens commanding,
Till the jewels of light,
Heavenly men beaming bright,

Appeared as one man,
Who complacent began
My limbs to infold
In his beams of bright gold;
Like dross purged away,
All my mire and my clay.
Soft consumed in delight,
In his bosom sun-bright
I remain'd. Soft he smil'd,
And I heard his voice mild,
Saying: 'This is my fold,
O thou ram, horn'd with gold,
Who awakest from sleep
On the sides of the deep.

On the mountains around
The roarings resound
Of the lion and wolf,
The loud sea and deep gulph.
These are guards of my fold,
O thou ram, horn'd with gold!'
And the voice faded mild,
I remain'd as a child;
All I ever had known,
Before me bright shone:
I saw you and your wife
By the fountains of life.
Such the vision to me
Appear'd on the sea.

Mrs Butts will, I hope, excuse my not having finished the portrait. I wait for less hurried moments. Our cottage looks more and more beautiful. And though the weather is wet, the air is very mild, much milder than it was in London when we came away. Chichester is a very handsome city, seven miles from us. We can get most conveniences there. The country is not so destitute of accommodations to our wants as I expected it would be. We have had but little time for viewing the country, but what we have seen is most beautiful; and the people are genuine Saxons, handsomer than the people about London. Mrs Butts will excuse the following lines: –

TO MRS BUTTS.

Wife of the friend of those I most revere,
Receive this tribute from a harp sincere;
Go on in virtuous seed-sowing on mould
Of human vegetation, and behold
Your harvest springing to eternal life,
Parent of youthful minds, and happy wife!

W. B.

I am for ever yours,

WILLIAM BLAKE.

397

Felpham, May 10, 1801.

MY DEAR SIR,

The necessary application to my duty as well to my old as new friends has prevented me from that respect I owe in particular to you. And your accustomed forgiveness of my want of dexterity in certain points emboldens me to hope that forgiveness to be continued to me a little longer, when I shall be enabled to throw off all obstructions to success.

Mr Hayley acts like a prince. I am at complete ease. But I wish to do my duty especially to you, who were the precursor of my present fortune. I never will send you a picture unworthy of my present proficiency. I soon shall send you several. My present engagements are in miniature-painting. Miniature is become a goddess in my eyes, and my friends in Sussex say that I excel in the pursuit. I have a great many orders, and they multiply.

Now, let me entreat you to give me orders to furnish every accommodation in my power to receive you and Mrs Butts. I know, my cottage is too narrow for your ease and comfort. We have one room in which we could make a bed to lodge you both; and if this is sufficient, it is at your service. But as beds and rooms and accommodations are easily procured by one on the spot, permit me to offer my service in either way; either in my cottage, or in a lodging in the village, as is most agreeable to you, if you and Mrs Butts should think Bognor a pleasant relief from business in the summer. It will give me the utmost delight to do my best.

Sussex is certainly a happy place, and Felpham in particular is the sweetest spot on earth; at least it is so to me and my good wife, who desires her kindest love to Mrs Butts and yourself. Accept mine also, and believe me to remain

Your devoted

WILLIAM BLAKE.

Sept. 11, 1801.

MY DEAR SIR,

I hope you will continue to excuse my want of steady perseverance, by which want I am still your debtor, and you so

398

much my creditor; but such as I can be, I will: I can be grateful, and I can soon send you some of your designs which I have nearly completed. In the meantime, by my sister's hands, I transmit to Mrs Butts an attempt at your likeness, which, I hope, she who is the best judge will think like. Time flies faster (as seems to me here) than in London. I labour incessantly, and accomplish not one-half of what I intend, because my abstract folly hurries me often away while I am at work, carrying me over mountains and valleys which are not real, in a land of abstraction where spectres of the dead wander. This I endeavour to prevent, and with my whole might chain my feet to the world of duty and reality. But in vain! the faster I bind, the better is the ballast; for I, so far from being bound down, take the world with me in my flights, and often it seems lighter than a ball of wool rolled by the wind. Bacon and Newton would prescribe ways of making the world heavier to me, and Pitt would prescribe distress for a medicinal potion. But as none on earth can give me mental distress, and I know that all distress inflicted by Heaven is a mercy, a fig for all corporeal! Such distress is my mock and scorn. Alas! wretched, happy, ineffectual labourer of Time's moments that I am! who shall deliver me from this spirit of abstraction and improvidence? Such, my dear Sir, is the truth of my state, and I tell it you in palliation of my seeming neglect of your most pleasant orders. But I have not neglected them; and yet a year is rolled over, and only now I approach the prospect of sending you some, which you may expect soon. I should have sent them by my sister; but, as the coach goes three times a week to London, and they will arrive as safe as with her, I shall have an opportunity of enclosing several together which are not yet completed. I thank you again and again for your generous forbearance, of which I have need; and now I must express my wishes to see you at Felpham, and to show you Mr Hayley's library, which is still unfinished, but is in a finishing way and looks well. I ought also to mention my extreme disappointment at Mr Johnson's forgetfulness, who appointed to call on you but did not. He is also a happy abstract, known by all his friends as the most innocent forgetter of his own interests. He is nephew to the late Mr Cowper, the poet. You would like him much. I continue painting miniatures, and I improve more and more as all my friends tell me. But my principal labour at this time is engraving plates for *Cowper's Life*, a work of magnitude, which Mr Hayley is now labouring with all his matchless industry, and which will be a most valuable acquisition to literature, not only on account of Mr Hayley's composition, but also as it will contain letters of Cowper to his friends – perhaps, or rather certainly, the very best letters that ever were published.

My wife joins with me in love to you and Mrs Butts, hoping that her joy is now increased, and yours also, in an increase of family and of health and happiness.

I remain, dear Sir,

Ever yours sincerely,

WILLIAM BLAKE.

Felpham Cottage, of cottages the prettiest,
September 11, 1801.

Next time I have the happiness to see you, I am determined to paint another portrait of you from life in my best manner, for memory will not do in such minute operations; for I have now discovered that without nature before the painter's eye, he can never produce anything in the walks of natural painting. Historical designing is one thing, and portrait-painting another, and they are as distinct as any two arts can be. Happy would that man be who could unite them!

P.S. – Please to remember our best respects to Mr Birch, and tell him that Felpham men are the mildest of the human race. If it is the will of Providence, they shall be the wisest. We hope that he will next summer joke us face to face.

God bless you all!

Felpham, January 10, 1802.

DEAR SIR,

Your very kind and affectionate letter, and the many kind things you have said in it, called upon me for an immediate answer. But it found my wife and myself so ill, and my wife so very ill, that till now I have not been able to do this duty. The ague and rheumatism have been almost her constant enemies, which she has combated in vain almost ever since we have been here, and her sickness is always my sorrow of course. But what you tell me about your sight afflicted me not a little, and that about your health, in another part of your letter, makes me entreat you to take due care of both. It is a part of our duty to God and man to take due care of His gifts; and though we ought not think *more* highly of ourselves, yet we ought to think *as* highly of ourselves as immortals ought to think.

When I came down here, I was more sanguine than I am at present; but it was because I was ignorant of many things which have since occurred, and chiefly the unhealthiness of the place. Yet I do not repent of coming on a thousand accounts; and Mr H., I doubt not, will do ultimately all that both he and I wish – that is, to lift me out of difficulty. But this is no easy matter to a man who, having spiritual enemies of such formidable magnitude, cannot expect to want natural hidden ones.

Your approbation of my pictures is a multitude to me, and I doubt not that all your kind-wishes in my behalf shall in due time be fulfilled. Your kind offer of pecuniary assistance I can only thank you for at present, because I have enough to serve my present purpose here. Our expenses are small, and our income, from our incessant labour, fully adequate to these at present. I am now engaged in engraving six small plates for a new edition of Mr Hayley's *Triumphs of Temper*, from drawings by Maria Flaxman, sister to my friend the sculptor. And it seems that other things will follow in course, if I do but copy these well. But patience! If great things do not turn out, it is because such things depend on the spiritual and not on the natural world;

and if it was fit for me, I doubt not that I should be employed in greater things; and when it is proper, my talents shall be properly exercised in public, as I hope they are now in private. For till then I leave no stone unturned, and no path unexplored that leads to improvement in my beloved arts. One thing of real consequence I have accomplished by coming into the country, which is to me consolation enough: namely, I have re-collected all my scattered thoughts on art, and resumed my primitive and original ways of execution in both painting and engraving, which in the confusion of London I had very much lost and obliterated from my mind. But whatever becomes of my labours, I would rather that they should be preserved in your greenhouse (not, as you mistakenly call it, dunghill) than in the cold gallery of fashion. The sun may yet shine, and then they will be brought into open air.

But you have so generously and openly desired that I will divide my griefs with you that I cannot hide what it has now become my duty to explain. My unhappiness has arisen from a source which, if explored too narrowly, might hurt my pecuniary circumstances; as my dependence is on engraving at present, and particularly on the engravings I have in hand for Mr H., and I find on all hands great objections to my doing anything but the mere drudgery of business, and intimations that, if I do not confine myself to this, I shall not live. This has always pursued me. You will understand by this the source of all my uneasiness. This from Johnson and Fuseli brought me down here, and this from Mr H. will bring me back again. For that I cannot live without doing my duty to lay up treasures in heaven is certain and determined, and to this I have long made up my mind. And why this should be made an objection to me, while drunkenness, lewdness, gluttony, and even idleness itself, does not hurt other men, let Satan himself explain. The thing I have most at heart − more than life, or all that seems to make life comfortable without − is the interest of true religion and science. And whenever anything appears to affect that interest (especially if I myself omit any duty to my station as a soldier of Christ), it gives me the greatest of torments. I am not ashamed, afraid, or averse to tell you what ought to be told – that I am under the direction of messengers from heaven, daily and nightly. But the nature of such things is not, as some suppose, without trouble or care. Temptations are on the right hand and on the left. Behind, the sea of time and space roars and follows swiftly. He who keeps not right onwards is lost; and if our footsteps slide in clay, how can we do otherwise than fear and tremble? But I should not have troubled you with this account of my spiritual state, unless it had been necessary in explaining the actual cause of my uneasiness, into which you are so kind as to inquire: for I never obtrude such things on others unless questioned, and then I never disguise the truth. But if we fear to do the dictates of our angels, and tremble at the tasks set before us; if we refuse to do spiritual acts because of natural fears or natural desires; who can describe the dismal torments of such a state! – I too well remember the threats I heard! – 'If you, who are organized by Divine Providence for spiritual communion, refuse, and bury your talent in the earth, even though you should want natural bread, – sorrow and desperation pursue you through life, and after death shame and confusion of face to eternity. Every one in eternity will leave you, aghast at the man who was crowned with glory and honour by his brethren, and betrayed their cause to their enemies. You will be called the base Judas who betrayed his friend!' – Such words would make any stout man tremble, and how then could I be at ease? But I am now no longer in that state, and now go on again with my task, fearless though my path is difficult. I have no fear of stumbling while I keep it.

My wife desires her kindest love to Mrs Butts, and I have permitted her to send it to you also. We often wish that we could unite again in society, and hope that the time is not distant when we shall do so, being determined not to remain another winter here, but to return to London.

I hear a Voice you cannot hear, that says I must not stay,
I see a Hand you cannot see, that beckons me away.

Naked we came here – naked of natural things – and naked we shall return: but while clothed with the Divine mercy, we are richly clothed in spiritual, and suffer all the rest gladly. Pray, give my love to Mrs Butts and your family.

I am yours sincerely,

WILLIAM BLAKE.

P.S. – Your obliging proposal of exhibiting my two pictures likewise calls for my thanks; I will finish the others, and then we shall judge of the matter with certainty.

Felpham, Nov. 22, 1802.

DEAR SIR,

My brother tells me that he fears you are offended with me. I fear so too, because there appears some reason why you might be so. But when you have heard me out, you will not be so.

I have now given two years to the intense study of those parts of the art which relate to light and shade and colour, and am convinced that either my understanding is incapable of comprehending the beauties of colouring, or the pictures which I painted for you are equal in every part of the art, and superior in one, to anything that has been done since the age of Raphael. All Sir J. Reynolds' *Discourses to the Royal Academy* will show that the Venetian finesse in art can never be united with the majesty of colouring necessary to historical beauty; and in a letter to the Rev. Mr Gilpin, author of a work on Picturesque Scenery, he says thus: – 'It may be worth consideration whether the epithet picturesque is not applicable to the excellences of the inferior schools rather than to the higher. The works of Michael Angelo, Raphael, &c. appear to me to have nothing of it: whereas Rubens and the Venetian painters may almost be said to have nothing else. Perhaps *picturesque* is somewhat synonymous to the word *taste*, which we should think improperly applied to Homer or

Milton, but very well to Prior or Pope. I suspect that the application of these words is to excellences of an inferior order, and which are incompatible with the grand style. You are certainly right in saying that variety of tints and forms is picturesque; but it must be remembered, on the other hand, that the reverse of this (*uniformity of colour* and a *long continuation of lines*) produces grandeur.' So says Sir Joshua, and so say I; for I have now proved that the parts of the art which I neglected to display, in those little pictures and drawings which I had the pleasure and profit to do for you, are incompatible with the designs. There is nothing in the art which our painters do that I can confess myself ignorant of. I also know and understand, and can assuredly affirm, that the works I have done for you are equal to the Caracci or Raphael (and I am now some years older than Raphael was when he died). I say they are equal to Caracci or Raphael, or else I am blind, stupid, ignorant, and incapable, in two years' study, to understand those things which a boarding-school miss can comprehend in a fortnight. Be assured, my dear friend, that there is not one touch in those drawings and pictures but what came from my head and my heart in unison; that I am proud of being their author, and grateful to you my employer; and that I look upon you as the chief of my friends whom I would endeavour to please, because you, among all men, have enabled me to produce these things. I would not send you a drawing or a picture till I had again reconsidered my notions of art, and had put myself back as if I was a learner. I have proved that I am right, and shall now go on with the vigour I was in my childhood famous for. But I do not pretend to be perfect; yet, if my works have faults, Caracci's, Correggio's, and Raphael's have faults also. Let me observe that the yellow-leather flesh of old men, the ill-drawn and ugly young women, and above all, the daubed black and yellow shadows that are found in most fine, ay, and the finest pictures, I altogether reject as ruinous to effect, though connoisseurs may think otherwise.

Let me also notice that Caracci's pictures are not like

Correggio's, nor Correggio's like Raphael's; and, if neither of them was to be encouraged till he did like any of the others, he must die without encouragement. My pictures are unlike any of these painters, and I would have them to be so. I think the manner I adopt more perfect than any other. No doubt they thought the same of theirs. You will be tempted to think that, as I improve, the pictures, &c. that I did for you are not what I would now wish them to be. On this I beg to say that they are what I intended them, and that I know I never shall do better; for, if I were to do them over again, they would lose as much as they gained, because they were done in the heat of my spirit.

But you will justly inquire why I have not written all this time to you. I answer I have been very unhappy, and could not think of troubling you about it, or any of my real friends (I have written many letters to you which I burned and did not send). And why I have not before now finished the miniature I promised to Mrs Butts? I answer I have not till now in any degree pleased myself, and now I must entreat you to excuse faults, for portrait-painting is the direct contrary to designing and historical painting in every respect. If you have not nature before you for every touch, you cannot paint portrait; and if you have nature before you at all, you cannot paint history. It was Michael Angelo's opinion and is mine. Pray give my wife's love with mine to Mrs Butts. Assure her that it cannot be long before I have the pleasure of painting from you in person, and then that she may expect a likeness. But now I have done all I could, and know she will forgive any failure in consideration of the endeavour. And now let me finish with assuring you that, though I have been very unhappy, I am so no longer. I am again emerged into the light of day; I still and shall to eternity embrace Christianity, and adore Him who is the express image of God; but I have travelled through perils and darkness not unlike a champion. I have conquered and shall go on conquering. Nothing can withstand the fury of my course among the stars of God and in the abysses of the accuser. My enthusiasm is still what it was, only enlarged and confirmed.

I now send two pictures, and hope you will approve of them. I have inclosed the account of money received and work done, which I ought long ago to have sent you. Pray forgive errors in omission of this kind. I am incapable of many attentions which it is my duty to observe towards you, through multitude of employment, and through hope of soon seeing you again. I often omit to inquire of you, but pray let me now hear how you do, and of the welfare of your family.

Accept my sincere love and respect.

I remain yours sincerely,

WILLIAM BLAKE.

A piece of seaweed serves for barometer, and gets wet and dry as the weather gets so.

DEAR SIR,

After I had finished my letter, I found that I had not said half what I intended to say, and in particular I wish to ask you what subject you choose to be painted on the remaining canvas which I brought down with me (for there were three), and to tell you that several of the drawings were in great forwardness. You will see by the inclosed account that the remaining number of drawings which you gave me orders for is eighteen. I will finish these with all possible expedition, if indeed I have not tired you, or, as it is politely called, *bored* you too much already; or, if you would rather, cry out, Enough, off, off! Tell me in a letter of forgiveness if you were offended, and of accustomed friendship if you were not. But I will bore you more with some verses which my wife desires me to copy out and send you with her kind love and respect. They were composed above a twelvemonth ago, while walking from Felpham to Lavant, to meet my sister: –

With happiness stretched across the hills,
In a cloud that dewy sweetness distils,

407

With a blue sky spread over with wings,
And a mild sun that mounts and sings;
With trees and fields, full of fairy elves,
And little devils who fight for themselves,
Remembering the verses that Hayley sung
When my heart knock'd against the root of my tongue,
With angels planted in hawthorn bowers,
And God Himself in the passing hours;
With silver angels across my way,
And golden demons that none can stay;
With my father hovering upon the wind,
And my brother Robert just behind,
And my brother John, the evil one,
In a black cloud making his moan;
Though dead, they appear upon my path,
Notwithstanding my terrible wrath:
They beg, they entreat, they drop their tears,
Fill'd full of hopes, fill'd full of fears;
With a thousand angels upon the wind,
Pouring disconsolate from behind
To drive them off, and before my way
A frowning Thistle implores my stay.
What to others a trifle appears
Fills me full of smiles or tears;
For double the vision my eyes do see,
And a double vision is always with me.
With my inward eye, 'tis an old man grey;
With my outward, a thistle across my way.
'If thou goest back,' the Thistle said,
'Thou art to endless woe betray'd;
For here does Theotormon lower,
And here is Enitharmon's bower,
And Los the Terrible thus hath sworn,
Because thou backward dost return,
Poverty, envy, old age, and fear,
Shall bring thy wife upon a bier.
And Butts shall give what Fuseli gave,
A dark black rock, and a gloomy cave.'

I struck the thistle with my foot,
And broke him up from his delving root;
'Must the duties of life each other cross?
Must every joy be dung and dross?
Must my dear Butts feel cold neglect
Because I give Hayley his due respect?
Must Flaxman look upon me as wild,
And all my friends be with doubts beguil'd?
Must my wife live in my sister's bane,
Or my sister survive on my Love's pain?
The curses of Los, the terrible shade,
And his dismal terrors make me afraid.'

So I spoke, and struck in my wrath
The old man weltering upon my path
Then Los appeared in all his power:
In the sun he appeared, descending before
My face in fierce flames; in my double sight,
'Twas outward a sun, – inward, Los in his might.
'My hands are labour'd day and night,
And ease comes never in my sight.
My wife has no indulgence given,
Except what comes to her from heaven.
We eat little, we drink less;
This earth breeds not our happiness.
Another sun feeds our life's streams;
We are not warmèd with thy beams.
Thou measurest not the time to me,
Nor yet the space that I do see:
My mind is not with thy light array'd;
Thy terrors shall not make me afraid.'

When I had my defiance given,
The sun stood trembling in heaven;
The moon, that glow'd remote below,
Became leprous and white as snow;
And every soul of man on the earth
Felt affliction, and sorrow, and sickness, and dearth.

Los flam'd in my path, and the sun was hot
With the bows of my mind and the arrows of thought:
My bowstring fierce with ardour breathes,
My arrows glow in their golden sheaves;
My brother and father march before,
The heavens drop with human gore.

Now I a fourfold vision see
And a fourfold vision is given to me;
'Tis fourfold in my supreme delight,
And threefold in soft Beulah's night,
And twofold always. May God us keep
From single vision, and Newton's sleep!

I also enclose you some ballads by Mr Hayley, with prints to them by your humble servant. I should have sent them before now, but could not get anything done for you to please myself; for I do assure you that I have truly studied the two little pictures I now send, and do not repent of the time I have spent upon them.

God bless you!

Yours,

W. B.

P.S.– I have taken the liberty to trouble you with a letter to my brother, which you will be so kind as to send or give him, and oblige yours, W. B.

April 25, 1803.

MY DEAR SIR,

I write in haste, having received a pressing letter from my Brother. I intended to have sent the Picture of the Riposo, which is nearly finished much to my satisfaction, but not quite. You shall have it soon. I now send the four numbers for Mr Birch with best respects to him. The reason the Ballads have been suspended is the pressure of other business, but they will go on again soon.

Accept of my thanks for your kind and heartening letter.

You have faith in the endeavours of me, your weak brother and fellow-disciple; how great must be your faith in our Divine Master! You are to me a lesson of humility, while you exalt me by such distinguishing commendations. I know that you see certain merits in me, which, by God's grace, shall be made fully apparent and perfect in Eternity. In the meantime I must not bury the talents in the earth, but do my endeavour to live to the glory of our Lord and Saviour; and I am also grateful to the kind hand that endeavours to lift me out of despondency, even if it lifts me too high.

And now, my dear Sir, congratulate me on my return to London with the full approbation of Mr Hayley and with promise. But alas! now I may say to you – what perhaps I should not dare to say to any one else – that I can alone carry on my visionary studies in London unannoyed, and that I may converse with my friends in Eternity, see visions, dream dreams, and prophecy and speak parables, unobserved, and at liberty from the doubts of other mortals: perhaps doubts proceeding from kindness; but doubts are always pernicious, especially when we doubt our friends. Christ is very decided on this point: 'He who is not with me is against me.' There is no medium or middle state; and if a man is the enemy of my spiritual life while he pretends to be the friend of my corporeal, he is a real enemy; but the man may be the friend of my spiritual life while he seems the enemy of my corporeal, though not *vice versa*.

What is very pleasant, every one who hears of my going to London again applauds it as the only course for the interest of all concerned in my works; observing that I ought not to be away from the opportunities London affords of seeing fine pictures, and the various improvements in works of art going on in London.

But none can know the spiritual acts of my three years' slumber on the banks of Ocean, unless he has seen them in the spirit, or unless he should read my long Poem* descriptive of those

* (The Jerusalem.)

411

acts; for I have in these years composed an immense number of verses on one grand theme, similar to Homer's *Iliad* or Milton's *Paradise Lost*; the persons and machinery entirely new to the inhabitants of earth (some of the persons excepted). I have written this Poem from immediate dictation, twelve or sometimes twenty or thirty lines at a time, without premeditation, and even against my will. The time it has taken in writing was thus rendered non-existent, and an immense Poem exists which seems to be the labour of a long life, all produced without labour or study. I mention this to show you what I think the grand reason of my being brought down here.

I have a thousand and ten thousand things to say to you. My heart is full of futurity. I perceive that the sore travail which has been given me these three years leads to glory and honour. I rejoice and tremble: 'I am fearfully and wonderfully made.' I had been reading the CXXXIX. Psalm a little before your letter arrived. I take your advice. I see the face of my Heavenly Father: He lays His hand upon my head, and gives a blessing to all my work. Why should I be troubled? Why should my heart and flesh cry out? I will go on in the strength of the Lord; through Hell will I sing forth His praises: that the dragons of the deep may praise Him, and that those who dwell in darkness, and in the sea coasts, may be gathered into His kingdom. Excuse my perhaps too great enthusiasm. Please to accept of and give our loves to Mrs Butts and your amiable family, and believe me

Ever yours affectionately,

WILLIAM BLAKE.

Felpham, July 6, 1803.

DEAR SIR,

I send you the Riposo, which I hope you will think my best picture in many respects. It represents the Holy Family in Egypt, guarded in their repose from those fiends the Egyptian gods. And though not directly taken from a Poem of Milton's (for till I had designed it Milton's Poem did not come into my thoughts), yet it is very similar to his Hymn on the Nativity, which you will find among his smaller Poems, and will read with great delight. I have given in the background a building, which may be supposed the ruin of a part of Nimrod's Tower, which I conjecture to have spread over many countries; for he ought to be reckoned of the Giant brood.

I have now on the stocks the following drawings for you: – 1. Jephthah sacrificing his Daughter; 2. Ruth and her Mother-in-law and Sister; 3. The Three Maries at the Sepulchre; 4. The Death of Joseph; 5. The Death of the Virgin Mary; 6. St Paul preaching; and 7. The Angel of the Divine Presence clothing Adam and Eve with coats of skins.

These are all in great forwardness, and I am satisfied that I improve very much, and shall continue to do so while I live, which is a blessing I can never be too thankful for both to God and man.

We look forward every day with pleasure toward our meeting again in London with those whom we have learned to value by absence no less perhaps than we did by presence; for recollection often surpasses everything. Indeed, the prospect of returning to our friends is supremely delightful. Then I am determined that Mrs Butts shall have a good likeness of you, if I have hands and eyes left; for I am become a likeness-taker, and succeed admirably well. But this is not to be achieved without the original sitting before you for every touch, all likenesses from memory being necessarily very, very defective; but Nature and Fancy are two things, and can never be joined, neither ought any one to attempt it, for it is idolatry, and destroys the Soul.

I ought to tell you that Mr H. is quite agreeable to our return, and that there is all the appearance in the world of our being fully employed in engraving for his projected works, particularly Cowper's *Milton* – a work now on foot by subscription, and I understand that the subscription goes on briskly. This work is to be a very elegant one, and to consist of all Milton's Poems with Cowper's Notes, and translations by Cowper from Milton's

Latin and Italian Poems. These works will be ornamented with engravings from designs by Romney, Flaxman, and your humble servant, and to be engraved also by the last-mentioned. The profits of the work are intended to be appropriated to erect a monument to the memory of Cowper in St Paul's or Westminster Abbey. Such is the project; and Mr Addington and Mr Pitt are both among the subscribers, which are already numerous and of the first rank. The price of the work is six guineas. Thus I hope that all our three years' trouble ends in good-luck at last, and shall be forgot by my affections, and only remembered by my understanding, to be a memento in time to come, and to speak to future generations by a sublime allegory, which is now perfectly completed into a grand Poem. I may praise it, since I dare not pretend to be any other than the secretary; the authors are in Eternity. I consider it as the grandest Poem that this world contains. Allegory addressed to the intellectual powers, while it is altogether hidden from the corporeal understanding, is my definition of the most sublime Poetry. It is also somewhat in the same manner defined by Plato. This Poem shall, by Divine assistance, be progressively printed and ornamented with prints, and given to the Public. But of this work I take care to say little to Mr H., since he is as much averse to my Poetry as he is to a chapter in the Bible. He knows that I have writ it, for I have shown it to him, and he has read part by his own desire, and has looked with sufficient contempt to enhance my opinion of it. But I do not wish to imitate by seeming too obstinate in poetic pursuits. But if all the world should set their faces against this, I have orders to set my face like a flint (Ezekiel iii. 8.) against their faces, and my forehead against their foreheads.

As to Mr H., I feel myself at liberty to say as follows upon this ticklish subject. I regard fashion in Poetry as little as I do in Painting: so, if both Poets and Painters should alternately dislike (but I know the majority of them will not), I am not to regard it at all. But Mr H. approves of my Designs as little as he does of my Poems, and I have been forced to insist on his leaving me, in both, to my own self-will; for I am determined to be no longer pestered with his genteel ignorance and polite disapprobation. I know myself both Poet and Painter, and it is not his affected contempt that can move to anything but a more assiduous pursuit of both arts. Indeed, by my late firmness, I have brought down his affected loftiness, and he begins to think I have some genius: as if genius and assurance were the same thing! But his imbecile attempts to depress me only deserve laughter. I say thus much to you, knowing that you will not make a bad use of it. But it is a fact too true that, if I had only depended on mortal things, both myself and my wife must have been lost. I shall leave every one in this country astonished at my patience and forbearance of injuries upon injuries; and I do assure you that, if I could have returned to London a month after my arrival here, I should have done so. But I was commanded by my spiritual friends to bear all and be silent, and to go through all without murmuring, and, in fine, [to] hope till my three years should be almost accomplished; at which time I was set at liberty to remonstrate against former conduct, and to demand justice and truth; which I have done in so effectual a manner that my antagonist is silenced completely, and I have compelled what should have been of freedom – my just right as an artist and as a man. And if any attempt should be made to refuse me this I am inflexible, and will relinquish any engagement of designing at all, unless altogether left to my own judgment, as you, my dear friend, have always left me; for which I shall never cease to honour and respect you.

When we meet, I will perfectly describe to you my conduct and the conduct of others towards me, and you will see that I have laboured hard indeed, and have been borne on angels' wings. Till we meet I beg of God our Saviour to be with you and me, and yours and mine. Pray give my and my wife's love to Mrs Butts and family, and believe me to remain

Yours in truth and sincerity,

WILLIAM BLAKE.

415

Felpham, August 16, 1803.

DEAR SIR,

I send seven Drawings, which I hope will please you. This, I believe, about balances our account. Our return to London draws on apace. Our expectation of meeting again with you is one of our greatest pleasures. Pray tell me how your eyes do. I never sit down to work but I think of you, and feel anxious for the sight of that friend whose eyes have done me so much good. I omitted, very unaccountably, to copy out in my last letter that passage in my rough sketch, which related to your kindness in offering to exhibit my two last pictures in the Gallery in Berners-street. It was in these words: 'I sincerely thank you for your kind offer of exhibiting my two pictures. The trouble you take on my account, I trust, will be recompensed to you by Him who seeth in secret. If you should find it convenient to do so, it will be gratefully remembered by me among the other numerous kindnesses I have received from you.'

I go on with the remaining subjects which you gave me commission to execute for you; but I shall not be able to send any more before my return, though, perhaps, I may bring some with me finished. I am at present in a bustle to defend myself against a very unwarrantable warrant from a justice of peace in Chichester, which was taken out against me by a private in Captain Leathes' troop of 1st or Royal Dragoons, for an assault and seditious words. The wretched man has terribly perjured himself, as has his comrade; for, as to sedition, not one word relating to the King or Government was spoken by either him or me. His enmity arises from my having turned him out of my garden, into which he was invited as an assistant by a gardener at work therein, without my knowledge that he was so invited. I desired him, as politely as possible, to go out of the garden; he made me an impertinent answer. I insisted on his leaving the garden; he refused. I still persisted in desiring his departure. He then threatened to knock out my eyes, with many abominable imprecations, and with some contempt for my person; it affronted my foolish

416

pride. I therefore took him by the elbows, and pushed him before me till I had got him out. There I intended to have left him; but he, turning about, put himself into a posture of defiance, threatening and swearing at me. I, perhaps foolishly and perhaps not, stepped out at the gate, and, putting aside his blows, took him again by the elbows, and, keeping his back to me, pushed him forward down the road about fifty yards – he all the while endeavouring to turn round and strike me, and raging and cursing, which drew out several neighbours. At length, when I had got him to where he was quartered, which was very quickly done, we were met at the gate by the master of the house – the Fox Inn – (who is the proprietor of my cottage) and his wife and daughter, and the man's comrade, and several other people. My landlord compelled the soldiers to go indoors, after many abusive threats against me and my wife from the two soldiers; but not one word of threat on account of sedition was uttered at that time. This method of revenge was planned between them after they had got together into the stable. This is the whole outline. I have for witnesses: – the gardener, who is ostler at the Fox, and who evidences that to his knowledge no word of the remotest tendency to Government or sedition was uttered; our next-door neighbour, a miller's wife (who saw me turn him before me down the road, and saw and heard all that happened at the gate of the inn), who evidences that no expression of threatening on account of sedition was uttered in the heat of their fury by either of the dragoons. This was the woman's own remark, and does high honour to her good sense, as she observes that, whenever a quarrel happens, the offence is always repeated. The landlord of the inn and his wife and daughter will evidence the same, and will evidently prove the comrade perjured, who swore that he heard me, while at the gate, utter seditious words, and d— the K—, without which perjury I could not have been committed, and I had no witnesses with me before the justices who could combat his assertion, as the gardener remained in my garden all the while, and he was the only person I thought necessary to take with me. I have been before a bench of justices at Chichester this morning; but they, as the lawyer who wrote down the accusation told me in private, are compelled by the military to suffer a prosecution to be entered into, although they must know, and it is manifest, that the whole is a fabricated perjury. I have been forced to find bail. Mr Hayley was kind enough to come forward, and Mr Seagrave, printer at Chichester; Mr H. in £100, and Mr S. in £50, and myself am bound in £100 for my appearance at the quarter-sessions, which is after Michaelmas. So I shall have the satisfaction to see my friends in town before this contemptible business comes on. I say contemptible, for it must be manifest to every one that the whole accusation is a wilful perjury. Thus you see, my dear friend, that I cannot leave this place without some adventure. It has struck a consternation through all the villages round. Every man is now afraid of speaking to, or looking at, a soldier: for the peaceable villagers have always been forward in expressing their kindness for us, and they express their sorrow at our departure as soon as they hear of it. Every one here is my evidence for peace and good neighbourhood; and yet, such is the present state of things, this foolish accusation must be tried in public. Well, I am content, I murmur not, and doubt not that I shall receive justice, and am only sorry for the trouble and expense. I have heard that my accuser is a disgraced sergeant: his name is John Scholfield. Perhaps it will be in your power to learn somewhat about the man. I am very ignorant of what I am requesting of you; I only suggest what I know you will be kind enough to excuse if you can learn nothing about him, and what I as well know, if it is possible, you will be kind enough to do in this matter.

Dear Sir, this perhaps was suffered to clear up some doubts, and to give opportunity to those whom I doubted to clear themselves of all imputation. If a man offends me ignorantly, and not designedly, surely I ought to consider him with favour and affection. Perhaps the simplicity of myself is the origin of all offences committed against me. If I have found this, I shall have learned a most valuable thing, well worth three years' persever-ance. I *have* found it. It is certain that a too passive manner, inconsistent with my active physiognomy, had done me much mischief. I must now express to you my conviction that all is come from the spiritual world for good and not for evil.

Give me your advice in my perilous adventure. Burn what I have peevishly written about any friend. I have been very much degraded and injuriously treated; but if it all arise from my own fault, I ought to blame myself.

> O why was I born with a different face?
> Why was I not born like the rest of my race?
> When I look, each one starts; when I speak, I offend;
> Then I'm silent and passive, and lose every friend.
>
> Then my verse I dishonour, my pictures despise;
> My person degrade, and my temper chastise;
> And the pen is my terror, the pencil my shame;
> All my talents I bury, and dead is my fame.
> I am either too low or too highly priz'd;
> When elate I'm envy'd, when meek I'm despis'd.

This is but too just a picture of my present state. I pray God to keep you and all men from it, and to deliver me in His own good time. Pray write to me, and tell me how you and your family enjoy health. My much-terrified wife joins me in love to you and Mrs Butts and all your family. I again take the liberty to beg of you to cause the enclosed letter to be delivered to my brother, and remain sincerely and affectionately

Yours,

WILLIAM BLAKE.

FURTHER READING

William Blake

Allan Cunningham: *The Lives of the British Painters*, 1830
Algernon Charles Swinburne: *William Blake: A Critical Essay*, 1868
Alexander Gilchrist: *William Blake: Pictor Ignotus*, 2nd edition, 2 vols., 1880
Anne Gilchrist: 'William Blake', in *The Dictionary of National Biography*, 1886
Arthur Symons: *William Blake*, 1907
Mona Wilson: *The Life of William Blake*, 1927
Northrop Frye: *Fearful Symmetry: A Study of William Blake*, 1947
David Erdman: *William Blake: Prophet Against Empire*, 1954
Geoffrey Keynes (editor), *The Letters of William Blake*, 1968
G.E. Bentley: *Blake Records*, 1969; and *Blake Records Supplement*, 1988
James King: *William Blake: His Life*, 1991
Peter Ackroyd: *Blake*, 1995
Morris Eaves (editor), *The Cambridge Companion to William Blake*, 2003

Anne and Alexander Gilchrist

Alexander Gilchrist: *The Life of William Etty, RA,* 1853
Anne Gilchrist: *A Memoir of Alexander Gilchrist,* 1880
Herbert Gilchrist: *Anne Gilchrist, Her Life and Writings,* 1887
Marion Walker Alcaro: *Walt Whitman's Mrs G: A Biography of Anne Gilchrist,* Associated University Presses, 1991

INDEX

424

Bulwer-Lytton, Edward: *Lucretia* 297
Bunhill Fields 61, 65, 106, 386, 392;
  WB's grave 388–9
Bunyan, John 201, 388
Bürger, Gottfried August: *Lenore*
  149–50
Burgoyne, Sir John 83
Burke, Edmund 106, 276
Burke, Haviland 391
Burney, Dr Charles 38
Burney, Edward 101
Burns, Robert 167; *Poems in the
  Scottish Dialect* 31, 133; published by
  Cromek 253–4; 'Tam O'Shanter' 133
Butts, Thomas 152, 159; cools towards
  WB 300; WB's letters to 394–419;
  on WB's nakedness 124–5; WB's
  patron 124, 218, 240, 244, 261, 265,
  301, 357, 383; and WB's state of
  mind 345
Byfield (engraver) 291

Cadell (publisher) 36, 51
Cadell and Davies (publisher) 234,
  254, 256
Calvert, Edward 320, 329; attends
  WB's burial 388; on WB's sanity 345
Campbell, Thomas 184; *Pleasures of
  Hope* 133
Canova, Antonio 7
Canterbury Pilgrimage (WB, fresco)
  225, 243–4, 261; commissioned by
  Cromek 218–19; 258; engraving 24,
  246, 249–50, 362; exhibited 244;
  Lamb's opinion of 246; part of
  engraving published 262–3; pencil
  sketch 218–19; prospectus for
  engraving 246–7
Carpaccio, Vittore 282
Carpenter, Mr (of British Museum)
  261
Carter, Elizabeth 50
Carter, John 23
Cary, Henry Francis 366; notion of
  WB's madness 266, 346; purchases
  WB drawing 391

Chamberlayne, William 298
Chambers, Sir William 11
Chantrey, Sir Francis 135, 256, 257,
  371; buys copy of *Songs* 382; declines
  Paradise Regained 358
Chapone, Mrs Hester 38, 50
Charlotte, Queen 33, 235
Chatterton, Thomas (Thomas
  Rowley) 7, 30
Chaucer, Geoffrey, *Canterbury Tales*
  246, 249, 262; Stothard's painting
  of 217, 219; see also Canterbury
  Pilgrimage
Cheetham (Paine's biographer) 105
Chichester Quarter Sessions 189
'Chimney Sweeper, The' (WB, poem)
  82
Chodowiecki, Daniel Nikolaus 150
Christ in the Sepulchre Guarded by
  Angels (WB, painting) 233
Christie's 10
Churchill, Charles 16
Claude Lorraine 333–4
Clennell, Luke 255, 256
Cobbett, William 7
'Cold and the Pebble, The' (WB,
  poem) 130
Coleridge, Samuel Taylor 31, 131, 184;
  The Two Founts 360; WB meets
  358
Collection of Old Scottish Songs
  (Cromek) 254–5
Collings, S: WB's engravings after
  60
Collins, Mrs (of Hampstead) 378
Collins, William 28, 301, 335; death
  269; monument to 96; on WB's
  gentlemanliness 329
Connoisseur, The 288
Constable, John 382
Cooke, John 25
Cooper, Abraham 301
Copley, John Singleton 39, 63
Corbould (designer) 101
Corregio, Antonio Allegri 279
Cosway, Richard 39, 63, 216

INDEX

Printed by RR Donnelley at Glasgow, UK